Indonesia

Indonesia

The Great Transition

Edited by
John Bresnan

ROWMAN & LITTLEFIELD PUBLISHERS, INC.
Lanham • Boulder • New York • Toronto • Oxford

ROWMAN & LITTLEFIELD PUBLISHERS, INC.

Published in the United States of America
by Rowman & Littlefield Publishers, Inc.
A wholly owned subsidiary of The Rowman & Littlefield Publishing Group, Inc.
4501 Forbes Boulevard, Suite 200, Lanham, Maryland 20706
www.rowmanlittlefield.com

PO Box 317, Oxford, OX2 9RU, UK

A Study of the Weatherhead East Asian Institute, Columbia University

British Library Cataloguing in Publication Information Available

Library of Congress Cataloging-in-Publication Data

Indonesia : the great transition / edited by John Bresnan.
    p. cm.
    Includes bibliographical references and index.
    ISBN 0-7425-4010-3 (cloth : alk. paper) — ISBN 0-7425-4011-1 (pbk. : alk. paper)
    1. Indonesia—Politics and government—1998– 2. Indonesia Economic conditions—
1997– I. Bresnan, John, 1927–
    DS644.5.I4815 2005
    959.8—dc22

                                                                2005015350

Printed in the United States of America

♾™ The paper used in this publication meets the minimum requirements of American
National Standard for Information Sciences—Permanence of Paper for Printed Library
Materials, ANSI/NISO Z39.48-1992.

Contents

List of Tables

Acknowledgments

This volume was made possible by a grant from the United States–Japan Foundation for the study of political and economic developments in Indonesia as seen from the perspectives of Japanese and American scholars and analysts. The project was conceived by Ann Marie Murphy, then a doctoral candidate at Columbia University, and was chaired jointly by Takashi Shiraishi of Kyoto University and John Bresnan of Columbia University. Many Japanese and Americans visited Indonesia in the course of the project and met in a series of international conferences over a period of years beginning in 1999. All were students of Indonesian matters, some with long histories of residence and research in that country. Australian participation was included in some conferences, and Indonesian participation was included throughout. Papers were presented at each conference, and reports coauthored by Murphy and Bresnan were published by the Weatherhead East Asian Institute of Columbia University in a series entitled Transition Indonesia. An effort was made to share the findings with the governments of Japan and the United States. The present volume was prepared for the express purpose of contributing to a deeper American understanding of contemporary Indonesia, which the project principles judged a high priority. The editor and contributors would like to thank the participants of several nationalities who gave generously of their time to engage in the multinational dialogue that led to this publication. The editor also wishes to thank his colleagues at the Weatherhead East Asian Institute for their unfailing encouragement; members of the institute staff who gave always valuable assistance in the preparation of the volume, in particular Madge Huntington, Elizabeth Demissie, Jasmine Polanski, Arie Bram, and Sarah Lee; and graduate students Scott Harold and

Jessica Wilson. The editor and contributors also wish to thank the anonymous readers who read drafts of their manuscripts and offered comments that
have helped them make the text as accurate and balanced an introduction to
contemporary Indonesia as they could make it.

Abbreviations

ABRI   Angkatan Bersenjata Republic Indonesia (Armed Forces of the Republic of Indonesia)

BCA   Bank Central Asia

Bulog   Badan Urusan Logistik (Bureau for Logistical Affairs)

DDII   Dewan Dakwah Islamiya Indonesia (Indonesian Council for Islamic Preaching)

DPD   Dewan Perwakilan Daerah (Council of Provincial Representatives)

DPR   Dewan Perwakilan Rakyt (Council of People's Representatives)

GAM   Gerakan Aceh Merdeka (Free Aceh Movement)

Golkar   Golongan Karya (Functional Groups)

IBRA   Indonesian Bank Restructuring Agency

ICMI   Ikatan Cendekiawan Muslim Indonesia (Indonesian Association of Muslim Intellectuals)

Inpres   Instruksi Presiden (Presidential Directive)

KKN   *korupsi, kolusi, nepotisme* (corruption, collusion, nepotism)

LSM   Lembaga Swadaya Masyarakat (Self-supporting Social Agency)

MPR   Majelis Perwakilan Rakyat (Assembly of People's Representatives)

NU   Nahdlatul Ulama (Renaissance of Muslim Clergy)

OPM   Organisasi Papua Merdeka (Free Papua Organization)

PDI   Partai Democrasi Indonesia (Indonesian Democracy Party)

PKI   Partai Komunis Indonesia (Indonesian Communist Party)

PNI   Partai Nasional Indonesia (Indonesian National Party)

POLRI   Polisi Republic Indonesia (Republic of Indonesia Police)

PPKI	Panitia Persiapan Kemerdekaan Indonesia (Committee to Prepare Indonesian Independence)
PPP	Partai Pembangunan Persatuan (United Development Party)
PT	Perusahan Terbatas (Limited Company)
SARA	*suku, agama, ras, antar-golongan* (ethnic group, religion, race, intergroup relations)
SBY	Susilo Bambang Yudhoyono
SESKOAD	Sekolah Staf dan Komando Angkatan Darat (Army Staff and Command School)
TNI	Tentara Nasional Indonesia (Indonesian National Military)

Southeast Asia

Indonesia

Rangoon ★

Vientiane

THAILAND

LAOS

VIETNAM

Bangkok ★

CAMBODIA

Phnom Penh ★

● Ho Chi Minh City

Andaman Sea

Gulf of Thailand

South China Sea

Sabang

Lhokseumawe ●

Aceh

MALAYSIA

● Medan ★ Kuala Lumpur

Kepulauan Anambas

Kepulauan Natuna

BRUNEI
Bandar Seri Begawan ★

MALAYSIA ⸱ **Sarawak** ⸱ **Kali**
T

● Kuching

Sumatera Utara

Strait of Malacca

SINGAPORE

Kepulauan Riau

Riau

Kepulauan Lingga

Pontianak ●

Kalimantan (Borneo)

Bukittinggi ●

Kalimantan Barat

Kalimantan Tengah

Padang ●

Sumatra

Sumatera Barat

Jambi ●

Bangka

Bangka & Belitung

Palembang ●

Belitung

Banjarmasin ●

Kalimantan Selatan

Sumatera Selatan

Bengkulu

I N

Java Sea

D O

Lampung ●

Sunda Strait

★ Jakarta

Banten

Jawa Barat

Jawa Tengah

Semarang ●

● Surabaya

Jawa Timur

Bali
Bali

Yogyakarta ●

J a v a

Denpasar ●

Lombok Strait

Lombok

I N D I A N
O C E A N

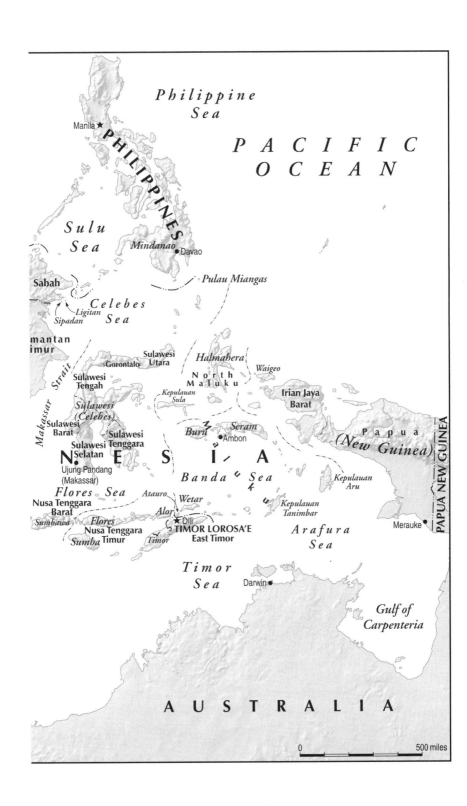

Prologue

It has long been customary to introduce a book about Indonesia by arguing that the country is important. Indonesia's population, we are reminded, is the fourth largest in the world. It is the source of petroleum, natural gas, and hard minerals. It is located strategically between the landmass of Asia and the continent of Australia, straddling the sea-lanes that link the Pacific and Indian Oceans.[1] At the same time, it has been customary to warn that Indonesia is difficult to know. Its languages and ethnic groups are famously heterogeneous. Indonesia has experienced "revolution, parliamentary democracy, civil war, presidential autocracy, mass murder and military rule" in its first half century; it is not a history with much coherence.[2] For these and other reasons, including distance and language barriers, Indonesia has not generated a literature to serve the general reader interested in world affairs. In the absence of such a literature, there has been little interest in Indonesia outside specialist circles, and Indonesia is best known for being little known, even to its neighbors.

There is no longer good reason for this Indonesian exceptionalism. High rates of economic growth between the mid-1960s and mid-1990s fed major social change, including the development of a modern corporate sector and an urban middle class, making it more like other societies and economies. Moreover, since the fall of a long-ruling autocrat in 1998, Indonesia has been in the midst of a multifaceted transition of historic proportions. It has been in transition from decades of authoritarian government, following a wave of democratic openings that many states have experienced in recent decades. It has been in transition from years of secular government to a new era of struggle over the role of Islam in politics, a matter common to predominantly Muslim societies elsewhere in the world. Indonesia also has been in transition from a

1

financial crisis, searching for resilience in the face of globalization, as are most nations of Asia, Africa, and Latin America. These processes of change are making Indonesia more relevant to the interests of three groups: (1) students of modern history and the social sciences with a concern for the problems of postcolonial states, (2) scholars in comparative studies of Asia, and (3) members of the general public who seek a scholarly introduction to contemporary Indonesia, its legacies, and its prospects. The five scholars who contribute to this book joined together to help make the new Indonesia that is emerging more accessible to all three of these groups.

The term "crisis" does not exaggerate the dire nature of conditions in Indonesia in 1998. The social order, the political regime, and the economic system of Indonesia all teetered on the verge of collapse. Each of these near implosions had its own history, but each also impacted on the others, greatly increasing the chaos that ensued. The restoration of public order, the reform of institutions of governance, and the beginning of social and economic recovery were still under way when the tsunami struck the Indonesian province of Aceh on the island of Sumatra in December 2004. The tsunami added another layer of complexity to the process that serves as the subtitle for this volume, one the contributors have called "the great transition."

This recent history raises many questions. Why did the regional financial crisis of 1998 have its most severe impact in Indonesia? What does the violence of 1998 and since tell us about Indonesian society and the Indonesian state? What do the crisis and the transition from it have to say about the relevance of the nation-state in the twenty-first century; about Islam and democratic politics; about a negotiated route to democratic governance; about corruption and global finance? What do they tell us about the prospects for Indonesia's contribution to stability or instability in Southeast Asia and in the wider region of East Asia and the Pacific? And what impact will the tsunami and its devastation have on these prospects?

Indonesia's civil and military elite was, by the mid-1990s, seriously disaffected by the preferential treatment accorded to a small circle of family and friends of President Suharto. He was one of the world's longest-surviving heads of state, and many of the elite had come to see their interests as no longer bound up with his. Having guided the economy with a steady hand through three decades of extraordinarily rapid growth, Suharto by 1998 was behaving erratically. He reversed policy after policy in the interests of his family. All through the early months of the year, he was faced with strong pressure from the International Monetary Fund to allow subsidized fuel prices to rise in order to bring the government budget into balance. Suharto at first resisted this pressure and sought refuge in a currency board, widely viewed as unsuitable for Indonesia's financial condition. In early May, with no advance notice, he capitulated and canceled the subsidies entirely, stunning the population, and left the country for an international conference.

Two nights of rioting and looting followed on May 13–14, during which more than 1,000 people lost their lives in the capital city of Jakarta alone. Thousands of Chinese businessmen, targets of much of the violence, moved capital abroad and fled the country with their families. University students, four of whom had been shot and killed while demonstrating against the government, were mobilizing for mass action to bring the capital to a standstill. These numbers may seem insignificant in comparison with the more than 100,000 killed by the 2004 tsunami, but they were highly significant in the political environment of Jakarta in 1998.

Abandoned by one group of former supporters after another, and assured that the armed forces would continue to protect his person and his name, Suharto resigned on May 21. Even before he stepped down, communal violence was occurring in some localities. In the political vacuum created by his fall, incidents of ethnic and religious violence broke out in many places across the country, often setting members of the Muslim majority and Christian minority against each other; more thousands lost their lives in these communal breakdowns. The armed forces did little to prevent these developments; on the contrary they were accused of precipitating some of them or permitting them to happen. With this last prop to government no longer respected by the civilian elite, it was thought for a time that the country might break into separate pieces.

The very thought raised the question of what was holding the country together. Indonesia was among the most varied of nations, with several thousand inhabited islands and hundreds of ethnic groups, each with its own language or dialect, making national unity the major goal of the first president, Sukarno. Does the geography of the archipelago work for or against Indonesian unity? What has been the political impact of language distribution, including the many first languages and the single national language? How important is shared history? Donald Emmerson pursues such questions as these in chapter 1 of this book.

Emmerson also addresses the three separatist challenges to Indonesia's physical integrity that were active when Suharto fell. Most international attention directed at Indonesia prior to the 2004 tsunami focused on East Timor. This half island was not part of the former Dutch East Indies, but was a Portuguese colony invaded by the Indonesians in 1975 and annexed as a province. The movements for independence in Aceh in the far northwest of Indonesia and Papua on the eastern extremity were of longer standing. What motivated the leaders of these cases of extreme dissidence? How was Jakarta responding? What are the prospects for independence in the case of Papua, and how did East Timor impact on these prospects? What are the prospects in the case of Aceh, and what impact might the tsunami have on them?

The legacy of violence continues to hang over Indonesian society, with sporadic fighting in several widely separated locations. Yet Indonesians have long considered themselves, and have been considered by others, to be a people markedly tolerant of social difference. In chapter 2 Robert Hefner explores how Indonesians have lived in relative harmony with religious and other social differences over the centuries. Today the vast majority of Indonesian Muslims, who make up 88 percent of the population, hold to nonconfrontational ways of interacting with others.

There nevertheless have been incidents of violence in the name of Islam in modern Indonesian history. A violent Islamist movement in the 1950s and 1960s, the Darul Islam, aimed to turn Indonesia into a Muslim state. The power vacuum that followed Suharto's fall opened Indonesia once again to the recruitment and training of armed Muslim militias. One group, the Laskar Jihad, became involved in Muslim–Christian violence in the Maluku islands, escalating the scale of dead and wounded. The suicide bombing of a resort in Bali in October 2002, in which more than 200 foreign tourists lost their lives, was attributed to a secret network of radicals known as Jema'ah Islamiyah. Subsequent bombings at a hotel and an embassy in Jakarta had further repercussions for Indonesian politics, its economy, and its foreign relations. Hefner reflects on why an "uncivil" Islam made a fresh appearance after 1998, and what is required to restore a "live and let live" ethic to the social order.

Suharto's fall left the country for a time without a political institution that could contain the spreading disorder. The presidency had lost its legitimacy, and the legislature had been a rubber stamp since 1957, when the first period of democratically elected government ended with a declaration of martial law. In 1998 the armed forces experienced internal division and disgrace for serving Suharto's personal interests at the expense of the people.

In chapter 3 Annette Clear analyzes, institution by institution, how authority was restored to government and how political life was significantly democratized. She analyzes the presidencies of Suharto's three immediate successors, all of whom served less than full terms; the restoration of freedom of speech and assembly; the successful parliamentary elections of 1999 and 2004; the growing strength of parliament vis-à-vis the executive branch; the massive devolution of authority, personnel, and revenues to local governments; the loss by the armed forces of some of their privileges; and the election of the president by the direct vote of the people for the first time in Indonesian history, resulting in the landslide victory of Susilo Bambang Yudhoyono in 2004. Clear assesses the extent to which these reforms are taking hold, considers the delayed case of judicial reform, and reflects on the question of where the armed forces are heading in the governance of Indonesia.

Was Suharto's fall inevitable? Why did Indonesia suffer greater damage than any other nation in the financial crisis that swept most of East and Southeast Asia between 1997 and 1999? How did corruption become so extensive in Indonesia? How did it affect the crisis in the economy? John Bresnan, in chapter 4, deals with these questions in recounting Indonesia's descent into de facto bankruptcy. He also assesses the Indonesian government's response restructuring the banking industry and why the process went awry; privatizing state enterprises and why it has not worked; making corporate owners accountable for fraudulent behavior and why they have escaped; and leaving uncertain how the cost of the bank bailout will be paid or when. He also assesses the performance of the International Monetary Fund and how Indonesia can restore its resilience in the face of continuing globalization.

The social, political, and economic aspects of the crisis have had a strong impact on how Indonesians see the rest of the world and how they can protect their interests. The regional strategic situation has been changing with China's economic rise, Japan's declining role, and disaffection with U.S. policy in the Middle East. Indonesia's success or failure in resolving its domestic problems meanwhile has had implications for its immediate neighbors, the Association of Southeast Asian Nations (ASEAN, which it once championed), and major extraregional powers with an interest in this region, including the United States. To these issues was added at the end of 2004 the impact of the Indian Ocean tsunami. Against an analysis of major periods and issues in Indonesian foreign policy history, Ann Marie Murphy assesses in chapter 5 the meaning of recent developments for Indonesia's prospective role in Southeast Asia and the Muslim world.

That the Indonesian people managed to contain the disorder and begin to enact key reforms is a central theme of this volume. The evidence assembled by the five authors describes a crisis of very large proportions seven years before the tsunami occurred, and traces a process of self-correction that, while it still has a long way to go, has registered some impressive achievements in its first years. National pride has been restored by the success of political reforms, although separatism remains a major issue. Communal violence has subsided, but terrorism in the name of Islam remains a serious threat. Political institutions have in large measure been democratized, but experience in making them work is still limited. Bank ownership has been largely restructured and macroeconomic stability has been achieved, but growth has not yet been sufficient to stem unemployment. Indonesia's role in international forums, once counted a major national asset, has been muted by the need to focus on urgent domestic tasks, of which reconstruction from the ravages of the tsunami is only one.

In an epilogue drawing on the chapters of this volume, the editor assesses the interrelated challenges confronting Indonesia's leaders as they look to the future. He concludes that the subtitle of this volume—*The Great Transition*—will apply to Indonesia, if it is fortunate, for years to come. New and reformed institutions, whether social, political, or economic, will require time to become established. Meanwhile, much depends on individual leaders. It is partly a matter of luck whether and how these might rise to meet the needs of a people. To that extent, he concludes, Indonesia's future remains hostage to good fortune. He also asks whether it is not time for Indonesia to be considered a "normal" country and brought more fully into the general literature on world affairs, an outcome he hopes this volume will help to advance.

NOTES

1. Karl Pelzer and Ruth McVey, *Indonesia* (New Haven: Human Relations Area File Press, 1963), preface, no page number.

2. Clifford Geertz, "Afterword: The Politics of Meaning" in Claire Holt, ed., *Culture and Politics in Indonesia* (Ithaca, N.Y.: Cornell University Press, 1972), 319.

1

What Is Indonesia?

Donald K. Emmerson

Indonesia is likely the worst of the nations now limping toward greater control of their own destiny. . . . Will the disastrous national disintegration that we have had for the past few years ever be mended . . . ? What should we do to rebuild optimism in an acutely pessimistic country?

—Ahmad Syafi'i Maarif, "Can Indonesia Survive until 2050?"[1]

We must begin again from zero.

—Semar, a character in *Republik Bagong*, a satirical play[2]

I'm a kid and I need to go to school. I have nothing now. I'm working for the future.

—Fifteen-year-old Syarita, on the day her school reopened following the deaths of five of her relatives and more than 150,000 others in an earthquake and tsunami that struck the province of Aceh on December 26, 2004[3]

Indonesia is a country that has been through a lot. In 1997–1998, its forests were blazing, its currency was sinking, its economy was shrinking, and its president resigned. In 1999–2000, democratic elections were held for the first time since 1955, a referendum in East Timor overwhelmingly rejected Indonesian rule, and the presidency changed hands again. In 2001–2002, the president was impeached, the speaker of the house was found guilty of corruption, and Islamist terrorists killed more than 200 people on Bali. In 2003–2004, terrorists struck again in Jakarta, Indonesians went back to the polls three times, including a first-ever presidential election, and on December

26, 2004, the northwestern tip of Sumatra took the brunt of an earthquake plus tsunami deadlier in lives lost than any natural disaster to strike the archipelago since 1815.

Capital flight, a laggard economy, widespread corruption. Political demonstrations, communal violence, secessionist movements. Constitutional innovation, radical decentralization, five presidents in seven years. These challenges and changes render understandable the quotes at the beginning of this chapter—Syafi'i Maarif's cry of despair and Riantiarno's back-to-zero-ism, but also the hope of a better future in Syarita's determination to start her life again.

This chapter explores aspects of Indonesia's identity—some of the ways in which Indonesia has been, remains, and will continue to be more than zero. The qualifier "some" is crucial. Indonesia's identities are a vast and plural subject, whereas the scope of this chapter is necessarily limited. In selecting certain ways of seeing Indonesia for a brief treatment here, I did not try for comprehensiveness. I decided instead to highlight four broad aspects of identity: a *spatial* Indonesia visualized along physical, social, and political lines; a *centrifugal* Indonesia that could someday disintegrate, as Syafi'i Maarif and others have feared; a *historical* Indonesia variously influenced by its precolonial, colonial, and nationalist pasts; and a *personal* Indonesia as imagined or experienced by individual Indonesians.[4] In addition to meriting review in their own right, these understandings of Indonesia will, I hope, complement the discussions of religion, politics, economy, and foreign affairs in the rest of this book.

In a volume on contemporary affairs, history typically comes first. Especially in a book that contemplates a country's future, the first author might want to fill in the history, freeing the other authors to focus on the present and the future. But these contemporary concerns make the past too important to assign to a single chapter. Today and tomorrow cannot possibly be understood without first comprehending yesterday, not to mention the years, decades, and centuries that have gone before. Necessarily, therefore, from their various perspectives, my co-contributors take Indonesian history richly into account. In doing so, they have left me free not to ignore history but to approach my subject, Indonesian identity, from a point of view that visualizes Indonesia in space rather than tracing it over time. The decline of geography as a discipline in the United States and the corresponding paucity of spatial approaches to Indonesia in American writing also influenced my choice of geography over history as a principal (though hardly exclusive) lens.

That said, two main arguments I make toward the end of this chapter are unapologetically historical in nature. First, Indonesia was a state before it became a nation. In consequence, rather than the nation straightforwardly growing a state through which to organize itself, the Indonesian nation has been called into being by—and substantially for—a preexisting state. "Self-determination" in this context is therefore only a partial truth. Certainly the idea of Indonesia has proven its resilience against considerable odds. The country is not about to break into pieces. But in *only one* of Indonesia's multiple possible futures does the state-nation finally and fully become the nation-state.

The second argument stems from the first: If the state matters so much, it also matters greatly who controls the state. The modern political history of Indonesia can be simplified as a prolonged struggle for control over the state and hence for possession of a major basis for shaping the identity of the nation. Seeing and, when it suited them, exaggerating these high stakes, elite actors at key moments have made sudden moves to forestall the feared actions of others. Some of these preemptive moves have had great, even devastating consequences. As a historical legacy, the sheer efficacy of elite preemption amounts to a lingering temptation away from the rule of law.

A crucial element in building immunity against this temptation was the constitutional and other reforms accomplished in 1999–2004, including the elections of 1999 and 2004 and the experiment in decentralization that began in 2001. These reforms held out the hope of constraining the autonomy and impunity of elite actors so that they could no longer, in the name of forestalling a hypothetical future disaster, create a real one now. In this respect, it was not merely the benign or malign content of Indonesia's futures that mattered as the country tested its reforms in national, regional, and local elections in 2004 and its mettle in 2005 coping with the tsunami's aftermath in Aceh.[5] There was also a need to reduce the sheer number of futures for the country that observers, accustomed to the arbitrariness of unaccountable elites, could plausibly entertain.

This chapter does not begin with such large—and debatable—ideas. It starts with rocks—geophysical Indonesia. The country is introduced spatially in terms of its coherence, distinctiveness, and commonality. Topics covered include geographic and linguistic patterns of identity, and the status of borders historically and now. Treated next are decentralization and pressures for secession in Aceh and Papua as they may affect Indonesian identity. Indonesia as a Javanese empire, a Dutch legacy, and a nationalist artifact are considered next, followed by a glimpse of images of Indonesia in the minds and lives of a small and unrepresentative but thought-provoking group of younger Indonesians. Throughout, tying these otherwise disparate materials together, is the title question: What is Indonesia?

Among some readers already familiar with Indonesia, the question may seem too obvious to bother asking. Indonesia is a country. End of story.

Cognoscenti, on the other hand, may consider the question misconceived. They may fear it invites a would-be definitive summation of the "true" reality of Indonesia. As if a notion so varied and complex in its meanings as "Indonesia" could be reduced to the limits of a singular noun, as in "Indonesia is a country." End of story? Hardly. *Beginning* of an *endless* story.

If I thought Indonesia were banal, I would not have written this chapter. And asking a deceptively simple question hardly precludes — I hope it invites — the discovery of just how many, diverse, and debatable are the identities that have been and could be attributed to Indonesia. My purpose is not to single out among these images and possibilities the one "real" Indonesia. But neither are they all equally proven or plausible. Complexity is not a synonym for "anything goes."

How much does go? Is enough already known and agreed about Indonesia for its multiple identities to have been culled to the point where only the most factual survive? Not at all. Identities are not testable propositions; they embody belief. And even if they were, the stock of certain and detailed knowledge about Indonesia still leaves much to be desired.

Compared with that of the United States, the surface of Indonesia is less well mapped, and its history since 1945, when its existence as an independent state was first declared, has been documented in less detail. To this extent, it is easier to imagine Indonesia. One is less restrained by what is known beyond dispute. Observers vary in how much they know. Errors about Indonesia's most basic characteristics can persist among educated Americans and Europeans because of the greater incidence in such populations of ignorance about Indonesia than about the United States, say, or the United Kingdom.

To illustrate the latter point, look up "Indonesia" in the 2002 edition of the *Shorter Oxford English Dictionary*. There is no entry for "Indonesia," but "Indonesian" is defined as a native inhabitant of "Indonesia, a large island group in SE Asia, and now esp. of the federal republic of Indonesia, comprising Java, Sumatra, southern Borneo, western New Guinea, the Moluccas, Sulawesi, and many other smaller islands." Far from being true "now," this statement was never true. During the few and only months when Indonesia was a federal republic — from December 27, 1949, until the formal abrogation of that arrangement on August 17, 1950 — authority over western New Guinea remained in Dutch hands. It is hard to imagine such a basic factual error in the *OED*'s entry for, say, "Britain."[6]

Indonesia's huge size makes the extent of the literature on it seem paltry by comparison. Much about the country remains unclear, including matters that one might expect to have been settled long ago. Consider what happens, for example, if we "simply" count the islands and part islands inside the boundaries of Indonesia in search of a total figure that can stand as an empirically fixed and lasting physical answer to the question that entitles this chapter.

According to Robert Cribb in his invaluable *Historical Dictionary of Indonesia* (1992), "The country . . . consists of approximately 13,669 islands the size of a tennis court or larger; the exact number changes frequently due to siltation and volcanic eruptions."[7] Eight years later, in his no less useful *Historical Atlas of Indonesia*, Cribb updated his earlier estimate while further emphasizing its mutability. Indonesia, he wrote,

> is formally considered to consist of 17,508 islands. (With the recent loss of East Timor's two offshore islands, Atauro [Kambing] and Jaco, the official figure is presumably 17,506.) This figure was decided in 1994 and replaced the earlier official figure of 13,667, set in 1963. Only about 3,000 of these islands, however, are said to be inhabited and only about 6,000 are officially named, though many more certainly have unrecognized local names. In reality the number of islands—however an island is defined—is in constant flux.

Cribb noted, for example, how siltation at the mouths of rivers could form new offshore islands or join old ones to the mainland, and how coral islands could be submerged through mining and erosion.[8] Had he been writing in 2005 he might have added to this map-changing list the creative destruction of the massive earthquake and tsunami that shook and battered northwestern Sumatra in 2004. Two years before, in December 2002, the International Court of Justice adjudicated Indonesia's and Malaysia's claims to Sipadan and Ligitan in the western Celebes Sea by awarding both islands to Malaysia. Two months later, however, new satellite photographs of all pieces of land at least 30 square meters large suddenly boosted Indonesia's total to 18,108.[9]

Uncertainty, flux, and therefore subjectivity thus compromise even this most tangible embodiment of Indonesia. Perfect bedrock—exactly known, forever fixed—is a holy grail. There is no single, nontrivial, debate-silencing answer to the question, What is Indonesia?

INDONESIA IN THREE DIMENSIONS

What is Indonesia? is a question about identity. But what is identity?

Coherence, *distinctiveness*, and *commonality* are three spatial dimensions that help an observer compare and assess assertions of identity. Coherence is the extent to which the contents of a phenomenon are patterned rather than random. Distinctiveness is the extent to which the phenomenon stands out against the environment around it. Commonality is the extent to which the contents of the phenomenon are similar rather than disparate. By these criteria, the extent to which a phenomenon has an identity depends on the extent to which it meets them.

Arguing Coherence

However many islands Indonesia has, on a summary map they form no consistent pattern. The country's shape is not, for example, symmetrical.[10] But one way of arranging the jumble of islands has endured: the perception of Java (including Madura and typically Bali as well) as an "inner" or "core" island compared with the "outer" or "peripheral" ones—in Dutch colonial parlance, the Buitengewesten, or outer territories—that make up the rest of the country.

The suitability of these designations cannot be judged without reference to history, demography, political economy, and culture. Readers may, nevertheless, wish to glance at the map of Indonesia in this book to see for themselves, simplified on a flat page, how convincing or far-fetched this pattern of core and periphery appears to be. To my eyes, in purely cartographic terms, the case for an inner–outer pattern that puts Java at its core is imaginable but not compelling.

The spatial salience of core and periphery depends on their being easily distinguished. This would be true, for example, if the core were the largest island and the peripheral islands were all markedly smaller. But that is not the case. Java is only the fifth largest island or part-island inside Indonesia. The biggest such feature in the country is Kalimantan, the Indonesian bulk of Borneo.

For such a pattern to be complete, the periphery should entirely surround the core. That too is not the case. Would-be peripheral islands circumscribe Java only from its northwest clockwise around to its east. Java itself is too far west to be literally central. Nor is there much to be gained by searching for a core island of any consequence at the geographic center of Indonesia; the candidates are mere specks.

Not far away from that exact center are the million-plus inhabitants of Makassar, the largest Indonesian city east of Surabaya. Could Indonesians sometime in this century counterbalance the superiority of Jakarta by moving their capital to Makassar, closer to the physical midpoint of the country? In 2003 this prospect remained wildly unlikely. But in the long run it is not impossible. As the largest country in Southeast Asia by area and population, Indonesia is comparable wholly or partly to Brazil in Latin America or Nigeria in Africa. It may not be frivolous to recall the migration of the capitals of these states, respectively, from coastal Rio de Janeiro to central Brasilia and from coastal Lagos to central Abuja.

One might also look for a center and fringe pattern in the extent to which Jakarta dwarfs the rest of Indonesia's urban areas. The larger a metropolitan core and the thinner its urban periphery, one could argue, the greater the chance that the latter will depend on and be dominated by the former—a case of inegalitarian coherence. With a year 2000 population officially estimated at 8.4 million, greater Jakarta is by far the most populous urban zone in Indonesia. Yet the share of all city dwellers who live in the capital area may not be much over 10 percent. The only country in Southeast Asia with a lower rate of urban primacy is Malaysia, and Malaysia is also the region's only federation.[11] In this comparative light, one could interpret Indonesia's recent and radical experiment with decentralization as a belated political acknowledgment of a demographic fact.

Indonesia's major coastal and near coastal cities, considered clockwise from west to east, do form a flat and foreshortened circle that runs from Palembang northeast to Banjarmasin, continues farther east to Makassar, then halts and turns southwest to Denpasar, farther west through Surabaya and Semarang to Jakarta, and finally northwest back to Palembang. The resulting oval circumscribes the Java Sea, but stops well short of the Flores and Banda Seas—the vast eastern extension of Indonesia's ostensible maritime core.

With a single exception, the Indonesian islands and part islands to the east of Sulawesi or Java are all much smaller than the big four that lie in the center or to the west: Sulawesi, Kalimantan, Java, and Sumatra. The exception is Papua, the huge and mountainous half island that traditionally has been Indonesia's most sparsely populated province.[12]

Will Indonesia develop these eastern towns and hinterlands enough to pull its urban oval eastward, beyond Sulawesi and Bali, toward a more symmetrical identity for the country? It is hard to say. The eastern zone has long been considered the main frontier for demographic, economic, and infrastructural expansion. Developing the eastern islands was a priority for President Suharto in the 1990s. In 2000–2004 eastern Indonesia was the only region with its own cabinet post—first junior and then state minister to accelerate the development of Eastern Indonesia. But it was one thing to acknowledge the center's previous neglect of the east, and quite another to remedy it.

If the zone's potential is fulfilled, some eastern coastal towns could become thriving cities. If that happens, the urban–littoral oval around the Java Sea will expand to include the Banda Sea as well, improving the symmetry and possibly also the cohesion of a sea-centered identity for Indonesia. The historical lagging of the east behind the center west may not be reversed, however.[13] And a failure to tie these eastern lands and peoples more dynamically and equitably to the rest of Indonesia could have significant long-term consequences. These could even include a further shrinkage of Indonesia's eastern border—"further" in relation to East Timor's already having left the republic in 1999 and gained its own independence, as Timor Lorosa'e (or Timor Leste), in May 2002.

In strictly spatial terms, then, Indonesia does not obviously cohere. And even if the centrality of the Java and Banda Seas implies a maritime heart, where does the periphery of Indonesia stop and its external environment begin? Water is a continuous field, unlike the coast of an island. Separated only by the narrow Sunda Strait, Sumatra and Java clearly delimit much of southern Indonesia and place the Indian Ocean outside the country. But where are the boundaries of Indonesia to be drawn? along the northern semicircle from west to east, in the Andaman Sea, the Malacca Strait, the South China Sea, the Celebes Sea, the Philippine Sea, the Pacific Ocean, the Arafura Sea, and the Timor Sea? Visualized in core sea terms, Indonesia may gain internal coherence at the expense of its distinctiveness.

Arguing Distinctiveness

The designation of islands as inside or outside Indonesia seems arbitrary. Why should Sipadan and Ligitan, off the northeast coast of Borneo, be Malaysian despite their proximity to Indonesian Kalimantan, while Miangas, northeast across the Celebes Sea, is Indonesian notwithstanding its proximity to Philippine Mindanao? Small wonder that Indonesia contested Malaysian sovereignty over Sipadan and Ligitan, while the Philippines claims the waters around Indonesian Miangas. These are tiny bits of land. But purely in terms of proximity—ignoring the Spanish and Dutch colonial histories that conditioned the demarcation of the Philippines from Indonesia—why should the second largest of all the Philippine islands, Mindanao, not be Indonesian? More anomalous still is the inclusion of the Natuna-Anambas islands inside Indonesia, given their location between western and eastern Malaysia and north of a straight line drawn from the Malaysian capital (Kuala Lumpur) to the capital of Malaysian Sarawak (Kuching).

Opinions vary as to how many of Indonesia's outermost islands and islets could become sites of territorial disputation with neighboring states. An Indonesian journalist has estimated that Miangas is only one of some eighty such potentially controversial features.[14] Ownership of Sipadan and Ligitan became an issue between Jakarta and Kuala Lumpur only in 1969, after President Suharto succeeded President Sukarno and cooperation replaced confrontation in Indonesian–Malaysian relations. Those relations remained amicable enough to keep the matter on a back burner until 1997 and finally to yield, in that year, an agreement between the two governments to submit the dispute for arbitration by the International Court of Justice. In December 2002, when the Court awarded sovereignty over both islands to Malaysia, Indonesia's foreign minister accepted "as final and binding" the rejection of his country's claim.[15]

Such equanimity is not assured when it comes to resolving disagreements elsewhere along the fringe of Indonesia. More influential as a precedent could be the court's prior reasoning, not only regarding Sipadan and Ligitan but also, more than half a century earlier, its approval of Dutch rather than American sovereignty over Miangas. Critical on both occasions was the criterion of *effectivité*—the actual and effective exercise of state authority over a disputed territory by any one claimant.[16] If there is a lesson here for Jakarta, it may be that Indonesia's borders are best shored up not by relying on maps displaying contiguity or treaties showing cession, but by expanding and activating, archipelago wide, the presence of the state.

As for the differentiating power of Indonesia's four land borders, none of them consistently separates what is distinctively Indonesian from what is not. The line between Indonesian and Malaysian Borneo, the two that delimit Indonesian West Timor from the enclave and half island that make up independent East Timor, and the one between Indonesian Papua and independent Papua New Guinea (PNG) are definitively clear on standard *political* maps of Southeast Asia.[17] In the absence of patterns representing other variables, these borders seem definitively clear-cut. But this need not be true—and it can be spectacularly untrue—of other displays.

Consider, for example, what happens to these four demarcations when they appear on *ethno-linguistic* maps. Large areas of similarity representing broad classifications of indigenous languages surround the political lines on both sides. So do the smaller areas where those languages are spoken. This "double erasure" of sovereignty by speech is most evident in Borneo, where the Indonesian–Malaysian border runs through a broad zone of "Austronesian" languages and through specific subzones as well, including "Malayan," "Land Dayak," "Kayan-Kenyah," and "Apo Duat." But the case for speech over sovereignty holds as well for Indonesia's eastern land borders. Farthest to the east, for example, the aptly named Trans-New Guinea phylum of local tongues overwhelms the distinction between Indonesia and PNG, although some much smaller phyla are unique to one side or the other.[18]

How, then, is sovereignty related to speech? Data on where languages are located were gathered some time ago, and subsequent migration may have moved a linguistic frontier closer to a political one. More importantly, detailed ethno-linguistic maps of the sort cited here locate "indigenous" languages, omitting the products of language mixing (pidgins) and the secondary languages (lingua franca) that make communication possible among people whose first languages differ. Often spread by trade, pidgins and lingua franca may be widely spoken, sometimes widely enough to qualify as "national" languages. Taking such instances into account will tend more closely to align political with linguistic borders.

But not if the same mixed or secondary language is widely used on both sides of the border. The Malay language spoken in Malaysia and the Indonesian one spoken by Indonesians (Bahasa Indonesia) are not identical. Their respective lexicons differ more than those of American and British English, for example. Yet the divergence of Indonesian and Malay falls well short of mutual incomprehension. Nor have the governments in Jakarta and Kuala Lumpur tried to increase the linguistic distance between them. On the contrary, the two sides agreed in 1972 to use the same spelling rules—a "decolonizing" convergence in which Indonesian was purged of orthographic conventions held over from Dutch days. These transnational consistencies reduce, in effect, the linguistic sharpness of Indonesia's western political rim.

If Indonesian distinctiveness is attenuated in the west by the overlapping of Indonesian and Malay, circumstances along the farthest eastern perimeter of Indonesia are very different. In the southeast, notwithstanding Jakarta's imposition of Bahasa Indonesia on East Timor before the latter's independence, the zone in which Tetum is spoken does roughly distinguish that country from its Indonesian neighbor. Farther east, the interlinguistic boundaries between New Guinea Pidgin and Bahasa Indonesia roughly coincide with the PNG–Indonesian border.[19] Likely to strengthen this correlation is the implementation of the decision by East Timor's constitutional convention to enshrine Tetum and Portuguese, but not Indonesian, as official languages of the new country.[20]

In modern times—the heyday of the nation-state—sovereign borders probably have reinforced differences in speech at least as often as similarities in speech have weakened sovereign borders. Such a pattern is especially likely to hold true for a nascent country that has just escaped the long and brutal embrace of a much larger neighbor. Indonesian domination of East Timor has, nevertheless, left its imprint on local discourse.

Prior to its invasion and occupation by Indonesia beginning in 1975, East Timor had been part of Portugal's empire. By the time independence was finally achieved, after nearly a quarter century of rule from Jakarta, the Indonesian language had become far more widely known than Portuguese. A survey in 2001 found Tetum, Indonesian, and Portuguese spoken, respectively, by 82, 43, and merely 5 percent of East Timorese households.[21] Unlike Portuguese, Tetum lacks a diverse modern vocabulary and long-standardized rules of spelling and usage. Independence meant that official documents, formerly written in Indonesian, would now be couched in Portuguese, ensuring their incomprehensibility without translation in the eyes of virtually the entire population. Younger citizens of the new state, schooled in Indonesian and ignorant of Portuguese, felt especially disadvantaged.

Future good relations with Jakarta could erode in Timor Lorosa'e the opprobrium associated with Bahasa Indonesia as the language of a recent oppressor. Indonesian, along with English, is already considered a "working language."[22] Bad relations, however, could further downgrade Indonesian over time while upgrading Tetum, or expanding English, reinforcing in discourse the political separation of the two countries. Most probably, the usage of Indonesian will fade but not disappear.

"One nation, one people, *one language*" announced the nationalist authors of the Youth Oath in Batavia (later Jakarta) in 1928, although the italics are mine. As an assertion of Indonesian identity, the phrase would become famous—almost a mantra. Measured by the extent to which its boundaries distinguish it linguistically from its environment, however, Indonesia is not compellingly singular. Especially in the west, speakers of the same language, or of languages in the same group, tend to flank the sides of its sovereign borders.

It will not be easy to nationalize discourse in Timor Lorosa'e. Tetum, Portuguese, English, Indonesian . . . One nation, one people, *four* languages. And this in a microstate with a population one-third of 1 percent the size of Indonesia's.[23] Can East Timor afford to acknowledge multiple tongues without risking an identity made solid by decades of Indonesian repression? Or does its legal concession to pluralism reflect real schisms—historical, generational, social, political—whose exacerbation by the "victory" of a single language would threaten the nascent state? Decades from now, will its linguistically eclectic but Portuguese-privileging first constitution be praised as tolerant, or faulted as divisive?

I raise these questions not to answer them but to underscore how fortunate Indonesia has been to avoid them. Bahasa Indonesia as a nationalist choice may not have rescued Indonesia from otherwise certain ruin. But it is hard to picture the republic having survived this long in Javanese. Indonesians were also able to strengthen their identity by virtue of having a consensus in favor of Indonesian well prior to independence.

Movable Borders?

In spatially vast countries such as the United States and Indonesia, pride can be taken in the breadth of national space. A vocal example occurs when American and Indonesian pupils on patriotic occasions sing of their countries' respective widths, "from sea to shining sea" and "from Sabang to Merauke." The latter pair names an island off the northwestern tip of the westernmost province of Indonesia (Aceh) and a town in the southeastern corner of its easternmost counterpart (Papua).

The connotations of these phrases differ, however. Even though it had been part of the Netherlands East Indies, Papua was formally attached to Indonesia only in 1963. By then, a unitary Indonesian republic spanning the rest of the former Indies had been independent for more than a decade. The reference to Merauke in the national anthem thus connotes a nationalist struggle to enlarge the new state. The revolution more or less led by Sukarno in 1945–1949 was, of course, anticolonial. In cartographic terms, however, Sukarno's later campaign to push the country's eastern border farther east had a neocolonial goal: to return that border to its original, colonial location.

One might argue that "Polynesian Hawaii," a small archipelago, has been to core-continental-Caucasian America what "Melanesian Papua," a large landmass, has been to core-maritime-Malay Indonesia—a peripheral and thus also potentially member of a different sphere of meaning and belonging. Compared with the Papuan independence movement, however, Hawaii's nativist movement is modest in purpose, method, and size. Unlike native Hawaiians, who form a minority in their home state, Papuans are still a majority in their home province.

Exactly how much of a majority is not clear. Migration from the rest of Indonesia appears to have enlarged the proportion of Papua's residents who were born outside the province from only 4 percent in 1971 to about 20 percent by 1990 and 33 percent by 2001. At this rate of acceleration, Papuans could become a minority in their homeland by 2006.[24] Straight-line extrapolations that depend on so many variables are almost always wrong. But the fear of becoming outnumbered in their own home province is all too credible among Papuan nationalists.

As already noted, Papuans are Melanesians. A family of ethnic groups scattered widely across the southern Pacific Ocean, Melanesians tend to differ from Malays in skin color, facial features, and hair—not to mention the churches that further differentiate Indonesia's Christian-majority Papuans from its majority-Muslim Malays.

Barriers to Papuan let alone Melanesian identity remain formidable, however. New Guinea's mountainous, communication-impeding terrain and corresponding language diversity have worked to inhibit the growth of broadly "Melanesian" solidarity both within the province of Papua and across the decades-old international border between Papua and PNG. In this context, the Free Papua Organization has focused on national independence for the Indonesian province of Papua within its existing borders. Nor have the authorities in Port Moresby, PNG's capital, been willing to risk the consequences of laying a claim to their huge neighbor's eastern flank. In 2005 it was still fanciful to think that the vertical line bisecting New Guinea could be erased on behalf of a "greater Melanesian" state combining Papua and PNG.

On a map, the western extension of Papua vaguely resembles the head of a bird. In 2003 Jakarta drew a new line down the bird's neck, declared the head a new province, and named it Irian Jaya Barat—West Irian Jaya. The Indonesian part of New Guinea, formerly one province, became two: West Irian Jaya and Papua, respectively the head and body of the bird. ("Papua" in this chapter refers to the territory occupied by the one province before 2003 and by the two provinces afterward.) This development will be discussed below. Suffice it for now to acknowledge the split as a possible further impediment to pan-Papuan identity.

Indonesian nationalists inclined to scan the eastern fringes of their unitary republic for pieces that might someday break off, as East Timor did, may take some comfort in the view to the far west. There, where another zone of rough (Malay-Muslim) resemblance straddles an international boundary (with Malaysia), can the sharp clarity of Sumatra's northern coastline be said to help "keep" Aceh inside Indonesia, notwithstanding that province's secessionist challenge to Jakarta?

Certainly, on a geophysical map, Indonesia's westernmost border appears far less arbitrary than its easternmost one. Aceh is land's end and ocean's beginning, despite belonging to the ethnically Malay world that spans the Malacca Strait and being called "the front porch of Mecca" for its long-standing Muslim identity and, relative to the rest of Indonesia, least distance from the hub of global Islam.

Yet the maritime passageway separating Indonesia from Malaysia is not a barrier to air and sea travel and does not prevent Acehnese and Malaysians from communicating by phone, fax, mail, or e-mail. What keeps Aceh from declaring and pursuing a "greater Malay" identity in common with Malaysia is much less the province's coastline than a host of other factors. These include Aceh's history as an independent sultanate in its own right; its record of resistance to outside rule; its willing participation in the Indonesian revolution; its troubled but long-standing incorporation into the rest of independent Indonesia; the very different colonial and postcolonial experience of what is now peninsular Malaysia; and the consistent unwillingness of Malaysian governments to claim Aceh as theirs, given not only the risk of war with Indonesia but also the likelihood that Acehnese themselves would reject such an imperial presumption. The devastating earthquake and tsunami that struck the province in December 2004 may have made it even more dependent on aid through and from, and thus its ties to, Jakarta. Whatever Aceh may be, it is not the front porch of Kuala Lumpur.

Nor is geography destiny. The politically centrifugal forces at work in Papua and Aceh should not be underestimated. But if the arbitrariness of Indonesia's border with PNG has not fostered a "greater Papuan" project, neither does the geophysical clarity of the Sumatran coast and the Malacca Strait explain why Acehnese secessionists lack Malaysian horizons.

As for the chances of a narrower independence for Papua and Aceh proper, in 2005 these prospects seemed less realistic than they had just a few years before when financial collapse, political conflict, and communal violence had threatened to derail Indonesia's "great transition" from authoritarian rule.

A Borderless World?

The case being made here for the importance and durability of Indonesia's sovereign borders is necessarily cursory. But it cannot be left without taking into account one particularly bold and sweeping argument against it: that a boundary-indifferent model of the polity held sway in precolonial Southeast Asia and has been reintroduced (or at any rate refurbished) by globalization in the postcolonial era. From this standpoint, the Dutch, British, and German officials who drew an almost ruler-straight line down the middle of New Guinea in agreements reached around the turn of the twentieth century were not only violating the geophysical integrity of that island. They were also transgressing the border blindness of a much earlier and authentically "Indonesian" conception of the polity. In this view, as the globe has been increasingly crisscrossed by flows of people, goods, and information—globalization—the bounded state as a colonial legacy in Southeast Asia is being superseded by postmodern versions of this originally borderless polity. Thus reconsidered, the idea of Indonesia as the physical and social space inside a delimited frame could in future turn out to have been a Western conceit whose time came and is now going, soon to be gone.[25]

The precolonial polity at issue here is called a mandala. Not Southeast Asian but Indian in origin, a mandala is at once a pattern and a metaphor. In the first of these meanings, it is a concentric diagram—in Sanskrit, *mandala* meant circular or round—with spiritual and ritual significance for followers of certain Hindu and Buddhist traditions. Its shape appears to have been reflected in the architecture of the circular Buddhist shrine known as a *stupa*, and in the religio-political practice whereby a ruler circumambulated such a shrine, as if to encircle the universe and thus reaffirm his power over it. (Leave aside the ambiguity implicit in physically tracing a manifest boundary while laying claim to limitless space.) This identification of a microcosmic structure with a macrocosmic realm seems also to have symbolized the totality of existence and thus the erasure of any distinction between "inner" and "outer" being.

Arguably the best known and visually most impressive Buddhist shrine anywhere is Borobudur, located northwest of the court city of Yogyakarta in central Java. Built in the eighth and ninth centuries C.E. under the aegis of the Sailendra dynasty then ruling the area, Borobudur proceeds upward from a square base through a five-level stepped pyramid to a set of seventy-two

Buddha-enclosing stupas arranged on three concentrically circular levels that sustain, at the top, a final, central stupa enclosing empty space. The original meaning of the monument remains obscure. Enhancing a mandala-based impression, however, is the resemblance of Borobudur to a sacred mountain. Given the volcanic character of Java's landscape, making a mountain stand for power and its concentration may predate even the arrival of the Indic mandala.

It is difficult to fix unambiguously the defining features of the mandala in its second meaning: as a metaphor for the kind of polity that existed in precolonial times in what is now Indonesia and which could someday succeed the Indonesian nation-state—or state-nation—in a form at least vaguely reminiscent of the ancient original. As it has been reconstructed and reinterpreted backward over the intervening centuries on the basis of limited archeological and mythological evidence, a precolonial mandala polity is a loose system of rule. The system is not demarcated territorially in space. Nor is it regularized dynastically over time. It is based instead on the contingent ability of a particular ruler to display, project, and maintain religio-personal primacy in a larger and unbordered realm in which the unconditional claims of other such rulers in other such centers overlap and conflict.[26] The farther one travels from the exemplary center of such a mandala, the less influential its ruler is likely to be.

Present-day Indonesia has not been modeled on a mandala, at least not overtly. The Western-derived project of the nation-state has been the leitmotiv of modern Indonesian political history: to constitute and emancipate from colonial control a colonially demarcated country; to configure it on maps not as a radiant center, whose light fades with distance, but as an evenly and uniformly sovereign entity clear "from Sabang to Merauke"; and to embody such sovereignty not in the personality of a god-king (however self-legitimating the pretensions of Sukarno or Suharto may have been) but in abstractions (characteristically, though not always, "the nation" for Sukarno and, for Suharto, "the state").

Mandala-style polities have nevertheless played roles in the rhetorical construction of Indonesian identity. The early history of Indonesia's islands included, by the surviving evidence, many instances of apparently mandala-like polities whose fragility limited their longevity. There were, however, two exceptions to the short shelf life of the archipelago's precolonial polities. Srivijaya, ostensibly a mandala polity centered in what is now the city of Palembang in southeastern Sumatra, endured for several centuries prior to its eleventh-century decline. Majapahit, based in eastern Java and debatably also a mandala polity, lasted some three centuries, shining brightest in the fourteenth century before its own long if uneven dwindling into the sixteenth. These two empires of sorts (and especially Majapahit) were notable too for the spatially greater extent of their influence, however difficult it is to infer from fragmentary and often indirect evidence just how far their presences were felt.

Claims to national identity are often transhistorical, seeking in history a prefiguring of the nation and a validation of the struggle on its behalf. In this context Srivijaya and Majapahit have afforded Indonesian nationalists in the twentieth century a grand, enduring, and therefore usably prototypical past.

What recommended these examples was not their content, mandala-like or otherwise, but their breadth in space and their durability over time. That said, however, it is worth asking why, in this mythologizing, Majapahit upstaged Srivijaya. The reasons include the greater accumulation of evidence regarding Majapahit compared with the earlier Srivijayan polity. But it also clearly mattered that Majapahit was a Javanese realm centered on Java.

Whether modern Indonesia resembles a Javanese empire is a topic treated later in this chapter. Here I merely want to note the affinity between a core and periphery understanding of Indonesian identity that appreciates the core and a mandala that sanctifies it. In this context, compared with Javanese Majapahit, the Sumatran focus of Srivijaya would have reduced its eligibility in the eyes of nationalists ransacking history in search of a proto-Indonesia. Both Srivijaya and Majapahit offered mythological Indonesia a welcome distinctiveness for which the Dutch could never claim credit. But only Java-focused Majapahit supplied core island coherence as well.

This brings me to commonality, the third and last of my suggested dimensions of identity.

Arguing Commonality

Is Indonesia the most diverse country on earth? Not necessarily. It is, however, among the most diverse countries on many dimensions.

Especially striking is the variety of fauna and flora. If the numbers of different species of mammals, birds, marine life, and flowering plants known to exist in data-available countries as of the late 1990s are compared, Indonesia emerges with the highest average ranking.[27] Notable in this respect is the broad zone of biotic transition that groups the islands between Kalimantan and Bali to the west and Papua to the east. Known as Wallacea, this longitudinal swath combines the Asian animals and plants of western Indonesia with the Australian forms typical of the archipelago's easternmost end—a legacy geologically traceable to the collision of eastern and western continental plates some 19 million years ago.[28]

Indonesia is no less famous for its human diversity, and in a chapter on national identity, linguistic variety is an especially relevant case in point. Estimates of the number of languages presently spoken in Indonesia vary greatly, for lack of adequate information on a complex and changing situation, and due to ambiguities as to exactly what a language is and how to distinguish one from another. Nevertheless, according to a comprehensive, detailed, and reasonably up-to-date survey by the Summer Institute of Linguistics (SIL), a total of 726 indigenous languages were spoken in the 1980s and early 1990s as mother tongues—first languages—in Indonesia.[29]

But this impression of Babel needs qualification. Comparatively, as an instance of language variety in the world, Indonesia is not the most diverse country. Far from it. The late linguist Joseph Greenberg developed a method of calculating the probability that in a given country two randomly selected individuals will have different mother tongues. The index runs from 0 (no diversity) to 1 (maximum diversity). By this measure, according to SIL, twenty-seven countries are linguistically more varied than Indonesia, whose Greenberg score is "only" .83.[30]

The most language-diverse country in the world by this method turns out be Indonesia's immediate eastern neighbor, Papua New Guinea, whose Greenberg rating is an almost perfectly heterogeneous .99. With a population of barely more than 5 million, PNG has more spoken first languages—823—than Indonesia with its 227 million-plus people. Nor is PNG exceptional in this respect within the Melanesian sphere. Second most diverse are Vanuatu (.97) and the Solomon Islands (.97), while New Caledonia (.84) is polylingual as well. Variety is evident too in East Timor (.88).

Also intriguing is the distribution of linguistic diversity inside Indonesia. If the country is divided into seven zones and these are listed in declining order of linguistic differentiation, the sequence is Papua (.94), Maluku (.94), Sulawesi (.87), Sumatra (.86), Nusa Tenggara (.85), Kalimantan (.78), and finally Java and Bali (.66). Indonesia as a whole is linguistically various, but the variegation is spatially peripheral. Relative to the core, it inhabits the rim. If Java and Bali form that "inner" core, and the other six zones just listed are "outer" islands, the imbalance is striking. With less than 40 percent of the total population, the outer islands nevertheless originated and/or today mainly locate 97 percent of the country's indigenous languages. Java and Bali, where more than 60 percent of Indonesians live, account for merely 3 percent of the indigenous languages. Furthermore, diversity by this measure is concentrated in the sparsely populated east. Less than 2 percent of Indonesians live in Papua or Maluku, yet more than half—54 percent—of the country's autochthonous languages are based there.[31]

The extent of exclusivity or overlap (e.g., in vocabulary) among the 726 "different" languages identified by SIL is not clear. And even in the extremely unlikely event that all of them are mutually unintelligible, one cannot infer incomprehension in general from first-language incompatibility. Two randomly chosen individuals may speak wholly different first languages while conversing for years in a second language, such as Bahasa Indonesia.

Also unclear is the extent to which these data take recent migration into account. Were they updated to incorporate fully the arrival of non–Javanese speakers on Java, would that island's diversity score be higher? What of the countertrend whereby Javanese speakers "transmigrate" to the outer islands? Would the effects of this two-way traffic on linguistic diversity be self-canceling? Not necessarily, and surely not exactly.

Nevertheless, for the present purpose of large-scale spatial comparison, better evidence almost surely would not overthrow the conclusion reached here: that the rim of non-Javanese outer islands and Melanesian eastern islands is more first-language diverse than the core of Java and Bali. Corroborating the latter conclusion is another, far more summary estimate, which halves the number of "languages" thought by SIL to be found in Indonesia but, in effect, restates the greater concentration of diversity per capita and per square kilometer in Melanesian Indonesia.[32]

Identity through Language

What do these findings imply for national identity? The mere existence of variety does not foretell conflict. *Complementary* diversity can, on the contrary, imply cohesion, especially if it is also legitimate in the eyes of those involved. Within the life experience of an individual Indonesian there can indeed be a kind of "fit" between a first language and the lingua franca, Indonesian, used by that person to bypass first-language barriers. The development of Malay-based Bahasa Indonesia, from the premodern facilitation of coastal trade, linking ports, to the modern expression of national sentiments, linking citizens, has reinforced its essentially *public* role. First languages, which for most Indonesians were not Malay, were over this same period increasingly used for discourse in *private*.

Now consider the dynamic possibilities that could affect this relationship. The first, though not necessarily the most plausible, is stable complementarity. By that I mean the long-accustomed and unproblematic habit of allocating one's "mother tongue" mainly for use among first-language-sharing kin or neighbors, while reserving Bahasa Indonesia for less intimate settings and more formal occasions, including school, work, the media, and public gatherings. Bilingualism need not imply schizophrenia. One can be no less "Indonesian" for speaking Javanese or Batak or something else at home, and no less "Javanese" or "Batak" for using Indonesian at work or in school. In conditions of stable complementarity, the usage of any given language, national or local, can expand or contract over time without provoking controversy.

The second possibility is unstable complementarity, which could in theory intensify tension in either of two directions: animosity toward the national language as, say, a mechanism of exploitation and repression in the name of "Indonesian" unity; or alienation from one's childhood language as lexically inadequate and socially rustic or even "feudal"—the latter a charge sometimes leveled at the status-linked levels of Javanese. Language choices in this context could be zero-sum: One could, for instance, cultivate an "authentically" local language against Jakarta's apparently self-serving imposition of "artificial" Indonesian—or, for "patriotic" reasons, actively prefer and promote Indonesian over a divisively "parochial" local tongue.

What does in fact seem to be evolving is not a pattern of hostility at all, but a broadly stable complementarity in which the knowledge and use of Bahasa Indonesia has expanded rapidly while, by and large, the vernaculars have grown in usage more slowly, or remained more or less stationary, or lost ground.

Regarding the national language, the statistical evidence is striking. Census figures show a dramatic gain, during President Suharto's "New Order" regime, in the proportion of Indonesians able to speak Indonesian—from 40.5 percent in 1971 to 60.8 percent in 1980 to 82.8 percent in 1990.[33] The first of these figures is low enough to seem shocking. How could a country as large and as multiply varied as Indonesia have remained intact if in 1971, some two decades after its recognition as a republic, three-fifths of its citizens did not even speak its language?

In terms once popularized by Marshall McLuhan, the medium affects the message.[34] The medium provides vocabulary and grammar, supplies denotations, and evokes connotations. It preselects the potential audience to which the message can be intelligibly addressed. But form does not magically drive content toward behavior. A separatist can use the "national" language to denounce Indonesia and incite separation, just as a nationalist can express and mobilize loyalty to Indonesia in a "local"—or a foreign—tongue.

Movements for independence in Aceh and Papua illustrate the use of Indonesian against Indonesia. The Free Aceh Movement (Gerakan Aceh Merdeka, or GAM) and the Free Papua Organization (Organisasi Papua Merdeka, or OPM) today deploy in their own Indonesian-language names a word, *merdeka*, meaning "free," that Indonesians associate with their own earlier struggle for freedom from Dutch rule.

Linguistic form need not limit political content. The New Order's priority on expanding fluency and literacy in Indonesian and its concomitant neglect of local languages did have a politically limiting purpose: to help inoculate the population against appeals to racial, ethnic, religious, and class-based chauvinisms presumed to endanger national unity, state security, and, not coincidentally, the position of the strongman in charge of the state, general-turned-president Suharto.[35] But if simply knowing Bahasa Indonesia had been powerfully and lastingly centripetal in its political effects, the New Order's success in spreading knowledge of the national language should have precluded what, in fact, unfolded after Suharto resigned in 1998 and his regime unraveled: waves of resentment expressed against Jakarta, including one that swept East Timor out of the republic in 1999 and others strong enough to suggest domino effects that threatened, in the eyes of some at the time, to doom the republic.

THE END OF INDONESIA?

Here is how historian Robert Cribb began the published version of a paper he gave at a conference convened in Australia in 2000, at the height of uncertainty about Indonesia's future:

"East Timor is no longer a part of Indonesia. Aceh and Papua are seething with secessionist tension. The resource-rich provinces of Riau and East Kalimantan have put in ambit claims for independence, and talk has even been heard of independence demands from Bali and Sulawesi. The Indonesian experiment, a multiethnic state stretching more than 5,000 kilometres from east to west, is under challenge today as never before, and all over the Asia-Pacific region defense analysts are pondering the question of whether the early 21st century will see the disintegration of Indonesia in the way that the late 20th century saw the disintegration of the Soviet Union and Yugoslavia. For the first time since the Second World War, there is a serious possibility that the extended archipelago to Australia's north [roughly from PNG through Malaysia] could be divided not into five or six states as at present, but into a dozen or more."[36]

Four years later, in 2004, Indonesia's prospects appeared to be much less dire, but the conditions in Aceh and Papua were anything but improved. In Aceh, a ceasefire brokered by a Swiss organization in December 2002 had collapsed in the face of mutual mistrust and charges of failure to honor commitments. In May 2003 Jakarta had declared martial law in the province and launched a massive air, sea, and land offensive to destroy GAM. In Papua, where repression also continued, the Indonesian military had been implicated in the November 2001 killing of Papuan leader Theys Eluay and the August 2002 killing of two Americans working in an international school. Meanwhile, the global "war on terrorism"—triggered by Al Qaeda's attacks on the United States in September 2001 and sustained by subsequent incidents, including the bombing on Bali in October 2002 that took more than 200 lives—

strengthened Jakarta's hand by tending to reinforce international antipathy toward violence in the service of self-determination.

In 2000–2004 no serious impetus toward independence developed in Riau, East Kalimantan, Bali, and Sulawesi, all mentioned by Cribb as sites of conceivable future fracture. Most of the autonomist stirrings in these diverse settings were better understood as political entrepreneurship meant to maximize local advantage within Indonesia. Extracting such benefits required a continuing domestic relationship with the national capital from which they could be obtained. Enhancing such opportunism was the potentially far-reaching experiment in decentralization that accompanied the democratization of Indonesia, as politicians rushed to dismantle Suharto's center-out, top-down, one-way legacy of rule.

Linguistic Stability

With so much to contest in such a turbulent transition, it is remarkable that Indonesians did not also bicker over language. Such conflicts were strikingly absent from the multiple crises—economic, political, environmental—that struck Indonesia more or less simultaneously at the close of the twentieth century. Nor, in the opening years of the twenty-first, did linguistic concessions or impositions figure among the factors working to lessen or contain the centrifugal forces that had so recently seemed to be tearing the country apart.

In 2001 the People's Representative Council (the national legislature) that Indonesians had elected in 1999 adopted a new law on Aceh. It granted expanded autonomy to what it called the Province of the Country of Aceh, Abode of Peace (Propinsi Nanggroe Aceh Darussalam). If the name was confusing, the ambivalence behind it was clear. While Aceh would, for example, be allowed to embody its unique character in a logo or flag of its own choosing, the law warned that such a device did not constitute an expression of sovereignty.[37]

At the eastern extremity of Indonesia, renaming also took place. What Jakarta had once referred to as Irian Barat (West Irian) and then Irian Jaya (Great Irian) would now be called Papua. The shift was not toward an etymologically more indigenous term. It was Portuguese travelers who had bestowed the name that evolved into "Papua." But because the long use of "Irian" in the Indonesian language by Indonesian governments, politicians, and media had tainted that term among so-called Irianese, Jakarta's shift to "Papua" was seen as a concession to autonomist local sensibilities.[38] Yet even as anti-Jakarta concerns rose in the regions, the Indonesian language itself remained unproblematic.

Remarkable too is the fact that in the seventy-five years since it was first proclaimed in the Youth Oath of 1928 as the unifying "one language" of

Indonesia, Bahasa Indonesia has remained the mother tongue—as opposed to the second language—of a small minority of Indonesians. In 1928, by one estimate, Indonesian was the first language of only some 10 percent of all Indonesians, compared with nearly 40 percent whose first language was Javanese.[39] More than half a century later, in 1980, when census takers counted the number of Indonesians who spoke Indonesian at home, that figure equaled only 12 percent of the total population. Ten years later, in 1990, census data showed only 15 percent of the population using Indonesian at home, a proportion still far less than the 38 percent reported to be speaking Javanese in that private setting.[40]

This is not to suggest that the proclaimers of the Youth Oath failed. They were not so naive as to expect Indonesia, with its myriad mother tongues, to become monolingual. As a national project, Bahasa Indonesia was not intended to replace different first languages; it was an overlay to allow communication among people who would retain opportunities to speak them. The suitability of Indonesian as the material from which such a connective network could be made—its potential importance as a second language—depended in part on its actual unimportance as a first language: on its not having been, and not becoming, the private property of any major ethnic group.

In 1928 the future of Bahasa Indonesia and the country to which it referred could not be foreseen. Fortunately for Indonesian unity, over the rest of the century the national language was publicized but not privatized, and thus remained distinctively national.[41]

Vernaculars can, of course, be heard or read in public settings. Speakers at public gatherings in a given place flavor their Indonesian with vernacular phrases. Locally written and circulated Indonesian-language newspapers carry occasional pages or columns in a local language. Nor is the national language absent from private life. Especially in urban areas or among educated younger-generation Indonesians, Bahasa Indonesia may be used alongside or instead of a mother tongue. In addition to those in originally Malay-speaking areas, some urban Indonesians may have been raised hearing the national language consistently enough for it to have become their "mother tongue."

Yet the stable complementarity of first and second languages in Indonesia has been well established and seems assured. There is no serious prospect that any of Indonesia's first—mainly private—languages, including the most popular of these, Javanese, will dislodge or even rival Indonesian as the country's second—mainly public—means of expression. President Suharto flavored his Indonesian-language discourse with homilies in Javanese. In 2003 President Megawati Sukarnoputri was criticized for her use of Javanisms in speeches she gave in Indonesian.[42] But neither leader was so foolish—or so parochial—as to try displacing Indonesian with Javanese in the public arena. The country's history had made that a preposterous endeavor. When Javanese writers commented on the state of the Javanese-language press, far from lauding its expansion, they lamented its shrinkage and feared its extinction.[43]

As for possibly destabilizing future movement in the other direction, the still small proportion of Indonesians who speak Indonesian at home, and whose children might thus be expected to hear that language first, could continue to increase. But that is most likely to occur in urban settings among households of diverse linguistic backgrounds. The slow expansion of Indonesian from second- to first-language status therefore, if it continues, will tend not to be concentrated in any one ethnic group.[44]

I have already noted that Indonesia's periphery is linguistically more diverse than its core. From this one might be tempted to infer that Indonesian is less widely spoken in the outer islands compared with Java and Bali, and therefore that national unity is endangered, inasmuch as the fringe, less socialized into using the national language, should be more inclined to break away. But the evidence is not there, and the reasoning is wrong.

If knowledge of Indonesian in 1990 is mapped across all twenty-seven provinces then in existence, the extremes were East Timor, where 54 percent spoke the language, and greater Jakarta, where 100 percent did. East Timor, located far from Jakarta on the definitely "outer" island of Timor, became independent a decade later, while the capital city's political and economic centrality made it the most "Indonesian" place in the country and the least likely to secede. By this comparison, language resembles destiny.

The extremes are misleading, however. Comparing the twenty-five provinces on this spectrum between East Timor and greater Jakarta, the outer island jurisdictions turn out to have been, on the whole, proportionally more able to use Indonesian than the core provinces of West and Central Java, Yogyakarta, East Java, and Bali.

The two places with secessionist movements, Papua (then still called Irian Jaya) and Aceh, were among the relatively less Indonesian-speaking provinces. Papua and Aceh had the same rates, respectively, as Central and West Java. Yet on a scale from 0 to 100 percent, these "low" rates were remarkably high: 79 for Papua and 84 for Aceh. These numbers suggest nothing even approaching a rejection of the Indonesian language.[45]

Quite the contrary. The spectacular linguistic diversity of Papua, already noted in this chapter, makes Indonesian worth embracing as a useful lingua franca, and one that is no less usable in rallying and expressing sentiment against Indonesian than for it. Growing knowledge of Bahasa Indonesia in Papua during the New Order may also reflect the arrival of migrants from other provinces who were more likely to speak it than indigenous Papuans were. Aceh is different. But because of its historic location within the Malay world, a rejection of Indonesian has been less plausible in Aceh as well. And again, using the Indonesian language need *not* mean accepting Indonesia the

country, which many or most Acehnese have mixed to critical feelings about
and some would indeed reject if given the chance.

This chapter has argued that space is not destiny in any simple sense. Neither is speech. Without belittling the language optimism of the Youth Oath in
1928, or the role of Indonesian in creating Indonesia, the country's fate in this
century will involve a great deal more than who speaks what. The spatial distribution of first and second languages, including the ability to speak the national language, suggests if anything a relatively stable complementarity. A
failure of national *linguistic* identity is a highly unlikely basis for expecting
Indonesia to unravel.

Decentralization

In this seemingly stable political language game, however, there is a wild
card—decentralization—and it has been played, for better or worse, by the
central government in Jakarta, beginning in 2001 with the implementation of
laws meant to boost regional autonomy.[46] The experiment is a bold propositional gamble that in addition to improving governance, granting more power
to local authorities will increase their motivation to remain inside Indonesia,
rather than whetting their appetite for exit. Four years later, in 2005, it was
still too early to confirm this argument in any definitive way.

A short-term judgment was entirely possible, however. The circumstances
and aftermath of Suharto's downfall reflected a wholesale delegitimation of
his centralized regime. Impressions of economic collapse, political collapse,
moral collapse—the latter signaled by sometimes horrifically violent mobs—
made it easy to understand why one might wish to quit such an obviously failing state. Meanwhile the means to act on such alienation appeared in the form
of free media, where regional resentments could be voiced, and in the championing of democratic rights, including the right to vote in competitive national elections in June 1999 and, for East Timorese, the right to vote themselves, in effect, out of the republic a few months later.

Yet in early 2005 there were still only two real independence movements
inside the country: the already familiar ones in Aceh and Papua. Also familiar but considerably less significant were the occasional reexpressions of
residual sentiment in favor of the sovereign republic that had been championed by some Christians in southern Maluku in the 1950s. Considering all
that Indonesia had so recently been through, including an estimated 13 percent shrinkage of its economy in 1998, the lack of new separatist campaigns
was surprising, even amazing.

It would be wrong to attribute this lack of new moves to leave Indonesia
solely to cooptation, that is, to the power of autonomy, including financial

transfers, to tempt the regions back from the brink of independence. That would overstate the proximity of the brink to begin with, by underestimating the staying power of the idea of Indonesia and by exaggerating the extent to which East Timor's departure was seen elsewhere in the republic at the time as a chance to follow suit.

That said, however, decentralization did become a reason for staying put, especially in places well endowed with natural resources and thus with elites hoping for the income from those resources, formerly transferred to Jakarta, to be rerouted in their direction. Thirty percent of central government spending was devolved to the governments of cities and regencies or districts. A district endowed with natural resources—oil and gas, hard minerals, tropical forest—was assured of a major share of the revenue accruing to the central government from their exploitation. Regional protests and expressions of regional identity against Jakarta in this context were not demands to break away from the center so much as acts of leverage on it.

The downside of decentralization has been fractionation: a proliferation of bounded units within the same space. This aspect of the process has received much less attention than the rules of transfer have, even though it could wind up draining resources, magnifying corruption, and reducing efficiency at the local level.

The Indonesian government is a building with five floors. At the top is the national administration headquartered in Jakarta. Provincial, district, subdistrict, and village levels of authority complete the hierarchy. The decentralization laws that were adopted in 1999 more or less bypassed the provincial level. Authority was instead transferred mainly to the next lower floor—the districts.[47]

Apparently this choice was made to avoid the risk of giving too much power to units as large and therefore potentially as dangerous as provinces. That centripetal concern could be spun patriotically as a laudable desire to empower people closer to the ground while denying larger-scale constituencies and resources to future warlords bent on splitting the nation. But the decision could also be read cynically as an effort by Jakarta to claim generosity while retaining primacy, knowing that the country's districts were too many and too small ever to coalesce successfully against central domination. Common to both explanations was the idea that the centrifugal thrust of democratization could be limited by checking the provinces from below.

Regionalism and Religion

Whatever the exact rationale for empowering the districts, doing so greatly amplified their value. Under the terms of Laws no. 22 and 25 of 1999, districts were authorized to assume and fund responsibilities previously discharged by the central government in all sectors save foreign relations, national defense and security, national monetary and fiscal policy, and religious affairs. The laws did allow for the central government to adopt and implement policies as needed with regard to development planning, national state administration, training and manpower issues, the exploitation of natural energy resources, advanced technologies of a "strategic" nature, environmental conservation, and national standards. But that did not necessarily imply a central usurping of district authority over those subjects.

Presumably to implement their new responsibilities, districts were empowered to exercise governmental authority over potentially lucrative matters such as capital investment, industry and trade, public works, agriculture, manpower, and education, among other topics. Districts were also entitled to manage national energy resources located within their borders. And they were assured—on paper—of financing, infrastructure, and personnel sufficient to discharge their newly enlarged responsibilities. Suddenly, from jurisdictions with little clout under Suharto's centralized regime, Indonesia's districts had become valued assets—and estimable prizes in political competition.[48]

In 1999 Indonesia held democratic elections to local councils in 306 districts. The autonomy laws were implemented beginning in 2001. The number of districts rose above 350 by 2002, to around 430 in 2004. The formation of each new district created a new set of executive, administrative, and legislative positions to be filled and implied an additional budget to be spent. More districts meant more jobs, patronage, and influence—turf—for local politicians and for national ones seeking local support. Local businesses reportedly experienced 10–15 percent increases in the cost of doing business, especially in the transport of goods on local roads. Members of the national legislature in Jakarta were happy to approve subdividing the political map. And they were willing as well to enlarge the number of fully recognized provinces from twenty-six in 1999 (after East Timor's departure) to thirty-two in 2004.[49]

In a country with hundreds of local ethno-linguistic identities, would political subdivision wind up creating hundreds of little platforms to match—platforms where minorities could become majorities and cease having to compromise for the sake of consensus within larger frames, including the national one? Would these new roosts be used by petty rulers to refurbish, for political and economic gain, nativisms and atavisms inimical to the growth of civil society? Would subdivision as the underside of decentralization thus breed conflict and undermine democracy?

The carving of new subdistricts, districts, and provinces from 1999 onward sparked or fueled conflicts along ethnic or religious lines in several outer islands. Viewed overall, however, drawing more and more lines on political maps seemed more likely to spawn wastage than warfare. In years to come one could imagine the entrenching, in some parts of the country, of an illiberal kind of democracy in which elections rotated power and money through more or less self-serving local oligarchies. If it is not slowed or checked, such a trend could spread through Indonesia the sort of decentralized bossism that has tended to characterize politics next door in the Philippines.[50]

But localism need not always be regressive. Decentralization in Indonesia has been driven by forethought as well as backlash. Alongside the negative case for dismantling Suharto's top-down, center-out regime lies a positive hope—that bringing government closer to society will make politicians more accountable, more informed, and more effective. Early evidence of conflict and corruption to the contrary notwithstanding, in 2005 it was still too early to label that hope entirely naive.

Responsibility for religious affairs was not decentralized. Matters of faith were too sensitive for Jakarta to relinquish authority over them. But keeping them within Jakarta's ambit for purposes of policy and administration hardly settled their relationship to Indonesian identity. That relationship need not bear extensive scrutiny here; religion is thoroughly treated elsewhere in this book. I will, however, introduce the subject in relation to identity, summarize the geography of belief, and question the implications of religion for the territorial integrity of Indonesia, including the political importance of faith in majority-Muslim Aceh and majority-Christian Papua.

Room for Religion

Islam in Indonesia has enjoyed a cultural efflorescence for some time now. Arguably the seeds for this revival were sown in the later 1970s, when a buoyantly oil-driven economy enabled the New Order to support Islam as a religion in a range of ways, including building mosques and religious schools and subsidizing pilgrimages to Mecca. By the 1980s, an Islamic religious revival was under way, and in the second half of that decade it was strengthened as President Suharto grew more interested in Islam and less wary of Muslim organizations, or at least those he thought he could control. In the 1990s it became conventional to think of Indonesia as having taken an "Islamic turn."[51]

In 1971, according to that year's census, 88 percent of Indonesians were Muslims. In view of the subsequent invigoration of Islam as a religion, one would have expected this figure to grow. It did not. Census data for 2000 show the proportion unchanged—still 88 percent. The continuity suggests that the revival of Islam in Indonesia has involved quality more than quantity, internal substantiation more than external conversion. Religious minorities are in no demographic danger. Christians, not Muslims, were the fastest-growing religious community in the country between 1971 and 2000.[52]

If Indonesia remains democratic, its national identity could become more Islamic. That shift, if it happens, will reflect the religion's overwhelming majority status. Translating majorities into governments is what democracies do. More interesting, however, will be the content of that more Islamic identity, as it may have been shaped over decades by the increasing manifestation of Islam in the private and public lives of Muslims. A "civil Islam" in which piety is not a political project will have markedly different effects on Indonesian identity compared with an "uncivil Islamism" that demands a strictly and legalistically Islamic state.

The traditional moderation of Islam as practiced in Indonesia favors the milder outcome. In the legislative elections of 2004, compared with those held in 1999, Islamist parties did better, but they remained a fairly modest minority. In the country's first-ever direct presidential elections in 2004, candidates identified with Islam did not fare well. The winner, retired General Susilo Bambang Yudhoyono, and his second-round opponent, incumbent President Megawati Sukarnoputri, were Muslims with secular backgrounds, outlooks, and styles. Isolated acts of Islamist violence have appalled most Indonesians. Moderate Muslims and non-Muslim minorities will continue to provide a national constituency for tolerance.

That constituency is, however, unevenly distributed across the archipelago. Followers of different faiths can be found throughout the country, but their concentrations are not random. Christianity, for example, has a distinctly eastern cast. In 2000 the most Christian provinces (and the proportions living there who reported being Christian) were all in eastern Indonesia: East Nusa Tenggara (88 percent), Papua (76 percent), North Sulawesi (69 percent), and Maluku (50 percent).[53]

On a map, Indonesia extends horizontally from 95° to 141° longitude. The country is bisected longitudinally at 118°. Back in 1971, with one exception, Christians were an absolute or near majority in every province wholly located east of a north–south line drawn just two degrees east of that midline, at 120° longitude. Conversely, in that year, with one exception, Muslims were an absolute majority in every province wholly located west of that same near middle meridian. (The exceptions were, respectively, Muslim-majority Southeast Sulawesi and Hindu-majority Bali.)[54] But these statistical differences lacked political force. The ensuing three and a half decades proved that Indonesia was not about to split nearly in half along religious lines. Economic expansion, social moderation, and the centralized institutions and antisectarian vigilance of the New Order all contributed to that proof.

Since the end of Suharto's rule and the onset of democratization, however, fractionation has tended to undermine religious diversity—not by deepening the national contrast between east and west but by creating, throughout the country, new and smaller jurisdictions whose internal pluralism, religious or ethnic, is less than that of the units they replace.

After 1998, for example, two new provinces were established in eastern Indonesia. Gorontalo was carved out of North Sulawesi; North Maluku was subtracted from Maluku. The effect on intraprovincial religious diversity was dramatic. North Sulawesi, immediately prior to its division, had been 50 percent Muslim and 49 percent Christian. In its place stood Gorontalo with a 98 percent Muslim majority and a truncated North Sulawesi with a 69 percent Christian majority. Maluku had been 62 percent Muslim, 37 percent Christian. Its division yielded North Maluku with an 85 percent Muslim majority and a reduced Maluku almost evenly split between Muslims at 49 percent and Christians at 50 percent. From two provinces, each shared by a larger Muslim population and an also large Christian one, four provinces had been gerrymandered—two largely Muslim, one largely Christian, and only one in which the two communities were evenly balanced.[55]

The great majority of instances of fractionation did not result in violence, and when violence did occur, it sometimes preceded fractionation. Nor did a demographic balance between religious communities necessarily guarantee provincial security. The intercommunal bloodshed that flared in parts of the Maluku archipelago in 1999, when the islands were still one province, became a reason to divide it. The migration of Muslims into formerly Christian-majority southern Maluku, far from heralding a stable parity, stoked Christian fears. Also, religion was but one ingredient in the mixtures of ethnic, economic, and political identifications and resentments that set off and helped to sustain these and other seemingly faith-driven clashes.

So in 2005, the question remained: Would fractionation weaken or strengthen Indonesian national identity, or leave it unchanged? Particularly worth watching in this respect will be what Jakarta does or does not do when a given province or district relies on its religious or ethnic majority to enact laws and engage in practices that cater to that majority, including the introduction of discriminatory laws.

In the case of Aceh, renowned for its Islamic character, Jakarta did not wait for the Acehnese to erect a scaffolding of Islamic rules to challenge national ones. The central authorities moved instead to offer to satisfy what they assumed was an Acehnese thirst for Islamic law. A concessionary gesture catering to that thirst, they hoped, would stimulate badly needed Acehnese loyalty toward Indonesia. Arguably, however, they misread the importance of religion in that long-suffering province.

Aceh and Indonesia

Aceh's location has greatly affected its history. Its westernmost position at the northwest entrance to the Malacca Strait and the farther western (Arabian) provenance of Islam made Aceh the logical first landfall of that religion in the archipelago—although the earliest known physical evidence of a Muslim presence comes from an eleventh-century headstone in eastern Java.[56] The first recognizably Muslim polity was Pasai on Aceh's north coast not far from present-day Lhokseumawe. Upon his conversion to Islam in 1297, Pasai's Sultan Malek Saleh became the first Muslim ruler in what is now Indonesia. A succession of sultanates continuing into the twentieth century made Aceh unique among the components of Indonesia in having the longest unbroken record of statehood. That record included fierce resistance against the "infidel" Dutch in the Aceh War (1873–1903).

Islam has become an integral part of what it means to be an Acehnese. Religion and ethnicity are intimately linked in a two sides of a coin pattern that is not unlike the coincidence of being Muslim with being Malay that prevails across the strait in peninsular Malaysia. That said, however, it is important to keep in mind that while Muslims account for an estimated 97 percent of the total population in Aceh, only half of that total are thought to be ethnically Acehnese.[57] And the society is much more than merely Muslim. Historically its indigenous elites have included teachers of Islam who were identified strongly with their religion. But they have interacted, sometimes violently, with inland aristocrats, who have themselves been distinguished from coastal traders, not to mention the further differentiation of Acehnese society that has taken place over the course of Indonesian independence. Even on "Mecca's front porch" there are differences when it comes to understanding Islam, interpreting its laws, and projecting its political role.

Official Indonesian perceptions of Aceh have not always taken these subtleties into account. In 1998–2000, in the tumultuous and democratizing aftermath of the New Order, which included East Timor's long-delayed self-determination, Aceh's independence became less unimaginable than it had been under Suharto. In Jakarta, opinions differed as to what to do. Some of the politicians I interviewed thought of the Acehnese as so single-mindedly Muslim that allowing them to enact Islamic law for themselves might be enough to keep the province inside Indonesia. Reflecting that hope, the autonomy law for Aceh adopted by the national legislature in 2001 provided for a Court of Islamic Law with authority over Muslims.[58]

If Aceh could be essentialized as homogeneously, single-mindedly Muslim by some Indonesians in Jakarta, it was even easier for Americans to do so from the other side of the Pacific Ocean. This was especially so in the more

Manichean atmosphere of suspicion toward Islam that followed al-Qaeda's calamitous strikes against the United States on September 11, 2001, and the gruesome success of Indonesian jihadists in Bali a year and a month later. But in seeking justice if not freedom from Jakarta, the Acehnese were not mono-maniacally counterposing against Indonesia a radically Islamist vision of the world. Nor were they about to launch a war against Christians in Indonesia or elsewhere. Arguably, Islam had so imbued Acehnese society, and for so long, that it was taken for granted in a way quite alien to the obsessions of Osama bin Laden in Afghanistan or the insecurities of jihadists on Java.

Had Aceh's elite been Muslim exclusively, nothing else would have mat-tered. Instead, the diversity of Acehnese society sustained diverse vantage points and arguments. Some university students would tolerate no option save independence. Other students wanted self-determination as a democratic right whose exercise Suharto's fall had made possible. In this latter group, the means mattered as much as the end. If (against all expectations) a genuine ref-erendum in Aceh endorsed the prolongation of provincial status quo, so be it. Members of the Acehnese business community who had prospered during the New Order thanks in no small part to their connections to that regime were inclined to see in the movement for independence a means of persuading the central government to make profitable concessions, including redirecting rents from Jakarta toward Aceh and thus prospectively into their own hands. Among the ulamas there were differences regarding the Islamic legal frame to be administered under special autonomy, between those who rejected Jakarta's offer as an insincere bribe and those who saw it as an opportunity for employment and influence.[59]

Ryamizard's Rule

Violence in Aceh did not necessarily accelerate momentum toward separa-tion. Responding to widespread brutality by Indonesian police and soldiers, many Acehnese probably wanted the removal of Indonesian forces from Aceh at least as much as that of Aceh from Indonesia. Ten thousand or more, mostly civilians, had died since the rebels' declaration of Acehnese independence in 1976. GAM's tendency to perpetrate brutalities of its own had left some Acehnese unable to reserve their scorn for Jakarta alone. In these eyes, mounting noncombatant deaths and damages made freedom less inevitable than it made peace desirable. If Aceh does remain within the republic, future historians may review this period for evidence as to why. One conclusion they may draw is that, along with cooptation, repression worked.

That, at any rate, was the calculation behind the Indonesian effort to wipe out GAM that began, as noted, in May 2003—one of the largest, if not the largest, military operations undertaken by Jakarta since invading East Timor in 1975. In declaring martial law in the province, the central government swept aside any pretense of civilian rule. With it went the niceties of cooptation through autonomy sweetened by Islamic laws. In the words of the hard-line army staff chief, General Ryamizard Ryacudu,

> *No region can be allowed to break away.* That includes Aceh and Papua. Even if those making noises [for independence] number up to a million, this is a country of more than 220 million people. Our job is to safeguard unity. Our job is to destroy GAM's military capability. Issues of justice, religion, autonomy, social welfare, education—those are not the Indonesian military's problems.[60]

Neither, it seemed, did the military have to worry about public opinion opposing the decision to storm GAM. Among Indonesians outside Aceh, support for using force to suppress separatism there ran between 70 and 80 percent in some polls.[61] Seen from the United States, it was tempting to picture the war becoming, for Jakarta, a domestic "Vietnam" where mounting casualties among civilians and government troops would in time shrink and reverse the popularity of a military solution to the point of Indonesian withdrawal and acquiescence to independence.

Don't bet on it. During Indonesia's transition from New Order rule, the conflict in Aceh has fluctuated along three parallel tracks—suppression, cooptation, and negotiation—in ways inimical to success on any one of them. Like strong wind pushing a kite higher, abuses associated with suppression tend to fortify the opposition to be suppressed. But GAM cannot defeat Jakarta militarily, and probably never will. Cooptation might work if peace is assured. But violent methods, mainly by Jakarta but also by GAM, assure that it is not. Successful negotiations presuppose trust. But trust is sapped by the abuses that accompany insurgency and repression, and by bad faith— Jakarta's when it tries to buy rather than earn Aceh's fealty, GAM's when it burns the schools that Jakarta builds and Aceh needs, and both sides when they use negotiated pauses in the fighting to prepare for more of it. Megawati's Aceh is more like Vladimir Putin's Chechnya than it is like Lyndon Johnson's or Richard Nixon's Vietnam.

The interlocking stalemates that have thwarted a resolution of the conflict in Aceh might be broken, in theory, by democratization and internationalization. A thriving Indonesian democracy should foster military reform and thus break the vicious zigzag from harm to hatred as a rationale for additional harm. A fully democratic Indonesia should honor the democratic right of self-determination and thus permit a referendum to take place. Sufficiently concerned foreigners should be able to entice and pressure both sides toward peace and compromise.

Against the grain of such hopeful logic, however, stands the capacity of democracy not to moderate but to express and intensify Indonesian nationalism. In the years of transition from Suharto's rule, especially after the pride-wounding "loss" of East Timor, what might be called "Ryamizard's rule" would have made a popular campaign slogan: No region can be allowed to break away. It is not clear how many Indonesians would have noted the deficiency of a national identity that had to forbid by fiat what it should have made unnecessary, even inconceivable, by success. Self-reflective or not, the appeal and the intransigence of Ryamizard's rule showed how determined Indonesian nationalism could be.

The devastation of much of Aceh's coastline on December 26, 2004, by a Richter scale 9.0 earthquake and the tsunami that it triggered was much too recent in January 2005 to allow an observer to know how the aftermath would affect GAM's prospects and Aceh's relations with Jakarta. In the short run, the central government's hand was strengthened. By wiping out lives and infrastructure in the province, the disaster suddenly made the province far more dependent on Jakarta than it had been before. The channeling of emergency aid through the national authorities greatly empowered them. In contrast, GAM's ability to gain credit by helping with relief and reconstruction was hampered by small numbers, few resources, and enemy status in the eyes of some 50,000 government troops, including many brought in to respond to the calamity and, not least, to prevent the rebels from using it to their own ends. But it was also clear that, over time, Jakarta's advantage could be frittered away in red tape, corruption, and renewed brutality against Acehnese suspected of favoring independence.

Either way, the disaster was a major early test of the ability of President Yudhoyono and Vice President Jusuf Kalla, in office only since October 2004, to perform well in a crisis. Soon after the waves struck in December, GAM offered a cease-fire, which mostly endured in the early weeks despite clashes. In January in Jakarta, the president surprised observers by consulting with foreign ambassadors on ways to resolve the conflict and by authorizing negotiations to that end under the auspices of a Finnish NGO later that month. At the same time, however, he championed an even stronger military, arguing that such a force might have crushed the rebels in Aceh long ago. Amplifying the ambiguity of such mixed messages were differences inside GAM and among non-GAM Acehnese groups and views and, in Jakarta, between Yudhoyono and his politically powerful and ambitious vice president.

Whatever the balance of promise and danger in this cauldron of possibilities, in early 2005 Aceh was not poised to leave Indonesia, and Islam was not the engine driving the Acehnese toward such a result. Grievances stemming from Jakarta's brutality mixed with rancor over its avarice were. For decades

Aceh had been an important source of natural gas. Nearly all of the profits from exporting that resource had been transferred out of Aceh—to the national government, its national oil company (Pertamina), and the latter's foreign partner in the province (ExxonMobil). And this in a period when, if these "missing" returns from oil and gas were excluded from the province's per capita economy, Aceh lagged most of the comparably reduced provincial economies in the rest of the country.[62] Following Jakarta's earlier failure to reward the province materially for helping to fight the Indonesian revolution against the Dutch, this treatment fed a deep sense of injustice among Acehnese.

The sheer scale of Aceh's travail in the wake of the tsunami drew an outpouring of empathy and support from other Indonesians. To that extent, however perversely, the province's suffering strengthened the country's identity. In Jakarta, grand plans were floated: to raze and rebuild the badly damaged provincial capital, Banda Aceh, along dramatic high-modern lines, while assuring for hundreds of thousands of homeless coastal Acehnese material conditions even better than what nature had destroyed. If these plans were realized with honesty and sensitivity to local needs, perhaps the economic development of Aceh could accomplish what repression, negotiation, and offers of autonomy had not—the final, successful integration of the province into Indonesia.

But more than 98 percent of all Indonesians had not been directly affected by the disaster. Once scenes of pain and wreckage no longer filled the media, would the political will to transform the province remain, or would it too fade away? How much of an estimated $4 billion in pledges of aid by foreign governments would never be made good, or be transferred but then siphoned off, as natural gas receipts had been?[63] In a country known for corruption, Aceh's administration has been especially corrupt. When the tsunami struck, the province's governor was being detained in Jakarta on corruption charges. Was that an encouraging sign of a national government finally willing to discipline its own? Or the tip of a national cancer too endemic to remove?

Papua and Indonesia

Acehnese and Papuans alike have resented Jakarta. But the farthest eastern and western ends of the republic differ in many other respects, including religion. In 2000 Aceh and Papua were, respectively, 98 percent Muslim and 79 percent Christian. But just as Islam alone did not explain Aceh's revolt against Indonesian authority, neither did Christianity fully account for Papuan separatism.

The numerically dominant Protestant congregations in Papua were organizationally divided. In the transition from the New Order, no charismatic religious leader arose to evoke and rally a common Papuan identity. It would have taken someone of uncommon skills to unite a population whose largest ethnic group amounted to merely 12 percent of the province's people and consisted not of Papuans but Javanese.[64] Ethno-linguistic diversity in a population spread thinly across dispersed settlements on mountainous terrain complicated the formation and expression of a would-be Papuan nation, even one limited to the western half of New Guinea. Other such complications included the repression, intimidation, cooptation, and manipulation of "its" Papuans by Jakarta.

Historically, ethnic Papuans' sense of being removed from Indonesian identity dates back to their nearly complete absence from the nationalist struggle to create it. The anti-Dutch revolution, a formative experience for a generation of Indonesians, including many Acehnese, passed Papuans by. They were kept under Dutch control until Indonesia threatened invasion and the Netherlands, the United States, and the United Nations arranged for the territory's transfer to Jakarta in 1963. The deal included a proviso that Papuans themselves would eventually be consulted on the matter. In 1969 the Indonesian government orchestrated an "act of free choice" whereby a thousand Papuans handpicked and coached by Jakarta ratified adherence to Indonesia—an event later ridiculed by Papuans as an "act of no choice."[65] No such history complicated the Indonesian status of Aceh.

Papua and Aceh do share a history of having their natural resources exploited lopsidedly to Jakarta's benefit. Papuan concerns in this respect have focused on the mining of the world's most valuable deposit of gold and third most valuable deposit of copper, near Timika not far inland from the eastern province's west central coast. Under a generous agreement signed early in the New Order by Indonesian officials eager for foreign investment, an American firm, now called Freeport-McMoRan Copper & Gold, dug and ran the mine and became the biggest taxpayer in Indonesia. The company also became the largest employer in the province, although skilled positions were mostly taken by non-Papuan Indonesians. In 2003 only a fourth of all Freeport employees in Papua were ethnically Papuan.[66]

Locally filled Freeport jobs and Freeport-funded community development projects accounted for an insignificant fraction of the profits obtained, and very little of the rest was returned to the province. Following the example already given for Aceh—subtracting the contribution of mining to Papua's regional product per capita to reflect Jakarta's retention of revenue from that source—Papua also badly lagged the country.[67] Ranked by poverty, Papua fared even worse; an account released in 2003 judged the province the poorest in Indonesia.[68]

For ethnic Papuans, stigmatization based on race and culture compounded material exploitation. The Acehnese in principle shared their Malay–Muslim character with most other Indonesians. The distinctively Melanesian features and customs and Christian beliefs of Papuans, in contrast, enhanced their vulnerability to stereotyping and disdain.

In November 2001, a few months after doing so for Aceh, President Megawati signed into effect a special autonomy law for Papua. It granted the province authority over sectors other than foreign policy, defense and security, fiscal and monetary policy, religion, justice, and "other sectors to be determined in consonance with laws or equivalent regulations"—the latter potentially a large loophole.[69] The law granted such autonomy to Papua as a single province. If this law were implemented in ways favorable to Papuans, its provisions might go some distance toward meeting their demands. Especially generous was the promise to channel up to four-fifths of the returns from local resource extraction back into the province.

By 2001, however, decentralization for Papua had already shown its darker side as fractionation. In 1999 Indonesia's legislature had adopted a law splitting Papua into three provinces. Papua's sheer physical size—much larger than Aceh's—did make it harder to rule as one province. But the move could also be taken—among Papuan and foreign observers, it was taken—as a ploy meant to thwart secessionist Papuan unity against Jakarta.

Three Provinces from One?

Initially stalled by strong Papuan opposition, fractionation resurfaced as an official Indonesian priority in January 2003. One might have thought that Law no. 21 of 2001, which granted special autonomy to Papua and made no mention of its being divided, would have superseded the earlier Law no. 45 of 1999, which had authorized Papua's trisection. But not according to Presidential Instruction (Inpres) no. 1 of 2003, which ordered the implementation of the 1999 legislation. Confusion ensued in Jakarta and Papua alike. The Department of Home Affairs basically denied responsibility for the president's decision. Nevertheless, on February 6 in Manokwari, Papua, the first of three provinces intended to replace Papua was announced at a ceremony reportedly attended by thousands of local supporters of the new jurisdiction. No official from either the Papuan capital, Jayapura, or Jakarta was present, however. A few days later in Jakarta, Papuans demonstrated against Inpres no. 1 and vowed to ask Indonesia's Supreme Court to rule it illegal.

In mid-February 2003, following a closed meeting, the People's Representative Council endorsed turning Papua into three provinces. By then, Home Affairs was on board. The minister of that department and the head of the legislature explained that the 2001 law had not superseded and did not contradict the 1999 law. Prior to the 2001 law granting special autonomy, in this official view, the 1999 law had already validly established the division of Papua. Said the minister, "It's a fait accompli."[70]

It was not. In 2004 where one province had been, there were not three but two: a new province named West Irian Jaya and the large remaining part of the old one, still called Papua. West Irian Jaya includes Tangguh, a large field of natural gas being developed for export to China. The lead foreign company in this project, BP (British Petroleum), has taken steps meant to avoid the troubles that have plagued Freeport. All the same, a new military hierarchy assigned to the new province may try to tap the gas project for informal rents in ways reminiscent of Freeport's experience. That could entrench and enrich corrupt security personnel at a time when Indonesia urgently needs the opposite—military reform.

A new province means a new bureaucracy to be staffed, legislative seats to be filled, and openings for entrepreneurs to meet increased demand for goods and services. That could be good for economic growth. But it could also strengthen the dominance of ethnic non-Papuans whose résumés and connections to Jakarta make them more employable than the indigenous population, many of whom lack formal education and are not used to working for wages.

In Jakarta in May 2000, I asked a leading Indonesian official with responsibility over Indonesia's regions whether he worried more about Aceh or Papua (Irian Jaya) leaving the republic. He did not hesitate before answering, Papua. His reasoning featured religion. Aceh was Muslim. Papua was Christian. Indonesia was weak. The Christian West, and the United States especially, did not care about Muslim Acehnese. Christian Papuans were another matter. If Papua did eventually leave, it would be because foreigners had pried it loose.[71]

Sympathy for fellow Christians does animate some Western supporters of Papuan independence. But the Indonesian violation of human rights in Papua counts for more in eliciting anger in the basically secular societies of Australia, the United States, and Europe. Gross violations in Aceh, compared with Papua, have been two-way, implicating not only Indonesian forces but, to an extent, GAM as well. Nor is there an event in Acehnese history that delegitimizes Jakarta's rule as notoriously as does the "act of [un]free choice" whereby Jakarta sealed the absorption of Papua into Indonesia. For Aceh there is nothing comparable to the Western guilt by historical association created by the involvement of the Dutch and American governments and the United Nations in that bit of realpolitik.[72] The earthquake and tsunami of December 2004 triggered Western sympathy for the plight of the Acehnese. Nevertheless, as of early 2005, among all of Indonesia's provinces, the most susceptible—or least immune—to being "East Timorized" by rising international pressure toward a referendum on independence was not Aceh but Papua. Religion was relevant to that ranking but not decisive.

What, then, of the "end of Indonesia"? In 2005 it was ludicrous to expect the country's outright disassembly, something comparable to the shattering of the Soviet Union into fifteen pieces in 1991. In Aceh and Papua, secession was not in sight. In the rest of Indonesia, Ryamizard's rule—No region can be allowed to break away—was still too popular. Sometime in the future, the costs of retaining the rim could finally escalate beyond the core's willingness or ability to pay them, or beyond the inclination of appalled foreigners to tolerate the abuse of Indonesians by Indonesia. But in 2005 that tipping point was still nowhere in sight. And if it were ever reached, Indonesia seemed more likely to lose an extremity than its identity.

As the country struggled to cope with the pangs and dilemmas of reform, on the other hand, the "end of Indonesia" in the sense of a new national purpose, a matter not of form but content, that uncertainty remained in full and urgent view.

IMAGES OF INDONESIA

In the following section I will briefly explore and evaluate three concrete answers to the question, What is Indonesia? The answers are, a Javanese empire, a Dutch legacy, and a nationalist artifact.

The pool of answers from which these particular images are drawn is large. Indonesia can be variously pictured as an endangered ecology, a fledgling democracy, a corrupt oligarchy, a cultural compromise, a communal shambles, an Islamic society, an Islamist hatchery, a civil society, an uncivil society, a lawless anarchy, a recovering economy, a laggard economy, a reforming polity, a stumbling polity, a secular state, a garrison state, a "messy state," or a "pivotal state" for the United States, Southeast Asia, the Muslim world, and so on.[73]

Images of Indonesia as a Javanese empire, a Dutch legacy, and a nationalist artifact are not necessarily superior to the many other possible answers to my title question. But they are more clearly historical, and in that respect may usefully complement the spatial and centrifugal Indonesias scanned earlier in this chapter and the contemporary events discussed later in this book.

Javanese Empire?

The case for this image of Indonesia runs roughly as follows. The Javanese are by far the largest ethnic group. Their homeland, Java, is the most developed island, and not by coincidence. Hypocritically, behind a nationalist facade, the Javanese have dominated and exploited the periphery on the core's behalf, entrenching and advantaging themselves against the interests of other Indonesians. Indonesia is an internally neocolonial recreation of another Javanese empire, Majapahit. But compared with that one, this one is far more intrusive and brutal. For decades, officially sponsored transmigration from Java to the outer islands proliferated colonies of Javanese, threatening the land rights and livelihoods of the resident non-Javanese. And when, as in Aceh and Papua, the non-Javanese resisted such treatment, the Javanese waged fierce war to retain their empire intact—or even to expand it, witness the invasion, annexation, and prolonged repression of East Timor.

But the movement against Dutch rule was transethnic from the outset. Nationalism superseded more parochial identifications, including Javanism. Ethnically disparate but socially elite young men from the Netherlands East Indies studying in Holland banded together, drawn by their shared status as outsiders in Europe to consider themselves insiders from Indonesia. The choice of a national language bypassed Javanese. In exhortatory speeches and writings, some nationalists invoked Majapahit as glorious proof of Indonesian greatness. But the most extravagant of these, Muhammad Yamin, was Minangkabau, not Javanese. And that precolonial empire was too ancient, too vague, too vast, and, yes, too Javanese to be taken seriously as a blueprint of the unified modern future the nationalists desired. As for the priority on improving the welfare of Java's residents, it grew not from Javanese selfishness but from Dutch concern, however belated and superficial, to address the entwining of poverty with overpopulation on that island. Transmigration too was originally a Dutch idea.

For the cosmopolitan mixed-blood nationalist Sukarno, however much Javanese traditions might help sustain the idea of Indonesia, they could never be allowed to supersede it. His successor, Suharto, was less urbane, less educated, and "more Javanese" in genealogy and style. Among Indonesia's six presidents, only Suharto was regularly likened to a Javanese sultan.[74] More than any preceding regime, his army-based New Order centralized state power on Java, in the government in Jakarta, and exploited the resources of the outer islands while penetrating their societies, including the officially sponsored resettlement of mainly Javanese transmigrants.

Yet the public ideology of Suharto's Indonesia was not Javanism. It was a transethnic and transreligious creed, *pancasila* (the Five Principles), devised to encompass subnational identities, not to privilege one of them over the rest. (First articulated by Sukarno in 1945, the principles may be summarized as belief in one God, a just and civilized humanity, Indonesian unity, democracy through representative deliberation, and social justice.) Nor did the New Order limit the scope of its main preoccupations—development and security— to speakers of Javanese.

In terms of physical infrastructure, manufacturing jobs, and educational access, among other indicators, the island of Java and the metropolis of Jakarta were relatively favored over the outer islands. But in 2000 the Javanese accounted for merely one-tenth of the 44 million Indonesians in West Java (including Banten) and one-third of the 8 million in Jakarta. To be sure, nearly four-fifths of the 35 million Indonesians in East Java and almost all of the 34 million in Central Java (including Yogyakarta) were Javanese.[75]

These data invite comparison. If Suharto's Indonesia had been a Javanese empire geared to putting the interests of its Javanese citizens first, Central Java (including Yogyakarta) should have done best, followed by East Java, Jakarta, and West Java (including Banten) in that order. Instead, among these four populations in 1990, after more than two decades of New Order rule, the highest per capita gross regional products (GRPs) were in Jakarta and West Java (including Banten), where the Javanese were proportionally *least* present. East Java and Central Java (including Yogyakarta), on the other hand, scored lowest on this economic scale despite hosting proportionally the *most* Javanese. As for the rest of the country, the only outer island province with a Javanese majority, Lampung, was the fourth worst off by this measure of any of the twenty-seven provinces then in existence. Nor, under Suharto, were provinces "rewarded" with more growth in gross regional product per head— or less poverty—according to how Javanese their populations were.[76]

Other points could be made. Proponents of the Javanese empire thesis might expect Aceh and Papua to have suffered demographic colonization in the form of large influxes of ethnic Javanese. The already cited estimates of Indonesian migration into Papua are alarming from a nativist standpoint. Yet the census in 2000 found Aceh and Papua only modestly diluted by Javanese, with minorities of 16 and 12 percent of their respective populations reporting that ethnicity.[77]

If Indonesia were an oppressively Javanese empire, non-Javanese Indonesians throughout the country should have rooted for the independence of Aceh and Papua. On the contrary, these outcomes have been and remain almost wholly unsupported by Indonesians, including the majority who are not Javanese. Under the New Order one might have attributed this silence to fear. But the rise of freedom of speech did not trigger a crescendo of public willingness to let Aceh and Papua go. If there was a trend outside of these places, it ran in the opposite direction: toward retaining Indonesia's borders by whatever means, including force. Public sympathy for the victims of Aceh's tsunami in 2005 could incubate demands for greater fairness and transparency in Jakarta's dealings with the province without creating support for independence.

If non-Javanese Indonesians felt victimized inside a Javanese empire, they should have applauded East Timor's bravery in voting to leave the republic and perhaps also endorsed a new presidential term for the man who had proposed the referendum and allowed it to be held at the end of August 1999. He was B. J. Habibie, the first Indonesian president from an outer island (Sulawesi). Instead, in the People's Consultative Assembly in Jakarta, wounded national pride tipped the political balance against him. Already unpopular as a former protégé and crony of Suharto's, and now also blamed for East Timor's disaffiliation, Habibie lost his presidential bid in the face of a backlash among nationalistic politicians who were by no means only Javanese.

Java and the Army

There are, all the same, two reasons not to dismiss out of hand the idea of Indonesia as a Javanese empire. The first is straightforward: If by Javanese we mean not the ethnic group but the ethnically various core island, there can be no doubt that Java compared with the rest of Indonesia has been a magnet— for spontaneous migration, job-creating investment in manufacturing, and a massive and ongoing influx of rents. The latter accrued in New Order days to administrative, political, and business elites on Java, especially in Jakarta, from the exploitation of natural resources along the periphery and from the willingness of the regional clients of these central elites to pay for access and favor in the country's top-down political economy.

Perhaps the world's largest ongoing experiment in decentralization will succeed. Perhaps Indonesia will empower its regions, including the neglected eastern islands, to the benefit of core and periphery alike. In that event, Indonesia will resemble a Java-centered empire less than at any time since independence. But decentralization could also fail, if it does no more than multiply sites for bossism, corruption, and coercion—not just a single big Suharto, from whom at least consistency might be expected, but hundreds of little ones plotting in all directions in fiefdoms around the archipelago. In that event, Jakarta-on-Java would have an incentive to recapture its former primacy, and if it did, the country might even segue from democracy back toward authoritarian rule.

Uncertainties surrounding the future role of the army are a second reason not to deny categorically the idea of Indonesia as a Javanese empire. Historically and today in Indonesia, the army has enjoyed more influence than the air force, navy, and police combined. And notwithstanding its explicitly national scope and mission, the army has had a special relationship to Java and the Javanese.

It was on Java in 1945 that the Indonesian national army was first established. Java was the epicenter of the ensuing revolution to stop the Dutch from reappropriating their former colony. The men who commanded the army during those formative years of popular struggle (1945–1949) were Javanese. Subsequent commanders included non-Javanese, notably Abdul Haris Nasution (1950–1952; 1955–1962), and the army did nationwide recruitment. But insofar as the "1945 generation" of topmost generals in Jakarta defined their task in the 1950s and 1960s as protecting the new republic from the communist left and the Islamist right, their outlook was compatible with, and partly inspired by, an elitist Javanist ideology. That outlook was too conservative to tolerate a social revolution, but too loosely Muslim—lax, mystical, secular—to imply anything but alarm at the prospect of an Islamic state. This "extreme centrist" position became orthodox under Suharto—a Javanese general and a prime exponent of "1945 values"—from the onset of his regime.

Javanism, in this limited sense, receded as the New Order aged and Islamic consciousness grew. In the 1990s Suharto reduced the political and psychological distance he had maintained between himself and Islamist circles. In the face of mounting opposition in 1998, he could have entrusted his aging regime to another Javanese general, Try Sutrisno, whom Suharto had promoted on a fast track—from army chief in 1986–1988 to armed forces commander in 1988–1993 to vice president in 1993–1998. Instead, Suharto chose the Sulawesi-born civilian Habibie as his vice president in March 1998, only to hand him the presidency in May when escalating protests and defections finally convinced the New Order's founder to step down.

Not one of the ensuing three civilian presidents—Habibie, Wahid, Megawati—could or would serve up again the unique dish of despotism and syncretism garnished with favorite Javanese sayings that Suharto had been known for. Of the trio, only Abdurrahman Wahid was fully Javanese by descent and childhood upbringing. And his background and specialty were Islamic; his outlook was liberal and democratic; and through study, teaching, travel, and conversation he had broadened his knowledge far beyond Suharto's.

The Army and Megawati

If the "1945 generation" is history, however, its values are a legacy that could in future be refurbished in response to prolonged turmoil. In 2005, eight democratizing years after the end of Suharto's anticommunist regime, full legitimacy had still not been restored to the leftist politics he had so assiduously repressed. The officer corps remained impervious to arguments for thoroughgoing social change. And their resistance to upending the status quo could only be stiffened by what they saw as the potential for anarchy in the clashes and protests that had proliferated in Indonesia's new climate of freedom. Not to mention the centripetal effect of Acehnese and Papuan rebellions on military thinking already hardened by the loss of East Timor.

As for the Islamist right's deviation from "1945-style" nationalism, by 2003 the symbols and discourses of the majority religion had become ubiquitous in public life. Beginning in the 1980s, Suharto himself had been willing to promote more (and more actually practicing) Muslim officers to leading military positions. But piety in Islam's name was one thing, violence quite another. Indonesians did not respond to the Bali bombing of October 2002 with sympathy for the bombers. Far from auguring wider support for a jihad by extremist Muslims against their perceived enemies, the attack shocked the moderate majority into at least tacitly repudiating such acts.

Considering the militarization of Indonesia under Suharto, one might have expected the army during democratization to have become a pariah. Far from it. In 1998–2003 the army managed its own transition in a manner at once brutal and adroit. It did not launch a coup to thwart or oust the country's new civilian leaders. It refused to be used by one of those civilians, Abdurrahman Wahid, whose liberal views in the end did not prevent him from ordering the military to implement a state of emergency that would have undermined democracy. And the army bowed to some reforms, including the elimination of its blocs of appointed seats inside elected assemblies.

But the army retained its multilevel territorial commands virtually intact. It managed to escape significant punishment for the atrocities it had committed under Suharto. In East Timor in September 1999, local militias sponsored by the Indonesian army went on a rampage to protest the rejection of Indonesian rule by the Timorese people in a referendum at the end of August. Perhaps a thousand people died and most of the territory's infrastructure, such as it was, was destroyed. Yet as of 2004, Indonesian courts had acquitted or overturned the sentence of every one of the thirteen Indonesian officers, including four generals, who had been charged in Indonesia of complicity in those atrocities.[78]

From 1998, in any case, the relevant subject of public concern had tended to segue from the brutality of the army's past, which had triggered angry calls for justice, toward Indonesia's future, endangered by secession and disorder and therefore calling not for the army's punishment but for its replenishing as the nation's indispensable guardian and savior. No better illustration of this shift could be found than the popularity, among Indonesians outside Aceh, of Megawati's decision to assail and destroy, once and for all, the Aceh freedom movement beginning in May 2003. For most politically aware Indonesians, keeping their country together had become more important, or at any rate more urgent, than rendering their army humane.

As for a "Java-first" backlash against the outer islands, it is hard to see how that could occur short of a steep and prolonged escalation in the central government's losses, in blood and treasure, in Aceh, in Papua, and along the rest of the periphery—losses sufficient to gut the willingness of the majority on Java to keep on fighting for Indonesia. Far from validating Indonesia as a Javanese empire, however, that drastic change of subject would amount to a confession of futility that its core island and largest ethnic group could keep the republic alive.

Indonesia as a Javanese empire? If by that is meant the centrality of Java, yes, notwithstanding historically rival polities off Java and the present experiment in devolution. But Javanism as ethno-ideological hegemony, no, notwithstanding Suharto's aphorisms and how culturally Javanistic Indonesia may still appear in the eyes of some non-Javanese. Modernization, Islamization, and now democratization have, in different ways, made assertively "feudalistic" Javanism quaint.

Dutch Legacy?

Compared with the ambiguities of Javanism and empire, this face of Indonesia seems straightforward. Half a millennium separates the demise of Majapahit as a unified royal house (1456) from the birth of Indonesia as a sovereign unitary state (1950).[79] As a far more recent polity, the Netherlands East Indies should have been more consequential for the republic than any precolonial exemplar, even if it did take the Dutch three centuries from the founding of Batavia (1619) to bring the length and breadth of the islands fully under their control. And that control was more pervasive and capacious— again, therefore, more consequential as a legacy for Indonesia—than anything Majapahit could have managed.

Compared with Majapahit and the Indies, Japan's occupation of the islands during World War II lasted the blink of an eye. Already in 1944–1945, as the tide of war in the Pacific turned against them, the archipelago's Japanese occupiers began considering the idea of Indonesian independence. In March 1945 they announced that an all-Indonesian body would be convened to explore that prospect. In July, this body voted, in effect, to implement the maximalist vision of Indonesia championed by Muhammad Yamin. Three-fifths of the 66 delegates chose to extend the new state far beyond the Dutch East Indies. Their design for Indonesia encompassed all of the Indies *plus* the Malayan peninsula, northern Borneo, eastern Timor, the rest of New Guinea, and unnamed "surrounding islands." Only one-fifth wanted to keep the proposed country to the limits of its colonial antecedent.[80]

In this enlargement of what Indonesia might have become, one senses the triumph of a profusely reimagined Majapahit over confining Dutch colonial horizons. Decades later, following the New Order's brutal ingestion of East Timor, the natural desire in the West to denounce that annexation reinforced a conventional view of Indonesian nationalism as the desire for sovereignty over the lands and waters that the Dutch had placed inside the Indies—no more (or less) than that. This view legitimated as authentically nationalist the campaign of arms and words led by Sukarno to "return" western New Guinea to Indonesia-the-Indies, and the cession of that half island to the republic by Holland via the United Nations in 1963. Seen from this same perspective— the republican movement as an affirmation of Dutch-drawn borders—the grabbing of Portuguese East Timor was an act of imperialism that, far from implementing Indonesian nationalism, betrayed it.

The lavish dream of a nationalist majority in 1945 cannot justify what a militarist minority—Suharto and his generals—did to East Timor beginning in 1975. But the breadth of that earlier vision does offer a different point of departure for understanding Indonesian history since 1945. The more one acknowledges the genuine appeal of "greater Indonesia" to Sukarno, Yamin, and others among the founders of the republic, the harder it is to treat the persisting sense of geopolitical entitlement on the part of successive Indonesian regimes as anomalous—a regrettable deviation from a solid and confident consensus to stay within boundaries owed to the Dutch. That sense of larger entitlement also reflected a volatile insecurity derived from the country's massive size and considerable resources compared with its physical fragmentation and material weakness. In this image, Indonesia was invincible and vulnerable at the same time.

Consider, in this light, the exercises pursued by Sukarno in the early 1960s against the formation of independent Malaysia west of Indonesia and for the absorption of western New Guinea far to the east. The more one accepts Indonesia as the legitimate successor to the Indies, the easier it is to treat the confrontation against Malaysia as an imperialist intervention beyond once Dutch lines and to distinguish it sharply from the nationalist restoration of Papua to its rightful place inside them. The more sensitive one is, on the other hand, to the sheer sweep of Indonesian nationalist ambition in 1945 as an illustration of entitlement, the easier it becomes to understand both campaigns as having unfolded within what were then the still not yet consolidated limits of Indonesian identity. Nationalism and imperialism are not contradictory.

The jumbo version of Indonesia envisioned by the independence body in Jakarta in July 1945 did contradict geostrategic realities. Day by day, allied battlefield successes were dismantling Japan's ability to allow Indonesian nationalists to realize their larger dream, quite apart from Japanese willingness to do so. Nor, as Sukarno soon found, was Japan willing to entertain the independence of a "greater Indonesia." And what if Japan were defeated and forced to relinquish once European Southeast Asia to its prewar overlords? Indonesia's nationalists could hardly expect not just the Dutch in the Indies but also the British in Malaya and Borneo, the Portuguese in East Timor, the Australians in New Guinea, and the proprietors of those unspecified "surrounding islands" to donate their holdings to Jakarta.

In the second week of August 1945, the Japanese occupiers of the region made clear their refusal to countenance any such scheme, whereupon Sukarno and his fellow nationalists retracted the boundaries of their proposal to match, after all, the edges of the Indies.

Demarcation was only one of Holland's contributions to Indonesia. Not least among the others were the physical accoutrements of modernity—roads and ports, trains and ships, schools and offices. That legacy supports a view of Indonesia as having inherited from its colonial past more of a state, especially an administrative state—in Dutch, a *Beamtenstaat*—than a society, least of all a functioning civil society committed to a democratic identity for Indonesia.

I share this view of Indonesia as having been innovated from the top down. For a society already endowed with a strong self-identity in this chapter's terms—coherent, distinctive, common—forming a state would have been less of an innovation than a completion: the natural political expression of a prior social fact. The same process in reverse is riskier. Building a national consciousness from the top down—starting from a state in the absence of a self-identifying society—can founder for a range of reasons, including the possible exacerbation of social divisions by elite rivalries, or vice versa. In this respect, reviewers of Indonesian identity formation ought not to have expected too much.

Historical sequences are not neatly sequential. State and social identities can and do overlap, interact, develop in tandem. Indonesia does, nonetheless, seem an artificial construct relative to Thailand, arranged around the central plain ethnic Tai and their monarchy, or Vietnam, organized around the ethnic Viet and their self-definition as something other than Chinese. Although the Javanese are a 45 percent plurality of Indonesians, 75 and 88 percent of the citizens of Thailand and Vietnam are ethnically Thai and Viet, respectively.[81] Compared with the caution of Indonesian nationalists who could not afford to be too blatantly Javanist in building their proposed republic lest they alienate its non-Javanese, no such restraint complicated the use of core Thai and core Viet identities as matrices for those nation-states.

Among other precolonial kingdoms in what would become the Indies, Majapahit did have inspirational value as proof of an indigenous ability to organize loose polities prior to the European arrival. But the Dutch bequeathed to their Indonesian successors the essentials: a frame, some physical infrastructure, an indigenous bureaucracy, in short, the makings of a more or less modern state.

It is not that the Dutch played no role in stimulating the growth of an Indonesian society. The roads they built facilitated travel. Economic activities, even in a racially divided colony, had socially mobilizing effects. So did the educational opportunities that the colonizers made available, however belatedly and selectively, to their native subjects. By publishing or allowing the circulation of Malay-language materials—serials, books, pamphlets—the Dutch facilitated literacy in what would become Bahasa Indonesia, the "one language" so patriotically cited by the authors of the Youth Oath of 1928.

Nevertheless, in the wake of World War II, what the Dutch left to their successors was not an integrated society, let alone a democratic polity, but a colonially imposed state. Those who took charge of the independent country could not rely on the vigor and viability of a nationally self-aware and socioeconomically mobile population, or of a large and liberalizing indigenous middle class, to decolonize and democratize this inheritance. Politicians with such goals in mind had to contend with two key institutions, the bureaucracy and the military, that were in varying degrees and ways holdovers from the colonial past. Not that the politicians themselves were necessarily sincere or credible reformers. The "solidarity maker" label conventionally assigned to Sukarno is often inferred from his charismatic personality, notably his oratory.[82] But it can also be understood structurally as a reflection of a real need to play a kind of sociological catch-up, fashioning the horizontal empathy and awareness—the national identity—that had for so long lagged behind the colonial emphasis on vertical control, administration, extraction.

Indonesia as a Dutch legacy? Definitely yes. The Dutch drew lines around a place that became a space. Through modern technologies of transport and communication, they began the process of linking the elements within that space to each other and to elements beyond it. At first inadvertently, and then a bit more consciously during their late in the game "ethical policy," they fostered limited social mobilization, while fearing and trying to check or coopt its destabilizing political consequences. They became a common opponent against which Indonesians could rally. Most lastingly, however, they bequeathed a frame and the challenge of how to administer the congeries inside it. And in this last sense, the Dutch left behind a question: Can a formation that began its sovereignty as a state-nation become a nation-state?

Nationalist Artifact

How does one grow a nation to fit a state? Indonesia answered that question by building its national consciousness more or less from the top down and the center out. But for that strategy to work, nationalists first had to occupy the top and the center of the ex-Dutch state in the name of their independent nation-to-be. Three obvious routes to this pinnacle were a revolution, a coup, and a negotiation. All three paths figured in the story of how, in 1945–1949, Indonesians took from the Japanese what the Dutch had left behind.

But a fourth and merely symbolic ascent was also possible: a declaration that henceforth an independent nation-state did, in fact, exist. And in Jakarta at the end of the Pacific War the symbolism of such a step had the virtue by necessity of avoiding the twin difficulties of physically usurping power from the Japanese or peacefully negotiating power away from it. For in August 1945, in the strange days immediately following their final defeat and surrender, the Japanese occupiers remained in charge of the ex-Indies yet were beholden to the Allies, including the very Dutch whom they had ousted or interned at the start of the war.

Timing a declaration of independence can be crucial. How can a nationalist leader, committed to making and heading a sovereign nation-state, lessen the risk of eclipse by indigenous rivals and foreign powers with competing claims to sovereignty—claims that the leader considers rebelliously subnational, mistakenly national, or neocolonially antinational in character? Preemption is an obvious if preliminary answer: to promulgate "national" independence first, under one's own leadership, before anyone else can advance an alternative sovereignty or block any sovereignty at all for the state in question.

Such a strike-first nationalist hopes to conjure citizenship by fait accompli. He (historically less often she) relies on one or both of two conjectures. Looking inward at the population his proclamation has just instantly "nationalized," he calculates that those who support the new identity, or at least cannot be mobilized to oppose it, will so outnumber or outweigh proponents of rival identities as to make the "national" one stick, at least until it can be furnished with specific and attractive content. Comparably, looking outward at the world, he figures that his independence by manifesto will elicit foreign support and deter foreign opposition, or at least be treated by outsiders as a fact on the ground—a circumstance that has to be taken into account. In the longer run, such a preemptive nationalist hopes to influence, ideally to control, the terms of ensuing action and discourse.

Japan surrendered to the Allies on August 15, 1945, Indonesian independence was announced by Sukarno and Mohammad Hatta two days later, on August 17, 1945. The next day, a Japanese-sponsored Committee to Prepare the Independence of Indonesia (PPKI) at its inaugural meeting named the two men president and vice president, respectively, of the barely proclaimed republic.

What made this timing so urgent was not the fear of being upstaged from within by a subnational competitor for loyalty but the fear of being sidelined from without by the imminent closure of a unique window of opportunity opened by the denouement of the war in the Pacific—the lag in time between Japan's defeat and Holland's return. In June 1945 in South Sulawesi, the Japanese allowed the formation of a National Party under the aegis of the Sultan of Bone. In July the Japanese set up a version of the PPKI in Sumatra. But the occupiers constrained the Sumatran body and soon changed their minds about the Bone initiative and suppressed it entirely. Nor is there reason to believe that the leaders involved in either instance, had they been free to forge subnational sovereignties, would have done so.[83]

If Indonesia makers in Jakarta in August 1945 were not bothered by indigenous competitors with smaller sovereignties in mind, however, their own priorities differed. A group of younger nationalists urged revolutionary struggle to forge the nation in the act of inspiring it from within. Some of their elders stressed instead the need for international support to consolidate the state through diplomatic recognition by other states. In the end, Sukarno and Hatta signed a two-sentence declaration: "We the Indonesian people hereby declare the independence of Indonesia. All matters concerning the transfer of power etc. will be executed in an orderly manner and in the shortest possible time."[84] The first sentence validated *the nation* from the bottom up as a unilateral act of avowal by a preexisting Indonesian people. The second sentence reflected a top-down desire to accomplish the transition of *the state* from Japanese to Indonesian auspices with sufficient discipline to forestall anarchy, yet speedily enough to greet the victorious Allies on their arrival with a display of sovereignty too convincing to be denied, let alone reversed.

On the afternoon of August 17, revolutionary youths seized the Japanese radio facility in Jakarta and announced the proclamation of independence to "the Indonesian people" in whose name it had, that same morning, been made. Responses from listeners were enthusiastic, especially on Java. By month's end, buildings and even arms had been wrested from Japanese control in all the major cities on that central island. Java became the epicenter of the revolution, in contrast to those outer islands where the returning Dutch were able to regain some influence, however temporarily. All the more reason for Sukarno to have insisted, as he publicly and repeatedly did, on the transinsular, transethnic, transreligious breadth of the Indonesian identity he and his fellow nationalists were trying to create. And, yes, their nationalism was meant to preempt rivals before they could emerge.

Eventually they did emerge. Against first-strike nationalism, other identities struck back. In subsequent years and decades, clear into the twenty-first century, multiple movements with diverse agendas arose to challenge the originally declared republic. Notable nonetheless is how long it took for the two most formidable and enduring territorial challenges, in Aceh and Papua, to acquire fully secessionist form. That occurred not on Sukarno's presidential watch (1945–1967) but during Suharto's (1967–1998). And although the republican facts on the ground created by the nationalists of 1945 were not enough to prevent a Dutch return, they encouraged U.S. pressure on Holland to accommodate Indonesian sovereignty, as finally happened in December 1949. By then, the sheer drama of the revolution against the Dutch had generated ample material for later use in elaborating a heroic national mythology—grist for civics textbooks, holiday speeches, postage stamps, and other sites of celebration.

Struggling over the State

One who strikes first tries to create an advantage in conditions that (in the attacker's eyes) combine danger with uncertainty. In predawn darkness on October 1, 1965, in Jakarta, squads apparently under the command of an ostensibly leftist lieutenant colonel in the army, Untung, went to the homes of seven leading and more or less anticommunist army generals, killed three (including the army chief of staff), and kidnapped three more who were killed soon after. The conspirators also took and killed an adjutant of the seventh targeted general, having mistaken the junior officer for his boss. Shortly afterward a radio announcement informed listeners that Untung's troops had moved to forestall a coup that was being planned by a "council of generals" sponsored by the U.S. Central Intelligence Agency. Several hours later the Untung group announced the formation of a revolutionary council with ultimate authority over the country pending elections.

Omitted from the cabal's list of foes was General Suharto, who took control of the decapitated army, used circumstantial evidence and propaganda to blame the killings on the Indonesian Communist Party (PKI), and sponsored the destruction of the PKI within a broader antileftist purge that took hundreds of thousands of lives. The number who died may have reached half a million—perhaps more, possibly fewer. By 1968 Suharto was fully ensconced in the presidency. Sukarno, kept under house arrest, died of natural causes two years later.

The exact causes, actors, and motives behind this conspiracy remain controversial. They may never be fully known. But preemptive calculation certainly played a role. In an atmosphere of rising political tension in the capital, supposedly impending conspiracies were increasingly the subject of rumor and speculation. By mid-1965 there were communists who feared a strike against them by an anticommunist "council of generals." Conversely, there were anticommunists who feared becoming the victims of treachery at the hands of Indonesia's large and increasingly militant left. In early August when President Sukarno collapsed briefly in public, doubts as to his ability to stop such plots made them seem more likely. Whether these conspiracies afoot were real or not, anxieties about them were real enough to motivate preemptive moves.[85]

The kidnappers and killers of October 1 meant, or were meant to, create powerful facts on the ground, in the expectation that establishing those facts would oblige key actors to adapt to them. Not least among such facts was an army ostensibly rendered egalitarian by decapitation. The conspirators thought they were ridding their country of a top layer of corrupt, high-living generals poised to sabotage the Indonesian revolution in secret concert with its American and British enemies. Arguably, in the conspirators' view, these foreign enemies were poised to divide and recolonize the republic in a manner not unlike what the Dutch had been so deviously up to in the 1940s—and what August 17 as a fact on the ground had been meant to prevent.

It may seem odd, even repugnant, to compare what Lieutenant Colonel Untung and his men did in Jakarta with the patriotic sentences that Sukarno and Hatta had signed and proclaimed two decades before. The two episodes differed greatly in empirical terms; and morally, in 1965, there was nothing to applaud. But both of these otherwise different cases showed the importance and persistence, alongside Indonesia as an imagined community, of Indonesia as an improvised response to imagined contingency. Twenty years after the assertion of their independence, Indonesians in whose name it had been made still did not enjoy levels of predictability, transparency, and safety high enough, or a society prosperous enough, or a state accountable enough (including officers subordinated to civilian rule and politicians committed to peaceful means) either to prevent a savage first strike or to stop it from being used to excuse a catastrophe when Suharto struck back. The left's decimation in that slaughter was another, far bloodier fait accompli.

These actions pose a dilemma that continues to bedevil Indonesia conceived as a nationalist artifact built from the top down and the center out. A struggle over control of the state is logically prior to the struggle to root that state in a nation. But in the absence of institutionalized procedures for political change and the peaceful settlement of grievances, the Indonesian state stayed up for grabs: in 1945–1949 during the revolution; in 1950 when an anti-Jakarta revolt broke out in Ambon; in 1952 when the army staff chief tried to have parliament dismissed; in 1956–1958 when army rebels rose against Jakarta on several outer islands; and in 1957 when Sukarno declared a state of war and siege that expanded the military's role. Two years later he shut down parliamentary rule, replaced Indonesia's provisional constitution, and dispersed its elected but deadlocked institutions. The upshot was yet another regime for Indonesians to cope with—an undemocratic "guided democracy" guided by none other than Sukarno himself, later named president for life.

Seen in this context, what made 1965–1966 so exceptional was the number of its victims and the sweep of its consequences, not the fact of another conspiracy in progress. Actually, there were two of them: Untung's effort and Suharto's artfully legality-seeking coup disguised as a countercoup that installed, top-down, an authoritarian "new order" on an already much-reordered country.

Future historians may still conclude that Suharto's resignation in 1998 and democratic elections the following year finally broke this cycle of autocratic improvisation from above. In 2001 at least, such optimism was premature. It was precisely the erratic and unilateral style of President Abdurrahman Wahid that had alienated the elected legislature and people's assembly to the point of instituting proceedings to remove him from office. Since February Wahid had sought military support for a state of emergency that would have served as a preemptive first strike against the looming contingency of his own impeachment. On July 22 he threatened to freeze the People's Assembly, suspend the country's second-largest political party, and hold new national elections, despite the lack of a constitutional basis for such actions.

His military having refused to go along, Wahid decided to go it alone. Soon after midnight on July 23, he issued a presidential decree. It declared an emergency, dissolved the People's Assembly, and promised elections in 2002. By sunset that same day, the chief justice of the supreme court had declared the move unconstitutional, and the assembly members whose ouster Wahid had announced had impeached him unanimously and replaced him with his vice president, Megawati Sukarnoputri. Intransigent to the end, Wahid threatened to force Megawati's government to drag him kicking and screaming from office, but finally relented and left of his own accord.

Is the system to blame for the actions of individuals and groups within it? Even if the state has failed in Indonesia, why implicate the nation in that disappointment? Arbitrariness and illegality at the top may require only procedural adjustments. If so, the four composite amendments to the constitution that were adopted in 1999–2002 could turn out to have been remedy enough. Certainly the legislative and direct presidential elections of 2004 further normalized Indonesia's fledgling democracy—a sunnier identity for Indonesia.

But not even successful reform will erase the historical question: Why has it taken Indonesia such a long and turbulent time to institutionalize an effective and responsive political system? Nationalists should not be faulted for conditions they could not affect. Hindsight can be unfairly harsh. But one of the possible answers to this question does point toward a more or less consistent inability, perhaps an unwillingness, possibly even a fear on the part of successive elites to build, downward from the top, a nation to which the inherited state—their state, with themselves on top—could then be held accountable. As for effectiveness, it is disquieting to think that the New Order's most lasting intellectual legacy could be the surely false idea that Indonesians can have a dynamic economy, or a democratic polity, just not both at once.

Indonesia as a nationalist artifact? Indeed, and with some success. The entity that Sukarno and Hatta announced in 1945 was not, and did not become, an ethnically Javanese empire in disguise. By 1963, with western New Guinea regained, Indonesian nationalism had managed to extend its field to the territorial limits of its Dutch legacy. In these senses, the nation did fit the state. But too many Indonesian leaders had too little interest in closing a different gap: between the intensity of their sometimes dangerous maneuvers in the capital and the paucity of their efforts to involve the vast rest of the country in, together, making a nation worth sharing. Aside from Indonesia's two democratic experiments—in the 1950s and from the late 1990s—the results were more state-first than nation-based.

Personal Meanings

As a nationalist undertaking, Indonesia recapitulates political history: the formation of the Indonesisch Verbond van Studeerenden (Indonesian Students Society) in the Netherlands in 1917; the morphing of the Indische Vereeniging (Indies Association) into Perhimpunan Indonesia (Indonesian Association) in 1922; the paradigmatic launching of the Youth Oath of 1928. And so on through the world depression (1930s); the Japanese occupation (1941–1945); the Indonesian revolution (1945–1949); parliamentary democracy (1950–1957); a transition between regimes (1957–1959); guided democracy (1959–1965); another transition (1965–1967); the New Order (1967–1998); and the latest transition, through four presidencies—B. J. Habibie (1998–1999), Abdurrahman Wahid (1999–2001), Megawati Sukarnoputri (2001–2004), and Susilo Bambang Yudhoyono (2004–)—toward whatever, and whomever, lies ahead.

This sequence highlights the milestones of national politics—changes of regimes and leaders—as if they were the prime drivers of Indonesian identity. The drama of high politics implies a "great tradition" of identifications that government officials have invoked on patriotic holidays.[86] This Indonesia has been about dates, heroes, emblems: 1928 and 1945; the legendary revolutionary general, Sudirman, and the champion of independence, Sukarno; the mythological garuda bird emblazoned on the national seal and the five principles of *pancasila* coined by Sukarno and sanctified by Suharto.

"Little traditions" of Indonesia, meanwhile, have resulted from the filtering of high-nationalist ideology through local identities, including local histories and local symbols—and local mixtures of affinity and grievance toward the metonymy of Jakarta as the country. Beyond these constructions lies Indonesia as individually experienced and imagined by its inhabitants. Alongside collective traditions of what Indonesia means, these personal versions also merit attention.

In 2001, in the middle of Indonesia's rocky transition, first-year students at Atma Jaya University in Yogyakarta were given a questionnaire.[87] Table 1.1 presents one of the questions and organizes the answers to it by topic and subtopic. The question (in Indonesian) was: "When you hear the word 'Indonesia,' what first occurs to you—what do you associate it with?"

Table 1.1. Representing Indonesia: Some Free Associations

Question: When you hear the word "Indonesia," what first occurs to you—what do you associate it with?

Category and Subcategory	Frequency of Occurrence	
	Number	Percentage
A. Nature and Geography	84	46.2
1. Natural resources	22	12.1
2. The archipelago	20	11.0
3. Mother Nature	17	9.3
4. Natural beauty	16	8.8
5. Flora and fauna	5	2.7
6. Tropical location	3	1.6
7. Asian location	1	0.5
B. Conflict and Failure	53	29.1
1. Political and economic chaos and crises	20	11.0
2. Feelings of shame (country no longer peaceful)	12	6.6
3. Poverty, crime, and social fragility	6	3.3
4. Street demonstrations	4	2.2
5. Unstable and irresponsible government	3	1.6
6. National collapse due to foolish and venal elites	3	1.6
7. Corruption	3	1.6
8. Inter-ethnic conflicts	1	0.5
9. Need for an iron hand (a people's dictator who will fight for the people's prosperity)	1	0.5
C. Culture and Religion	23	12.6
1. Rich culture(s)	16	8.8
2. People and their hospitality	5	2.7
3. Crowded country	1	0.5
4. Islam	1	0.5
D. "Great Tradition"	22	12.1
1. Bhineka Tunggal Ika	21	11.5
2. Red and white flag	1	0.5
	182	99.4

Table 1.1 cannot be said to stand for Indonesian opinion. These were beginning college students in Central Java, of whom a majority were Christian—features that hardly match the national distributions of educational status, residential location, or religious affiliation. Without being representative, however, table 1.1 is germane. The question was left open-ended to attract personal meanings—whatever the respondents at that moment happened to associate with "Indonesia."

A first impression of table 1.1 is how few—just 12 percent—of the answers it presents lie in the "great tradition" of national-patriotic symbols. Also striking is how nearly all of those who did evince such an understanding of Indonesia identified their country with unity in diversity, or *bhinneka tunggal ika*. (Remarkably, only one person thought of the national flag.) Would "great tradition" references to *bhinneka tunggal ika* be more frequent in a comparable survey of Muslim Indonesians? Possibly not. One could at least hypothesize that, other things being equal, minority groups, including Christians, have more invested in meanings of "Indonesia" that emphasize cultural diversity than Muslim-majority Indonesians do.

A second impression is that the students' perceptions and feelings about Indonesia reflected the turbulence of the country's transition, so obviously and uncertainly under way at the time. But in view of those circumstances, is a 29 percent emphasis on conflict and failure higher than, lower than, or roughly equal to what might have been expected? One can also wonder, had a similar group of respondents been asked the same question annually as Indonesia's transition wore on, whether the lone vote in 2001 for benign despotism (B.9) would have remained alone.

A third noteworthy aspect of these answers is the considerable—46 percent—attention they pay to the natural attributes of Indonesia. Was this, in effect, a default category? Were these students driven toward natural phenomena that exist independently of human beings for lack of positive human achievements to cite in giving meaning to "Indonesia"? Or would nature have figured as prominently even in the absence of the shame-inducing bloodshed and other failings of human behavior that had occurred since the twilight of the New Order? The frequency with which these students associated Indonesia with its natural resources could be construed as optimistic, if those who replied in this vein were thinking of the gains in welfare achievable by wisely exploiting their country's gas, oil, minerals, forests, and water. My own guess is less presumptuous: that the table reflects a more general and independent tendency to associate Indonesia with its natural contents.[88] Whatever the explanation, the prominence of geography in these meanings of "Indonesia" would seem to offer some indigenous warrant for the visual-spatial orientation of much of this chapter.

A fourth impression is how differently these Indonesian students imagined their country compared with how their American counterparts might be expected to picture the United States: table 1.1 includes no mention of democracy. This omission also contrasts with the frequency, in American diplomatic rhetoric, of references to Indonesia as the world's "third largest democracy" or the "largest Muslim democracy." The issue at stake here is whether democracy, so central to American self-conceptions, will become a baseline referent for the *Indonesian* reconstruction of Indonesia.

Fifth and last is another intriguing absence in these results: *pancasila.* Has this term followed the fate of federalism in having become too guilty by association—*pancasila* with Suharto, federalism with colonialism—to be usable as a major part, let alone a keystone, of national identity?[89] The students' replies, of course, only raise this question; they do not answer it. Their silence on *pancasila* does match, however, a more general reluctance among politicians and officials to reinstall that particular emblem as the mainspring of national identity. *Pancasila* has not been abandoned. But it has been placed in abeyance since having been, under Suharto, compulsory.

What if the students whose responses occupy table 1.1 had been individually interviewed? Still different perceptions of Indonesia might have emerged. Relevant to this possibility are some conversations—not formal interviews—I had with college age and younger Indonesians in Jakarta in April 2001. When I asked them what Indonesia meant to them, they gave *none* of the answers in table 1.1. Nor did they talk about democracy, or *pancasila.* They spoke instead of the friends they liked to hang out with and the things they enjoyed doing together. "This," one said simply, "is where we live."

Is it helpful to speak of a "privatized" national identity in this most personal case? If so, is the lack of historical, political, or other "public" content in the conversational answers I elicited a symptom of retreat by these young Indonesians—unable as they may have been to take pride in a severely tarnished political tradition? Had they been shamed by their country's crises and failings into shrinking the semantic horizons of "Indonesia" toward the private, apolitical self?

I did not sense this. If anything, Indonesia as these informants had personally experienced it seemed in their accounts not a last recourse but a first one, not a fragile default but a solid design, not dutifully copied off the high doctrines of patriotism, nor filtered through a parochial localism, but inductively built up around lives actually lived—something quotidian, hence unproblematic.

Just as the survey in Yogyakarta was unrepresentative, so were my encounters in Jakarta. Had the latter taken place in Aceh, say, or Papua, and depending on who my informants were, the answers could well have differed, even sharply, from what I heard in the national capital. That said, the interactions I did have in 2001 were encouraging, if microscopically so, for the sustainability of Indonesian identity. Taking one's country for granted as one's home—where else did you think I would live?—does not imply the disintegration of Indonesian identity, and is at least compatible with an opposing view of Indonesia as a normal address. Conceivably, one could even take the Atma Jaya students' focus on natural attractions less as a refuge from high-national disillusion with Indonesia's performance than low-national pride in physical features, which are sure to outlast whatever regime happens to be in power and outlive those who have been corrupted by it.

Radically reglossing the now conventional reading of a nation as an imagined community, one might even say that the less imagined—more real—a community is, the greater the likelihood that it will endure. I live here.[90] These are my friends. Therefore, this is my country. End of story.

SOCIALIZING THE STATE

What does Indonesia need in the future? If a metaphor is called for, perhaps it should be borrowed not from construction but from ecology. That would imply a shifting of priorities—away from erecting a nation deductively to meet the specifications of yet another leader's abstract scheme, and toward the inductive cultivation of better governance in the service of society as it is. Not redesigning the nation but socializing the state. This may be something of what Robert Hefner has in mind in the next chapter when he writes of "scaling up" political civility in Indonesia.

In those parts of the country most scarred by tit-for-tat communal violence, of course, there may not be much local civility left to be "scaled up"—to be used as a basis for civilizing the state. And even in localities with a record of civic pluralism, specifically how should "scaling up" be undertaken, by whom, and on whose behalf? In hundreds of district-level jurisdictions, Indonesia's adventure with decentralization may be generating hundreds of different answers to this question as I write it.

Some of these answers will be promising enough to warrant deeper study and broader application. Others may show why in some deadlocked settings local enmities may have to be addressed from above in a process that involves "scaling down" national identity as a shared basis for badly needed empathy, or at least tolerance, between opposing groups. Noteworthy in this context in 2001–2002 was the crucial role played by national actors, including members of Megawati's cabinet, in facilitating peace-seeking agreements that for all their imperfections did help reduce communal violence in Sulawesi and Maluku.

Returning one last time full circle back to my beginning: What *is* Indonesia? It is many different things at once to different people for different reasons. It is a project endlessly shaped by multiple intentions. I have featured one version of the project: to rebalance a state-nation into a nation-state. But the futures of Indonesia are multiple enough to confound any one—or anyone's—interpretations, including mine here. Indonesia is a process that cannot be reduced to even a complex causal design. A transition is not a trajectory that ends conveniently in a destination.

Whatever else it may be, Indonesia is unpredictable. Seen as an omen of fragility, that is weakness. But as evidence of vitality, it is a strength. Beginning of story.

NOTES

In preparing this chapter I benefited from interactions with James Castle, Okky Choi, Robert Elson, Theodore Friend, Andreas Harsono, Ken Hoover, Terry Hull, Dwight King, Damien Kingsbury, R. William Liddle, Andri Manuwoto, Jean Taylor, Michael Malley, James Raphael, Rizal Sukma, and Leo Suryadinata, who bear no responsibility for its content, least of all its shortcomings. I am also grateful, with the same disclaimer, to Christian Cunningham, James Siegel, and several other colleagues who discussed the manuscript with me at a seminar at Cornell University in November 2003. Leonardus Eko Sudibyo provided invaluable survey research assistance. Last but most I thank John Bresnan for his advice, patience, and perseverance.

1. From a speech by the chairman of Indonesia's second-largest Muslim organization, Muhammadiyah, on May 20, 2002, as excerpted in the *Jakarta Post*, www .thejakartapost.com/special/os_26.asp.
2. Heard at a sold-out performance of the play, written by Riantiarno and staged by Teater Koma, in Taman Ismail Marzuki, Jakarta, on April 27, 2001; see also N. Riantiarno, *Republik Bagong: Sandiwara Teater Koma* (Yogyakarta: Galang, 2001), 139. In the title of the play Riantiarno used a laughably bumbling character in Javanese mythology, Bagong, to poke fun at the Indonesian republic (Republik Indonesia).
3. Quoted by Edward Harris, "Children Go Back to School in Indonesia," Associated Press, January 10, 2005.
4. See, for example, Justine Rosenthal, "Southeast Asia: Archipelago of Afghanistans?" *Orbis*, Summer 2003; David Rohde, "Indonesia Unraveling?" *Foreign Affairs*, July-August 2001; Donald Emmerson, "Will Indonesia Survive?" *Foreign Affairs*, May-June 2000; Anne Booth, "Will Indonesia Break Up?" *Inside Indonesia*, July-September 1999; and Booth, "Can Indonesia Survive as a Unitary State?" *Indonesia Circle*, June 1992.
5. For more on 2004 as a political watershed, see Muhammad Qodari, "Indonesia's 2004 Elections," *Journal of Democracy*, April 2005; and Donald Emmerson, "A Year of Voting Dangerously?" *Journal of Democracy*, January 2004, 94–108. On Jakarta's

response to Aceh's travail, see, for example, "Indonesia's Blueprint for Rebuilding Aceh," *Straits Times* (Singapore), January 19, 2005.

6. *Shorter Oxford English Dictionary* (5th ed.). The same error appeared in the previous edition.

7. Robert Cribb, *Historical Dictionary of Indonesia* (Metuchen, N.J.: Scarecrow, 1992), xv. Note how "the size of a tennis court" conveys a physical reality but also implies the subjective experience of a limited audience. Most Indonesians, never having seen a tennis court, could not be expected to know its size. But neither would most Indonesians be in a position to read, let alone purchase, Cribb's book. And to how many of them would it occur to count islands (of whatever size) as a way of answering the question, "What is Indonesia?"

8. Robert Cribb, *Historical Atlas of Indonesia* (Honolulu: University of Hawai'i Press, 2000), 10. The addition of Atauro and Jaco to reflect the forcible absorption of East Timor in 1975–1976 explains the discrepancy between "13,669" as of 1992 in the dictionary and "13,667" as of 1963 in the atlas.

9. "Indonesia 'Finds' 500 Islands," BBC News, February 20, 2003, news.bbc.co .uk/go/fr/-/1/hi/world/asia-pacific/2784461.stm. The BBC correspondent noted that, depending on the tides, islands photographed in the morning could have disappeared by afternoon.

10. Neither is, say, France. But compared with the islands and waters of Indonesia, France is easier to tidy into symmetry—specifically a hexagon. That is the shape that French schoolchildren may be asked to draw when first introduced to their national map, and what appears as background on the "national" side of "French" one- and two-euro coins. Physical reality does place limits on what can be persuasively said about it—or read into it.

11. The absolute and percentage estimates are drawn respectively from Leo Suryadinata, Evi Nurvidya Arifin, and Aris Ananta, *Indonesia's Population: Ethnicity and Religion in a Changing Political Landscape* (Singapore: Institute of Southeast Asian Studies, 2003), 140 (table 5.1.1) [henceforth abbreviated *IP 2000* because of its focus on the 2000 census]; and World Bank Development Data Group, *2002 World Development Indicators* (Washington, D.C.: World Bank, 2002), table 3.10.

12. In 2000, Papua's density was six persons per square kilometer, barely more than half the density of the next least peopled province, East Kalimantan (11), and less than two-thirds of 1 percent of that of Central Java (959), the densest province except for the provincial level but urban core areas of Yogyakarta (980) and Jakarta (12,635). Central Bureau of Statistics, *Statistics Indonesia*, www.bps.go.id/sector/population/ table3.shtml.

13. See Anne Booth, "Development: Achievement and Weakness," in Donald K. Emmerson, ed., *Indonesia beyond Suharto: Polity, Economy, Society, Transition* (Armonk, N.Y.: Sharpe, 1999), 119–23.

14. M. Senoatmodjo, "Pilipina Tak Mungkin Klaim Pulau Miangas," Suara Karya Online (Jakarta), January 12, 2003, www.suarakarya-online.com/news.html? id=54983.

15. "Press Statement: Minister of Foreign Affairs of the Republic of Indonesia," Jakarta, December 17, 2002, press release 737/04/XII/2002, Indonesian embassy,

Wellington, New Zealand, www.indonesianembassy.org.nz/News/PressRelease/
PressRelease-737-04-XII-2002.htm.

16. See Dr. Hasjim Djalal on Miangas, as quoted in "Pemerintah Bantah Gagal Soal
Sipadan-Ligitan," *Sinar Harapan* (Jakarta), December 18, 2002, www.sinarharapan
.co.id/berita/0212/18/sh01.html; and "Case Concerning Sovereignty over Pulau Ligitan and Pulau Sipadan (Indonesia/Malaysia): Summary of the Judgment of 17 December 2002," press release 2002/39bis, International Court of Justice, The Hague,
December 20, 2002, paragraphs 126–49, www.icj-cij.org/icjwww/idocket/iinma/
iinmaframe.htm.

17. Even on political maps, at very high ratios of inches to miles (or centimeters to
kilometers), rival placements of the same border segment by national authorities on either side of it may become visible. Also noticeable at close range should be the extent
to which a natural feature originally chosen to demarcate part of a border may since
have drifted, as has the westward bulge of the otherwise ruler-straight Indonesia-PNG
border where it briefly follows the Fly River.

18. The notion of a "double erasure" aside, this paragraph reflects designations on
maps 26 (phyla) and 43 (groups) in Stephen Wurm, "Australasia and the Pacific," in
Christopher Mosely and R. E. Asher, eds., *Atlas of the World's Languages* (London:
Routledge Reference, 1994), 91–156. On the complex matter of language classification, see 93–94.

19. See Wurm, "Australasia and the Pacific," maps 35–36 (New Guinea), 40
(Timor), and 43 (Borneo) on the one hand, and map 27 (Australasia) on the other, for
evidence at respectively lower and higher levels of classification. Especially clear for
New Guinea is the higher-level contrast in map 24 in S. A. Wurm and Shirô Hattori,
eds., *Language Atlas of the Pacific Area* (Canberra: The Australian Academy of the
Humanities with the Japan Academy, 1981).

20. As specified in section 13, article 1 of the Constitution of the Democratic Republic of East Timor adopted by the territory's elected Constituent Assembly on
March 22, 2002.

21. Dennis Schulz and Fernando de Freitas, "East Timor's Tower of Babel," *Sydney Morning Herald*, August 16, 2002, www.smh.com.au/articles/2002/08/15/
1029113984617.html.

22. Schulz and de Freitas, "East Timor's Tower of Babel."

23. As of 2002, population estimates for Indonesia and East Timor in 2002 were,
respectively, 228 million and 800,000; John W. Wright, ed., *The New York Times Al-
manac 2003* (New York: Penguin, 2002), 583 (Indonesia) and 557 (East Timor).

24. The figures for 1971 and 1990 are from official Indonesian sources as cited
by Chris Manning and Michael Rumbiak, "Irian Jaya: Economic Change, Migrants,
and Indigenous Welfare," in Hal Hill, ed., *Unity and Diversity: Regional Economic
Development in Indonesia since 1970* (Singapore: Oxford University Press, 1989),
89. The estimate for 2001 is by Human Rights Watch, *Indonesia: Violence and Political Impasse in Papua*, pt. 6, "Human Rights Developments in Papua Today," sec.
"Anti-migrant Violence by Papuan Militants" (New York: Human Rights Watch,
2001), 4, www.hrw.org/reports/2001/papua/PAPUA0701-06.htm. The extrapolation
is my own.

25. These controversial speculations have given rise to an ongoing discourse among historians, archeologists, anthropologists, and political scientists, among others, that runs well beyond Indonesian evidence to raise questions about the past and future identity of Southeast Asia as a region. The *locus classicus* of these conjectures is O. W. Wolters, *History, Culture, and Region in Southeast Asian Perspectives*, rev. ed. (Ithaca, N.Y.: Cornell University Southeast Asia Program/Institute of Southeast Asian Studies, Singapore, 1999).

26. This definition reflects my general understanding of the mandala polity as described by Wolters, *History, Culture, and Region*, passim. In distinguishing the mandala as a diagram and a metaphor, I have omitted a third usage advanced by Wolters: the mandala as a name attached to a specific polity, such as Srivijaya, in a surviving epigraphic or written record (141). The obvious question, to what extent "mandala" as a contemporaneous name implied for its users the same rich content of "mandala" the retrospective metaphor, I prefer to leave open. Wolters himself acknowledged (without accepting) the argument made by Jan Wisseman Christie that the mandala model was too static to describe accurately Java's polities over half a millennium— from the ninth to the fourteenth centuries. Christie, "Negara, Mandala, and Despotic State: Images of Early Java," in David G. Marr and A. C. Milner, eds., *Southeast Asia in the 9th to 14th Centuries* (Singapore: Institute of Southeast Asian Studies, 1986), 85–86, as referenced in Wolters, 138.

27. Based on 1996–1997 data on absolute numbers of species in 141 countries in World Bank Development Data Group, *2002 World Development Indicators* (Washington, D.C.: World Bank, 2002), table 3.4 (mammals [2nd], birds [3rd], plants [4th]), and a reported ranking (marine diversity [1st]) in Lluminado Varela Jr., "Rescuing ASEAN's Mega-biodiversity," *New Light of Myanmar*, September 15, 2002, citing the ASEAN Regional Centre for Biodiversity Conservation; bracketed ordinals indicate Indonesia's ranking. On overall biodiversity, Indonesia has been ranked as (a) 1st or 2nd; (b) 3rd; and (c) "among the top five." These estimates are from (a) Rochadi Abdulhadi, "Problems and Issues Affecting Biodiversity in Indonesia," *ASEAN Biodiversity* [Los Baños, Philippines], 1: 1–2 (January–June 2001), 33; (b) Varela Jr., "Rescuing"; and (c) Rexie Jane Parreño, "The ASEAN Regional Centre for Biodiversity Conservation," *ASEAN Biodiversity* [Los Baños, Philippines], 1: 1–2 (January–June 2001), 8.

28. Cribb, *Historical Atlas*, tables 1.3 and 1.24 on 12 and 22, respectively. The zone is named after nineteenth-century British naturalist Alfred Russel Wallace, who first noted the contrast.

29. The figure of 726 is from www.ethnologue.com/show_country.asp?name= Indonesia. See also Barbara F. Grimes, ed., and Joseph E. Grimes, consulting ed., *Ethnologue* (Dallas: SIL International, 2000). After noting a widely used estimate of around 200 indigenous languages (Cribb, *Historical Dictionary*, 260), Robert Cribb put the number at more than 350 (see n. 33 below). The meaning of "indigenous" can also vary from source to source. SIL's listing, for example, excludes European tongues but includes several varieties of Chinese, presumably on the grounds that Indonesian citizens who grew up speaking English and/or who now use English as their primary language are negligible in number compared with those for whom a Chinese

language filled and/or fills that role. The meanings of "mother tongue" and "first language" also may vary. Unless otherwise noted, on this topic, SIL's website supplied the data and the indices cited in the next few paragraphs of text. References to Java in these paragraphs include the island of Madura.

30. Other SIL scores include China .48; United States .35; Japan .03; and zero each for South and North Korea. A better known and simpler ranking of countries by "ethnic homogeneity" yields a different list, but also places Indonesia as the twenty-eighth most diverse. Ethnic heterogeneity in the latter source appears to have been defined as the percentage of the population of a country who speak the same primary language. George Thomas Kurian, *The Illustrated Book of World Rankings* (Armonk, N.Y.: Sharpe Reference, 1997), 52–53.

31. If Sulawesi is added to Papua and Maluku, this 54 percent is further enlarged. These three easternmost areas together host 70 percent of Indonesia's indigenous languages. Linguistic and population data used in reaching these conclusions were, respectively, compiled by SIL and drawn from official statistics for 1985 cited by Hal Hill and Anna Weidemann, "Regional Development in Indonesia: Patterns and Issues," in Hal Hill, ed., *Unity and Diversity: Regional Economic Development in Indonesia since 1970* (Singapore: Oxford University Press, 1989), 13 (table 1.1.4).

32. According to this summary source (Cribb's *Historical Atlas*, 30), more than 350 indigenous languages are spoken in the republic—200-plus that are Austronesian and another 150-plus that are Melanesian. Presumably, by this estimate, many of the "languages" named and mapped by SIL would be considered "dialects."

33. Sources for the 1971 and 1980 figures are *Sensus Penduduk 1971, Series E* (Jakarta: Biro Pusat Statistik, 1974–1975), table 1.13; *Sensus Penduduk 1980, Series S* (Jakarta: BPS, 1981), no. 2, table 1.16.3, as cited by Christine Drake, *National Integration in Indonesia: Patterns and Policies* (Honolulu: University of Hawaii Press, 1989), 62. I calculated the 1990 figure from data in *Penduduk Indonesia: Hasil Sensus Penduduk 1990, Series S2* [henceforth abbreviated *SP 1990*] (Jakarta: BPS, 1992), table 20.3. Here and below, in all census-based references to language use by some percentage of a population, that universe—100 percent—does not include persons who were under five years old when the census was taken. The 2000 census had no questions about language, although respondents were asked to identify themselves ethnically.

34. Marshall McLuhan, "The Medium Is the Message," in *Understanding Media* (New York: McGraw-Hill, 1964), 7–21.

35. These ostensibly divisive forces were known by an acronym, *sara*, that stood for *suku* (ethnicity), *agama* (religion), *ras* (race), and conflict *antar-golongan* (among groups, including class conflict). Race was distinguished from ethnicity to acknowledge prejudice against Indonesians of Chinese descent, in contrast to ethnic tensions among supposedly native (non-Chinese) citizens. Prejudicial allusions to these identities in public were strongly discouraged.

36. Robert Cribb, "Independence for Java? New National Projects for an Old Empire," in Grayson Lloyd and Shannon Smith, eds., *Indonesia Today: Challenges of History* (Lanham, Md.: Rowman & Littlefield, 2001), 298.

37. *Undang-Undang Republik Indonesia Nomor 18 Tahun 2001* [henceforth abbreviated *UURI 18 (2001)*], effective August 9, 2001, *State Gazette*, Republic of

Indonesia, 2001, no. 114, article 8, clause 2, www.nad.go.id/default.php ("Artikel 'Menuju Aceh Baru'").

38. Historical details are recounted by Decki Natalis Pigay, *Evolusi Nasionalisme dan Sejarah Konflik Politik di Papua* (Jakarta: Pustaka Sinar Harapan, 2000), 93–97. The official shift to "Papua" has not been fully observed. In January 2005 on the Department of Home Affairs website, different pages listed the territory as "Papua" and "Papua/Irian Jaya"; www.depdagri.go.id.

39. Drake, *National Integration*, 62.

40. The 1980 figure is from Drake, *National Integration*, 62, citing *Sensus Penduduk 1980*. The figures for 1990 were calculated from *SP 1990*, 189. It is not clear to me whether the 1928 estimate referred to the language used at home or to the language that respondents remembered having learned first.

41. Also helping the national potential of Indonesian were the global unimportance of Dutch, the declining power of the Dutch state, and the unwillingness of Dutch colonizers to evangelize their language among the indigenes. Based on the different experience of the Philippines, one can speculate that if Americans had gone on to colonize the Indies as well, Indonesian might later have faced in English a rival to become the population's second language.

42. Suharto's Indonesian-language autobiography included a fifteen-page glossary of Javanese expressions for the convenience of non-Javanese-speaking readers. Soeharto, *Pikiran, Ucapan, dan Tindakan Saya*, as told to G. Dwipayana and Ramadhan K. H. (Jakarta: Citra Lamtoro Gung Persada, 1989), 570–84. See also R. E. Elson, *Suharto: A Political Biography* (Cambridge: Cambridge University Press, 2001), 298–99. In January 2003, a university lecturer in West Java criticized Megawati for inserting Javanese words and phrases into her Indonesian-language public speeches. What especially disturbed him was her use of Javanisms in a verbal lashing of her critics before cadres of her political party ("Megawati Criticized for Often Using Javanese Words," *Jakarta Post*, January 31, 2003). Perhaps comparably, Javanese terms were more likely to surface in Suharto's speech on the rare occasions when he expressed anger in public. Compared with an impersonal lingua franca, a vernacular spoken since childhood seems naturally more suited to voicing strong emotion. And Megawati was speaking not in the presidential palace but inside her personal residence in South Jakarta.

43. For example, Sakdani Darmopamudjo, "Pers Berbahasa Jawa Tinggal Kenangan," *Suara Merdeka* (Semarang, Central Jawa), February 14, 2002, www.suaramerdeka.com/harian/0202/14/kha2.htm. The article was written and published in Indonesian in an Indonesian-language daily read mainly by Javanese. See also Khaidir Anwar, *Indonesian: The Development and Use of a National Language* (Yogyakarta: Gadjah Mada University Press, 1980), 136–45 ("Indonesian versus the Regional Languages").

44. In 1990, young people age 5 through 24 were slightly more likely than their immediate elders (age 25 through 49) and more than twice as likely as the eldest (age 50 and higher) to have Indonesian as their mother tongue. Looking ahead, this "youth wedge" of "childhood Indonesia" seems more likely to enlarge or level off than shrink. Proportions by age group were calculated from *SP 1990*, 162.

45. The preceding three paragraphs reflect calculations using the census data in *SP 1990*, 195 (table 20.2). East Timor aside, proportionally the fewest Indonesian speakers were in West Nusa Tenggara (68), East Java (75), Bali (76), South Sulawesi (77), East Nusa Tenggara (78), Irian Jaya/Papua (79), Central Java (79), Yogyakarta (80), Aceh (84), West Java (84 each), and so on upward through the rest of the country. See also the summary maps in Drake, *National Integration*, 63 (for 1980), and Cribb, *Historical Atlas*, 37 (for 1990).

46. Adopted by the national legislature in 1999, these were Law no. 22 on regional government and Law no. 25 on regional finance.

47. The laws distinguish cities (*kota*) from regencies (*kabupaten*), but as autonomous regions they are functionally equivalent and are, for convenience, grouped together here as districts.

48. This paragraph reflects my reading of *Undang-Undang Republik Indonesia Nomor 22 Tahun 1999*, effective May 7, 1999, *State Gazette*, Republic of Indonesia, 1999, no. 60, especially articles 7, 8, 10, and 11, www.gtzsfdm.or.id.

49. By fully recognized, I mean by the Department of Home Affairs, which listed thirty provinces on its website, www.depdagri.go.id, as of mid-2003.

50. On the Philippines, see John Sidel, *Capital, Coercion, and Crime: Bossism in the Philippines* (Stanford, Calif.: Stanford University Press, 1999).

51. For details, see Robert W. Hefner, *Civil Islam: Muslims and Democratization in Indonesia* (Princeton, N.J.: Princeton University Press, 2000), 84, 122, 128, 135, 167.

52. *IP 2000*, 104 (table 4.1.1). The percentage breakdowns in 2000 were Muslims 88, Christians 9, Hindus 2, and Buddhists 1. The average annual rates of growth in percent in 1971-2000 were Christians 2.5, Muslims 1.9, Hindus 1.6, and Buddhists 1.5.

53. *IP 2000*, 115–16 (table 4.3.2).

54. The relevant historical statistics are in *IP 2000*, 115–16 (table 4.3.2).

55. These percentages were calculated from 2000 census data by Suryadinata et al. in *IP 2000*, 109–10 (table 4.2.2) and 115–16 (table 4.3.2).

56. Mary Somers Heidhues, *Southeast Asia: A Concise History* (London: Thames & Hudson, 2000), 77. Despite this evidence of an early Muslim presence in eastern Java, the first conversions to Islam almost certainly occurred to the west, along Sumatra's northern coast.

57. *IP 2000*, 15 (table 1.1.2.4). More than year 2000 census data from other provinces, these figures should be treated with caution. The security situation in Aceh in 2000 prevented enumerators from counting more than half the population. Estimates cited here are projections from that base. See *IP 2000*, 158. According to the census of 1990, Aceh was 98 percent Muslim in that year; *SP 1990*, 24.

58. *UURI 18 (2001)*, articles 25–26. The court was clearly subordinated to Jakarta in being "a part of the [Indonesian] national justice system" and "based on Islamic law within the [Indonesian] national legal system" (art. 25). Indonesia's president, acting as the national head of state, was given the authority to hire and fire the court's judges on the advice of the minister of justice in his or her national cabinet (art. 26). The content of the Islamic laws the court would administer was left for future determination. Permitting such laws as a way of enticing Acehnese allegiance to a larger framework was not a new idea. It had precursors dating from colonial times.

59. The drafters of special autonomy for Aceh did specify that the Islamic court would be "free of influence from any quarter"; *UURI 18 (2001)*, art. 25. They may have had in mind the risk that local groups might try to take over the new legal structure and use it to promote separation from Indonesia.

60. "'No Region Can Break Away': Interview with Ryamizard Ryacudu," *Time Asia*, June 2, 2003, www.time.com/time/asia/magazine/article/0,13673,501030602-454532,00.html; italics added.

61. John Cherian, "Crackdown in Aceh," *Frontline*, June 7–20, 2003, www.frontlineonnet.com/fl2012/stories/20030620000806400.htm; "Make or Break for Jakarta," *Australian*, May 24, 2003, www.theaustralian.news.com.au/printpage/0,5942,6481781,00.html.

62. In 1990, for example, excluding oil, gas, and mining, nearly two-thirds of Indonesia's twenty-seven provinces enjoyed per capita regional products larger than Aceh's; Hal Hill, *The Indonesian Economy*, 2nd ed. (Cambridge: Cambridge University Press, 2000), 222–23 (table 1.11.1).

63. Cited by Jane Perlez, "Asia Letter: As Aceh Aid Pours in, How Will It Be Spent?" *International Herald Tribune*, January 27, 2005.

64. Breakdowns by religion and ethnicity appear in *PI 2000*, 161–63.

65. See, for example, John Saltford, *United Nations Involvement with the Act of Self-Determination in West Irian (Indonesian West New Guinea) 1968 to 1969* (undated, but not completed before 2000), www.fpcn-global.org/downloads/act-of-free-choice-papua/un-papua-1968-69.pdf.

66. Council on Foreign Relations, Center for Preventive Action, *Indonesia Commission: Peace and Progress in Papua* (New York: Council on Foreign Relations, 2003), 7, www.cfr.org.

67. Indonesia's currency is the rupiah (R). In 1990, after deleting mining, oil, and gas, the per capita regional products of Papua (R 742) and Aceh (R 737) were a trivial five rupiahs apart. Hill, *Indonesian Economy*, 222–23 (table 1.11.1).

68. Japan International Cooperation Agency, Planning and Evaluation Department, *Country Profile Study on Poverty: Indonesia*, March 2003, 7, www.jica.go.jp/english/global/pov/profiles/pdf/ind_eng.pdf.

69. *Undang-Undang Republik Indonesia Nomor 21 Tahun 2001*, effective November 21, 2001, www.papuaweb.org/goi/otsus/files/otsus-id.html.

70. "Irian Jaya: House Endorses Division of Papua Province," *Jakarta Post*, February 14, 2003, www.indonesia.nl.

71. He was not alone among Indonesians in fearing this scenario. Another observer acknowledged the fears of "Muslim hard-liners" who blamed the West for driving off Catholic East Timor and suspected a Western–Christian "conspiracy against Indonesia's Muslims . . . to divide Indonesia into two parts: The western part for the Muslim population and the eastern part for the Christians." Lela E. Madjah, "Indonesia, a Nation Divided by Faith," *Jakarta Post*, June 26, 2000, www.thejakartapost.comj/special/os_04.asp.

72. In 1999 the foreign minister of the Netherlands promised to initiate a reconsideration of what had actually transpired in the "act of free choice" three decades before. A member of the Dutch parliament who had advanced the same idea looked forward

to a time when such a reappraisal might enable the Dutch people finally to "look the Papuans straight in the eyes." *Algemeen Dagblad* (Rotterdam), December 10, 1999, as cited by Saltford, *United Nations Involvement*, 20. Six years later, however, such wishful rethinking still lacked clear policy consequences. Revising history for conscience's sake and revising Indonesia for Papua's were not the same thing.

73. Indonesia in the eyes of Thomas L. Friedman epitomizes a state that is "too big to fail; too messy to work." Friedman, "Wahid's New-Look Indonesia Is Frankly a Mess," *International Herald Tribune*, October 4, 2000, 8. For Robert S. Chase, Emily B. Hill, and Paul Kennedy, Indonesia was a "pivotal state," defined as "a hot spot that could not only determine the fate of its region but also affect international stability." Chase, Hill, and Kennedy, "Pivotal States and U.S. Strategy," www.sais-jhu.edu/depts/econ/chase/pivotal.html. See also John Bresnan's chapter on Indonesia in Chase, Hill, and Kennedy, eds., *The Pivotal States: A New Framework for U.S. Policy in the Developing World* (New York: Norton, 1998).

74. Compare, in this respect, Keith Loveard, *Suharto: Indonesia's Last Sultan* (Singapore: Horizon, 1999), with the skepticism of Elson, *Suharto*, viii.

75. Based on census data reported in *IP 2000*, 34 (table 2.1.2). Banten later became a province in its own right.

76. These judgments summarize data in Hill, *Indonesian Economy*, 222–23 (table 1.11.1); *IP 2000*, 34 (table 2.1.2); and Menno Pradhan, Asep Suryahadi, Sudarno Sumarto, and Lant Pritchett, "Measurements of Poverty in Indonesia: 1996, 1999, and Beyond," Social Monitoring and Early Response Unit (SMERU), June 2000, 18 (table 4), www.smeru.or.id/report/workpaper/measurement/measbyond.pdf. The 1990 census did not ask about ethnicity.

77. *IP 2000*, 34 (table 2.1.2). Difficulties in gathering census data in these provinces probably imply a margin of error larger than for other provinces. Such error may, however, point toward an overestimation of Javanese strength, insofar as Javanese might have been more inclined than Acehnese to receive census takers and less likely to reside in remote or insecure areas the enumerators could not readily enter. A large physical presence is not, of course, a necessary requisite of empire. (On non-indigenous Indonesian residents, see n. 25 above.)

78. "East Timor Says No to UN Tribunal," August 9, 2004, www.laksamana.net/vnews.cfm?ncat=45&news_id=7365. On the Indonesian military's responsibility for what happened, see, for example, Donald Emmerson, "Voting and Violence: Indonesia and East Timor in 1999," in *Indonesia beyond Suharto*, 357.

79. On the fate of Majapahit, see M. C. Ricklefs, *A History of Modern Indonesia since c. 1220*, 3rd ed. (Stanford, Calif.: Stanford University Press, 2001), 22.

80. Muhammad Yamin, ed., *Naskah-Persiapan Undang-Undang Dasar 1945* ([Jakarta:] Jajasan Prapantja, 1959), 1:212–14.

81. U.S. Central Intelligence Agency, *World Factbook 2002*, www.cia.gov/cia/publications/factbook.

82. See Herbert Feith, *The Decline of Constitutional Democracy* (Ithaca, N.Y.: Cornell University Press, 1962).

83. This judgment reflects evidence in George McTurnan Kahin, *Nationalism and Revolution in Indonesia* (Ithaca, N.Y.: Cornell University Press, 1952), 121–22, 127, 177, 355.

84. Cribb, *Historical Dictionary*, 193.

85. This conclusion reflects interviews done in Jakarta in 1968. Among published sources, see Elson, *Suharto*, 94–98.

86. On "great" and "little traditions" as applied to civilizations, see Robert Redfield, *Peasant Society and Culture: An Anthropological Approach to Civilization* (Chicago: University of Chicago Press, 1956), 70.

87. For his cooperation in administering it, I am grateful to Leonardus Eko Sudibyo.

88. Indonesian university students commonly organize themselves into clubs to hike, camp, and otherwise enjoy the outdoors. I am grateful to Anna Tsing for suggesting this interpretation.

89. The Dutch experimented with federalism as a weapon against the unitary nationalism of the insurgent Indonesian republic in the years following World War II.

90. See Benedict R. O'G. Anderson, *Imagined Communities: Reflections on the Origin and Spread of Nationalism* (New York: Verso, 1991).

2

Social Legacies and Possible Futures

Robert W. Hefner

As Indonesia was swept by ethno-religious violence in the late 1990s, many observers were shocked to find that a national project regarded as secure a few years earlier suddenly seemed in trouble. The fact that Indonesia has great religious divides and more than 300 ethnic groups has complicated the task of forging an enduring and inclusive framework for nationhood. But the country's pluralism also makes the establishment of such a framework imperative if Indonesia is to survive. In this chapter I want to look at the historical genealogy of Indonesia's diversity with an eye toward learning what clues the past may offer into the country's social future.

My discussion builds on two general observations. First, contrary to some recent laments in the Western media, Indonesia still enjoys an array of social resources that transcend locality, ethnicity, and religion, and provide a potential foundation for national integration. Some of these cultural precedents reach far back into history; others are of recent provenance. Second, having acknowledged these cultural resources, I go on to argue that their consolidation into a viable national framework will ultimately depend on more than past legacies or present-day "civil society." In the 1990s, in the aftermath of the collapse of authoritarian regimes in East Asia and Eastern Europe, political analysts came to emphasize that formal elections and legislatures are alone not enough to "make democracy work."[1] Analysts stressed that citizen groupings and civil society are also vital for strengthening democratic and pluralist habits of the heart. In much the same spirit, researchers set out for distant locales to explore the ways in which long-established traditions of public association and cooperation can provide a "social capital" for nation making and democracy.

After outbreaks of ethno-religious violence in places like Indonesia and Eastern Europe, however, we now understand that civil society and social capital too are not enough to make democracy, or for that matter a cohesive national politics, work. Undemocratic elites in state and society may defy the pluralist aspirations of the broader citizenry. Equally serious, the social capital created in vibrant public spheres may be put to any number of ends, including antidemocratic ones. After all, the associations and solidarities of German national socialism generated considerable social capital; however, few believe it helped the Weimar Republic function more democratically. To state the point more theoretically, social groupings located in civil society are capable of pursuing sectarian and even violent self-interests, not just "civil" ones.[2] Even where associations are democracy friendly, they are still not enough to guarantee democratic decency. To achieve the latter requires, to borrow a phrase from John Hall, a "package deal" of state and society, culture and social practice.[3] In particular, the achievement requires that the values and organizations consistent with pluralism and democracy be "scaled up" beyond the local into a culture and practice of citizenship continually reinforced and protected by collaborations across the state–society divide.[4]

If civil collaboration across the state–society divide is one of the most important ways to stabilize a nation and achieve a democratic peace, violent and sectarian alliances across the same divide are one of the most efficient ways to diminish both. Recent history provides us with many examples of societies attempting democratic transitions only to be denied that dream by antireformist elites. In deeply plural societies, one of the most common techniques whereby some parties push back reform is what we might call sectarian trawling—playing up ethnic and religious tensions in society so as to undermine broad-based coalitions aiming at political change.[5] In the 1990s, civility-destroying tactics like these were deployed with tragic effect in Rwanda, Bosnia, and Kosovo, among other places. Indonesian history offers numerous examples of a similar process. Again and again in the thick of political battle, some political players have thrown their rivals off balance by reaching out into society, exacerbating sectarian tensions, and mobilizing angry citizens along ethnic or religious lines.[6]

Notwithstanding official claims to the contrary, such runs on the nation's civic capital occurred during several periods of political crisis during Indonesia's New Order period (1966–1998). Some among the regime's supporters did not hesitate to engage in what Indonesians refer to as the *politik pecah-belah*, "the politics of split and separate." Whether it was whipping up Muslim (and other religious communities') anger in a campaign to destroy the Communist Party during 1965–1966; warning of Muslim extremism in the 1970s to win the backing of Christians and secular Muslims; or, during

1997–1998, portraying the democracy movement as an instrument of Judeo-Christian imperialism, a few in and around the Suharto administration never shied from making ethno-religious appeals. There is evidence to suggest that although it had complex local genealogies, some of the incidents of ethno-religious violence that swept Indonesia after the collapse of the Suharto government in May 1998 were made worse by similar trawling expeditions. Now, however, the tactic was not limited to a few governing elites, but was used by sectarian-minded rogues in "civil" society.[7]

It is not just Jakartan elites, then, who have exploited sectarian tensions for their own ends. Inasmuch as this is so, any effort to explain the prospects for nationhood and democracy in Indonesia must strike a delicate balance between recognizing the centrality of the state to political culture making, while also rejecting the "blame the state" explanations that were a staple of Indonesian studies in the 1980s and 1990s. Whatever its political missteps, the New Order improved education; made significant advances in family planning and public health; and built up the country's communications and transport infrastructure. These achievements boosted per capita income, fueled the growth of a new middle class, and spurred a great movement of people around the country. Migration and social mobility blurred ethnic boundaries and challenged established social hierarchies. No matter what the national leadership, these changes were destined to strain the country's traditions of commensality and tolerance.

As the historians Anthony Reid and Denys Lombard have amply demonstrated, the movement of peoples and cultures around the Indonesian archipelago is nothing new, and the region's peoples were accustomed to dealing with visitors of varied social backgrounds. For more than a thousand years, this island expanse has been a place where much of the population picked up and moved when opportunities beckoned. Moreover, the mobility of people, goods, and ideas created an unusually labile ethnic culture. Cultural innovations moved easily across communal borders. Along many such borderlands, the line where one ethnic group ended and another began was fuzzy. Some denizens of these hybrid zones found it easy to move from one ethnic or religious identity to another. In Denys Lombard's famous phrase, the Indonesian archipelago was a "crossroads" (*carrefour*) of peoples and cultures. The region developed a tradition of ethnic hybridity within civilizational commonality to go with the great cultural flow.[8]

As in many other parts of the world, colonialism introduced new restrictions on regional cultural flows; it also reified ethno-religious divides. The sharpening of communal divisions continued in the postcolonial era. Migration rearranged the country's cultural map. Social mobility upset local balances of power among ethnic and religious groupings. Political campaigns drew religious symbols into fiercely polarized contests. The changes continued in the New Order era; indeed the scale of social movement dwarfed anything seen in earlier periods. In light of the magnitude of these developments, the effort to develop a pluralist framework for national culture would have tested the capacities of even the most benign leaders. However, the actions of a few in and around the New Order leadership complicated the task considerably.

My goal in this chapter, then, is to refine our sense of the social challenges facing Indonesia today. I do so, first, by examining the historical legacy of this deeply plural Asian nation. I then review this plural heritage in light of modern efforts to scale up existing precedents into new frameworks for participation and citizenship. Finally, on the basis of this historical evidence, I throw caution to the wind and hazard a few predictions on what lies ahead for this unsettled Asian giant.

ETHNIC PLURALITY, CIVILIZATIONAL COMMONALITY

Witnessing the spate of ethno-religious violence that followed the fall of the Suharto government, some Western pundits have claimed there was nothing surprising about this turn of events. Like the former Soviet Union, they insisted, the idea of Indonesia was an artificial contrivance from the start. Once the strong man at its center fell, the country's disintegration was inevitable.

Certainly the first of these generalizations applies well enough to places like East Timor and Irian Jaya. These territories were never part of the struggle for Indonesian independence. They were forced into the nation largely against their will, many decades after the nationalist movement began. Ethnographies of the county's hinterlands remind us that many of the populations of interior Sulawesi, Kalimantan, and eastern Indonesia have also been ambivalent about the project of nation making.[9] Faced with an influx of meddlesome government officials, some locals have seen nation building as a cloak for Javanese domination. (Ethnic Javanese make up almost half of the country's population.) Other provincial peoples have watched as development and immigration have upset long-established balances of wealth and power among local social groupings. As with Madurese migrants in Dayak areas of Kalimantan, Muslim Bugis, and Makasarrese in once Christian Ambon, or Javanese in West Papua, migrants have sometimes demonstrated business acumen greater than that of long-established locals. Sometimes too, government officials have favored the newcomers over indigenes. Not surprisingly, imbalances like these have left some local populations skeptical of a nation-building program that, as Jane Atkinson has said with reference to the Wana people of Central Sulawesi, looked like an "attempt to herd hitherto isolated ethnic minorities into the nationalist fold."[10]

However serious these problems, it is too simple to conclude that the idea of Indonesia is an empty modernist shell. With some 300 ethnic groups spread across 6,000 inhabited islands, the task of defining the nation has never been easy. However, long before Indonesia declared its independence in August 1945, many of its peoples were linked by community, language, and religion. These ties created an at least tentative foundation for the country's modern construction.

Culture Across Society

When Europeans first arrived in the Indonesian archipelago in the early sixteenth century, the territory they encountered was not one of timeless traditionalism and separated populations, but a bustling maritime realm with a thousand-year history of commercial and cultural exchange. With its vast trade in rice, cloth, precious metals, and spices, the archipelago had long been, with the eastern Mediterranean, one of the world's great maritime emporia.[11] In the 1500s, the most important trade routes linked Muslim principalities in the east of the archipelago with larger ports in its west. Greatest among the latter states was the entrepôt of Malacca on the Malay peninsula, described by European visitors as the "the Venice of Asia." Aside from Hindu Bali and a few pagan polities to the east, by the seventeenth century most of the archipelago's trading centers were Muslim ruled. Notwithstanding Muslim political dominance, "the Southeast Asian trading city was a pluralistic meeting point of peoples from all over maritime Asia."[12] Its visitors included Arabs, Chinese (Muslim and non-Muslim), Indians (Muslims and Hindus), tribal animists, a few Christians, and even regular trade delegations from Japan.[13]

This great movement of people, commodities, and culture contributed to the archipelago's most distinctive social trait: its ethnic plurality within civilizational commonality. Whether in matters of dress, dance, coinage, gender relations, gong music, social etiquette, or the institution of slavery, most of the archipelago's societies drew on a common civilizational stream, even while maintaining varied ethnic identities. This pattern of ethnic plurality within civilizational commonality stands in marked contrast to the more severe process of ethnic homogenization that took place over much the same period in China. On China's southern frontier, minority peoples, many of whom were closely related to ethnic groups in mainland Southeast Asia, were continually pressed into a Han ethnic prototype.[14] To take an example from another part of Asia, we know that pluralist interaction in multiethnic India

created a complex system of ethno-religious segregation, not social homogenization. Religious and ethnic pluralism was maintained, yes, but at the price
of a caste hierarchy that naturalized inequality and separated people by purity,
kinship, and occupation.

That neither of these two options prevailed in the Malay archipelago, and
that there was instead a pattern of flexible ethnicity within civilizational commonality, is evident from several additional historical facts. From the fifteenth to the seventeenth century, for example, Malay became the primary
language of interethnic interaction across much of the coastal archipelago.
Once a local language spoken on the west coast of Borneo, the Malay peninsula, and the east coast of Sumatra, from the sixteenth onward Malay became
the "preeminent language of scholarship, commerce, diplomacy, and religion."[15] In this it resembled Latin in late medieval Europe, except that Malay
was a popular oral as well as an elite literary language. Literary Malay was
not without its linguistic rivals. Although most wrote in Malay or Javanese,
the elite among Muslim scholars could also read and write Arabic. Because
of the political dominance of the Hindu–Buddhist kingdom of Majapahit in
the fourteenth and early fifteenth centuries (prior to its conquest in 1525 by
an alliance of Muslim principalities from Java's north coast), Javanese cultural forms also flowed out into the archipelagic stream. Javanese shadow
puppetry, mysticism, court ceremony, dance, and literary genres were known
across the island world. The Javanese-inspired Panji stories even made their
way to Burma and Thailand.[16]

Compared with Javanese or Arabic, however, Malay had an advantage because it was not merely a literary or courtly idiom but a public language of
the market, the mosque, and maritime travel. Malay was spoken in all of the
major trading ports of Southeast Asia, including those in Thailand and Cambodia.[17] The breadth of its diffusion prompted the Dutch colonial government
to choose Malay rather than Javanese or Dutch as the official medium for native affairs in the Netherlands East Indies.

Religion before Islam

Religion too was part of the archipelago's great civilizational flow. In the
first millennium of the common era, Buddhism and Saivite Hinduism (with
Vishnuite elements) had made their way to court centers throughout the region, becoming the religion of state in most of the west-central archipelago's
kingdoms.[18] The diffusion of these religions was part of a broader, albeit selective, appropriation of Indian cultural styles by local courts. Not all societies were drawn into this process of state formation, and not all the states
that emerged relied on Indian cultural prototypes. Bugis principalities in

southern Sulawesi—destined to become mercantile powers in the sixteenth and seventeenth centuries—developed a distinctive political culture outside the penumbra of Indian forms. Among their many achievements prior to their seventeenth century conversion to Islam, the Bugis created one of the world's major epics, the *La Galigo* cycle.[19]

In most of the states in the central and western archipelago in the premodern era, however, court traditions of dance, law, religion, and architecture showed the influence of Indian cultural styles recast in Southeast Asian molds. In its ritual pomp and ceremony, the pre-Islamic court served as a meeting place between the celestial heavens, the human world, and the underworld. Court ceremonies maintained the cosmological balance required for the fertility of the land and the prosperity of its people. In its concern for world origins and the harmony of the spirit and human worlds, this ceremonial complex built on ideas widespread across the archipelago well before their recasting in Hindu–Buddhist form.[20] Stripped of their Hindu–Buddhist references and given a light Islamic gloss (loosely based on Islamo–Persian models of kingship), much of this tradition survived the wave of Islamization that swept the archipelago from the thirteenth to seventeenth centuries.[21]

Although bits and pieces of the Hindu–Buddhist tradition filtered out from the courts into popular culture, the cultural transfer was selective. Although aristocrats adopted Hindu caste titles in premodern Java and Bali, most of the commoner population did not. Among the courtly elites who did adopt caste labels, there were few of the restrictions on diet, work, marriage, and commensality typical of the institution in India. Rather than an all-encompassing system of purity and hierarchy, caste seems to have been just another layer in the system of ranked titles used by political and religious elites.[22]

Similarly, although Sanskrit terms and Hindu-inflected rituals made their way into local culture, kinship and gender relations across the archipelago remained strikingly different from their Indian and Chinese counterparts. Although a few societies, like the Minangkabau and Balinese, had unilineal descent groups, the most common kinship system across the archipelago was a bilateral or "cognatic" arrangement that eschewed lineal emphases to accord equal weight to maternal and paternal relatives. Even in societies featuring unilineal descent, family relations showed a matrifocal emphasis, in which the mother, not the father, was the social and emotional center of the family.[23] Fathers were accorded great respect, but they were, and to a degree are still today, less central than mothers in the day-to-day operations of the family.[24]

Other features of kinship and gender in the archipelago displayed a similar pattern of female prominence. Residence after marriage was, and in many rural regions still is, with or near the wife's kin. In striking contrast to the Indian and Chinese patterns, this arrangement provides young wives with protection and support during the first months of marriage, when marital disputes are most likely to occur.[25] Similarly, although formal politics showed the masculinist bias common throughout the premodern world, women were not restricted to the domestic sphere.[26] Village women controlled local food markets, orchestrated the household labor required for religious festivals, and were active as midwives, healers, and shamans. Popular gender ideals portrayed male and female as complementary and interdependent, not hierarchically asymmetrical.[27]

The arrival of Islam, Christianity, and, on the mainland, Theravada Buddhism, challenged aspects of this gender tradition. All three world religions imposed new limits on women's roles as celebrants of official religion.[28] European colonialism introduced other masculinist biases, especially in business, education, and government. In the late twentieth century, tourism, movies, and a globalizing sex commerce in women, children, and pornography placed additional pressures on women's standing. Many of these latter-day developments have been offset, however, by new opportunities for women in education, employment, and government. Although ever changing, the prominence of women in the family and some public spheres remains a distinctive feature of Indonesian society to this day.

Another indication of the uneven penetration of Hindu–Buddhist institutions into popular society is that the collapse of the great Indic kingdoms was quickly followed by the nearly total disintegration of the monasteries, hermitages, and temples once common across the Hindu–Buddhist heartland in Java and Sumatra.[29] Outside of Hindu Bali and several corners of eastern Java and Lombok, no explicitly Hindu institutions survived into the modern period. This pattern stands in striking contrast to events accompanying Islamization in India. There, even after Muslim conquest of the state, Hindu institutions held their own.[30] In Indonesia, by contrast, Hinduism as a great tradition collapsed. More than in India, it seems, Hinduism had depended on the culture and patronage of the royal courts. When these were Islamized, most of the local population followed suit.

ISLAM AND CIVILIZATION

The Islamization of the Indonesian archipelago ranks as one of the most important events in the cultural history of the Muslim world and early modern Southeast Asia.[31] Few changes have had a more profound impact on community and identity. Few are more important for understanding Indonesia today. The process of Islamization varied greatly by region. Not all the archipelago's people converted to Islam, and those who did often argued over what aspects of their culture were compatible with the new faith and just what it meant to be Muslim.

Royal Courts and Conversion

Although Arab Muslim traders had sailed to maritime Southeast Asia since the seventh century, it was not until the late thirteenth century that native peoples began to convert to Islam in large numbers.[32] The first converts were won on the northern coast of Sumatra. From there the new faith spread eastward following the archipelago's trade routes. By the seventeenth century, Islam was the religion of most coastal states, as well as some but not the majority of the archipelago's hinterland societies.

As with the collapse of the great Javanese kingdom of Majapahit around 1525, some Hindu–Buddhist courts were Islamized as a result of conquest. However, the more common pattern was for rulers to convert peacefully, with their subjects then following suit. "The Islamization process . . . occurred in the idiom of rajaship."[33] The Islamization of the courts was in turn linked to a broader change sweeping societies in the Indian Ocean region. By the thirteenth century the great trade linking the Indonesian archipelago to India and southern China had largely fallen into Muslim hands. With the commercial and cultural ascent of Islam, rulers throughout the region were drawn to the new religion.[34]

Where, as in several regional kingdoms, conversion had been facilitated by royal proclamation, the new religion's local social organization remained, in A. C. Milner's apt term, "raja centered."[35] This fact helps explain a number of unusual features of early Muslim culture in the archipelago. Although Hindu–Buddhist monasteries and temples collapsed with the coming of Islam, Indian-influenced arts and court traditions survived. Muslim nobles in much of the archipelago patronized shadow theater and dance troupes that drew heavily on localized variants of Indian-inspired drama. As late as the early twentieth century, Muslim courts on Java, the Malay peninsula, and Sulawesi continued to sponsor annual festivals in which, although preceded by a profession of the Islamic faith, court servants presented offerings to the guardian spirits of the air, the four corners, and the sea. The cultural impact of these ceremonies was not confined to the courts. The ceremonies legitimized the actions of folk ritual specialists who used offerings and invocations loosely modeled on those of the court. The archipelago had a surfeit of shamans, midwives, exorcists, and mystics who, while professing their allegiance to Islam, dabbled in an eclectic esoterica.

Ritual activities like these survived in part because, prior to the nineteenth century's great movements of Islamic reform, ordinary Muslims held varying views of just what their religion entailed. Most ordinary Muslims derived their understanding of religion from popular oral culture, not from the Qur'an, canonical commentaries, or government-supplied textbooks. As a result, the range of acceptable religious practices was much greater than it was to become after the modern era's movements of Islamic reform and state-mandated religious education.[36]

Notwithstanding this variation, from early on there were religious scholars (*ulama*) well versed in Islamic legal commentaries and committed to canonical traditions. Treatises on Islamic law were available in the archipelago from the sixteenth century, although they had a notably narrower readership than the mystical compendiums, devotional songs, and didactic treatises also available at the time.[37] Even in this early period, some rulers had a restrictive understanding of normative Islam. In the seventeenth century, for example, the powerful sultan of Aceh, Iskandar Thani, burned books of heterodox mysticism in front of the great mosque in Aceh; he also barred "pig-eating" Chinese from his territory.[38] From time to time in a few Muslim principalities (Aceh, Banten, and Makassar), rulers implemented aspects of Islamic penal law, executing apostates, amputating thieves' hands, and stoning adulterers.

Notwithstanding these examples, enforcement of Islamic law remained the exception rather than the rule. The more familiar pattern was for rulers to assert the right to define the public practice of Islam, and to do so in a selective, self-interested manner. Some rulers did not bother to establish Islamic courts. Among those who did, their judges often accorded greater authority to local custom (*adat*) than to canonical law. Equally important, when appointing court magistrates (*qadi*), rulers often recruited officials from their own relatives, not the ranks of independent scholars (*ulama*). In these and other respects, then, "the centrality of the ruler is the dominant characteristic of the Muslim South-East Asian state."[39]

Although varied in expression, Islam had spread across coastal regions of the archipelago and into parts of the interior by the time of the European arrival in the sixteenth century.[40] Among coastal states in the west and central archipelago, only Bali resisted the Islamic trend. Balinese rulers appear to have been less heavily involved in the inter-island trade than their counterparts on nearby islands. The one notable exception to this generalization was the slave trade, where Balinese played a major role.[41]

Conversion paved the way for later religious changes. Some among the Muslim faithful were soon linked by pilgrimage and education to the Muslim Middle East. Although in the fifteenth and sixteenth centuries, travel between the two regions involved mystic-minded Sufis more than it did legal-minded jurists, the profile of pilgrims eventually changed. The eighteenth and nineteenth centuries saw the rise of Wahhabi reformism in Arabia, as well as non-Wahhabi reformism in other parts of the Middle East. Both movements quickly spread to the Indonesian archipelago and helped shift the center of doctrinal gravity among Muslims.[42] Ironically, the consolidation of European colonial power in the nineteenth and early twentieth centuries greatly accelerated these reformist trends.

Islam and Indonesian Civilization

In modern times, some Muslim writers have cited the centrality of Islam in archipelagic civilization to argue that the proper basis of the Indonesian nation should be Islamic law (*shari'a*), not multiethnic or multireligious nationalism. In the 1940s and 1950s, Muslim party leaders made just this argument when they inveighed against the nationalist "five principles" or *pancasila*, the pluralist ideology on which the nation was officially founded. Whether the Indonesian state should be based on *shari'a* is, of course, a normative issue, not one that can or should be resolved by historical analysis. Normative issues aside, however, it is clear that while Islam was central to what we today regard as Indonesian civilization, it was intertwined with other cultural streams in complex ways.

In recent years, historians, anthropologists, and even political scientists have begun to examine culture across great expanses of time and space. They have come to realize that civilizations are not composed of fixed values or postulates shared by all people. Even in circumscribed locales, culture is best thought of as intrinsically plural or, in Ulf Hannerz's phrase, an "organization of diversity."[43] Every culture has multiple streams and organizations. As the Norwegian anthropologist Fredrik Barth has observed, from the perspective of any single actor or group of actors in society, civilization is less "one complete, logically compelling package or structure," than it is "a surfeit of cultural materials and ideational possibilities available from which to construct reality."[44] Civilization creates not so much a unitary mind-set or system of shared meanings, but an ongoing exchange in which participants are obliged to "deal with other people's meanings."[45]

This pluralistic and contestive understanding of civilization is helpful for thinking about the role of Islam in Indonesian civilization. The archipelago has long been one of the world's great crossroads of civilization. As such, it has been defined less by the presence of a unitary system of meanings or a single set of religious ideas than by the openness of its member societies to a great flow of peoples, objects, and ideas. For the past few centuries, Islam has been a key part of that great civilizational dialogue. But it has always been one stream in an even vaster cultural flow. As the historian Adrian Vickers has observed, when Hindu rulers in eighteenth-century Bali interacted with their Muslim Javanese counterparts, they emphasized not their Hinduism as opposed to the Javanese rulers' Islam, but the fact that both claimed descent from the great Javanese kingdom of Majapahit.[46] Elsewhere, as when Muslim Bugis interacted with animist Toraja, the exchange of goods, tribute, and occasionally brides superseded religious differences. This example reminds us that Islam was a powerful stream in archipelago civilization. But it was one among several streams and never uniform in its expression. Confronted as they were with diverse ethnic groups, devotions, and claims as to what composed Islam, most Muslims developed the habit of seeing social variation as a key feature of their religious community.[47] The Muslim habit of tolerating unity in religious diversity was to be put to the test in later years.

CENTERS, MARGINS, AND HYBRIDS

Even as it showed a pattern of plurality within commonality, there were clear limits to the archipelago's tradition of permeable ethnicity and cross-cultural flow. As illustrated in the diffusion of Islam, the archipelago's coastal regions (*pasisir*) and lowlands showed the greatest measure of cultural integration. Away from the coasts, however, roads were poor or nonexistent, and the sheer density of jungles, swamps, and volcanic ranges made land travel vastly more difficult than in, say, Western Europe. In premodern times, population was also sparse, half that of Western Europe and one-sixth of that of China.[48]

Social Ecologies

In addition to their differences with regard to inter-island traffic, archipelagan societies also differed in their social and natural environments. There were three major human ecological zones.[49] The first and most densely populated were the great wet rice (*sawah*) societies of Java and Bali. These inland territories enjoyed some of the most productive agricultural lands in the preindustrial world. Especially among their ruling elites, these societies were also known for their hierarchical traditions of language and social interaction, a legacy that has marked them to this day. Some of these traditions preserved bits and pieces of earlier Hindu–Buddhist traditions. In Muslim regions, however, courtly traditions of refinement, mysticism, and power came to show the influence of Persian and South Asian prototypes as well.[50]

The second major social ecological zone in the archipelago was its coastal or *pasisir* states. As in Aceh on the northern tip of Sumatra, the Malay lowlands of North Sumatra, Java's north coast, the Bugis and Makassarese king-doms in South Sulawesi, and the Banjar territories of South Kalimantan, these were also complex societies, but they were less densely populated, less cul-turally elaborate, and more outward looking than interior Java and Bali had become after the arrival of the Europeans. The *pasisir* regions combined as-pects of inland agrarian society with the more mobile and free-spirited world of the open seas and uplands. For example, by comparison with the great ex-panses of fertile *sawah* in interior Java and South Bali, rice agriculture in the coastal states was circumscribed by rugged landscape, dense rain forests, and the limited availability of water and appropriate soil. Not far from areas of wet rice cultivation, then, peasants and ethnic minorities engaged in dry field or swidden agriculture. The residents of these latter borderlands typically maintained social systems apart from their *pasisir* neighbors, less cued to the cultural traffic of the archipelagic ecumene. Their mainstream neighbors, by contrast, tended to be heavily involved in maritime trade, considerably more than their counterparts in interior Java and Bali.[51] In the celebrated kingdom of Malacca on the Malay peninsula, the bulk of state revenues were derived from commerce, not agriculture.

Settlement patterns and class structures reflected this pluralistic pattern. For a brief period in the seventeenth century prior to the European advance, some among these coastal states developed social systems in which rulers were obliged to share power with wealthy merchants. As with the kingdom of Makassar in South Sulawesi, a few states even imposed strict limits on royal authority.[52] As the French historian Denys Lombard has shown too, during this same period some *pasisir* societies experienced a burst of cultural creativity in which literary and religious works expressed a height-ened concern for individual dignity.[53] In the eighteenth and nineteenth centuries, European colonialism and their native allies united to extinguish these liberalizing trends.

The third of the archipelago's great socioecological zones was that of the nonstate peoples living in remote interiors and uplands. Although upland peasants in the densely populated territories of Java and Bali practiced fixed-field fallow agriculture, their counterparts on many of the outer islands en-gaged in full-blown swidden cultivation—cutting the forest, farming for a year or two, and then moving on as soil fertility declined. As with the Toraja of Sulawesi, a few societies developed pockets of wet rice cultivation as well. Upland peoples complemented their farming activities with hunting and gath-ering in the jungles, trading precious forest goods with lowland peoples. Mountain peoples on Java and in Bali had long since been assimilated to low-land ethnic identities. Outside of Java and Bali, however, most peoples of the uplands and interior maintained an ethnic identity apart from coastal society, although the degree of separation varied widely.[54] The peoples of these interior regions did not live "in virtual isolation from the outside world."[55] Even small populations in interior Kalimantan were linked by language, trade, tribute, and marital exchange to coastal society. Rather than physical isolation alone, then, it was the hinterland peoples' desire for autonomy and fear of slave raiding and pillage that kept them, relatively speaking, separated from their coastal neighbors.[56]

Under Dutch colonialism, this stand-apart quality made highland and interior peoples easy targets for Christian missionization. For most of their 350 years in the archipelago, the Dutch discouraged Christian evangelism among established Muslim populations, recognizing that it could undermine the "security and order" necessary for European enterprise.[57] As the Dutch consolidated their rule in the archipelago's hinterlands in the late nineteenth century and early twentieth centuries, however, the state gave the green light to missionaries. It did so in part to aid in the territories' pacification by carving out Christian enclaves that, it was hoped, might prevent the creation of a continuous Islamic expanse.[58] With their rule in Java secure after the mid-nineteenth century, the Dutch even tolerated a modest missionary presence among the nominally Islamized or *abangan* population of the Javanese hinterland.[59] Where uplanders or inlanders converted to Christianity, the cultural change hardened ethnic divides and caused tensions with Muslim neighbors in a manner that has affected social and political relations to this day.

Sojourners and Other Strangers

In addition to the ethnic minorities of the interior, there were other populations in the archipelago who held themselves apart from the region's permeable ethnicity and easy cultural flow. Although in premodern times many assimilated to local ways, in the modern period Arabs, Indians, Chinese, and other sojourner minorities kept a careful distance from native society. Some did so, and do so still today, because they were "entrepreneurial minorities" whose business success depended on tightly coordinated networks of partners and kin.[60] Others were sojourners intent on accumulating savings and then returning to their place of birth. And still others remained apart for reasons of religion, marital custom, affinal exchange, patriarchal authority, or descent purity.

Among these Asian immigrants, the Chinese had a special position. They were the most numerous of the archipelago's "non-Indonesian" minorities. Still today, although cross-cut by subethnic divisions of language and cultural heritage, Chinese are the third or fourth largest of Indonesia's ethnic groups, numbering some 7 million. After the coming of the Europeans, the Chinese also achieved the distinction of being the most economically powerful ethnic group, a privilege they enjoyed even more in the postcolonial era.

Chinese had been coming to Southeast Asia since well before the colonial era. Chinese merchants played an important role, for example, in the revival of trade that underlay the "age of commerce" from the fifteenth to seventeenth centuries.[61] Some among the Chinese were Muslim, and many in pre-European times had close cultural ties to the native population. Several of the Muslim "saints" (*wali*) identified as having brought Islam to Java were Chinese or part Chinese, although this history is disputed by some Muslim scholars.[62]

The social incentives for Chinese assimilation, however, decreased in later centuries. Prior to the late nineteenth century, most Chinese migrants were unaccompanied men. Those who settled permanently took local wives, most of whom could not speak Chinese. Although the offspring of these mixed marriages tended to identify as ethnic Chinese, they were *peranakan* Chinese, closely related in physical type and cultural custom to their neighbors.[63] The long-standing tendency of Chinese immigrants to accommodate to local cultural ways weakened, however, in the late nineteenth and early twentieth centuries. The sheer numbers of Chinese immigrants, the presence of Chinese women in their ranks (albeit in numbers much smaller than men), and Dutch policies of ethnic and racial segregation all "provided a milieu that discouraged assimilation."[64]

There was a political dimension to the nonassimilationist trend as well. The Dutch collaborated with some of the more absolutist-minded local rulers, most notably in Java, to curb the activities of indigenous traders, transforming what had been a vibrant trade into a monopoly franchised by native rulers and the Dutch. Because they were less likely than locals to challenge colonial rule, and because they had a long tradition of enterprise, Chinese were given the lion's share of the Dutch-managed concessions, including tax farms in such lucrative enterprises as the opium trade. Policies like these only widened the gap between natives and Chinese, causing resentments that occasionally exploded in bitter racial attacks.[65]

In short, in the early modern period there were already precedents for what we might call, anachronistically, Indonesian culture and society. But precedents were not felt uniformly across the archipelago. Upland and forest peoples heard the distant din of archipelago traffic but declined its most powerful appeals. For Chinese and people of the hinterland, the clearest symbol of social difference was religion, and these groups continued to hold themselves apart from Islam. The division between Muslim and non-Muslim was to become an even more significant divide in the twentieth century, as the flexible plurality of the precolonial era gave way to the simpler polarities of colony and nation.

FROM COLONIAL TO POSTCOLONIAL PLURALISM

However significant the proto-Indonesian heritage that preceded it, Indonesian pluralism assumed its modern form during the colonial period. The Dutch introduced new elements into the diverse streams of archipelago civilization. Their actions had deeply unintended consequences, the legacy of which is apparent still today.

Containing Islam

Although the details of colonial policies changed over time, in the later phases of their rule the Dutch resolved to block the spread of Islam to non-Muslim areas of the archipelago.[66] They feared that an expanded Muslim community would strengthen opposition to European rule. This anxiety was reinforced by the prominence of Islamic appeals in the Dutch–Java War of 1825–1830, the Padri rebellion in western Sumatra (1803–1837), the Banten revolt in 1888, and the Aceh war in northern Sumatra (1873–1906).[67] Despite their best efforts, however, Dutch programs to block Islam's advance met with limited success, actually accelerating the Muslim advance in some regions.

A key element in the government's efforts to contain Islam had to do with the reform of native legal traditions across the archipelago. Under the direction of Cornelis van Vollenhoven, the "*adat* [customary] law school" worked under state directive to develop what amounted to a state-mandated system of legal pluralism that amplified differences rather than commonalities among Indies peoples. A classic example of the colonial "invention of tradition," European experts divided native peoples into nineteen legal communities.[68] Islamic law was acknowledged in each community's legal culture only to the extent that colonial scholars determined that local custom (*adat*) explicitly acknowledged Islamic law.[69]

In this manner, colonial authorities reified the distinction between customary *adat* and Islam and slowed the spread of Islamic legal institutions. As James Siegel's study of Aceh and Taufik Abdullah's of Minangkabau both demonstrate, however, the distinction on which this policy was based, between a purely endogenous "custom" (*adat*) and a putatively exogenous "Islam," misrepresented the degree to which Islam and custom had fused in many societies.[70] In the decades preceding the European conquest, legal traditions in West Sumatra had begun to accord a greater role to textually based Islamic norms. It was developments like these that prompted Dutch authorities to implement their *adat* policy in the first place.

Consistent with this policy, from the mid-nineteenth century on the Dutch also sought to restrict public expressions of Islamic piety among native administrators in their service (known as *priyayi*), while also promoting Christian conversion among populations not yet Muslim. The former program was pursued to greatest effect in Java, where educational programs aimed at the children of native elites taught Western values of progress and secularity in opposition to Islamic ideals.[71] More subtly, the Europeans also encouraged the de-Islamization of Java's courtly arts.[72]

The colonial peace, however, facilitated other social developments that undermined these official programs. In the seventeenth and eighteenth centuries, large portions of the as yet uncolonized archipelago had been ravaged by warfare. Although at first colonialism only added to the dislocation, the colonial peace eventually allowed a steady growth in native population. The Pax Nederlandica also facilitated a great wave of migration by Islamic traders, scholars, and teachers into inland areas of Java, Sumatra, Kalimantan, and Sulawesi, where Islamic institutions had previously been weak or nonexistent. As colonial commerce provided new opportunities for natives, the ranks of educated Muslims swelled. So too did the number of natives making the pilgrimage to Mecca.[73] The stage was thus prepared for the Islamic reform that was to sweep native society in the late nineteenth century.

Dutch efforts to promote Christianity among non-Muslims met with equally mixed results. In their rush to incorporate peripheral territories into their colony, in the late nineteenth century Dutch authorities gave a freer rein to Christian missionaries. In the Karo highlands of North Sumatra and the interior of Central Sulawesi, colonial officials previously indifferent to missionization turned to Christian missions to administer and educate local natives.[74] Not all mission programs were successful. In the Tengger highlands of East Java, mission programs to non-Muslims had a limited impact because the new religion was seen as "European" and not native. Elsewhere, as in the Batak regions of interior Sumatra, mission programs were offset by significant conversion to Islam.[75]

Among the interior non-Muslims of Sulawesi, Kalimantan, and eastern Indonesia, however, the relative absence of Muslim institutions and the closer cooperation between mission and state allowed for a greater evangelical success. In her ethno-historical study of animism, Christianity, and state development in Central Sulawesi, Lorraine Aragon observes that just prior to the arrival of the Dutch in the late nineteenth century, relations between animist highlanders and coastal Muslims "did not entail the religious and social rift that the Dutch colonial government began to create."[76] In those precolonial years, non-Muslim chiefs in the highlands maintained close ties of "trade, tribute, and occasional military alliances" with lowland sultanates. In an effort to stop the spread of Islam to the highlands, the Dutch put an end to these exchanges, hoping to "replace the authority of the lowland Muslim kingdoms with their own."[77] The Dutch also initiated an ambitious program of Christian school building, eventually winning much of the highland population to Protestantism. This same politicization of religion, however, only accelerated conversion to Islam in the remaining non-Muslim enclaves in the lowlands, where Muslim leaders responded to the Dutch threat by intensifying religious programs of their own.

The Rise of Reform

Still another development that undercut colonial ambitions was the rapid spread of Islamic reform in the late colonial era. The movement began in the archipelago's fast-growing towns and cities. In the late nineteenth and early twentieth centuries, Indonesians from diverse ethnic backgrounds flocked to urban centers to take advantage of employment opportunities in industries processing newly introduced cash crops. Where market towns arose, Muslim schools soon followed. A new class of Muslim merchants funded the schools, promoting a cosmopolitan culture typically opposed to local customs and hierarchies.

Taufik Abdullah and John Bowen's studies of the Minangkabau and Gayo highland regions of Sumatra, respectively, provide us with a vivid sense of the impact of reformism.[78] Rooted less in the sedentary village than in the mobile world of the market and pilgrimage, the town population welcomed reforms that downplayed the authority of traditional religious scholars and the court while emphasizing "the self-sufficiency of scripture and the moral responsibility of the individual."[79] The reformers dismissed traditional practices of saint veneration, ritual healing, spirit offerings, and Qur'anic magic as "innovations" (*bid`a*) inconsistent with the Qur'an and the traditions (*sunna*) of the Prophet.

Founded in Yogyakarta, Java, in 1912, the modernist Muslim organization, Muhammadiyah, soon established itself at the forefront of the movement to reorient Islam and society. The organization's founders included a lower-ranking official from the Yogyakartan court and Muslim traders from the Minangkabau region of West Sumatra. With this solidly multiethnic base, the movement spread rapidly across Java and Sumatra. By the mid-1920s it had reached Sulawesi and Maluku. The Muhammadiyah eschewed formal politics, concentrating its efforts among the poor, the sick, and the orphaned, as well as in religious education. In contrast to traditional Qur'anic education, Muhammadiyah schools had age-based grades on the model of European schools. Muhammadiyah schools also taught science, mathematics, world history, and geography. Through initiatives like these, the Muhammadiyah sought to create modern Muslim subjectivities, while still encouraging its followers to identify with the broader Muslim community (*umma*). Whether in Yogyakarta, West Sumatra, or British Singapore, these themes of modernity, identity, and individual responsibility resonated well with the uprooted and multiethnic population.[80]

The reformists' emphasis on self-study and individual responsibility also presented a challenge to the classically trained scholars (*ulama*) long regarded as the preeminent custodians of Islamic learning.[81] With the establishment of the Nahdlatul Ulama (the Renaissance of Islamic Scholars) in East Java in 1926, however, traditionalist Muslim scholars responded to the modernist challenge. The traditionalists defended the privileged role of scholars by pointing out that Islam is a religion of law, and knowledge of the law requires mastery of its classical commentaries. Traditionalists also defended their emphasis on the spiritual pedigree of religious leaders. For the traditionalists, religious teachers were part of a long line of holy men and saints (*wali*) leading back to the Prophet Muhammad. The rivalry between modernist and traditionalist Muslims has remained a key feature of Indonesian politics and society to this day.

Despite their mutual suspicions, the traditionalists adopted many of the modernists' reforms, especially in matters of education. In the 1930s, many traditionalist schools began to include secular subjects in their curricula. Traditionalist leaders also joined with modernists in establishing missionlike programs of religious "appeal" (*dakwah*) designed to improve the piety of ordinary Muslims. Both groups sought to do away with traditions of healing and spiritual mediumship that involved addressing (or, worse yet as far as normative Islam is concerned, being possessed by) ancestral or guardian spirits. In the early decades of the twentieth century, public rituals aimed at placating guardian and ancestral spirits were still common in some Indonesian Muslim communities. Over the course of the twentieth century, reformists succeeded in abolishing such syncretistic rituals in most of the archipelago.[82]

By the late 1920s, then, traditionalist and modernist leaders alike had begun to speak about the need for change in native society, including European rule. The Muslim leadership hoped to position itself at the forefront of this movement for change. To their great disappointment, however, Muslim leaders soon discovered that the space they hoped to occupy had other residents, equally affected by the native encounter with European civilization. The stage had been set for what was to become one of Indonesia's most intractable contests, between Muslim and secular visions of nation and modernity.

PUBLIC CULTURE DIVIDED

With the growth of towns and commerce across the archipelago, some non-Europeans began to experiment with new forms of public association. Inspired by the republican movement in China, Chinese residents were the first to do so, organizing civic associations to support the nationalist cause in China and to press for rights in the East Indies.[83] Native Indonesians quickly followed suit, however, establishing a number of organizations dedicated to improving native rights. Most of these native associations were "protonationalist" rather than nationalist, in that they were organized around ethnicity or religion, and had ambitions more modest than the creation of a nation-state. Founded in 1908, the first of the native organizations, the Taman Siswa, lobbied for the extension of educational programs reserved for elite children to the whole Javanese population.[84] Similarly, the Sarikat Islam (Islamic Association; see below), founded in 1912 in Solo, Central Java, aimed to help native traders press their economic interests against Chinese merchants.

Religion and the Public Sphere

However varied their aims, these associations represented an important new development in native society. A "public sphere" of dialogue and debate was emerging, and the actions of native Indonesians showed that they wanted to be part of it.[85] The key characteristic of this public sphere was that people from outside the ranks of the political and religious establishment sought to assert their right to voice opinions and make a difference on everything from education and business to government affairs. Not everyone was granted entrance rights to the sphere; nor were all those who were admitted equal. The terms of admission and participation were to be hotly debated for many decades to come.

The emergence of a vernacular press a few decades earlier had helped lay the foundation for this new public sphere. The native-language press began in the royal city of Surakarta in Java in the 1850s, with the publication of two Javanese-language newspapers by European printers. The founding of the newspapers was a response to new freedoms made possible after the colonial government's promulgation of the Press Act of 1854. Europeans and Eurasian publishers dominated the press until the 1880s, when an economic recession forced several papers into bankruptcy sale to *peranakan* Chinese. Over the next few years *peranakan* Chinese captured a growing share of the newspaper market. By publishing in Malay, the Chinese publishers were able to reach a non-Chinese readership. This was serendipitous because the ranks of native readers were also expanding as a result of school programs launched after the passage of the Fundamental Education Decree of 1871. By the early 1900s, there was a large vernacular press oriented to the concerns of nonelite natives.[86]

As John Bowen observes in his study of the public sphere in the Gayo region of Aceh, for Indies Muslims the most important milieu for discussion of public issues was Islamic schools and associations, not the newspapers, coffeehouses, and women's salons highlighted in Jürgen Habermas's study of the public sphere in early modern Europe. "It appears to have been largely through events designated as 'religious' that Gayo began to engage in critical public discussions about society."[87] Although originating in Islamic circles, the concerns raised in these discussions went well beyond religion, touching on everything from the proper forms of dress and greeting to matters of government. Taufik Abdullah and Howard M. Federspiel have demonstrated that Islamic schools elsewhere played an equally vital role in reshaping attitudes on tradition, knowledge, and public authority.[88] Studies of Indonesian Christians and Hindus suggest that religious institutions played a similar role in their communities at this time, encouraging people to raise new questions about important questions of public life, not just religious worship.[89]

Soon the emerging public sphere began to develop deep ideological divides of its own. The most important pitted those who believed that public life should be organized on a multireligious or "religiously neutral" basis against those convinced that Islam must provide an all-encompassing model for state and society.[90] Proponents of the latter view cited the fact that most of the East Indies' population was Muslim to assert that its social and political organizations should be as well.

Islam and Religiously Neutral Nationalism

This opposition between Islamic and religiously neutral nationalism was complicated by the fact that the Muslims, who composed almost 90 percent of the Indies population, could not agree on the best role for religion in public life. The disagreement was particularly intense in Java, where the Muslim community was split between people of normatively orthodox persuasion, known as *santri* (Javanese, "student of an Islamic boarding school" but used by extension for all observant Muslims),[91] and "Javanist" (*kejawen*) Muslims of nominal or syncretistic orientation (also known as *abangan* [literally, red]).[92]

As commentators on other parts of the Muslim world have long emphasized, Muslim societies are often divided into groups distinguished by strictness of religious observance and depth of education.[93] The most common distinction pits literate scholars (*ulama*) and their followers against those inclined to adopt a mystical, populist, or intermittent profession of the faith. For many of the latter, the focus of their religious attention lies in occasional healing rituals, the veneration of saints, and the petitioning of saints and guardian spirits. There were, of course, individuals and communities who bridged this too-neat divide. Across Muslim Africa and the Middle East into South Asia, popular Sufi leaders made use of rituals of worship and healing that resonated well with the concerns of ordinary Muslims.[94] Notwithstanding these hybrids, a key feature of Muslim civilization around the world has long been the tension between Muslims of varying degrees of education and religious commitment.

Seen from this broader perspective, the diversity and contest of Muslim Java were not exceptional. Indeed, in West Africa, Central Asia, and South Asia, Muslim culture prior to the twentieth century had syncretistic influences every bit as deep and pervasive as those in Java. What was unusual about the Javanese Muslim community, however, was the degree to which political rivalries in the late colonial era pushed tensions between observant Muslims (*santri*) and their secular counterparts to the brink. By the early twentieth century, a few nominal Muslims had even begun to wonder whether they were really Muslim at all.[95]

The rivalry between these groups escalated after 1912, with the founding of the first mass-based native movement for political change, the Sarikat Islam (SI). Initially organized to challenge Chinese commercial dominance, the SI soon extended its aims to include demands for native political rights. Although outside Java, SI tended to have an Islamic and modernist Muslim face, in Java the organization was marked by fierce struggles between those committed to Islamic ideals and others drawn to socialism and religiously neutral nationalism.[96] The struggle peaked in 1921 with the adoption of new membership rules requiring leaders of the so-called red SI to resign from the organization.

This, then, was the beginning of a rivalry that has shaped Indonesian politics to this day. The competition reached new heights during the Japanese occupation (1942–1945) and the war for independence (1945–1949). The Japanese wooed native Indonesians to their cause by organizing Muslims and religiously neutral nationalists into patriotic associations and militias; both were ostensibly designed to rally native support for the Japanese war effort.[97] Rather than dampening competition between the two communities, however, these programs intensified it. Tensions erupted again in meetings held in the months leading up to the declaration of independence on August 17, 1945, as native leaders discussed plans for the new state. Islamic nationalists wanted the state to require Muslim citizens to perform their religious duties. Non-Muslims and secular nationalists insisted the state should be neutral on religious matters, making Islam but one religion among equals. The argument was to become the basis for bitter rivalries among political parties during the 1950s and early 1960s.

Communalism and Elite Factionalism

In the years following Indonesian independence, the contest between secular and Islamic visions of Indonesia became the basis for mass political mobilizations on a scale never before seen in Indonesian history. As the country prepared for elections in 1955 (to be followed by another round in 1957), the major political parties established organizations in the countryside. They did so in the hope of winning the support with which they might break the political stalemate in the capital.

Notwithstanding the populist discourse of most parties, the mass mobilizations of the 1950s tended to be top-down affairs. Taking their cues from the leadership in Jakarta, the main parties "threw themselves into expanding not merely their own memberships but those of affiliated associations of youth, women, students, farmers, workers, intellectuals, and others"; they "competed fiercely for influence in every sphere of life and on a round-the-clock basis."[98] As the competition intensified, relations among party leaders at the national level deteriorated. Whereas in the first years of the republic, national politics had been marked by fluid alliances, the worsening competition created two primary political blocs, the one largely secular nationalist, and the other Islamist. There was "little acceptance of common fundamentals" to mediate between the two.[99]

In this manner, ideological rivalries in the capital reached deep into popular society and exacerbated preexisting tensions there. In many parts of the country, local communities were split into vertical factions organized along ideological lines. Indonesians referred to the vertical segments as *aliran*, or "streams." Viewed from a national perspective, the dominant *aliran* streams had their own platforms, social organization, and political hierarchy. The injection of national ideological conflicts into local affairs politicized mundane social occasions, a fact that was vividly captured in Clifford Geertz's classic essay on the dispute accompanying the burial of a nominally Islamic man in Pare, Central Java in the 1950s.[100] In Javanist Islamic villages in East Java, where I did research in the late 1970s and 1985, elderly nationalists—who were now all quite eager to perform their Friday prayers—recounted that in the 1950s they stopped going to the mosque entirely because services had been taken over by their rivals in the Nahdlatul Ulama.[101] Conversely, many among the latter had come to view their Javanist neighbors as infidels.

The precise pattern of *aliran* competition varied by region. In Java there were four primary groups—nationalists, communists, traditionalist Muslims, and modernist Muslims. In many other parts of the country, however, only one or two *aliran* might be represented. Notwithstanding this regional variation, *aliran* politics had a profoundly destabilizing effect, harnessing local social relations to the fluctuating and agonistic tides of national politics. Worse yet, as the competition among *aliran* intensified in the early 1960s, some groups began to train paramilitaries. Ostensibly intended to provide crowd control and protection at public rallies, in Java the paramilitaries were drawn into bitter agrarian conflicts, especially after the Communist Party attempted to unilaterally enforce recently enacted land reform legislation. To the surprise of communist leaders, Muslim paramilitaries proved as effective as the communists', and the party eventually backed off from its campaign. A dangerous precedent, however, had been set. By the end of the campaign, several Muslim groups were receiving secret training from conservative officers in the armed forces. These Muslim groupings were to play a central role in the killings of communists in 1965–1966.

After fading briefly from the national scene, paramilitaries of this sort reappeared with a vengeance in the late 1980s and 1990s. Some factions in the Suharto administration recruited paramilitaries to strike at their enemies.[102] Other political parties and even some religious organizations did the same. As the central government weakened its hold on the provinces after Suharto's removal in May 1998, local bosses in several parts of the country battled their rivals, also relying on paramilitary gangs. In this manner, a paramilitary system that was once centrally coordinated was, so to speak, decentralized.

REGION AND *ALIRAN*

Rarely noted in discussions of the *aliran* phenomenon is that the cultural effect of this vertical mobilization was different in Java from what it was in Sumatra, Sulawesi, and most other islands. In Java, *aliran* rivalries slowed and in some regions even reversed the advance of reformist Islam, which had been on the ascent since the late nineteenth century. In Muslim areas outside of Java, by contrast, *aliran* accelerated Islamization and the suppression of syncretistic traditions. In non-Muslim communities outside of Java, finally, the *aliran* pushed non-Muslims into closer alliance with secular nationalists and led many casual non-Muslims toward more observant professions of their faith.

Java Disunited

Although scholars have often taken Javanese society as the prototype for aliranization, it was in many regards more the exception than the rule. The politicization of religious identities in Javanese society combined with the growing appeal of secular nationalism and socialism to embolden some nominal Muslims to deny their birth religion and embrace new faiths. The Javanese were converting to Christianity in significant numbers in the 1950s. After independence, Indonesian churches struggled to rid themselves of colonial stigma by shifting clerical responsibility to native ministers. The transition smoothed mission efforts and put the Christian churches in good position to take advantage of the tumult following the violence of 1965–1966.

The more striking religious trend in the early independence period was not conversion to Christianity, however, but the wildfire growth of new Javanese religions popularly referred to as mystical cults of interiority (*kebatinan*). Mysticism has a long history in the archipelago, including among Muslims. Some Muslim mystical groups place great emphasis on daily prayers, the annual fast, and payment of alms, in addition to mystical exercises. Only the most conservative Muslim reformists object to groups like these. Indeed, at the height of the Islamic resurgence in the 1980s and 1990s, neo-Sufi mystical groups enjoyed a growing popularity.[103] However, Java has long had other mystical traditions, some of which draw on pre-Islamic traditions of a pantheist or vaguely tantric nature, in addition to Sufism.[104] In the nineteenth century, most practitioners of syncretistic mysticism of this sort still identified as Muslim. As reformist Islam gained strength, however, some among Java's mystics felt so estranged from reformist orthodoxy that they began to identify as non-Muslim. In keeping with the rationalizing spirit of the age, in the 1920s some organized public associations for the promotion of non-Islamic mysticism. A few leaders announced that they had received prophetic revelations and wondrous spiritual powers. Although some among these prophets were from rural backgrounds, the majority were recruited from the ranks of urban teachers, the middle class, and the arts community.[105]

In the two decades prior to Indonesian independence, most of the new religions remained localized, rarely attracting more than a few hundred devotees. In the 1950s, however, the most successful new religions underwent an organizational transformation that allowed them to recruit thousands of new followers. They formalized their leaderships, regularized caderization programs, and rationalized their rituals and doctrines. Part of the reason the new Javanese religions made such headway in the 1950s was that they had discovered a new patron: mystical leaders affiliated with the Indonesian Nationalist Party.

Since its establishment in 1946, the government-supported Ministry of Religion had been dominated by observant Muslims (*santri*). Officially the ministry also recognized Christianity, and in 1958 Balinese Hindus succeeded in getting Hinduism and Buddhism added to the list of officially recognized religions.[106] Even after this change of status, however, Buddhism and Hinduism received few of the government subsidies enjoyed by Muslims. Moreover, in the climate of growing sectarian competition that characterized the 1950s, some officials in the Nationalist Party (PNI) began to present their party as the only one dedicated to equal rights for all religions. The two large Muslim parties, Masyumi and Nahdlatul Ulama, had little interest in the legal plight of mystics, apostates, and adherents of tribal religions. The fourth major party, the Communist Party (PKI), shared the Nationalists' social base among non-Muslims and nominal Muslims. Unlike the PNI, however, the PKI preferred to downplay religious issues, portraying religion as a matter of personal preference rather than public import.

The Indonesian Nationalist Party (PNI) had some pious Muslims in its ranks, and from time to time the party launched desultory campaigns to increase its support in the Muslim community. As I learned from interviews with Nationalist officials in East and Central Java in the late 1970s, 1985, and 1999, however, some party officials were uneasy about their colleagues' support for Javanese new religions. However, the religious orientation of some of the party membership and the loose nature of party discipline in the provinces encouraged officials in a few regions to launch religious initiatives of their own. In Java and mixed ethnic regions outside Java (like South Sumatra and Lampung), these officials threw themselves into the campaign to win state recognition for new religions. A few party officials went further, providing the religious movements with funds, printing presses, and advice on how to train their membership. As far as Muslim leaders were concerned, the nationalist officials were engaged in nothing less than the promotion of apostasy.

According to most schools of Islamic law, apostasy is legally punishable by death.[107] Although this prescription has been only rarely enforced in archipelago societies, most pious today view apostasy as a grave sin. The act is seen as an attack on the Muslim community as a whole, not just as an individual choice. As the rivalry between secular nationalist and Islamic parties in Java escalated in the late 1950s, a few nationalist officials angered their rivals in the Muslim parties by escalating their assistance to Javanese new religions. The largest of these made no secret of their non-Islamic intentions. They went by names like Religion of Majapahit, the Javanese Buddha–Vishnu Religion, the Religion of Sacred Origins, and the Four Fivers (named for its tantric concern with the body and its four guardian spirits). At no prior time in modern Indonesian history had there been such a large-scale and politicized movement for apostasy from Islam.

Outer Island Divisions

The religious scene outside of Java showed little of this new religious dynamism. Many regions experienced a disruptive politicization as everyday concerns were drawn into *aliran* contests. Rather than apostasy and new religious movements, however, the trend outside Java was toward a battening down of religious hatches and a closer and more repressive linkage of ethnicity with religion.[108]

In these regions too, the key to the religious change lay in the linkages created between local religious groupings and translocal social forces. As political competition heightened in the late 1950s, President Sukarno began to look to the Communist Party for support, in part to counterbalance the growing power of the armed forces. Upset by the political drift of the central government, modernist Muslims in some territories joined forces with dissident elements of the armed forces to challenge Jakarta's policies and demand a devolution of power to the provinces. Between 1958 and 1959, regional rebellions broke out over just these issues, with some of the heaviest action taking place in Muslim areas of South Sulawesi, West Sumatra, and West Java.[109]

Although by 1960 the central government had regained control of most territories, the conflict had an enduring impact on religious trends in these regions. In their base areas, Muslim rebels had sponsored campaigns to suppress syncretistic or heterodox traditions. In South Sulawesi, for example, rebels blocked pilgrimage to spirit shrines, forbade pre-Islamic rituals, stoned adulterers, and even executed transvestite priests (*bissu*) associated with local syncretistic religion.[110] Prior to this period most ordinary Muslims had regarded traditions like these as compatible with Islam; the modernist rebels begged to differ. A similar heightening of religious controls took place in Aceh, West Sumatra, and West Java, all regions experiencing rebellion under the banner of Islam. The religious impact of these political changes was contrary to events in Java. Rather than strengthening syncretistic Islam and heightening religious heterodoxy, the troubles accelerated their suppression.

The rebel campaign had an impact even in non-Islamic territories adjacent to Muslim strongholds. In Sulawesi and Kalimantan, the rebels forced some practitioners of ethnic religions to convert to Islam. In upland Central Sulawesi, minorities responded to the pressures with a militant profession of their heretofore casual Christianity. Elsewhere, as among the Meratus Dayak of South Kalimantan, some locals converted to Islam and changed their ethnic identity.[111] Still others attempted to defend local traditions against Muslim accusations that they were polytheists by adopting the trappings of monotheism, complete with scriptures, formal ritual, and newly minted prophets.

The latter efforts would continue into the New Order era, with a few practitioners of minority religions attempting to protect their heritage by redefining it as Hindu. In the 1970s and 1980s, for example, the Ngaju Dayak of Central Kalimantan sought to legitimate their indigenous practices by claiming they were a local variant of Hinduism. A few traditional Karo in North Sumatra did the same.[112] As the Harvard anthropologist Mary Steedly has noted, the ritual and doctrinal changes that accompanied these efforts were often minimal: "'becoming Hindu' has meant little more than attending a few lectures sponsored by the Department of Religion on the monotheistic basis of Hinduism and the virtues of the Pancasila."[113] In this and many other parts of the country, the movement for affiliation with Hinduism made significant headway in the 1970s. By the 1990s, however, the movement had stalled and even regressed under the impact of the nation's growing Islamic resurgence.[114]

In the late 1950s, religious developments among the Hindu majority in Bali and Christians in Ambon, Flores, and eastern Indonesia resembled the situation of non-Muslims outside Java more than it did Muslim syncretists in Java. The politicization of religion placed the practitioners of minority religions on the defensive, even where the state recognized their religion. Although some in these communities remained indifferent to the demand that they reshape their faith according to state mandates, most in the religious and political leadership felt they could not afford to be so brazen. Even in Hindu Bali, reformists dressed their polytheistic religion in monotheistic garb. Western anthropologists often found this dryly modernist rationalization of Balinese religion contrived. However, in the eyes of its promoters, the reforms were necessary if Hinduism was to survive.[115]

Outside of Java, then, the political competition of the late 1950s and early 1960s pressed religion toward stricter organization and more rigid doctrinal controls. Where religion coincided with ethnicity, the politicization also hardened ethnic boundaries, continuing a process of ethno-religious formalization begun in the colonial period. On the eve of the New Order, then, local religion had been firmly drawn into raging national battles. From this historical perspective, the New Order government's habit of interfering in local religious affairs had good social precedent. What was distinctive about the New Order's politicization of religion was that it replaced the competing *aliran* with a new governmentality, based on the three state agencies of the military, the bureaucracy, and the ruling Golkar party. Although to many Western observers in the 1980s and 1990s its hegemony seemed assured, this new arrangement was to prove no more stable than the old.

DEPOLITICIZATION VIA ÉTATIZATION

The Suharto-led New Order regime came to power in the aftermath of a failed left-wing officers' coup in Jakarta on the night of September 30, 1965. In the months that followed, Muslim political organizations joined forces with the conservative wing of the armed forces in a campaign to destroy the Communist Party, which was accused of masterminding the Jakarta coup. Army handlers rallied Muslims to the campaign with the charge that the Communist Party had supported the coup with the aim of, among other things, wiping out

Muslim scholars and destroying religion. In Hindu Bali, military and religious officials claimed that the PKI was intent on destroying Hinduism.[116] Conservative Christians from the ranks of the anticommunist student movement also participated in the killings. However, more than their Muslim and Balinese counterparts, church officials distanced their congregations from the worst killing, a fact not lost on some survivors of the violence. Six months into the anticommunist campaign, about a half million people had died, and the Communist Party lay in ruins.[117]

In the month following the campaign, the new government announced five new policies for cultural affairs. First, it signaled its determination to do away with the cultural ground out of which communism had grown. On the assumption that religion was the best way to inoculate people against the threat, state officials launched "building up" (*pembinaan*) programs that required all citizens to receive instruction in state-authorized religions. In implementing this program, New Order policies shifted much of the responsibility for religious affairs from societal organizations to the state. Officially at least, the policy was designed to stop the politicization of religion. It did indeed diminish party involvement in religion, but with a concomitant increase in state meddling. Moreover, because regime supporters were themselves divided along sectarian lines, the arrangement also made local religious administration vulnerable to factional rivalries in the state.

Second, the regime signaled its intention to "depoliticize" society by restricting party-based political activity to towns and periods of electoral campaigning two months prior to national elections. All village-based political organizations established in the final years of the Sukarno era were abolished. The rural population was supposed to be transformed into a "floating mass" undistracted by politics and committed to national development. Not coincidentally, the official government party, Golongan Karya or Golkar, was exempted from these restrictions and allowed to operate year round across the country. Government officials from the capital down to the village administration were required to prove their "nonpolitical" commitments by joining Golkar. By the late 1980s (after Golkar was opened to individual membership), one-third of the voting public had applied for party membership.[118]

Third, New Order leaders made clear their desire to maintain the loyalty of their Muslim allies while undermining the influence of Muslim political organizations. This ambition required the state to strike a delicate balance between its ambition to eviscerate Muslim political parties, on one hand, and its willingness to make cultural concessions to Muslims, on the other. The balance was not always easy. At the beginning of the New Order, Muslim political parties were subject to draconian restrictions, the most important of which was the decision not to lift the ban on the largest of the Muslim parties, the Masyumi. The country's two large Muslim social organizations, the Nahdlatul Ulama and the Muhammadiyah, however, had such large followings that the government hesitated to take direct action against them. As the New Order period advanced, the influence of these and other Muslim organizations increased, especially as Indonesia was swept by an Islamic resurgence in the 1980s. Surprised by the development, the government at first hesitated, but by the mid-1980s it was quietly reaching out to the leaders of major Muslim organizations. By the late 1980s, it had begun to extend contracts to Muslim businessmen, build mosques, refurbish Islamic schools, and distance itself from the mystical associations with which the president himself had once been associated.

Fourth, the New Order regime continued the Sukarno-era policy of promoting Indonesian national culture over and against regional and ethnic cultures. In most of the country, regional languages declined while reliance on Indonesian grew. Although government schools accelerated the process, the language's adoption by millions of citizens had as much to do with the social mobility and detraditionalization as it did government ambitions.[119]

By comparison with the spread of Indonesian, the official culture promoted by the government often resonated less well with much of the public. Modernist Muslims and non-Javanese complained that the culture wasn't really national because it owed more to a hegemonic Javanese culture than it did Indonesia as a whole. Many ordinary Javanese disliked the stiffness of New Order ceremonialism as well, however, seeing it as "the nationalizing of *elitist* Javanese values."[120] Javanese democrats viewed the government's programs as a repudiation of the egalitarian sensibilities popular among ordinary Javanese in the 1950s.[121]

Some spheres of popular culture, however, showed a striking ability to resist state controls. Classrooms and news broadcasts were subject to extensive state regulation, but the Islamic resurgence moved forward despite initial government disapproval.[122] By the 1980s, the growing popularity of Islamic greetings, dress, food, study groups, and the arts forced the government to pull back from its neo-Javanist formalism and adopt a more Islamic countenance (see below). But there were other cultural spheres that showed an energy and independence of their own. Indonesia's homegrown rock and roll, popular among middle-class youth, developed a reputation for "anarchic refusal to participate."[123] Aided by grants from international bodies like the Ford and Rockefeller Foundations, nongovernmental organizations developed programs for legal aid, women's rights, environmental defense, and consumer affairs.[124]

Fifth, and last, intent as it was on promoting rapid economic change, the regime moved quickly to improve the nation's educational, media, and transport system, all of which had deteriorated during the 1950s. Despite widespread corruption, investments in educational and economic infrastructures proved to be one of the New Order's most impressive achievements. Between 1965 and the early 1990s, the percentage of young adults with basic literacy skills skyrocketed from about 40 percent to 90 percent.[125] The increase in the percentage of people completing senior high school was equally dramatic, rising from 4 percent in 1970 to more than 30 percent in the late 1990s.[126]

Equally important, gender imbalances in education declined over these years, although full equality was far from being achieved. In 1961, the proportion of males with primary school education was 230 percent that of females; by 1990 the male proportion was only 15 percent higher. In secondary education too the percentage of males completing secondary school diminished from 150 percent of the female total in 1961 to 40 percent in 1990.[127] Today Indonesia's gender gap in education is modest by the standards of developing countries. Notwithstanding this impressive progress, the quality of public education in Indonesia still lags significantly behind that of other Southeast Asian countries. Government expenditures on education remain particularly low. In 1990, public expenditure in education as a percentage of GNP was only one third of that in the Philippines and one-sixth of that in Malaysia.[128] Indonesia's political and economic crisis of 1997–2002 further diminished state investment in education.

With the New Order's educational progress came growth in per capita incomes and, with it, the emergence of a new middle class.[129] By comparison with a generation earlier, the new middle class was less interested in government employment than in the private sector, reversing what had long been the dominant pattern in Southeast Asia.[130] Much of the private sector remained dependent on state contracts, however, and the middle class never provided a foundation for a democracy movement comparable to that in Taiwan and Korea in the 1980s. Moreover, crosscut by religion and ethnicity, the political interests of the new middle class seemed often contradictory. The growth of the Muslim middle class after the 1970s, for example, led a minority in the Muslim community to make illiberal demands for limits on the rights of Indonesian Chinese. Another segment of the Muslim middle class, however, became the carrier of the largest movement for liberal Islam in the Muslim world. In a similarly ambiguous manner, the spectacular expansion of print and electronic media prompted New Order officials to warn of the pernicious influence of Western consumerism and liberal ideas. Nonetheless, the New Order regime presided over Indonesia's opening to global media. Equally surprising, even as some media were transformed into large conglomerates, some of these businesses played a central role in the drive for cultural and political liberalization.[131]

BUILDING UP A NEW ORDER

The program that perhaps best illustrates the ambiguous effects of New Order cultural programs was its effort at building up (*pembinaan*) religious institutions. Initially aimed at former strongholds of the PKI, the program was subsequently extended to thinly populated interior forest regions in Indonesia's larger islands where dispersed populations practiced transhumant or swidden agriculture.[132]

Coordinated jointly by the Ministry of Religion and Ministry of the Interior, in Java the building-up program was intended, first of all, to root out communist ideology and replace it with a vigorously anticommunist understanding of the country's five principles, or *pancasila*. New Order interpretations of the *pancasila* downplayed its themes of economic equity and social justice while foregrounding the doctrine's "religious nature."[133] The government's interpretation of the *pancasila* obliged every citizen to profess one of five state-recognized religions: Islam, Protestant Christianity, Catholicism, Buddhism, or Hinduism. Each week schoolchildren received two hours of instruction in the religion of their choice. Those not yet professing a religion were required to pick one.

In keeping with these programs, the state allowed preachers from different religions to proselytize in villages targeted for "building up." In Java, the regime relied primarily on Muslim and Christian preachers for this activity, although in a few parts of Java Hindu preachers were also allowed to operate.[134] In remote provinces like interior Papua or Central Kalimantan, the state turned to the one group with the financial wherewithal to build roads and schools in these undeveloped territories, Western missionaries. In exchange for their development services, the missionaries were allowed to proselytize among natives who did not yet profess a state-recognized religion. By the standards of the larger Muslim world, the government's open door to Western missionaries was unusual, to say the least. The program caused enormous resentment among conservative Muslims.

Whatever the state's initial motives, the generous terms of its contract with missionaries did not last long. As Indonesia was swept by the early phases of the Islamic resurgence, the government imposed restrictions on mission activity in 1978.[135] When, in the mid-1990s, Suharto advisers reached out to conservative Islamists like the Indonesian Council for Islamic Preaching (Dewan Dakwah Islamiyah Indonesia, or DDII), the government reversed its policies, allowing conservative Muslim preachers into regions recently converted to Christianity or Hinduism.[136]

What conservative Muslims found so unfair about the building-up program in Java is that compared to their representation in Indonesian society as a whole (in 1966, roughly 6 percent and 1 percent respectively), Christians and Hindus enjoyed greater success in attracting converts than did Muslims. Between 1966 and 1976, almost 2 million ethnic Javanese, most from nominally Islamic backgrounds, converted to Christianity. Another 250,000 to 400,000 became Hindu. Conservative Muslims in the DDII pointed to the high rates of conversion as proof of a government plot against Islam.

The strongest influence on the Christian and Hindu success was not, however, a state conspiracy, but the politicization of religion in the late 1950s and the prominence of Muslims in the anticommunist killings of 1965–1966. Even in regions where there was no significant diversion from Islam, relations between ex-communists and Muslim organizations remained tense in the aftermath of the 1965–1966 violence. In villages of East Java where I worked in the 1970s, local Muslim leaders did not reach out to ex-communists but showed them in no uncertain terms that they were not welcome in the village. When the first ex-communists were released from prison in the late 1970s, some Muslims insisted that the prisoners should not be allowed to return to their natal villages. By contrast, Christian groups moved quickly to proselytize in detention camps and assist in the reintegration of ex-prisoners.[137]

Outside Java and Bali, the *pembinaan* program targeted non-Muslim areas of Irian Jaya, interior Kalimantan, and upland Sulawesi where swidden-cultivating minorities continued to adhere to religions not recognized by the state. As in Central Sulawesi, the Meratus mountains of South Kalimantan, and West Papua, the program often combined religious indoctrination with resettlement programs aimed at moving natives into settlements deemed more "civilized" and "orderly" (*teratur*): closer to roads and schools within reach of government officials.[138] The rapid penetration of international forestry firms into even remote regions heightened the pressure on upland- and forest-dwelling peoples. By the 1990s, most such populations had been relocated to state-mandated reserves. Most, at least officially, had given up their traditional religions for Christianity or Islam. Even among the (non-swidden) native population of Sumba, where as late as the 1970s "80 percent of the population continue to identify themselves for census purposes as worshipers of the traditional deities," the 1990s saw the nominal conversion of most of the population to Christianity and Islam.[139]

CHINESE AND OTHER OUTSIDERS

There were two groups for whom New Order religious policies proved especially vexing: Confucian Chinese and the adherents of Javanese mysticism (*kebatinan*) and new religions. During the first years of the New Order, the government launched programs to Indonesianize ethnic Chinese once and for all. Schools were the first target of these policies. In the late 1940s, there had been a significant expansion of Chinese-medium schools across the country. There were even indications the schools were beginning to "re-Sinify" Indonesian-born Chinese who spoke no Chinese (Indonesian-oriented Chinese known as *peranakan*). In 1957, the minister of defense banned Indonesian citizens from attending "alien" schools, thereby abolishing Chinese as the medium of instruction in schools catering to Chinese.[140] The last remaining Chinese-medium schools were closed in late 1965 in the aftermath of the failed left-wing officers coup. In 1974, the Suharto government imposed further restrictions on Chinese language instruction; literature and signs in Chinese characters were also forbidden.[141]

The New Order imposed similar controls on Chinese religion. The Department of Religion had never recognized Confucianism as a legitimate option for Indonesian citizens. Until 1966, however, most Chinese Indonesians were privately free to profess the religion of their choice. After 1966, however, all Chinese were obliged to affiliate with a state-recognized religion. Although government administrators allowed Confucian temples to operate, at school Chinese children were required to take courses in a state-sanctioned religion, which meant that they had to choose from among Islam, Protestantism, Catholicism, Hinduism, or Buddhism. Most Chinese opted for Christianity or Buddhism, though many resented the government's refusal to recognize Confucianism.

Practitioners of Javanese new religions and mysticism were also vulnerable to New Order controls. In the first years of the New Order, the regime banned hundreds of new religions and mystical groups, on the grounds that they had ties to left-wing organizations. Those who survived were subject to heightened government pressures to declare their affiliation with one of the five state-recognized religions. In schools, the mystics' children faced the same awkward choice as practitioners of Chinese religion. The children were required to take courses in religion, and Javanese mysticism and new religions were not among the options they could choose.

Although President Suharto himself dabbled in the mystical arts, he had little sympathy for the populist Javanisms that had flourished in the Sukarno era. Moreover, after Suharto reversed course and began to court Muslim leaders, the president distanced himself from the mystical organizations he had once supported. In a speech presented in late 1988, Suharto urged members of mystical organizations to return to their religion of birth (*agama induk*) and view mysticism as a complement to religion rather than an alternative. When, in 1989, the national congress of mystical associations declined to accept a chairman recommended by Suharto, the president responded by refusing to recognize the organization, rendering it effectively illegal. Javanese mystics were never again allowed to hold a national congress, and their influence in government circles declined drastically.

The folk Javanist religious traditions that had thrived in the 1950s and early 1960s experienced a similar fate under the New Order. By the 1980s anthropologists and journalists were reporting that normative Islam was making great progress in many former strongholds of secular nationalism, while public Javanism was in decline.[142] The change was not just a matter of government policy, of course. It also reflected broad changes in Javanese society. There was an individualistic economic ethic sweeping the countryside, one broadly incompatible with the corporatist communitarianism of traditional village ritual. Better educated and better traveled than their parents, many among the younger generation also found the old tradition's emphasis on village guardians and social harmony quaintly out of date. By the late 1980s, the communal rituals (*slametan desa*) celebrated at spirit shrines (*dhanyang*) two generations earlier had all but disappeared. The few that survive tend to be scaled-down affairs held in conjunction with annual Independence Day festivities. Overtly syncretistic aspects of village rituals, such as the presentation of offerings to spirits, have also been eliminated.

Although some people predicted the fall of the Suharto regime in May 1998 would lead to a revival of folk Javanism, no such development took place. As religion in the post-Suharto era was drawn back into political contestation, young people who disagreed with Islamist political agendas—including, it must be emphasized, many pious Muslims—have rallied around multireligious nationalism rather than the folk Javanisms of the 1950s.

THE CULTURE AND POLITICS OF RESURGENCE

The most dramatic development in the cultural field during the New Order, however, was the Islamic resurgence. Pushed to the political margins at the beginning of Suharto era, in the late 1980s Islam established itself as a dominant force in society. This was not the Islam, of course, of saint worship, wizened holy men, or esoteric Qur'an study. It was an intellectually mobile Islam whose leadership sprang from the college-educated and the mixed-ethnic middle class. As Islam moved to the public fore, moreover, debates raged as to what it should mean for women, public ethics, and the future of Indonesia itself.

From the beginning, Muslim opinion on these issues varied. Some of the most popular figures in the new Muslim middle class, like Nurcholish Madjid, were deeply committed to democracy, civil society, and women's rights.[143] Madjid even took exception to the requirement that Muslim women veil when outside the home. As demonstrated by the participation of Muslim students in the overthrow of President Suharto in May 1998, many pious youth also saw Islam as consistent with democratic values. Indeed, from the 1980s on, Muslim intellectuals were among the country's most ardent promoters of democratic ideals.[144]

At the same time, however, the resurgence also had a deeply conservative wing. Some among the latter were better organized and, especially in Suharto's final years, better financed than their moderate rivals. Conservatives insisted that implementation of Islamic law was the only way to move the country forward. Some among the conservatives were resentful of the social privileges enjoyed by Chinese and Christians, both of whom were disproportionately represented in the ranks of the middle class. The last years of the New Order were to see a bitter contest among moderates and conservatives for the hearts and minds of the Muslim community.

Muslims Divided

During the early years of the New Order, the traditionalist Nahdlatul Ulama (NU) was the most successful of Muslim organizations at maintaining its base in the face of strict government controls.[145] In the mid-1980s, the organization came under the influence of a charismatic and reform-minded leader, Abdurrahman Wahid. While counseling nonconfrontation with the government, Wahid sought to modernize NU by drawing urban activists and nongovernmental organizations into the effort to empower the organization's poor membership. During the 1980s, Wahid concentrated his efforts on economic and educational programs. Those familiar with him understood that Wahid, however good his intentions, had limited skills as an administrator. Though a deft political fighter, Wahid stumbled repeatedly with his social and economic programs.[146] This same lack of administrative skills was to hamper Wahid's presidency after his election in October 1999.

By 1990, Wahid had fallen out of Suharto's favor, after publicly criticizing the president and indicating he had no intention of uncritically backing the government. Rebuffed by Suharto, Wahid joined forces with the democracy movement to press for change. Suharto responded by trying to drive Wahid from the NU leadership and directing state resources away from Nahdlatul Ulama to rivals in the modernist Muslim community.

Indonesia's modernists tend to be more urban, affluent, and educated than their traditionalist counterparts. During the Suharto era, however, the modernists were more ideologically divided than the traditionalists. In the first years of the New Order, the modernist community's senior leadership shifted hard right in its political views. In the 1950s, the mainstream modernist leadership had seen itself as an ally of the West and a champion of an Islamic social democracy. In the 1960s, however, the modernists were subjected to harsh repression, first by Sukarno and then by Suharto. The senior leadership responded to this treatment by battening down its ideological hatches and asserting that Islamic law, not democracy, was the only solution to the country's problems. The rightward tilt of the senior modernists also reflected a hardening of attitudes in the Muslim world toward the United States in the aftermath of the 1967 war in Israel. In addition, finally, the darkened mood of the senior modernists reflected the fact that their support among Muslim businesspeople, long a moderating influence, had declined. The decline had many causes, but one contributing fact was that in its early years the Suharto regime tended to favor Chinese Indonesians over Muslim entrepreneurs.[147]

The senior modernists' hard line was expressed most vividly in the pronouncements of their main organizational vehicle, the Indonesian Council for Islamic Preaching, or DDII. The DDII denounced corruption, conspicuous consumption, Javanese mysticism, Muslim liberals, and the economic dominance of the Chinese. In its most florid statements, the DDII cited all of these things as proof of a vast conspiracy to "Christianize" Indonesia.[148] In its last five years, some in the New Order government concluded that the DDII's talk of Western conspiracies could be used for their own ends. Some among the president's advisers courted DDII hard-liners to counteract the reformist initiatives of Madjid, Wahid, and the democracy movement. Responding to the president's overtures, the DDII reconciled with the regime during 1994–1995. DDII organs applauded loudly when the president alleged that the democracy movement was dominated by Christians and Muslim secularists. They insisted the abuses of the early New Order were not Suharto's fault, but the work of Catholics, Javanists, and Jews.

The senior leadership, however, were not the only modernists on the national scene. Early on in the New Order, a junior leadership arose in opposition to the old guard. The group was under the informal leadership of Nurcholish Madjid, but its influence in the new Muslim middle class was broader than any single individual. The junior modernists and their supporters insisted there was no religious requirement to establish an Islamic state or even form Islamic parties. Rather than struggling to capture the state, the junior modernists insisted, Muslims should adopt a "cultural" strategy of deepening Islamic values in society.[149] In the final years of the New Order, the junior modernists echoed Wahid and the traditionalists in championing the idea that a true Muslim politics must be based on democracy and civic pluralism.

Despite their intellectual vigor, the junior modernists lacked a mass organization and were vulnerable to state pressures. In December 1990, the Suharto administration established a new Muslim organization known as the Association of Indonesian Muslim Intellectuals, or ICMI. Although a few traditionalists joined, ICMI was for all intents and purposes a modernist association.[150] During its first months, moderate and reform-minded modernists flocked to the organization, hoping it might accelerate political reform as well as Islamic revitalization. After 1993, however, the organization's leadership fell fully into the hands of Suharto allies, some of whom had little interest in Islamic affairs. When, a year later, several independent officers in ICMI criticized Suharto, they were quickly removed from their posts. The message seemed to be that there were limits to the president's "opening to Islam."

Having been marginalized from national politics for a quarter century, however, many among the mainstream modernist Muslim leadership found it hard to resist the offer of political influence, however circumscribed. A few also sincerely believed that by working with the president they could advance the cause of political reform. Between 1990 and 1993, then, the government forged a new relationship with the accommodating wing of the Muslim community. Suharto approved the founding of an Islamic bank, expansion of the authority of Islamic courts, the lifting of the prohibition on the Islamic veil (*jilbab*) in schools, the founding of an Islamic newspaper, the abolition of the state-run sports lottery, greater Muslim programming on television, increased funding for Muslim schools, and the replacement of the Catholic head of the armed forces with generals more sympathetic to Islam.[151] Conservative modernists applauded these concessions. Reform-minded Muslims countered that Islam's highest values could only be realized through democratic reform.

After 1994–1995, however, it became clear that if Suharto had ever intended a political "opening" (*keterbukaan*), it was quickly drawing to a close. The banning of three of the country's most respected newsweeklies in June 1994, the trial and imprisonment of the prodemocracy Muslim (and ICMI member) Sri Bintang Pamungkas in 1995–1996, and the ouster of Megawati Sukarnoputri from the leadership of the Indonesian Democratic Party in July 1996 showed that the president had no intention of relaxing his grip. Faced with a growing democracy opposition, Suharto aides expanded their secret collaboration with conservative Islamists. Flush with presidential funds, the hardliners launched bitter verbal attacks on Chinese, Christians, and the democracy movement. After the assault on Megawati Sukarnoputri's Democratic Party in 1996, they also attacked Muslims who protested the crackdown, accusing them of being pro-communist and anti-Islamic.

In the aftermath of the Asian economic crisis of late 1997, the political situation in Indonesia deteriorated rapidly, and the democracy movement gained new ground. Some of the president's supporters responded by ratcheting up their collaboration with conservative Islamists, including some who commanded well-organized paramilitaries. A few among these supporters distributed tens of thousands of copies of a booklet that alleged that the real cause of Indonesia's political crisis was a conspiracy hatched by "Jews, Jesuits, Americans, and Chinese."[152] The president had been targeted, the document alleged, because Suharto is a Muslim and was too independent for the cabal of Christians, Chinese, and Jews who control international capitalism. Shortly after this booklet's publication, hard-line Muslims upped the political ante by staging demonstrations at Jakarta's Center for Strategic and International Studies (CSIS), a research and policy institute funded in large part by Catholic Chinese (and once supportive of Suharto). In these and later demonstrations, Islamist hard-liners vilified Chinese and democracy activists as "rats" and "traitors" to the nation. A few militants even called for driving the Chinese from Indonesia.

A few weeks later, provincial officials began to make similar statements, blaming Chinese shopkeepers for the food shortages brought on by the continuing economic crisis. In the weeks that followed, Indonesia witnessed the worst attacks on Chinese businesses and Christian churches of the whole New Order era. The unrest came to a tragic climax on the nights of May 13–14, 1998, one week prior to Suharto's fall. In cities and towns across Indonesia, thousands of Chinese stores were destroyed. In Jakarta, dozens of Chinese women were raped, in what Indonesian human rights investigators later described as a deliberate campaign of terror.[153] In the following weeks more than 100,000 Chinese fled the country. The violence was a harbinger of the turmoil that was to mark the first years of the post-Suharto era.

ETHNO-RELIGIOUS CONFLICT AND THE FUTURE OF INDONESIA

In the months following Suharto's resignation, Indonesia seemed to stagger from one riot to another. At first, most incidents conformed to the pattern seen from 1995 to 1998. That is, they involved attacks by urban gangs, nominally identified as "Muslim," on Chinese and Christians. The sectarian violence was of a magnitude never seen in modern Indonesia.

However suspicious some incidents, the worst violence reflected, not controlled provocations, but general tensions in society compounded by the deteriorating political and economic situation. Well before Suharto's resignation, West Kalimantan had seen attacks by indigenous Dayaks (nominally Christian) on Muslim Madurese immigrants. In early 1997, some 500 people were killed. In 1999 and 2000, the violence exploded with a new fury, spreading to

Central Kalimantan. Hundreds were killed, most of them hapless Madurese immigrants.[154] In a similar pattern, gangs of Christian and Muslim youth in central Sulawesi took turns going at each other; hundreds died.[155] Meanwhile, there were anti-Chinese riots in Lombok and Medan; lynching of social deviants and petty criminals in East and West Java; attacks on intercity buses in west Java; and everywhere, it seemed, acts of wanton violence. Although rivalries among local bosses aggravated some of these conflicts, the violence reflected a general malaise in post-Suharto Indonesia.

The worst violence took place in Ambon and Maluku in northeastern Indonesia. Unlike other provinces, in the 1990s southern Maluku's population was evenly divided between Christians and Muslims. The region had already experienced localized clashes in the mid-1990s. In early 1999, however, the conflict escalated, spreading beyond Ambon city to other islands in the Maluku chain. In its initial phase the violence was not yet fully polarized along religious lines. It pitted a loose coalition of Muslim immigrants against an equally diverse alliance of native Christians and a few Muslims. Unfortunately, as the conflict escalated, it took on a more neatly communal pattern. Although for months they had held themselves above the fray, in late 1999 Catholics were pushed into alliance with Protestants after they were targeted for violence. A few communities where Muslims and Christians lived side by side held out against the bloodshed, preserving the tradition of Muslim–Christian cooperation for which Maluku had once been famous.[156] Sadly, however, several local leaders who did so were denounced as traitors to their religion; several were killed. The middle ground of civic pluralism was being deliberately narrowed.

In early 2000, the conflict in Maluku entered a new and less localized phase, as outsiders supplied money and arms to parties to the conflict. Conservative Muslims in the nation's capital provided support to a new paramilitary known as the Laskar Jihad (jihad paramilitary). The Laskar Jihad was a Yogyakarta-based paramilitary established in early 2000. Neo-Wahhabis with spiritual ties to conservative Saudis (and, despite their hard-line views, opposed to Osama bin Laden), the group enjoyed the backing of several influential military retirees, but the organization was never merely a puppet of a Jakartan elite.[157] When I interviewed the Laskar Jihad leader, Jafar Umar Thalib, at the end of July 2001, he made no secret of his unhappiness with some members of the armed forces command. Several had recently spoken out against Thalib's plan to extend his jihad to other areas of the archipelago, "anywhere the enemies of Islam have not learned they must relent." On the evidence of some commanders' statements as well as clashes with the Laskar Jihad by security forces in Maluku, it was clear that although it had some powerful backers, others in the armed forces were deeply unhappy with the Muslim paramilitary.

Notwithstanding this evidence of intraelite disagreement, assistance to the Laskar Jihad proved decisive at key moments in its campaigns. Despite appeals by President Wahid, the governor of Maluku, and the minister of defense, in April 2000 a large contingent of jihad fighters traveled across Java to Surabaya, with military escorts along much of the route. In Surabaya, the fighters boarded state-owned ferries for the passage to Maluku. In Maluku, they were greeted and given automatic weapons by soldiers dressed in civilian clothes. Shortly after the arrival of the jihad fighters, the troubled province saw a new round of killings. In one especially bloody incident, several hundred Christian villagers were massacred and their village razed.[158] The attack was revenge for an earlier Christian massacre, in which fighters had killed 250 women and children taking refuge in a mosque. By late 2002, violence like this had taken the lives of 10,000 people; 600,000 more had fled their communities.

Rather than an all-powerful state preying on a passive and innocent society, the violence in Maluku was the product of declining state capacity, heightened elite factionalism (at both the local and national level), and a rash of sectarian trawling by elements in state *and* local society. With the nation in economic crisis and the government's ability to provide basic security faltering, infighting among rival political elites spread rapidly from the capital to the provinces. Faced with the vacuum of power at the center and a scramble for political resources in the provinces, local bosses used whatever they could to bloody their opponents. The parallels between post-Suharto Indonesia and India in the 1990s are striking. As Thomas Blom Hansen has shown, there too a long-dominant ruling party began to decline, and this led to a scramble by rival bosses and bureaucrats to take advantage of the administrative vacuum. Some did so by scaling up religious sectarianism.[159]

In this way, the sectarian trawling that had played a strategic role at several points in the New Order reappeared in the post-Suharto era, but in a form much less directly subject to state control. Indeed, many decent officials in the military and bureaucracy wanted nothing of the sectarian violence, and in provinces like Yogyakarta and East Kalimantan they succeeded in containing it. Elsewhere, however, divide-and-conquer tactics were deployed in an even more pervasive and destabilizing form—not by all-controlling Jakarta actors, but by state and nonstate actors in the provinces. In the months following Suharto's fall, hundreds of Islamist paramilitaries sprang up in cities and towns across Indonesia. In the Central Java city of Solo alone (long a hotbed of Islamist activity), there were more than seventy militias operating by late 1999. Many of the country's Islamist militias had no more than a few dozen members. The largest, however, mobilized tens of thousands of followers. Armed Muslim activism on this scale had not been seen since the anticommunist killings of 1965–1966.

Again, however, it was not just radical Islamists who benefited from the sectarian turn in regional politics. The same developments fortified antiplu-ralist forces in Christian communities in Maluku, Kalimantan, and Central Sulawesi. Indeed, as noted above, some of the worst violence in the early post-Suharto period took place in Central Kalimantan, where hundreds of hapless Madurese immigrants, who happened to be Muslim, were massacred by indigenous Dayaks, who happen to be Christian or animist. It is important to emphasize the multireligious nature of the violence, not least of all be-cause, in the aftermath of September 11, 2001, in the United States, many for-eign analysts assumed that Indonesia's real problem was, *tout court*, radical Islamism. Such a conclusion is grossly mistaken. The afflictions of sectarian trawling and communal violence have their roots deep in Indonesian political history, and are not a monopoly of any religious or ethnic group.

Although Islamist paramilitaries had no monopoly on violence, from the perspective of those hoping that democratic Islam might flourish in the post-Suharto era, the rise of the Islamist paramilitaries had an especially debilitat-ing effect. Between 2000 and 2002, the two largest groups—the above-mentioned Laskar Jihad, and the Islamic Defenders Front (*Front Pembela Islam*)—enjoyed significant backing from civilian and military patrons.[160] From its founding on August 17, 1998, to its "suspension" in October 2002, the Islamic Defenders Front showed itself an especially willing ally of old-guard hard-liners. During 1999 and 2000, the group was the most potent civil-ian strike force in the nation's capital. It attacked democracy demonstrators, rallied in support of military officials accused of human rights violations, and struck fear into the hearts of a police force nervous about a militia with such powerful friends. The Laskar Jihad was also involved in political initiatives well beyond Maluku. In my interviews in August 2000 and July 2001, the group's leaders declared their intention to topple Abdurrahman Wahid, whom they called a communist. They also declared their opposition to democracy, which they insisted was contrary to Islamic law; and their determination to extend the field of jihad battle to the whole of Indonesia.

To the surprise of many observers, these two paramilitaries suspended op-erations in the days following the terrorist bombings in Bali in early October 2002. Sources close to the Laskar Jihad in Yogyakarta told me that the orga-nization's dissolution was a direct response to "advice" from its elite political backers.

The relative pliability of these two Islamist militias stood in stark con-trast to the country's third largest Islamist paramilitary—the Laskar Mu-jahidin (jihad fighter paramilitary), the armed wing of the Council of In-donesian Mujahidin, or MMI. The MMI is under the spiritual leadership of Abu Bakar Ba'asyir, a charismatic, Arab Indonesian religious scholar with a long history of opposition to the national government. Many of Ba'asyir's senior associates had ties to the Darul Islam movement, a rebel group that had declared an Islamic state and done battle with government forces in the 1950s.[161] In the months following the Bali bombings, some of Ba'asyir's youthful associates were arrested and confessed to the bombings. Western, Singapore, and Malaysian intelligence accused the militants of membership in a shadowy Southeast Asian terror network, the Jemaah Islamiyah. Abu Bakar Ba'asyir denied any complicity in the Bali violence, as well as membership in the Jemaah Islamiyah. At the same time, however, he continued to defend armed attacks on Americans, as he had done earlier in an interview with me in May 2002.

The difference between Ba'asyir's group and the Laskar Jihad and Islamic Defenders Front reminds us that militant Islamists are not cast from a single mold. Although the evidence is not yet all in, Ba'asyir and his associates have long made clear their opposition to collaboration with members of the armed forces and political establishment. At the same time, the underground wing of this organization is alleged to have ties to an international armed network, dedicated to the implementation of Islamic governance in Malaysia, Indonesia, and the southern Philippines.[162]

The example of Ba'asyir and the MMI raise two other points relevant to our understanding of post-Suharto Muslim politics. The first is that the majority of Indonesian Muslims remain moderate in their political views, notwithstanding recent acts of terrorist violence. Since Suharto's departure, the national assembly has twice rebuffed efforts to implement *shari'a*. Surveys show that the majority of Muslims continue to see their religion as compatible with democracy and human rights.[163] More significant yet, the parliamentary elections in June 1999 and April 2004 were both triumphs of moderation. In the first election, Islamists—most of whom are only moderately conservative at that—won just 16 percent of the vote. In the second election the Islamists increased their share of the vote to 21 percent, largely as a result of the remarkable surge of the Prosperous Justice Party (PKS). A disciplined young party respected for its clean candidates, the PKS campaigned, not on the grounds of implementing Islamic law, but on fighting corruption and improving the economy. The party also fielded the largest number of women candidates in the parliamentarian elections. The results of the 2004 elections are all the more notable, one might add, because they took place in the aftermath of a sharp uptick in anti-American sentiment following the invasions of Afghanistan and Iraq, both of which were deeply unpopular in Indonesia, even among Christians. Notwithstanding this sentiment, Indonesian voters showed a clear-headed ability to distinguish opposition to the United States from opposition to democracy.

The second observation follows from the first: although Indonesian Muslims remain moderate in their views, a conservative but not extremist Islamism is here to stay on the political landscape. Using a combination of democratic electoral and lobbying techniques, the Islamists will continue to press for their most cherished of ambitions, the implementation of Islamic law (*shari'a*). To judge by the results of the past two elections, the great majority of Muslims have yet to find this appeal interesting. However, if Indonesia continues to be plagued by sky-high rates of corruption and an ineffectual legal system, popular frustration may yet boost the fortunes of the *shari'a* ideal.

AN UNFINISHED PROJECT

The causes of violence during the first years of the post-Suharto period were complex. Since the late 1990s, a few radical Islamist groups have developed ties to armed jihadi internationalists. Thus far, however, and with the notable exception of the Bali bombings, these actors have been only minor players on the larger stage of the country's radical politics. A more significant influence on recent conflicts was the broader legacy of paramilitarism and extrajudicial violence. For a few years following Suharto's overthrow, these activities moved from the margins of Indonesian politics to, at least in some provinces, its center.[164] As Gerry van Klinken has argued in an important study of the Maluku violence, we should not "blame the state" for this development, as if that institution were an all-powerful and evil monolith standing over an always innocent society.[165] In troubled provinces like Maluku and Central Sulawesi, the alliances supporting the post-Suharto era were so complex that it is difficult to speak of a unitary "state" at all. At the same time, some actors in "civil society" did not hesitate to invoke sectarian appeals when they served their interests. Whether initiated by actors in state or society, however, political tactics like these ignored the best features of Indonesia's pluralist heritage while amplifying the worst.

What makes these activities all the more unfortunate is that there are many well-intended officials in the state and the armed forces who want nothing of sectarian politics. There are also impressive resources for nationhood and pluralism in society, including, most notably, in civic–religious associations like the Muhammadiyah and Nahdlatul Ulama. The elections of May 1999 and June 2004 demonstrated that the great majority of Indonesian voters are interested in parties committed to moderation and tolerance. The tragedy of sectarian violence, however, is that it creates an environment in which paramilitarist forces are able to exercise an influence in society greatly out of proportion with their numbers in society. The containment of this uncivil fringe will remain a challenge for Indonesian politics for some time to come. The good news is that, to judge by developments from 1999 to 2004, Indonesia is beginning to make progress in meeting this challenge.

The scale of the post-Suharto violence in Indonesia led some Western commentators to throw up their hands and conclude that the country was no more viable an entity than the former Yugoslavia or Soviet Union. Such a conclusion, however, fails to take note of the fact that there still are strong social resources for citizenship and nationhood in this great country, some of which reach far back in time, others of which are new. Forty years ago, Hildred Geertz observed, "The awareness of cultural variation is both profound and almost universal in Indonesia's peoples—they have lived with ethnic diversity for thousands of years."[166] The same is still true today. The fact that the Muslim community was and remains ethnically diverse means that most Muslims learned to live with the idea that people could clothe the practice of their faith in different garbs.

Certainly this pluralist legacy always had its limits. Some in the Muslim community, including most of today's militants, ignored the lessons of their own history and sought to impose a coercive unity on a diverse whole. Tactics like these got a new lease on life in the first years of the post-Suharto period, and damaged but did not destroy the country's tradition of Muslim moderation. Now, however, a few years into the post-Suharto period, the violence has subsided, and there are signs that a more effective and decentralized leadership is succeeding at containing social conflict and even beginning to enforce a few rules of the democratic game.

Another limit to Indonesia's pluralist legacy was that the heritage of ethnic plurality within civilizational commonality always made more space for some peoples than others. Chinese, upland peoples, swidden agriculturalists—these and other minorities had an uncertain relationship, at best, to the archipelago's central cultural streams. That uncertainty was exacerbated during the colonial era. Western colonialism rigidified ethno-religious differences. In upland and interior regions, missionaries stopped the free cultural flow between inland animists and coastal Muslims. Colonial policies also segregated the economic system along ethnic lines. Flush with new migrants and accorded new privileges by European rulers, the Chinese felt less of an incentive to accommodate to local ways. Meanwhile, native Indonesians resented the competitive ardor of the Chinese. Some rallied to Islam as an encompassing marker of their difference with Chinese and Europeans. Showing the legacy of Muslim pluralism once again, however, others, including many pious Muslims, looked to nationalism and democracy as the best compasses for the future.

For most of the twentieth century, the rivalry between Islamic nationalism and its religiously neutral rival was the country's most heated political contest. Some have argued that this disagreement has its roots in ancient hostilities between observant and nominal Muslims, and that this is what underlay the collapse of parliamentary democracy, the killing of 1965–1966, and the divide-and-conquer genius of the Suharto regime. If one accepts this primordialist premise, the idea of Indonesia does indeed seem doomed.

What this chapter has suggested, however, is that this primordialist viewpoint is too static, too culturalist, and insufficiently attentive to the sociology of Indonesian violence. What made for the collapse of parliamentarism, the violence of 1965–1966, and setbacks to reform in the early post-Suharto period was not just the depth of old divides but the disruptive force of new maneuvers. For some political elites in both state *and* society, the all-too-familiar reaction to impasses at the center was to try to better one's hand by reaching into society, exacerbating ethno-religious divides, and mobilizing armed supporters to strike at rivals. In times of political crisis, sectarian trawling of this sort has been an all too familiar feature of Indonesian politics, including the final days of the Suharto administration. Unfortunately too, sectarianism and paramilitarism did not end in 1998 but underwent a dangerous mutation. The divide-and-conquer sectarianism previously used at the center was now decentralized and, so to speak, democratized.

During the thirty-two years of the New Order, the message that coercion or even violence against one's opponents is an effective political tool was heard loud and clear in the provinces. Moreover, it was not just a matter of cultural communication; there was social organization as well. Across Indonesia, actors associated with New Order agencies organized networks of local toughs to deal with political enemies. Military officials in Medan and Jakarta in 1965 organized hoodlums into what was to become one of Indonesia's most powerful paramilitaries, the Pancasila Youth (Pemuda Pancasila). In Medan and Jakarta during late 1965, the Pancasila Youth were mobilized to strike at the Communist Party. In the 1980s and 1990s, after establishing branches in big cities, government officials relied on this same organization to strike at democracy protestors.[167] By the late 1990s, there were many such hybrids of political paramilitarism operating across the country. There was, however, a new ingredient in the formula as well. Now some of the paramilitaries were of a radical Islamist bent. Established in August 1998, the Islamic Defender's Front (FPI) quickly became the largest of these Islamist paramilitaries.[168]

Details aside, the phenomenon of the paramilitaries raises three points for Indonesia's future. First it shows that by the late New Order the tactic of paramilitarist mobilization had become commonplace in society, and was no longer the preserve of a few powerful politicians. In the months following

Suharto's fall, political toughs like the Pancasila Youth and the Islamic Defenders Front became linked in shifting alliances to government officials, business leaders, conservative religious groupings, and even members of the political opposition. Whereas before there were a few big bosses in Jakarta, now the provinces had many claimants for power, sometimes doing battle one with another. There is evidence to suggest that, in its early phases, the Maluku violence had more to do with turf wars of this sort than it did religious ideals as such.[169]

A second and more theoretical observation flows from this first, and points to the future. In recent years, the literature on democratic consolidations has emphasized the importance of reformist coalitions across the state–society divide in strengthening commitment to the rules of the democratic game.[170] This emphasis on reformist coalitions and democratic constitutionalism is a healthy corrective to the romanticism of the 1990s literature on civil society. Much activist and scholarly writing during that period portrayed civil society as a good and homogeneous thing, as opposed to the state, which was typically portrayed as singularly self-aggrandizing and undemocratic.

The problem with these portrayals is that they say nothing of how local society and civic associations can also be undemocratic, often as a result of ethnic, religious, and ideological tensions. Recent events remind us that some "civic" associations may only exacerbate sectarian animosities. History also shows that other organizations of this sort can diminish rather than enhance the available stock of "good" social capital. This makes it all the more imperative to enhance collaboration across the state–society divide, so as to scale up public commitments to universal citizen rights and the rules of the democratic game.

These observations underscore the nature of the challenge Indonesia now faces, and lead me to a third and concluding observation. Since the collapse of parliamentary democracy in 1957, and especially since the establishment of the New Order in 1966–1967, a few in the political elite have gotten into the habit of making alliances with militant groupings in society. These undemocratic collaborations across the state–society divide are politically unhealthy for several reasons, but one of the most important is that they push much of the give-and-take of politics underground and out of public scrutiny. In so doing, they undermine the rule of law and diminish efforts to build a public culture of democratic proceduralism.

At the same time, however, sectarian trawling and communal violence are so hugely destructive of human lives and energies that they exhaust all but the most hardened ideologues. In the elections of 1999, the Indonesian public signaled that it wanted nothing of the divide-and-conquer tactics of the Suharto era. There is evidence of a similar thirst for peace and civility among much of the civilian population in battle-scarred areas of Maluku and Sulawesi. Unlike Yugoslavia and the former Soviet Union, the idea of a multiethnic and multireligious Indonesia appears to have survived the trauma of the early post-Suharto period, even in regions recently shattered by communal violence.

Every nation is an unfinished project. In the case of Indonesia, we see a country rich with pluralist endowments. But it also has long had a divided and sometimes undisciplined political elite, "whose members must continue to concern themselves primarily with the struggle for power among themselves" rather than the rule of law or democratic alliances.[171] Faced with impasses in government, a small few among the elite made sectarian runs into society to inflame passions, mobilize supporters, and tip the balance of power at the center.

Herein lies the central challenge of Indonesia moving beyond the Suharto era. The country's problems are not the result of unchanging primordial divides. Compared with fifty years ago, Indonesia today has an energetic middle class, a free and professional press, a substantial educational infrastructure, and a battered but moderate Muslim majority who, in elections and daily interactions, demonstrate deep affection for their plural nation. Certainly Indonesian society continues to be divided by differences of religion and ethnicity. But most democracies have such divisions; the challenge is to devise a pluralist and democratic framework for their management. The main task in Indonesia in years to come, then, will be to get leaders in state *and* society to resist the temptation to reach out and polarize, and instead channel their energies into free and fair competition, public accountability, and the rules of the democratic game.

In the face of the ethno-religious violence of the early post-Suharto period, all this for a while seemed a Sisyphean task. But its prospects have recently improved, buoyed by the continuing belief of most of the citizenry in the sweet dream of a pluralist and free Indonesia. No less significant, the task has also been eased by the conviction among most of the Muslim public in the compatibility of Islam and democracy. Indonesia may not turn itself into a peaceful and fully democratic place any time soon. But many of its people appear to have learned from their rich social history. Their knowledge and aspirations will continue to breathe life into the hope for a plural and democratic Indonesia for some years to come.

NOTES

1. This frequently cited phrase is from Robert Putnam's influential *Making Democracy Work: Civic Traditions in Modern Italy* (Princeton: Princeton University Press, 1993).

2. A point made for the Indonesian context in Michael van Langenberg, "The New Order State: Language, Ideology, Hegemony," in Arief Budiman, ed., *State and Civil Society in Indonesia*, Monash Papers on Southeast Asia no. 22. (Clayton, Australia: Center of Southeast Asian Studies, Monash University, 1990), 121. The issue is addressed in more general theoretical terms in John A. Hall, "In Search of Civil Society," in *Civil Society: Theory, History, Comparison* (Cambridge: Polity, 1995); and Robert W. Hefner, "Multiculturalism and Citizenship in Malaysia, Singapore, and Indonesia," in *The Politics of Multiculturalism: Pluralism and Citizenship in Malaysia, Singapore, and Indonesia* (Honolulu: University of Hawai'i Press, 2001).

3. Hall, "In Search of," 2.

4. See Peter Evans, "Government Action, Social Capital, and Development: Reviewing the Evidence on Synergy," *World Development* 24, no. 6 (1996): 1120; Robert W. Hefner, *Civil Islam: Muslims and Democratization in Indonesia* (Princeton: Princeton University Press, 2000) chap. 2; and Juan J. Linz and Alfred Stepan, *Problems of Democratic Transition and Consolidation: Southern Europe, South America, and Post-Communist Europe* (Baltimore: Johns Hopkins University Press, 1996).

5. This theme runs through two recent volumes on antidemocratic violence: Bruce B. Cambell and Arthur D. Brenner, eds., *Death Squads in Global Perspective: Murder with Deniability* (New York: St. Martin's, 2000); and Jeffrey A. Sluka, ed., *Death Squad: The Anthropology of State Terror* (Philadelphia: University of Pennsylvania Press, 2000).

6. Perhaps the most original study of this problem in a part of Indonesia is Geoffrey Robinson, *The Dark Side of Paradise: Political Violence in Bali* (Ithaca, N.Y.: Cornell University Press, 1995).

7. See George J. Aditjondro, "Ninjas, Nanggalas, Monuments, and Mossad Manuals," in Sluka, *Death Squad*; and Robert Cribb, "From Petrus to Ninja: Death Squads in Indonesia," in Cambell and Brenner, *Death Squads*.

8. Anthony Reid, *Southeast Asia in the Age of Commerce*, 2 vols. (New Haven: Yale University Press, 1988); and Denys Lombard, *Le carrefour javanais: Essai d'histoire globale*, vol. 2, *Les reseaux asiatic* (Paris: Editions de l'Ecole des Hautes Etudes en Sciences Sociales, 1990).

9. On this theme in Kalimantan, see Anna Lowenhaupt Tsing, *In the Realm of the Diamond Queen: Marginality in an Out-of-the-Way Place* (Princeton: Princeton University Press, 1993); for upland Sulawesi, see Ken George, *Showing Signs of Violence: The Cultural Politics of a Twentieth-Century Headhunting Ritual* (Berkeley: University of California Press, 1996); and for Sumba, Joel C. Kuipers, *Language, Identity, and Marginality in Indonesia: The Changing Nature of Ritual Speech on the Island of Sumba* (Cambridge: Cambridge University Press, 1998); and Janet Hoskins, "Entering the Bitter House: Spirit Worship and Conversion in West Sumba," in Rita Smith Kipp and Susan Rodgers, eds., *Indonesian Religions in Transition* (Tucson: University of Arizona Press, 1987).

10. Jane Monnig Atkinson, "Religions in Dialogue: The Construction of an Indonesian Minority Religion," in Kipp and Rodgers, *Indonesian Religions*, 183.

11. Lombard, *Le carrefour*, 2:16–30.

12. Reid, *Age of Commerce*, 2:66.

13. Lombard, *Le carrefour*, 2:31–48; and Luis Filipe Ferreira Reis Thomaz, "The Malay Sultanate of Malaka," in Anthony Reid, ed., *Southeast Asia in the Early Modern Era: Trade, Power, and Belief* (Ithaca, N.Y.: Cornell University Press, 1993), 77–82.

14. For a discussion of the cultural dynamics of Han expansion from the perspective of China's Muslim minority, see Dru C. Gladney, *Muslim Chinese: Ethnic Nationalism in the People's Republic*, Harvard East Asian Monographs 149 (Cambridge: Harvard University Press, 1991).

15. James T. Collins, *Malay, World Language: A Short History* (Kuala Lumpur: Dewan Bahasa dan Pustaka, 1996), 23.

16. See Adrian Vickers, "Hinduism and Islam in Indonesia: Bali and the Pasisir World," *Indonesia*, October, 1987, 55. On the Panji tales, see Th. Pigeaud, *Literature of Java* (The Hague: Martinus Nijhoff, 1967), 1:206–9.

17. Reid, *Age of Commerce*, 1:233.

18. O. W. Wolters, *The Fall of Srivijaya in Malay History* (Ithaca: Cornell University Press, 1970).

19. Christian Pelras, *The Bugis* (Oxford: Blackwell, 1996), 4.

20. A point amply developed in J. Stephen Lansing, *The Three Worlds of Bali* (New York: Praeger, 1983).

21. On the role of Sufi and Islamo-Persian models of kingship on Southeast Asian Islamic states, see A. C. Milner, "Islam and the Muslim State," in M. B. Hooker, ed., *Islam in South-east Asia* (Leiden: Brill, 1983); and Mark R. Woodward, *Islam in Java: Normative Piety and Mysticism in the Sultanate of Yogyakarta* (Tucson: University of Arizona Press, 1989), 177–84.

22. One would have to do more historical work and provide a richer sociology to apply this generalization to the phenomenon of caste in contemporary Bali. In *The Spell of Power: A History of Balinese Politics, 1650–1940* (Leiden, KITLV Press, 1996), historian Henk Schulte Nordhold shows how the Dutch colonial administration could not accommodate the more labile system of social hierarchy indigenous to Bali. As a result Dutch officials pressed it into a "uniform system of three closed castes" (234–35). In a similar spirit, in *Adat and Dinas: Balinese Communities in the Indonesian State*, Southeast Asian Social Science Monographs (Oxford: Oxford University Press, 1993), the anthropologist Carol Warren shows how "the contemporary ethnography of Bali has tended to overemphasize hierarchic values in Balinese culture and vertical relations of patronage in Balinese social structure at the expense of a full appreciation of their egalitarian and horizontal counterpoints" (5). Many of Warren's insights could be extended to recent discussions of hierarchy in Java. These too have tended to neglect history, overemphasize hierarchy, and ignore the egalitarian counterpoints of Javanese tradition.

23. Hildred Geertz was the first to highlight matrifocality in *The Javanese Family: A Study of Kinship and Socialization* (Prospect Heights, Ill.: Waveland, 1961), a work that offers great insights into Indonesian gender and family.

24. On the peculiar way in which husbands and fathers are accorded greater respect in the home but not an equivalent measure of paternal power, see Nancy J. Smith-Hefner, "Women and Politeness: The Javanese Example," *Language in Society*

17 (1988): 535–54; Suzanne April Brenner, *The Domestication of Desire: Women, Wealth, and Modernity in Java* (Princeton: Princeton University Press, 1998), 149–70; and James Siegel, *The Rope of God* (Berkeley: University of California Press, 1969).

25. On this and related points, see Wazir Jahan Karim, "Bilateralism and Gender in Southeast Asia," in Wazir Jahan Karim, ed., *"Male" and "Female," in Developing Southeast Asia* (Oxford: Berg, 1995); for an ethnographic illustration of its dynamics, see Michael Gates Peletz, *A Share of the Harvest: Kinship, Property, and Social History among the Malays of Rembau* (Berkeley: University of California Press, 1988).

26. Aristocratic and high-status Muslim women in some societies provided an exception to this rule. See Barbara Watson Andaya, "Delineating Female Space: Seclusion and the State in Pre-modern Island Southeast Asia," in Barbara Watson Andaya, ed., *Other Pasts: Women, Gender, and History in Early Modern Southeast Asia* (Honolulu: Center for Southeast Asian Studies, University of Hawaii, 2000).

27. On the complementary nature of gender relations in the archipelago and Southeast Asia as a whole, see Karim, *"Male" and "Female"*; Aiwa Ong and Michael G. Peletz, eds., *Bewitching Women, Pious Men: Gender and Body Politics in Southeast Asia* (Berkeley: University of California Press, 1995); and Jane Monnig Atkinson and Shelly Errington, *Power and Difference: Gender in Island Southeast Asia* (Stanford: Stanford University Press, 1990).

28. See Reid, *Age of Commerce*, 2:162–64. The full range of ritual activities available to women was, of course, greater than those allowed in official religion. For illustrations of this complexity, see Ann Kumar, "Imagining Women in Javanese Religion: Goddesses, Ascetes, Queens, Consorts, Wives," in Andaya, *Other Pasts*; and Carol Laderman, *Wives and Midwives: Childbirth and Nutrition in Rural Malaysia* (Berkeley: University of California, 1983).

29. Our most detailed sense of the distribution and nature of Hindu–Buddhist institutions supported in the pre-Islamic period remains Th. Pigeaud, *Java in the Fourteenth Century*, 5 vols. (The Hague: Martinus Nijhoff, 1967).

30. This begs the question of the form in which Hindu traditions survived, and their accompanying social and political organization. Although disagreeing on some points, Peter van der Veer, *Religious Nationalism: Hindus and Muslims in India* (Berkeley: University of California, 1994); and Richard M. Eaton, *The Rise of Islam and the Bengal Frontier, 1204–1760* (Berkeley: University of California, 1993) agree in showing that the relationship between Muslims and Hindus remained, at the very least, unstable and agonistic; the outcomes of the interaction varied greatly in different areas of the Indian subcontinent.

31. For an overview of the political and cultural processes through which these religions arrived in the region, see Reid, "A Religious Revolution," in *Age of Commerce*, vol. 2.

32. Reid, *Age of Commerce* 2:133; G. W. J. Drewes, "New Light on the Coming of Islam to Indonesia?" *Bijdragen tot de Taal-, Land-, en Volkenkunde* 124 (1968): 433–59; and Stuart Robson, "Java at the Crossroads," *Bijdragen tot de Taal-, Land-, en Volkenkunde* 137 (1981): 259–92.

33. Milner, "Islam and the Muslim State," 30.

34. Reid, *Southeast Asia*, 2:144.

35. Milner, "Muslim State," 36.

36. On the concept of ordinary Muslims, see Michael G. Peletz, "'Ordinary Muslims' and Muslim Resurgents in Contemporary Malaysia: Notes on an Ambivalent Relationship," in Robert W. Hefner and Patricia Horvatich, eds., *Islam in an Era of Nation-States: Politics and Religious Renewal in Muslim Southeast Asia* (Honolulu: University of Hawai'i Press, 1997).

37. On Islamic law texts in the early Islamic period, see M. B. Hooker, "Islamic Law," in Hooker, *Islam*, 161; and Pigeaud, *Literature of Java*, 1:309; on Muslim devotional and mystical literature from the same period and afterward, see Pigeaud, *Literature of Java*, 76–113; and Anthony Day, "Islam and Literature in South-East Asia: Some Pre-modern, mainly Javanese Perspectives," in Hooker, *Islam*, 130–59.

38. See Anthony Reid, "Islamization and Christianization in Southeast Asia: The Critical Phase, 1550–1650," in Reid, *Early Modern*, 174–77.

39. See Milner, "Muslim State," 31. On Islamic law in the premodern period, see also Hooker, "Islamic Law"; on many of the same issues in a modern Malay context, see Michael G. Peletz, *Islamic Courts and Modernity in Malaysia* (Princeton: Princeton University Press, 2002).

40. The arrival of Europeans in the 1500s may have given an extra impetus to the advance of Islam. One of the first acts of the Portuguese was to launch a bloody conquest of the great Muslim port of Malacca in 1511. The assault dispersed the resident community of Muslim merchants and scholars to ports around the archipelago. A few years later, the Portuguese followed up this attack with an equally brazen campaign in the Maluku archipelago (in the northeastern corner of today's Indonesia), in an effort to corner the spice trade. The Dutch arrived at the end of the century and quickly joined the fray, attacking principalities in the Maluku region. In 1619 the Dutch laid siege to the trading port of Jayakerta (contemporary Jakarta) in western Java, where they had opened a trading post a few years earlier. For years they had a hostile relationship with the Islamic rulers of Banten to the west and Mataram to the east. Historical evidence indicates that in response to European attacks on ports at this time, Muslim rulers in Java, Sumatra, and eastern Indonesia heightened their efforts to spread the faith to remaining centers of non-Islamic rule. See M. C. Ricklefs, "The Arrival of the Europeans in Indonesia, c. 1509–1620," in *A History of Modern Indonesia*, 2nd ed. (Stanford: Stanford University Press; St. Leonards, Australia: Allen & Unwin, 1993), 22–31.

41. One aspect of the inter-island trade in which Balinese were deeply involved, however, was the traffic in slaves. Many slaves were prisoners of war, victims of the fierce dynastic battles that periodically raged on the island. See Henk Schulte Nordholt, *The Spell of Power: A History of Balinese Politics, 1650–1940* (Leiden: KITLV Press, 1996), esp. 41–44.

42. On the role of Muslim networks of education and pilgrimage in transmitting ideals of Islamic reform from the Middle East to Indonesia, see Azyumardi Azra, "The Transmission of Islamic Reformism to Indonesia: Networks of Middle Eastern and Malay Indonesian Ulama in the Seventeenth and Eighteenth Centuries" (Ph.D. diss., Columbia University, 1992).

43. Ulf Hannerz, *Cultural Complexity: Studies in the Social Organization of Meaning* (New York: Columbia University Press, 1992), 14.

44. Fredrik Barth, *Balinese Worlds* (Princeton: Princeton University Press, 1993), 4.

45. Hannerz, *Cultural Complexity*, 14.

46. Vickers, "Hinduism and Islam," 54–55.

47. Andrew Beatty, *Varieties of Javanese Religion: An Anthropological Account*, Cambridge Studies in Social and Cultural Anthropology (Cambridge: Cambridge University Press, 1999), provides a vivid account of just such a pluralist heritage in the Banyuwangi region of eastern Java. Sven Cederroth, "Perceptions of Sasak Identity," in Michael Hitchcock and Victor T. King, eds., *Images of Malay-Indonesian Identity* (Kuala Lumpur: Oxford University Press, 1997), illuminates the history and culture of an equally diverse Islamic tradition among the Sasak of Lombok. It is telling that in both regions divisions on matters of religion had a parallel impact on political alliances.

48. Reid, *Age of Commerce*, 2:15.

49. This categorization doesn't quite do justice to the diversity of the archipelago. Among other places, it leaves out the distinctive cultural and ecological traditions of southeastern Indonesia, including those captured in such important works as James J. Fox, *Harvest of the Palm: Ecological Change in Eastern Indonesia* (Cambridge: Harvard University, 1977); Janet Hoskins, *The Play of Time: Kodi Perspectives on Calendars, History, and Exchange* (Berkeley: University of California Press, 1993); and Kuipers, *Marginality*.

50. On Persian-models of kingship with the king's role as defender of the faith and a mystical perfect man, see S. Soebardi, *The Book of Cabolek: A Contribution to the Study of the Javanese Mystical Tradition* (The Hague: Martinus Nijhoff, 1975), 84; Woodward, *Islam*, 57–60, and A. C. Milner, "Muslim State," 35. The Muslim–Persian influence on kingship in the region in no way diminishes the fact that in this emphasis on the king the Muslim states "resembled their . . . [Hindu–Buddhist] predecessors," Milner, 32.

51. The principalities of Demak, Tuban, and others along Java's north coast (*pasisir*) and of Buleleng in northern Bali diverged from the "Javo-Balinese" pattern I'm describing here, combining elements of the latter with the coastal state pattern. For an anthropological study of one such region in north Bali, see Barth, *Balinese Worlds*.

52. See Reid, *Age of Commerce*, 2:251–66.

53. See Lombard, *Le carrefour*, 2:155–62.

54. Two examples of interior peoples closely related to their coastal neighbors in this way are the Laujé of north Central Sulawesi and the Makassarese Patuntung in South Sulawesi. On the Laujé, see Jennifer W. Nourse, *Conceiving Spirits: Birth Rituals and Contested Identities among Laujé of Indonesia* (Washington, D.C.: Smithsonian Institution Press, 1999); on the Makassarese Patuntung, see Martin Rossler, "Islamization and the Reshaping of Identities in Rural South Sulawesi," in Hefner and Horvatich, *Nation-States*.

55. The quote is from Hildred Geertz, "Indonesian Cultures and Communities," in Ruth T. McVey, ed., *Indonesia* (New Haven: Human Relations Araa Files, 1963), 31.

Geertz's forty-year-old article is one of the finest essays ever written on the people and cultures of Indonesia.

56. For examples of less porous points of ethnic passage in southeast Sumatra, see Barbara Watson Andaya, *To Live as Brothers: Southeast Sumatra in the Seventeenth and Eighteenth Centuries* (Honolulu: University of Hawai'i Press, 1993), 145–76; in North Sumatra, see Kipp, *Dissociated Identities*, 41–50; in uplands Central Sulawesi see Aragon, *Fields*, 47–112; and for interior Kalimantan, see Victor T. King, *The Peoples of Borneo* (Oxford: Blackwell, 1993), 195–231.

57. Philip van Akkeren, *Sri and Christ: A Study of the Indigenous Church in East Java* (London: Lutterworth, 1969).

58. See Aragon, *Fields*, 107; King, *Peoples*, 142; and Albert Schrauwers, *Colonial "Reformation" in the Highlands of Central Sulawesi, 1892–1995* (Toronto: University of Toronto Press, 2000).

59. Robert W. Hefner, "Of Faith and Commitment: Christian Conversion in Muslim Java," in Robert W. Hefner, *Conversion to Christianity* (Berkeley: University of California Press, 1993), 102–5.

60. On Chinese settlers and sojourners, see Anthony Reid, ed., *Sojourners and Settlers: Histories of Southeast Asia and the Chinese* (Honolulu: University of Hawai'i Press, 2001); on Asian "entrepreneurial minorities," see Christine Dobbin, *Asian Entrepreneurial Minorities: Conjoint Communities in the Making of the World Economy, 1570–1940* (Richmond, U.K.: Curzon, 1996); and Jamie Mackie, "Business Success among Southeast Asian Chinese: The Role of Culture, Values, and Social Structures," in Robert W. Hefner, ed., *Market Cultures: Society and Morality in the New Asian Capitalism* (Boulder: Westview, 1998).

61. Reid, *Age of Commerce*, 2: xiii.

62. See H. J. de Graaf and Th. Pigeaud, *Chinese Muslims in Java: in the 15th and 16th Centuries*, Monash Papers on Southeast Asia no. 32 (Clayton, Australia: Center of Southeast Asian Studies, Monash University, 1984); and Lombard, *Le carrefour*, 2:42.

63. See G. William Skinner, "The Chinese Minority," in McVey, *Indonesia*, 97–98.

64. Reid, *Age of Commerce*, 2:313.

65. See Peter Carey, "Changing Javanese Perceptions of the Chinese Communities in Central Java, 1755–1825," in *Indonesia*, 37:1–48, and James R. Rush, *Opium to Java: Revenue Farming and Chinese Enterprise in Colonial Indonesia, 1860–1910* (Ithaca, N.Y.: Cornell University Press, 1990).

66. The most comprehensive study of Dutch policies on Islam is Karel Steenbrink, *Dutch Colonialism and Indonesian Islam: Contacts and Conflicts, 1596–1950*, trans. Jan Steenbrink and Henry Jansen. (Amsterdam: Rodopi, 1993).

67. Ricklefs, *History*, 135–37.

68. Eric Hobsbawm and Terence Ranger, eds., *The Invention of Tradition* (Cambridge: Cambridge University Press, 1983).

69. Hooker, "Islamic Law," 176.

70. Siegel, *Rope*; Taufik Abdullah, "Adat and Islam: An Examination of Conflict in Minangkabau," in *Indonesia* 2:10; and Daniel Lev, *Islamic Courts in Indonesia: A Study in the Political Bases of Legal Institutions* (Berkeley: University of California Press, 1972), 250.

71. See Heather Sutherland, *The Making of a Bureaucratic Elite: The Colonial Transformation of the Javanese Priyayi* (Singapore: Heinemann Educational, 1979).

72. On Dutch colonial policy on Islam, see Harry J. Benda, *The Crescent and the Rising Sun: Indonesian Islam under the Japanese Occupation, 1942–1945* (Leiden: Foris, 1983), 9–31; on de-Islamization in Java's arts, see Laurie J. Sears, *Shadows of Empire: Colonial Discourse and Javanese Tales* (Durham, N.C.: Duke University Press, 1996), 34–74.

73. J. Vredenbregt, "The Haddj: Some of its Features and Functions in Indonesia," *Bijdragen tot de Taal-, Land-, en Volkenkunde* 118 (1962): 91–154.

74. For the Karo highlands of North Sumatra, see Kipp, *Dissociated Identities*; for interior Central Sulawesi, see Aragon, *Fields*, 93; and Schrauwers, *Colonial "Reformation,"* 40.

75. See Hefner, "Christian Conversion."

76. Aragon, *Fields*, 93.

77. Aragon, *Fields*, 98; see also Kipp, *Dissociated Identities*.

78. Taufik Abdullah, *Schools and Politics: The Kaum Muda Movement in West Sumatra (1927–1933)* (Ithaca: Modern Indonesia Project, Cornell University, 1971); John R. Bowen, *Muslims through Discourse: Religion and Ritual in Gayo Society* (Princeton: Princeton University Press, 1993).

79. Bowen, *Muslims*, 22.

80. On Islam's role in forging the terms for a new, multiethnic community in Singapore, see William R. Roff, "The Malayo-Muslim World of Singapore," in *The Origins of Malay Nationalism* (Kuala Lumpur: University of Malaya Press, 1967), 32–55.

81. On the culture and organization of traditional Islamic schools, see Zamakhsyari Dhofier, *The Pesantren Tradition: The Role of the Kyai in the Maintenance of Traditional Islam in Java*, Monograph Series, Program for Southeast Asian Studies (Tempe: Arizona State University, 1999).

82. However, the traditionalists did not join the modernists in decrying pilgrimage (*ziarah*) to the shrines of Muslim saints.

83. Leo Suryadinata, *Pribumi Indonesians, the Chinese Minority, and China*, 3rd ed. (Singapore: Heinemann Educational, 1992), 12.

84. Ruth McVey, "Taman Siswa and the Indonesian National Awakening," *Indonesia*, October 1967, 128–48; and Kenji Tsuchiya, *Democracy and Leadership: The Rise of the Taman Siswa Movement in Indonesia*, trans. Peter Hawkes. (Honolulu: University of Hawaii Press, 1987).

85. Jürgen Habermas, *The Structural Transformation of the Public Sphere: An Inquiry into a Category of Bourgeois Society*, trans. Thomas Burger (Cambridge: MIT Press, 1991); for an exploration of the emergence of a public sphere in nearby Malaysia, see A. C. Milner, *The Invention of Politics in Colonial Malaya: Contesting Nationalism and the Expansion of the Public Sphere* (Cambridge: Cambridge University Press, 1995); for an illuminating comparative exchange on liberal and Muslim views of the modern public spheres, see José Casanova, *Public Religion in the Modern World* (Chicago: University of Chicago Press, 1994); and Talal Asad, "Religion, Nation-State, Secularism," in Peter van der Veer and Hartmut Lehmann, eds., *Nation*

and Religion: Perspectives on Europe and Asia (Princeton: Princeton University Press, 1999), 178–96.

86. On the early decades of newspapers and the press in Dutch East Indies, see Ahmat B. Adam, *The Vernacular Press and the Emergence of Modern Indonesian Consciousness (1855–1913)*, Studies on Southeast Asia no. 17 (Ithaca, N.Y.: Cornell University Press, 1995).

87. Bowen, *Muslims through Discourse*, 326; Milner develops a related point in a Malay context in his *The Invention of Politics*.

88. See Abdullah, *Schools and Politics*; Howard M. Federspiel, *Persatuan Islam: Islamic Reform in Twentieth-Century Indonesia* (Ithaca, N.Y.: Modern Indonesia Project, Cornell University, 1970).

89. For an example of these issues in a Hindu-Balinese context during the independence era, see F. L. Bakker, *The Struggle of the Hindu Balinese Intellectuals: Developments in Modern Hindu Thinking in Independent Indonesia* (Amsterdam: VU University Press, 1993). For an example from a Christian community, see Kipp, *Dissociated Identities*. For a discussion of a related process in late colonial Java, see Takashi Shiraishi, *An Age in Motion: Popular Radicalism in Java, 1912–1926* (Ithaca, N.Y.: Cornell University Press, 1990).

90. The phrase "religiously neutral nationalism" was coined by Deliar Noer in *The Modernist Muslim Movement in Indonesia*, to refer to non-Islamic nationalists. The phrase is more appropriate than the more commonly used "secular nationalism," referring to nationalist rivals to the Islamic nationalists. Most of the former did not advocate a fully secularist Indonesia, but a religiously plural nation in which the country's religions play an important role in public life.

91. In Java, *santri* were also referred to as *kaum putihan*, the "white group," those who dress in the white clothing of pious believers.

92. See Clifford Geertz, *Religion of Java* (New York: Basic, 1960). Although in the 1950s the term "red" acquired a left-wing connotation, in its original use the term evoked politically neutral images of the earth, farming, and the peasantry.

93. Cf. Ernest Gellner, "Flux and Re-flux in the Faith of Men," in Gellner, *Muslim Society* (Cambridge: Cambridge University Press, 1981).

94. On the often agonistic relationship of Sufis to Islamic reformism in a context other than Southeast Asia, see David Westerlund and Eva Evers Rosander, eds., *African Islam and Islam in Africa: Encounters between Sufis and Islamists* (Athens, Ohio: Ohio University Press, 1997).

95. See M. C. Ricklefs, "Six Centuries of Islamization in Java," in N. Levtzion, ed., *Conversion to Islam* (New York: Homes & Meier, 1993), 100–128.

96. Kartodirdjo, *Protest Movements*, 142–85.

97. Benda, *Rising Sun*, 104–94.

98. The quote is from Benedict Anderson, "Old State, New Society: Indonesia in Historical Perspective," *Journal of Asian Studies* 42 (1983): 487.

99. Herbert Feith, "Dynamics of Guided Democracy," in McVey, *Indonesia*, 316. Although the primary political blocs had this sectarian coloring, not all alliances did. In the early 1960s, many Muslims and anticommunist nationalists joined forces against the Communist Party.

100. Clifford Geertz, "Ritual and Social Change: A Javanese Example," in *The Interpretation of Cultures* (New York: Basic, 1973), 146–62.

101. Hefner, *Mountain Java*, chap. 7.

102. See Loren Ryter, "Pemuda Pancasila: The Last Loyalist Free Men of Suharto's New Order," *Indonesia*, October 1996, 45–73.

103. See Julia Day Howell et al., "Indonesian Sufism: Signs of Resurgence," in Peter Clarke, ed., *New Trends and Developments in the World of Islam* (Somerset, U.K.: Luzac Oriental, 1998), 277–97.

104. Elements of this syncretistic tradition are subtly analyzed in Beatty, *Varieties*.

105. Important studies on the origins and development of Javanese mystical associations include Antoon Geels, *Subud and the Javanese Mystical Tradition* (Richmond, U.K.: Curzon, 1997), and Paul D. Stange, "The Sumarah Movement in Javanese Mysticism" (Ph.D. diss., University of Wisconsin, 1980). Paul Stange, "Legitimate Mysticism in Indonesia," *Review of Indonesian and Malaysian Affairs* 20 (1986): 76–117, shows there were regime pressures on mystical movements in the mid-1980s, pressing the groupings toward orthodox Islamic forms.

106. Officially, however, recognition was only given to streams in these religions that affirmed a belief in a monotheistic God.

107. Even today the question of how to deal with apostasy remains central to debates on human rights in Muslim societies. See Ann Elizabeth Mayer, *Islam and Human Rights: Tradition and Politics*, 2nd ed. (Boulder: Westview), 141–51.

108. Kipp and Steedly's studies of religion and politics in the Karo region of North Sumatra show that not all populations linked ethnicity and religion. As Karo entered the national religious marketplace, they opted to affiliate with different religions rather than unite around one. A similar differentiation of religion and ethnicity has taken place among other populations, such as the Meratus Dayak. See Kipp, *Dissociated Identities*; Steedly, *Hanging*; and, for the Meratus Dayak, Lowenhaupt Tsing, *In the Realm*.

109. On the rebellion in West Java, see C. van Dijk, *Rebellion under the Banner of Islam: The Darul Islam*, Verhandelingen van Het KITLV no. 94 (The Hague: Martinus Mijhoff, 1981); for South Sulawesi, see Barbara S. Harvey, *Permesta: Half A Rebellion* (Ithaca, N.Y.: Cornell University Press, 1977).

110. Pelras, *Bugis*, 284–86; this information is also based on interviews I conducted with local Muslim leaders in Makassar in August 2003.

111. See Aragon, *Fields*; Albert Schrauwers, *Colonial "Reformation"*; and Lowenhaupt Tsing, *In the Realm*.

112. On the Ngaju, see Ann Schiller, *Small Sacrifices: Religious Change and Cultural Identity among the Ngaju of Indonesia* (Oxford: Oxford University Press, 1997), especially 109–31. On the Hindu movement among Karo Batak (most of whom have today converted to Christianity and, in smaller numbers, Islam), see Kipp, *Dissociated Identities*; and Steedly, *Hanging*. On the Hindu movement in East Java, see Robert Hefner, *Hindu Javanese: Tengger Tradition and Islam* (Princeton: Princeton University Press, 1985); for Central Java, see Margaret Lyon, "Politics and Religious Identity: Genesis of a Javanese–Hindu Movement in Rural Central Java" (Ph.D. diss., University of California, 1977).

113. Steedly, *Hanging*, 69.

114. On the fortunes of Indonesia's Hindu movement, see Martin Ramstedt, "Indonesianisation, Globalisation, and Islamisation: Parameters of the Hindu Discourse in Modern Indonesia," *International Journal of Hindu Studies*, forthcoming.

115. Elsewhere, as in Sumba, the most "pagan" of territories in the entire archipelago in the 1970s, indigenous religion held its own during the first two decades of the New Order but then gave way to widespread conversion to Christianity and Islam in the 1990s. On Sumba in the early years of the New Order, see Hoskins, "Bitter House." On the recent large-scale conversion to Christianity, see Kuipers, *Marginality*.

116. See Robinson, *Dark Side*.

117. The best source on the killings remains Cribb, *Indonesian Killings*.

118. David Reeve, "The Corporatist State: The Case of Golkar," in Budiman, *Civil Society*, 154.

119. On the social dynamics of Indonesia's diffusion, see Kuipers, *Marginality*; and Errington, *Shifting Languages*. On the role of media in Indonesian national culture, see Sen and Hill, *Media*, and Karl G. Heider, *Indonesian Cinema: National Culture on Screen* (Honolulu: University of Hawaii Press, 1985).

120. Langenberg, "New Order State," 134; my emphasis.

121. As noted above, Carol Warren's criticism of the tendency of Balinese ethnography to "overemphasize hierarchic values in Balinese culture . . . at the expense of a full appreciation of . . . egalitarian and horizontal counterpoints" applies in spades to the ethnography and cultural studies of Java in the 1980s. Clifford Geertz, *Religion of Java*; and Robert Jay, *Javanese Villagers*, show that Javanese society in the 1950s was thick with egalitarian counterpoints and contestations. James Peacock, *Rites of Modernization: Symbolic and Social Aspects of Indonesian Proletarian Drama* (Chicago: University of Chicago, 1968) illustrates some of the ways in which egalitarian themes played in the popular arts. Dazzled perhaps by the light of New Order hegemony, in the 1980s some Western scholars lost sight of Javanese society's democratic counterpoints and diversity.

122. On the ideological training in Indonesian classrooms, see Saya S. Shiraishi, *Young Heroes*, 123–43; in the media, see Sen and Hill, *Media*.

123. The phrase is from Keith Foulcher, "The Construction of an Indonesian National Culture: Patterns of Hegemony and Resistance," in Budiman, *Civil Society*, 309.

124. On nongovernmental organizations, see Philip J. Eldridge, *Non-Government Organizations and Democratic Participation in Indonesia* (New York: Oxford University Press, 1995). Having been scorned as viruses through which communism is spread, labor organizations were among the last public associations to be allowed even a limited measure of associational liberty. On labor under the New Order, see Vedi R. Hadiz, *Workers and the State in New Order Indonesia*, Routledge Studies in the Growth Economies of Asia (London: Routledge, 1997).

125. Gavin W. Jones and Chris Manning, "Labour Force and Employment during the 1980s," in Ann Booth, ed., *The Oil Boom and After: Indonesian Economic Policy and Performance in the Suharto Era* (New York: Oxford University Press, 1992).

126. Terence H. Hull and Gavin W. Jones, "Demographic Perspectives," in Hal Hill, ed., *Indonesia's New Order: The Dynamics of Socio-Economic Transformation* (Honolulu: University of Hawaii Press, 1994).

127. See Hal Hill, *The Indonesian Economy since 1966: Southeast Asia's Emerging Giant* (Cambridge: Cambridge University Press, 1996), 206–7.

128. Hill, *Indonesian Economy*, 208.

129. See Howard W. Dick, "The Rise of a Middle Class and the Changing Concept of Equity in Indonesia: An Interpretation," *Indonesia* 39 (1985): 71–92; and Richard Tanter and Kenneth Young, *The Politics of Middle Class Indonesia*, Monash Papers on Southeast Asia no. 19 (Clayton, Australia: Centre of Southeast Asian Studies, Monash University, 1990).

130. See Ruth McVey, "The Materialization of the Southeast Asian Entrepreneur," in *Southeast Asian Capitalism* (Ithaca, N.Y.: Southeast Asia Program, Cornell University), 7–33.

131. On the ambiguous role of the New Order media, see Sen and Hill, *Media*, esp. 6–17.

132. On the uses of "building-up" programs to resettle migratory populations, see Tsing, *In the Realm*, 93; and Bernard Sellato, *Nomades et sédentarisation à Bornéo*, Etudes Insulindiennes Archipel no. 9 (Paris: Editions de l'Ecole des Hautes Etudes en Sciences Sociales, 1989), 119–23. Sedentarization programs like these had begun earlier during the Dutch administration.

133. See M. Bambang Pranowo, "Which Islam and Which Pancasila? Islam and the State in Indonesia: A Comment," in Budiman, *Civil Society*, 493.

134. See Robert W. Hefner, "Hindu Reform in an Islamizing Java: Pluralism and Peril," in Martin Ramstedt, ed., *Hinduism in Modern Indonesia: A Minority Religion between Local, National, and Global Interests* (London: RoutledgeCurzon, 2004).

135. Hefner, "Hindu."

136. On the New Order's early agreements with Western missionaries to "build up" remote regions of Kalimantan, Sulawesi, and Irian Jaya, see Lorraine Aragon, *Fields*; and, for West Papua, Charles E. Farhadian, "A Social History of Urban Dani Christians in New Order Indonesia" (Ph.D. diss., Boston University, 2000). On the DDII alliance with Suharto, see Hefner *Civil Islam*, 106–13; chap. 7.

137. The case of Hindus was different yet from that of Christians. Compared to the Christians, who made great headway among ex-communists, the Hindus were most successful converting people from the National Party previously active in mystical groups or Javanese new religions. After 1965–1966, some of the former PNI leaders publicly converted to Hinduism, often citing what they regarded as the affinity between Hinduism and Javanist mysticism. See Margaret Lyon, "Politics."

138. See Aragon, *Fields*; Tsing, *In the Realm*; and Farhadian, *A Social History*.

139. Hoskins, "Bitter House," 138; Kuipers, *Marginality*, 112–16.

140. Suryadinata, *Pribumi*, 151.

141. Suryadinata, *Pribumi*, 158.

142. See Robert W. Hefner, "Islamizing Java? Religion and Politics in Rural East Java," *Journal of Asian Studies*, October 1987, 3; Hung-Jun Kim, "Reformist Muslims in a Yogyakarta Village" (Ph.D. diss., Australian National University, 1996);

and M. Bambang Pranowo, "Creating Islamic Tradition in Rural Java" (Ph.D. diss., Monash University, 1991).

143. See Greg Barton, "The Emergence of Neomodernism: A Progressive, Liberal Movement of Islamic Thought in Indonesia" (Ph.D. diss., Monash University, 1995).

144. For a discussion of the reception of democratic ideals among Indonesian Muslim intellectuals, see Masykuri Abdillah, *Responses of Indonesian Muslim Intellectuals to the Concept of Democracy (1966–1993)* (Hamburg: Abera Verlag Meyer, 1997).

145. On the history and organization of NU, see Andrée Feillard, *Islam et armée dan L'Indonésie contemporaine* (Paris: L'Harmattan, 1995); and Martin van Bruinessen, *NU: Tradisi, Relasi-relasi Kuasa, Pencarian Wacana Baru* (Yogyakarta: LKiS, 1994).

146. See the discussion of NU's effort to develop a banking system in the early 1990s in Hefner, "Islamizing Capitalism: On the Founding of Indonesia's First Islamic Bank," in Mark Woodward, ed., *Toward a New Paradigm: Recent Developments in Indonesian Islamic Thought* (Tempe: Center for Southeast Asian Studies, Arizona State University, 1996), 291–322.

147. On Muslim entrepreneurs and New Order cronyism, see John Bresnan, *Managing Indonesia*; Richard Robison, "Industrialization and the Economic and Political Development of Capital: The Case of Indonesia," in McVey, *Capitalism*; and Robert W. Hefner, "Markets and Justice for Muslim Indonesians," in *Market Cultures: Society and Morality in the New Asian Capoitalisms* (Boulder: Westview, 1998), 224–50.

148. On the DDII, see Robert W. Hefner, "Print Islam: Mass Media and Ideological Rivalries among Indonesian Muslims," *Indonesia*, October 1997, 1–27; and Hefner, *Civil Islam*, chap. 6.

149. See Greg Barton, "Neo-Modernism: A Vital Synthesis of Traditionalist and Modernist Islamic Thought in Indonesia," *Studia Islamika: Indonesian Journal for Islamic Studies* 2, no. 3 (1995): 1–71.

150. On ICMI's founding, see Hefner, *Civil Islam*, chap. 6.

151. For an analysis of government concessions to Islam, see Bahtiar Effendy, "Islam and the State: The Transformation of Islamic Political Ideas and Practices in Indonesia" (Ph.D. diss., Ohio State University, 1994).

152. Hefner, *Civil Islam*, 202.

153. See Tim Gabungan Pencari Fakta, *Laporan Akhir: Peristiwa Tanggal 13–15 Mei 1998*, available at www.indonesia-house.org/archive/021903TPGF_end_report.htm.

154. See ICG Asia, *Communal Violence in Indonesia: Lessons from Kalimantan* (Jakarta: Asia Briefing, International Crisis Group, 2001).

155. See Lorraine V. Aragon, "Communal Violence in Poso, Central Sulawesi: Where People Eat Fish and Fish Eat People," *Indonesia*, October 2001, 45–80, and Human Rights Watch, "Breakdown: Four Years of Communal Violence in Central Sulawesi," *Human Rights Watch* 14, no. 9C (December 2002), at www.hrw.org/reports/2002/indonesia/indonesia1102.pdf.

156. The strength of Maluku's earlier traditions of tolerance, however, has been exaggerated in some recent press reports. The region saw a Christian-led secessionist

movement in the late 1940s and early 1950s, heightening tensions between Christians and the (then) Muslim minority. In the early 1990s, state policies favoring Muslims in contracts and appointments further heightened tensions between the two communities, particularly in the city of Ambon. On the earlier period, see Richard Chauvel, *Nationalists, Soldiers, and Separatists: The Ambonese Islands from Colonialism to Revolt, 1880–1950* (Leiden: KITLV Press, 1990); on the early 1990s, see Christian Kiem, "Re-Islamization among Muslim Youth in Ternate Town, Eastern Indonesia," *Sojourn*, February 1993, 92–127.

157. For a fuller treatment of the Laskar Jihad, see Robert W. Hefner, "Civic Pluralism Denied? The New Media and *Jihadi* violence in Indonesia," in Dale F. Eickelman and Jon W. Anderson, eds., *New Media in the Muslim World: The Emerging Public Sphere*, 2nd ed. (Bloomington: Indiana University Press, 2003).

158. See Tamrin Amal Tomagola, "The Halmahera of North Moluccas," in Olle Tornquist, ed., *Political Violence: Indonesia and India in Comparative Perspective*, SUM Report no. 9 (Oslo: Center for Development and the Environment, University of Oslo, 2000). The Indonesian sociologist George J. Aditjondro also published an extensive analysis in which he tied rival Jakartan elites to the Maluku violence. Rather than seeing Suharto alone as the instigator, Aditjondro, like the author, sees the influence of more general battles among rival elites in a context of declining central power and heightened regional competition. See George J. Aditjondro, "Gajah dengan Gajah Berlaga, Orang Maluku Mati di Tengah-tengah" [Elephants Battle Elephants, Maluku People Get Killed in the Middle], *Apakabar Indonesia-L*, January 23, 2000.

159. Thomas Blom Hansen, *The Saffron Wave: Democracy and Hindu Nationalism in Modern India* (Princeton: Princeton University Press, 1999), 204–6.

160. For a fuller treatment of the variety of Islamist paramilitaries, see Robert W. Hefner, "Muslim Democrats and Islamist Violence in Post-Soeharto Indonesia," in *Remaking Muslim Politics: Pluralism, Contestation, Democratization* (Princeton: Princeton University Press, 2005), 273–301.

161. See ICG Asia, *Al-Qaeda in Southeast Asia: The Case of the "Ngruki Network" in Indonesia* (Jakarta: Asia Briefing, International Crisis Group, 2002).

162. See ICG Asia, *Indonesia Backgrounder: How the Jemaah Islamiyah Terrorist Network Operates*, Asia Report no. 43 (Jakarta: International Crisis Group, 2002).

163. For an excellent summary of recent polling on Muslim views of Islam and democracy, see Jamhari and Jajang Jahroni, *Gerakan Islam Radikal di Indonesia* (Jakarta: PT Raja Grafindo, 2004).

164. See Siegel, "Suharto, Witches." Robert Cribb, "From Petrus to Ninja: Death Squads in Indonesia," in Cambell and Brenner, *Death Squads*, sees the possibility of a political motive to the first wave of killing, in a manner consistent with information I was given by East Javanese Muslim friends in 1998. Those reports indicated that some killings targeted NU and *abangan* villagers in an effort to stir up violence and spoil the chances for a Megawati–Wahid alliance. Again, whether such reports are true or not, Siegel's general observation on the strength of everyday animosities is an indisputable part of the problem.

165. See Gerry van Klinken, "The Maluku Wars: Bringing Society Back In," *Indonesia*, April 2001, 1–26. On specific linkages between the Maluku violence and

rival Jakarta elites, see John McBeth and Dini Djalal, "Ambon violence may have had its origins in Jakarta," Far Eastern Economic Review On Line, March 25, 1999. For a broader discussion of the theoretical importance but limits of the concept of civil society in democratic theory, see Hefner, "Multiculturalism."

166. Geertz, "Indonesian Cultures," 95.

167. Loren Ryter, "Pemuda Pancasila: The Last Loyalist Free Men of Suharto's New Order," *Indonesia*, October 1998, 45–73.

168. See Hatta Chumaidi, "Melihat dari Dekat Front Pembela Islam" [To see from close up the Islamic Defenders Front], Jawa Pos Online, February 22, 2000.

169. See ICG Asia, *Indonesia: The Search for Peace in Maluku*, Asia Report no. 31 (Jakarta: International Crisis Group, 2002); and George J. Aditjondro, "The Political Economy of Violence in Maluku, Indonesia," Munindo website, February 27, 2000.

170. Two important examples of this literature are Juan J. Linz, *The Breakdown of Democratic Regimes: Crisis, Breakdown, and Reequilibration* (Baltimore: Johns Hopkins University Press, 1978); and Juan J. Linz and Alfred Stepan, *Problems of Democratic Transition and Consolidation* (Baltimore: Johns Hopkins University Press, 1996).

171. Feith, "Dynamics," 399.

3

Politics: From Endurance to Evolution

Annette Clear

The people of Indonesia, in all their ethnic and religious variety, face the common task of reforming the Indonesian state so that it can meet their equally diverse needs and demands. This chapter examines the recent crisis of the Indonesian state. It begins with an analysis of how Indonesia came to have such a highly dysfunctional state at the turn of the twenty-first century that its very existence was questioned. This chapter then turns to how the Indonesian state survived and has emerged from this existential crisis. It also analyzes the historic development of Indonesia's political institutions, with an emphasis on the post-Suharto political reforms. Finally, with a deep appreciation of the unpredictability of such matters, this chapter tries to assess precisely what these recent changes, or evolutionary steps toward democracy, suggest for the politics of Indonesia in the coming decade or, perhaps, decades.

Indonesians are not short of targets to blame for the conditions that contributed to the crisis of the state. Many blame Suharto, the long-term authoritarian leader who resigned in disgrace in May 1998. Some blame Sukarno and the generation that led the nation to independence, proclaimed in 1945. Others fault the Dutch, who turned the East Indies into a profitable but increasingly rebellious colony before World War II. All have ample justification for doing so, but the fault lies not with one particular person or cause but rather in the combination over time of and interaction among all of these and other factors.

Similarly, no one factor can be given all the credit for the recent political reforms. Many organizations and individuals came together to contribute to the *reformasi* movement, thereby creating the opportunity for and implementing the package of institutional changes that have moved Indonesian politics away from authoritarianism and toward democracy.

The Europeans introduced the concept of government as an autonomous entity, acting independently of popular support. They did so by the rule they imposed on the people of the "spice islands" from the early 1500s and, more consequentially, on those of the former kingdoms of Central and East Java in 1830. Government autonomy was enforced with armed might in these and later conquests, and in Dutch repression of nationalist politics in the second and third decades of the twentieth century. It was against the background of remembrance, history, and myth arising from this experience that Indonesia declared its independence in 1945, was recognized as an independent state by the Dutch at the end of 1949, and became a member of the United Nations in 1950, joining the international community of states.

Five distinct phases of political institutional development can be identified in the history of independent Indonesia. The first phase of Indonesia's political history was its revolution against the Dutch colonizers who refused to accept Indonesia's declaration of independence. Indonesia's second phase, during Sukarno's presidency, was parliamentary democracy, but this ended abruptly when civil and military leaders in the outer islands rebelled in 1957. The third phase, still under Sukarno, was a strong presidency with increasingly authoritarian elements. Sukarno's presidency disintegrated when he was no longer able to restrain the rising mistrust between the Indonesian army and the Communist Party in 1965, and as many as 500,000 communists and other leftists were executed within a few months' time. With this violent transition to Suharto's presidency, a fourth phase in Indonesian politics began in which his New Order supported by the military imposed a thoroughly authoritarian system. This regime, however, began to unravel when an international monetary crisis destroyed the economic foundation of the regime's legitimacy in 1998.

Since then, a fifth phase—called *reformasi*, or reform—has been under way in which Indonesian society has sought to challenge and limit the powers of the presidency and army. In this phase, evolutionary reforms have attempted to establish, or in some cases reestablish, such political institutions as independent political parties, free and fair elections, meaningful legislative bodies, a corruption-free judiciary, a reform-minded civil society, and newly empowered local governments. The scale of institution building that is being attempted is truly massive, and there is uncertainty about the likelihood that these reforms will provide a durable democratic system of government for the Indonesian people.

The title of this chapter is not meant to suggest that the Indonesian state or its politics has been unchanged throughout its modern history. Indeed, change is evident during its more than fifty years of independence. And yet, the trend of these institutional changes through most of Indonesia's modern history has been in the further consolidation of authoritarianism—the strengthening of state institutions that were designed to control and demobilize Indonesian society. These authoritarian institutions were once thought to be the enduring elements of Indonesian politics. But in recent years, a variety of societal and political forces have challenged the endurance of Indonesia's authoritarianism and shaped the Indonesian state into a set of more democratic institutions that are designed to represent the political aspirations of the people of Indonesia more genuinely and effectively.

Let me define a few terms. A widely accepted definition of institution is "the formal rules, compliance procedures, and standard operating practices that structure the relationship between individuals in various units of the polity and economy."[1] In this chapter the focus will be on rules, procedures, and practices that shape the relationship between Indonesian society and its state. The political institutions that will be examined are the electoral process, the legislative bodies, the judiciary, civil society, regional autonomy, and the military. As for the less conventional terms "endurance" and "evolution," they do not merely convey the idea of change and nonchange, nor should one be construed as necessarily a positive or a negative dynamic. *Merriam-Webster's Collegiate Dictionary* defines "endurance" in several ways: permanence, duration; the ability to withstand hardship or adversity, especially the ability to sustain a prolonged stressful effort or activity; and the act or an instance of enduring or suffering. With regard to the idea of permanence or duration, this speaks to the process of consolidating the authoritarian institutions that came to characterize the New Order regime. Permanence or duration is not a condition of inaction, but rather the dynamic of political institutions' ongoing resistance to challenges to the regime. The second and third components of the definition allude to the experiences of the Indonesian people with these authoritarian institutions. In the late 1990s, Indonesian citizens decided they could no longer endure or tolerate the practices of the New Order regime and demanded Suharto's resignation as only one component of the larger program of *reformasi*.

The dictionary offers several definitions for "evolution": a process of change in a certain direction, unfolding; a process of continuous change from a lower, simpler, or worse to a higher, more complex, or better state; growth. Use of this term here more closely follows the dictionary definition because it means the ability of Indonesian social movements to bring about institutional change that is self-sustaining and in a democratizing direction. But using the term "evolution" rather than its cousin revolution is purposeful. The Indonesian people have implemented significant change in the rules, procedures, and practices that govern their lives, but these have been reforms rather than wholesale displacement of the entire governing structure. Although many Indonesians found fault with several aspects of the New Order regime, there were elements that they sought to reform rather than discard. The great transition of Indonesia has been a dynamic process of selecting, then reforming and transforming various institutions of the Indonesian state so that they can meet the diverse needs and demands of Indonesian society.

This chapter argues that while many of Indonesia's political institutions are now more democratic than they have been at any time since the 1950s, key reformed institutions remain fragile and vulnerable, and others remain authoritarian in critical respects. The resignation of Suharto at the culmination of economic and political crises in 1998 briefly suggested otherwise. Many members of the elite, especially young intellectuals, thought that the authoritarian institutions of Suharto's regime could not last—that a period of rapid change would take place in the quality of political life. Selected political institutions were indeed liberalized during the presidencies that followed Suharto. Even a fully functioning and substantive democracy seemed within reach.

But the political evolution that has taken place has been slow, often wavering in direction, at times even regressing, but nonetheless ongoing. The low expectations for B. J. Habibie's presidency were far surpassed, but the high expectations for his successor Abdurrahman Wahid were displaced by disappointment and disillusionment. Many features of Suharto's authoritarian rule remained, and Indonesian political institutions were not greatly altered by the presidency of Megawati Sukarnoputri. The structure of the country's political institutions has been significantly altered by a series of constitutional amendments passed by the MPR, in at least one case in spite of Megawati's objections. The First Amendment of 1999 dealt mostly with electoral reforms. The Second Amendment of 2000 had provisions that guaranteed a wider range of human rights protections for Indonesian citizens. The Third Amendment of 2001 and the Fourth Amendment of 2002 together produced a major restructuring of the government, defined the rules for the direct election of the president and vice president, as well as created a new national legislative body for regional representatives. It nonetheless remains to be seen whether these structural changes will translate into an equally fundamental transformation in how politics is practiced. Nevertheless hopes are high for the presidency of Susilo Bambang Yudhoyono, Indonesia's sixth president and its first president elected directly by the people. Yet they remain merely hopes at this point.

These circumstances raise the following questions: To what extent are authoritarian institutions enduring? In what critical ways are institutions from the New Order period evolving? What are the sources of change? And perhaps more boldly, what are the prospects for democracy in Indonesia's future?

Will the current reforms not only remain but also strengthen? An examination of the evidence for endurance and evolution in Indonesian political institutions should shed some light on these questions.

The first section explores how Indonesia's colonial and independent political history contributed to authoritarian aspects of the country's political institutions. The second section describes the multiple crises that brought an end to Suharto's New Order regime in 1998, highlighting the ways in which political and social forces in Indonesian society confronted the Indonesian state, not only instigating a transition away from authoritarianism but also creating the opportunity for a transition to democracy. The third section examines the institutional anatomy of the post-Suharto years, institution by institution. The fourth section assesses the balance between enduring and evolving elements in the structure of Indonesian politics and identifies the principal challenges that the people of Indonesia continue to face in advancing their *reformasi*.

ENDURING STRUCTURES

Indonesia at the beginning of its sovereign existence was widely perceived as a nascent democracy. Herbert Feith, in *The Decline of Constitutional Democracy in Indonesia*, identifies six features that he considers characteristic of democracy and present in Indonesian politics in the early 1950s: civilians played a dominant role; political parties were of great importance; political players showed respect for the constitution, which set the rules of the game; most of the political elite was committed to democratic symbols; civil liberties were rarely violated; and the Indonesian state rarely resorted to violence or coercion.[2] The 1955 general elections were regarded as the high point of democracy in this early period of Indonesian politics. The early years of the Sukarno presidency were dominated by civilians who had led Indonesia in its struggle for independence, aided by the democratic provisional 1950 constitution. Also, despite the military's critical role in fighting the Dutch, its leaders did not demand a prominent role in politics. Indonesian citizens were granted civil liberties and not victimized by state violence. Moreover, political participation was encouraged in the parliamentary elections of 1955. With twenty-eight political parties competing, four parties won 77 percent of the vote. The Indonesian National Party won 22.3 percent; the Masyumi, 20.9 percent; Nahdlatul Ulama, 18.4 percent; and the Indonesian Communist Party, 15.4 percent.

Despite these early indications that Indonesia was to enjoy popular government, enthusiasm for it soon faded among the Jakarta elite. A rebellion in

Sumatra and Sulawesi in 1957 against the policies of the central government led not to negotiations but to martial law and a forceful response, reducing the role of political parties and strengthening the role of the president and the army.[3] There was also an increasing fear that the Communist Party would fare better in subsequent elections, eroding the Nationalist Party's already slim margin of victory. To forestall these possible incursions into his power, Sukarno introduced his concept of guided democracy; reinstated the 1945 constitution, which gave increased power to the office of the president; and in due course was proclaimed president for life. Through these measures Sukarno began the process of limiting democratic participation and erecting the authoritarian institutions that would govern and restrain Indonesian society until the very end of the twentieth century. Harry Benda observed that Feith asked the wrong question, that the question was not why democracy had declined in Indonesia, but, given Indonesia's history, why anyone had thought it would work there in the first place.[4]

Suharto, who acquired executive power in 1966 in the wake of the killing of hundreds of thousands of supporters of the Indonesian Communist Party (PKI) by the military and paramilitary groups, turned the country's remaining political institutions into instruments of control. Political parties were the first to suffer. The PKI was banned. The parties that survived were forced to merge into just two groupings: the Indonesian Democratic Party (PDI) and the Development Unity Party (PPP). An army-created organization, the Functional Group (Golkar), became the government's electoral machine.[5]

The electoral process more broadly speaking suffered as well from Suharto's authoritarian restrictions. General elections were held every five years in highly choreographed events that were dubbed "festivals of democracy." They played an important role in creating an illusion of public support, thereby providing a fig leaf of legitimacy for the New Order regime. The superficiality of the process was made clear, however, by several factors. The first factor was that although there were general elections, most of the parliamentary members were in fact not elected by the Indonesian voters, but selected by Suharto and his closest advisers. While the specific numbers of elected and appointed members varied from term to term, in the larger legislative body the MPR, the appointed members always outnumbered the elected ones. A second factor was the New Order regime's use of the concept of the floating mass to severely restrict political participation. According to this 1972 doctrine, the Indonesian state expected citizens to participate in elections but prohibited them from being politically active in any nonelectoral period and through any means other than voting. Between elections, the population was to be a "floating mass." These strictures led to innovative forms of resistance. One subtle form of popular resistance was the *golongan putih or golput* movement that gained prominence in the 1992 elections.[6] *Golongan putih* literally means the "white group" and refers in this case to ballots that were white because voters chose to cast them blank. While other forms of popular resistance and protest against the New Order regime were evident through Suharto's presidency, the *golput* movement was one of the few symbolic protests specifically targeting the electoral process.

This keenly manipulated electoral process produced members for the Indonesian legislature called the Dewan Perwakilan Rakyat (DPR) or People's Representative Council, which served to rubber-stamp New Order policies. People joked that the functions of the DPR were the 4 Ds: "*datang* (attend), *duduk* (sit down), *diam* (be silent), *duit* (collect money/honoraria)."[7] The DPR was made up of a combination of elected members and appointed military representatives.[8] Every five years the larger Majelis Permusyawaratan Rakyat (MPR) or People's Consultative Assembly met to hear the president's accountability speech and to reelect the president. The MPR consisted of the DPR's 500 members, and an additional 500 members approved by Suharto and his most trusted advisers. Although both the DPR and the MPR were totally beholden to him, Suharto nonetheless relied frequently on presidential decrees to promulgate the policies of his choosing. Likewise, while the judiciary functioned principally to serve its own interests—in particular, to make money through its own corrupt practices—when called on, the judiciary did the bidding of Suharto to support his interest in controlling the polity and economy.

Civil liberties received only lip service during the Suharto regime. Political rights were frequently denied ostensibly for preserving Indonesian unity, but more accurately for consolidating Suharto's political power. Fear that Indonesia's diversity would threaten national unity was captured in the acronym SARA, which stands for *suku, agama, ras, antar-golongan* and refers to ethnicity, religion, race, and intergroup relations. The Indonesian state established the informal but strict rule that no issue relating to SARA was to be discussed or debated publicly. The outward purpose of the SARA prohibition was to prevent political passions from being aroused over real social cleavages, but it also served to disallow grievances against the New Order regime from being discussed, debated, or even spoken. Moreover, the SARA prohibition created an atmosphere of ideological hegemony, which instilled a fear of punishment in any potential regime opponent or critic.

Despite Suharto's efforts to control the entire political process, there were elements in the society that challenged his regime, notably Muslims. The Nahdlatul Ulama (NU) and the Muhammadiyah counted their membership in the tens of millions. Both engaged in large-scale education and welfare programs. The Himpunan Mahasiswa Islam (HMI) was the largest association of university students. All three of these organizations were at the heart of an effort on the part of the Suharto regime to bring Muslim associations to heel in 1985. Legislation of that year required all "mass organizations" to make *pancasila*, the national credo of five principles, their *azas tunggal*, or "sole foundation." Suharto's support of the legislation was part of an effort to build a state based on his personal integralist convictions, a state that would practice *pancasila* democracy, which he saw as an alternative to the failed multiparty system of the past. This was a democracy without opposition parties, one established by unanimity based on deliberation and consensus.[9]

The large, influential Muslim associations submitted to the demands of the government; they did not intend to be found illegal. But the gulf that *azas tunggal* opened between Suharto and the nation's preeminent Muslim organizations was not to be bridged. On the contrary, the leading Muslim organizations became training grounds from which much of the first effective political opposition to Suharto was to arise. Abdurrahman Wahid was leader of the NU and became an active critic of Suharto long before he became president in 1999. Amien Rais was the leader of Muhammadiyah when he began to support student demands that Suharto step down; he went on to found a new political party and became chairman of the first post-Suharto MPR. The student association, HMI, was at the center of the student protest movement, counting the largest number of members among student organizations on many campuses. These elements of civil society managed to persist, helped bring Suharto down, and thus were in a position to contribute to building the new political system after Suharto's departure.

Another source of activist politics in spite of the heavy-handedness of the regime was the small number of nongovernmental organizations (NGOs) that persevered in public advocacy, known in Indonesian as *lembaga swadaya masyarakat* (LSMs), or self-supporting social agencies. Most were engaged in volunteer work that ran parallel to government programs, but a few served to keep alternatives to government policy before the public. Notable among this latter group were the legal aid organization LBH (Lembaga Bantuan Hukum), the environmental advocacy group WALHI (Wahana Lingkungan Hidup Indonesia), and the donor advocacy group known as the International NGO Forum on Indonesian Development (INFID). International financial support was significant for these organizations, but it was a two-edged sword: their international support gave them some protection from official repression, but it also left them open to the charge that they were pawns of external actors.[10]

With these limited exceptions, Indonesia's political structure was run hierarchically from the top down. By the end of the long Suharto era, the structure was devoid of institutional alternatives to the presidency, the civil bureaucracy, and the armed forces. Sukarno had begun the process of selectively banning political parties and mass media, jailing his critics, and centering political authority in the presidency. Suharto went beyond anything the Dutch or Sukarno had done in the way of political repression, including the use of paramilitary militias and political detention without trial. Following the trend set by his predecessor, Suharto continued to expand the powers of the office of the head of state. But Suharto went beyond Sukarno when he used the presidency to gain substantial personal benefits for himself, his family, and his close friends.

This brittle structure was the political system in place when Indonesia experienced its multiple crises in 1998.

The Security Structure

The Indonesian military played a powerful role in helping isolate the Indonesian state from societal demands during the Suharto presidency. Commonly known in recent decades by the acronym ABRI (for Angkatan Bersenjata Republik Indonesia, or Armed Forces of the Republic of Indonesia), the military traced their origins to the guerrilla forces that struggled against the returning Dutch troops after negotiations broke down in 1945. These guerrilla forces, however, were not a unified, professional force. Instead, they survived through a horizontal system of independent units that were entirely local in their operations.[11] Rather than having a vertical or hierarchical chain of command, each group strategized more or less independently of the others. These local groups included auxiliary military organizations that had been established by the Japanese during their occupation of Indonesia (e.g., Defenders of the Fatherland, called Peta) or those that formed spontaneously following Sukarno's proclamation of independence. This scattered base was critical to the success of the guerrilla forces; one unit could be put out of action, but others would survive to fight another day. These groups did not join the Indonesian military, but rather became the very core around which TNI (Tentara Nasional Indonesia) units were formed.

The fragmentation of the early guerrilla forces was one reason why the Indonesian military did not play a strong role in formal Indonesian politics in the early years of independence. Internal factions preoccupied them while Sukarno and other civilian leaders began the process of creating institutions for governing the new nation. Of course the military's involvement in the revolution against the Dutch colonizers was fundamentally a political act, where security concerns were inextricably intertwined with political involvement. But it was not until after martial law was declared in 1957 that the armed forces staked out a claim to a role in formal politics at the national level. In a speech on November 12, 1958, the influential army chief of staff, General A. H. Nasution, exhorted the military to follow the middle way, that is, they should not seek to control political life but must not permit themselves to be totally removed from it either. This began the appointment of military personnel to a widening array of civilian posts in government.

The Indonesian military also was involved in governance as a result of its territorial command structure. In their ongoing analysis of the Indonesian military, the editors of *Indonesia* explain: "The doctrine of territoriality has its honorable origins in the guerrilla war conducted by (the military) against the Dutch colonial regime in 1945–1949. In that era, the military survived through . . . its necessarily deep involvement with its popular base."[12] The Army Staff and Command School (Seskoad) produced in March 1962 the doctrine of territorial warfare, which proposed a military command structure that paralleled every level of civilian government. The Indonesian territory was divided into seventeen regional command centers (*komando daerah militer*, or Kodam), and military commands were established at the subregional or provincial level (*komando resort militer*, or Korem), the district level (*komando distrik militer*, or Kodim), the subdistrict level (*komando rayon militer*, or Koramil), and the village level (*bintara pembina desa*, or Babinsa).[13] In this way, the military command structure largely mirrored the civilian administrative structure.

With these doctrinal and structural developments, ABRI was poised to wrest greater control of the governing responsibilities from the civilian administration. The opportunity arose with the events of October 1, 1965, which led to the fall of Sukarno and the rise to the presidency of Suharto. Once Suharto was president, he and his generals sought to consolidate their grip on political and economic power. At the start of his regime, the earlier middle way doctrine evolved into the *dwi-fungsi*, or dual function, doctrine, whereby the military was held responsible not only for the security of the country, but also for sociopolitical aspects of governing the country. A prominent retired army general explains: "The dual function doctrine under Suharto was the implementation of military overreach into the sociopolitical dimension in support of General Suharto's political power."[14]

Accordingly, the military was granted a formal role in politics with as much as one-fifth of all legislative seats in the People's Representative Council reserved for military personnel. (In return, military personnel were denied the right to vote.) The number of seats shifted over time, but the military consistently had direct representation in the Indonesian legislatures.[15] Military officers were appointed in increasing numbers to positions at the various governmental levels, from the national down to the village levels. This system of *kekaryaan*, or civil secondment, enabled ABRI to exert its influence far and wide. The military presence throughout the Indonesian polity and economy was extensive; by the mid-1990s: "About half of the provincial governors and one-third of district heads had military backgrounds. Military officers also sat as appointed members of the national and regional parliaments as well as the People's Consultative Assembly. Among the other nonmilitary positions filled by military officers were judges in the Supreme Court, heads of state corporations, and ambassadors."[16] Even though the military expanded its influence through these secondments, the *kekaryaan* system was deeply subversive of the military hierarchy because an outsider, the now civilian president, could select officers and reward them with civilian posts. Moreover, the military gained control over a significant portion of the economy, although a relatively minor portion compared to the Suharto family and Chinese Indonesians. Off-budget revenues, such as profits from logging and illegal taxes on mining and oil and gas extraction in the outer islands, were a crucial supplement to ABRI's official budget, as well as a means for military officers to acquire massive personal wealth. The desire to protect these economic resources contributed to ABRI's desire to retain a formal role in Indonesian politics.

ABRI leaders assumed that the greatest threats to Indonesian national unity came from within the country itself: from secessionist movements, religious radicalism, and communism, because all these would promote conflicts among the diverse groups scattered throughout the Indonesian archipelago. They perceived the repercussions of these internal threats to vary from disintegration of national unity and territorial integrity to wide-ranging social disorder and disruption of the country's economic life. Thus the military became a mechanism for internal security. While successful guerrilla tactics against the Dutch inspired the idea of territorial command, during the New Order regime this structure became an instrument of social monitoring and control.

The number of military officers and personnel was relatively small in proportion to Indonesia's large population, but the number was somewhat misleading. ABRI included not only the three traditional military forces—army, air force, and navy—but also the police, and later in the New Order regime and informally, militia groups. One illustration of ABRI's organizational alternatives was its use of local militias in East Timor. In order to integrate East Timor forcibly into Indonesia, the army trained, supported, and directed sizeable militias of young Timorese men. Another example was its reliance on unofficial but officially sanctioned groups such as the Pemuda Pancasila, whose members claimed they were defenders of *pancasila*; in reality such groups were little more than street thugs. The national leaders of Indonesia used these means to enforce their will on the body politic.[17]

The Economic Structure

The Dutch interest was initially economic, and even though it gradually expanded to other spheres, Dutch firms still dominated the modern sectors of the economy even after independence until 1957. In that year, as the Netherlands continued to drag its feet over transferring control of western New Guinea to Indonesian hands, the Jakarta government ordered Dutch citizens out of the country, and Indonesians took over all Dutch economic enterprises. Twelve years after it declared independence, Indonesia was now in control of its banks, trading houses, plantations, and modern manufacturing for the very first time. Under pressure from the international community, the Netherlands and Indonesia resolved the New Guinea issue in 1963, although some argue to this day that its resolution was inadequate and unjust. In the meantime, Sukarno announced a policy of confrontation against the newly founded neighboring state of Malaysia. Indonesia's foreign trade collapsed as a result of the campaign of threat and intimidation that ensued, and the Indonesian economy fell into international bankruptcy.

Indonesia's integration into the global political economy dates back to colonial times, but the nature of its current integration into the global political economy, that is, its unusually heavy dependence upon it, is very largely a product of the Suharto era. The country enjoys an abundance of natural resources, and the Indonesian state came to rely heavily on "rent" paid by foreign multinational corporations for access to those resources. Indonesia is the only Asian member of the oil producers' cartel, the Organization of Petroleum Exporting Countries (OPEC), and the Indonesian state controls the extraction of oil and natural gas by foreign firms through contracts with the state oil company, Pertamina. A single multinational, Freeport-McMoRan, dominates copper and gold mining; it is the largest corporate taxpayer in Indonesia. Indonesia also is a major exporter of forestry products and pulp for the manufacture of paper. All these industries are taxed unofficially by the armed forces.

A state is thought to suffer political repercussions from such financial arrangements. In a country with a *rentier* economy, the state is more dependent on revenues, that is, the rents, from external sources than domestic ones, and consequently the state remains autonomous from its society. In democracies, the collection of taxes offers critical opportunities for the establishment of linkages between a state and its society. If taxes are not collected, then societal actors lack the necessary leverage over their state to make political demands. And the Indonesian state, owing little accountability to a public it barely taxes, is largely autonomous in its distributive welfare functions. In a new twist on a familiar phrase, *rentier* state theory argues, "No representation without taxation." This is clearly the case in Indonesia. A strong domestic tax system is absent, thereby denying Indonesia's citizens the leverage to make political demands.

Another repercussion of Indonesian dependence on multinational corporations flows from their demands for protection of their assets. The Indonesian state has tended to translate these demands into military repression of those most grievously impacted by the operations of the foreign enterprises. The paucity of revenues returning to the localities and the brutality of Indonesian security personnel toward the local people have generated the strong resistance to Indonesian rule seen in such areas as Aceh and Papua.

Another important external source of revenue for the sustenance of the Indonesian state has been foreign aid. The Indonesian economy was in dire straits in the mid-1960s due to several years of bad harvests, a severe drop in foreign reserves, ineffective institutions, and a low state capacity for economic policymaking. These harsh economic conditions contributed to the political turmoil that Indonesia experienced as a result of Sukarno's increasingly reckless policies. The Indonesian government stopped paying interest on its international loans, and Sukarno told international donors to "go to hell" with their aid. While such measures appealed to nationalist pride, they epitomized Sukarno's narrowing options and in hindsight signaled the beginning of the end of his presidency.

When Suharto became president, one of the first things he set out to do was attract foreign aid and foreign private investment in order to stabilize the economic situation. His economic policymakers approached Japan for help. Japan was not only amenable to helping Indonesia; it also was willing to serve as a bridge to the Western donors. In September 1966, Japan hosted the first assembly of all Indonesia's foreign donors, except for those in the communist bloc, at which they agreed to separate debt restructuring from foreign aid discussions. At a second meeting in Paris in December 1966, what became known as the Paris Club of donors agreed to reschedule the Indonesian debt.

Through a gradual process of institutionalization, a consortium of donors, known as the Intergovernmental Group on Indonesia (IGGI), became the central player in foreign aid to Indonesia. Some member governments and their own domestic constituents, eager to secure their investments in Indonesia, saw the importance of keeping the Indonesian economy afloat. Moreover, donors such as the United States were extremely concerned with containing communism and thus in preventing its spread to Indonesia. At the start of the Suharto regime, as a result, the international community of industrial democracies committed significant amounts of aid to Indonesia. At its peak, around 1970, the Indonesian state was so heavily dependent on foreign donors that

70–75 percent of its development budget was funded by foreign aid.[18] With the help of the IGGI members, Indonesia emerged from the economic chaos of the final Sukarno years. And through the IGGI efforts to bail out the Indonesian economy, donor countries became involved in Indonesian economic policy making, and by extension, in Indonesia's domestic politics.

As one might expect, when the IGGI members pledged aid to Indonesia, the New Order regime interpreted this as international approval of its policies. One group of Indonesians particularly well regarded by the international donor community were the economists trained with funding from the Ford Foundation. Because many of them were educated at the University of California, Berkeley, these young economic technocrats became known as the Berkeley mafia. Adopting a market-oriented approach, they were responsible for the policies that reconnected the economy with its traditional trading partners and brought a return to stability and growth in Indonesia.

By the early 1970s, Suharto began to use state contracts and licenses as political patronage. It is assumed that he ensured army loyalty by these means, but military finances remain closed to public inspection; a recent civilian minister of defense has said that the government budget provides less than a third of the armed forces' annual funding. Suharto also provided significant economic opportunities and support to a group of Indonesians of Chinese descent. Although Chinese Indonesians accounted for only 3 percent of the population, it was widely believed that they owned as much as 70 percent of the urban private sector of the economy. This perception conveniently deflected attention away from the regime, making the entrepreneurial Chinese community an easy target for critics of the regime and a scapegoat for societal frustrations.

Suharto also channeled state contracts and licenses to his family and friends. His wife, Ibu Tien, was called "Ibu Tien percent" because of her personal gain from state projects. Major infrastructure contracts were awarded to his children's companies, such as the toll roads to the company of his elder daughter, Siti Hardijanti Rukmana, who was commonly known as Tutut. Suharto's golfing partner, Mohammed (Bob) Hasan, was given a prominent role in the timber industry. His adviser and last vice president, B. J. Habibie, ran the heavily subsidized Indonesian airplane development enterprise called Industri Pesawat Terbang Nusantara (IPTN). (People joked that the name of its plane, the N250, stood for two pilots, five flight attendants, and zero passengers.) While IPTN was certainly a component and beneficiary of the state's import-substitution industrialization (ISI) strategy to development, with Habibie at its helm and the other perks he received during the New Order, IPTN was perceived by the Indonesian public as a prime example of the regime's corrupt practices. Confirming many critiques of the regime's corrupt practices, a leaked World Bank memorandum revealed an estimated 30 percent leakage of bank loans to Indonesia.[19] While some condemned the World Bank for not monitoring its loans more carefully, its estimate was viewed as evidence that state resources were being drained away by government officials throughout the bureaucracy.

Suharto did understand that economic development was critical for political legitimacy. And Indonesia did make economic progress. In the early years, and later in times of limited resources, Suharto was likely to leave economic policymaking to his American-trained economic technocrats, and they provided incentives for private sector investment. When resources were ample, on the other hand, the technocrats were bypassed, and the government invested in heavy industry owned and operated by the state. But policy was changed cautiously and slowly, and the private sector found the process predictable. One achievement of this process was the emergence of an urban middle class; eventually this social group contributed to the downfall of the regime. A more detailed examination of the economic performance of the Suharto regime can be found in chapter 4 of this volume by John Bresnan. Overall, the material gains of the New Order until the middle of 1997 were outstanding by world standards.

Thus the structure of the economy, fueled by foreign aid and investment, supported the political institutions of the regime—the presidency, the military, and the politico-bureaucratic elite—and enabled the state to remain independent of the society and its demands—until the regime experienced a series of jarring crises.

INDONESIA'S MULTIPLE CRISES

The monetary crisis, dubbed *krismon* for *krisis moneter* in Indonesian, was the beginning of the unraveling of the New Order regime. A confluence of factors brought an end to Suharto's rule, but the regional financial crisis that began with the devaluation of the Thai baht in July 1997 was central. Shortly thereafter, the Indonesian rupiah came under similar attack and tumbled drastically from about Rp. 2,500 per U.S. dollar to a low of Rp. 17,000 per dollar at one point in January 1998, eventually stabilizing around Rp. 10,000 per dollar.

The Indonesian rupiah's rapid devaluation had disastrous repercussions for the economy as a whole. The huge dollar short-term debts that had been incurred by Indonesian corporations were no longer serviceable. Entire companies collapsed, leading to a loss of wages and jobs, and substantial economic dislocation throughout Indonesian society. The rupiah's fall also prompted the urban middle class to make runs on the local banks, which were debilitating because they depleted the banks' reserves. More broadly, the rupiah's devaluation made imported goods prohibitively expensive for the average consumer, and many Indonesians even found it difficult to purchase *sembako* (*sembilan bahan pokok*), or basic foodstuffs. The difficulties brought on by the currency devaluation were coupled with environmental damage from El Niño and forest fires in Sumatra and Kalimantan. Massive crop failure resulting from a drought strained markets even further. Indonesia had achieved rice self-sufficiency a decade earlier, but during this economic crisis it had to begin importing rice once again, this time with a collapsed currency. The Indonesian government was unable to act quickly because its letters of credit were not honored abroad.

The International Monetary Fund mobilized a package of financing to rescue the rupiah that was contingent on Indonesia's meeting numerous conditions in its domestic affairs. In the early months of 1998, Suharto justified his not complying with the IMF conditionalities by calling them an infringement on Indonesia's sovereignty. His vacillation reflected the conflict that existed between his desire to resuscitate the Indonesian economy and his equal desire to save the fortunes of his family and friends. A case in point was the national car project of Suharto's youngest son, Hutomo (Tommy) Mandala Putra. The project was in no way an Indonesian national enterprise; the cars were built by South Korea's Kia Motors and imported into Indonesia without the usual import duties. The arrangement angered many Indonesians and earned the indignation of other countries, including the United States and Japan. The Suharto regime resisted the IMF condition that this project be eliminated. In another case, Suharto's second son, Bambang Trihatmodjo, owned one of sixteen banks forced by the IMF to shut down. Bambang accused the minister of finance, Mar'ie Mohammed, of unjustly attacking his family, and then brazenly reopened the bank under a different name. Again, Suharto's daughter, Tutut, had a controlling interest in the business conglomerate Citra Group. Under the IMF agreement, Citra Group's triple-decker transport project in Jakarta was supposed to be canceled, but in early 1998 it was somehow resurrected in defiance of IMF conditionality. The Fund's involvement was essentially a no-win situation for the Suharto regime: When Suharto signed the agreement, it was perceived as intervention in domestic affairs; yet when Suharto and his family challenged the Fund's conditionalities, their continued corrupt practices angered Indonesian society.

The specter of rising poverty and looming starvation among the population was a great blow to a regime that had prided itself on its achievements in economic development and poverty alleviation. Indeed, Suharto had allowed himself to be called *bapak pembangunan*, or father of development. Corruption on the part of the Suharto family had been tolerated because the regime was effectively causing the economy to grow at the long-term rate of 7 percent a year. With the economy in a tailspin, the New Order regime had no means by which to legitimate its continued rule. Its reliance on corruption, collusion, and nepotism became known in Indonesian as KKN (*korupsi, kolusi dan nepotisme*), and this became the rallying cry for regime opponents.

Indonesia's *Krispol*

Indonesia's monetary crisis soon became a political crisis, or *krispol*, for Suharto's New Order regime. Indonesia's decision to turn to the International Monetary Fund for emergency funding briefly reassured the markets, but Indonesians had mixed reactions to the prospect of IMF assistance. On the one hand, some recognized the Fund as the only source of leverage to reform their regime because they viewed themselves as powerless in confronting the New Order government on their own. Many student leaders were pleased with the conditions put forth in the IMF agreement, particularly those calling for dismantling state monopolies and curtailing the business interests of the Suharto children. On the other hand, many other Indonesians felt that the conditions of restructuring, especially the tight monetary policy imposed by the agreement, compromised Indonesia's sovereignty. Dependence on foreign aid was already a source of embarrassment for many Indonesians and was denounced by some as a form of neocolonialism. This negative view of Indonesian dependence on foreign aid was epitomized by a photo of the managing director of the Fund, Michel Camdessus, during the signing of the IMF agreement. While the film footage shows Camdessus standing awkwardly, not knowing what to do with his arms, the photo that dominated the Indonesian press was Camdessus with his arms folded in a haughty, disdainful manner, hovering over Suharto as he signed the agreement.[20]

Suharto himself now became a factor. He was seventy-six years old and his wife had already passed away. News of his ill health in December 1997 had sent the stock market and rupiah plummeting. With word circulating that he would insist on running in 1998 for another five-year term as president, some wondered whether he had lost sight of his own mortality.

On campuses throughout the archipelago, students began staging large demonstrations in January 1998. They served as spokespersons for others in Indonesia's diverse society, translating economic frustrations into political demands. Slogans such as *Turunkan Harga*, or "Bring prices down," became *Turunkan Suharto*, or "Bring Suharto down." Even though most Indonesians had no personal recollection of an Indonesia not ruled by Suharto, some began to imagine an Indonesia without him. At the end of February, student protestors at Gadjah Mada University in Central Java burned Suharto in effigy—an act that would have been inconceivable even a few weeks earlier. Professors—including Amien Rais, who was already the head of the large Muslim organization Muhammadiyah, and who was to become the first post-Suharto head of the legislative body MPR—joined student protests on campus. The military accommodated the students' political protests on the condition that they remain on their campuses. Young political leaders not affiliated with universities were meanwhile being "disappeared" and tortured, many believed, by members of Indonesian Special Forces under the command of Lieutenant General Prabowo Subianto, a son-in-law of Suharto. The students managed not only to sustain their momentum, but also to weld their scattered protests into a nationwide movement for change.

As expected, but to the utter dismay of many New Order opponents, Suharto was reelected at the March 1998 meeting of the People's Consultative Assembly, whose members were all chosen or cleared by him. After his reelection and the election of B. J. Habibie as vice president, Suharto's announcement of his new cabinet was another blow to his credibility. Prominent in the lineup were his daughter Tutut as minister of social affairs, a new cabinet position, and his golfing partner and timber magnate Bob Hasan as minister of trade and industry. Suharto was no longer even paying lip service to addressing the needs of the nation. He appeared to be in retreat, surrounding himself with people he knew were loyal to him. In doing so, he was engaging in the very practices that people were protesting.

From Protests to Riots

Suharto's reelection, instead of disheartening student protestors, only seemed to increase their determination to reform the Indonesian polity. They reconsidered their strategies, their tactics, and most importantly their vision for Indonesia in a post-Suharto era. In the early weeks of this new term, calls for reform were so widespread that Suharto acquiesced in plans for a discussion of political reform, although he said that no changes would be implemented until the completion of his new term in the year 2003. This was an early indication that the situation was beginning to spin out of his control. Just two months later, he was ready to accept immediate reforms in what would prove a final and fruitless attempt to maintain his grip on power.

Before the students and the new opposition groupings that were forming could coalesce around a common strategy, late in the afternoon on May 4, 1998, the Indonesian government unexpectedly announced that fuel and electricity prices would increase up to 70 percent, effective at midnight that same day. The surprise announcement threw the nation into a frenzy. Student protests spilled from the campuses onto the streets, once again confronting a menacing military. The shooting and killing of four students at the elite Trisakti University in Jakarta stunned the nation.

The protests erupted into riots with widespread property damage and the deaths of some 1,000 people in Jakarta alone. Faced with seemingly insurmountable economic and political troubles, Indonesian society found an outlet for its mounting anger by lashing out at members of the Chinese Indonesian minority. Those Chinese Indonesians who could afford to do so fled the country, their departure aggravating the already difficult economic situation by adding to capital flight. From fiscal year 1996–1997 to fiscal year 1997–1998, private capital in Indonesia's capital account dropped from US$13.5 billion to negative US$11.8 billion.[21] Most Chinese Indonesians remained behind, however, because they were shop owners and not wealthy enough to escape abroad. They were left to face the wrath of the mobs roving the streets. Their shops and homes were burned, their inventories were looted, their churches were destroyed, many women were raped, and many families were ostracized by their non-Chinese neighbors.[22]

Indonesia's *Kristal*

These economic and political crises culminated in a total crisis or *krisis total*, hence *kristal*, for the New Order regime. Following the riots, over the period of a week, Suharto consulted with a stream of visitors to his home, steadily increasing the concessions he offered to stanch the flow of supporters away from him, but leading only to a continual heightening of the pressure that he resign. The rector and deans of the University of Indonesia politely conveyed the message on behalf of their students that he should step down. Harmoko, a longtime loyalist, and at this point the chairman of both the DPR and the MPR—his home in Central Java having been burned to the ground by rioters and the parliament building by now under siege by students—appeared on television, called for Suharto to resign, and then set a deadline for the end of the week, after which impeachment proceedings would begin. Army leaders evidently readied themselves for a transition. A delegation of Muslim leaders, selected by Suharto himself, including representatives of NU and Muhammadiyah, surprised him by adding to the chorus counseling resignation. A massive student demonstration at the National Monument, to be led by Amien Rais, was called off only at the eleventh hour for fear of bloodshed. Suharto's three former vice presidents all urged him to turn the government over to Vice President B. J. Habibie. A last-ditch effort to recruit a new cabinet to carry out reforms failed; only three out of forty-five people contacted were willing to serve. On receiving this news on the night of May 20, Suharto told General

Wiranto, who was serving as the armed forces chief and defense minister, and a few aides that he would resign the following morning. Wiranto almost certainly made the promise privately that night that he made publicly the next morning: the armed forces would protect Suharto's person and his honor. On May 21, 1998, in a brief palace ceremony, Suharto resigned and Vice President B. J. Habibie was sworn in as Indonesia's third head of state.

Suharto had fallen from power for many reasons: he had held on to the presidency too long; the financial crisis had destroyed the economic basis of his legitimacy; the IMF was unyielding in its demands; the students were too threatening to be contained without further bloodshed; military leaders were not prepared to face the public reaction that forceful intervention on the streets of the capital might lead to; a large number of civilian leaders, including educators, cabinet officials, party leaders, and religious leaders, withdrew their support rather than reaffirm it when it was sought; and Suharto himself, isolated from all but his family and few aides, steadily misjudged the seriousness of the opposition against him until the very end. It was a rapid and stunning slipping away of all the institutional supports of Suharto's authoritarian rule.

Suharto's resignation brought about the departure of the only political leader whom most Indonesians had known. He represented the Indonesian state; in many people's minds he *was* the Indonesian state. Without him, the condition of the Indonesian state soon became a matter of mounting concern. His first two successors in the presidency, serving briefly as they did, made little progress in crafting political legitimacy for the post-Suharto Indonesian state. Many Indonesians came to believe that a restoration of state authority was necessary—for the stabilization and eventual recovery of the economy, for the maintenance of Indonesia's territorial integrity, and even as a prerequisite for political reform. Two and a half years after Suharto stepped down, Thomas Friedman of the *New York Times* echoed elite Indonesian opinion when he declared during a visit to Jakarta that Indonesia was a "messy" state. He wrote:

> In messy states the old authority structure that allocated resources, enforced contracts and collected taxes . . . has been broken down but has not been replaced by a new authority that can play the same role. The result, in Indonesia and Russia, is rampant corruption and a fragmentation of power in which neither the army, the Parliament, the executive nor the remnants of the old order have the strength to assert their will. Messy states: too big to fail; too messy to work.[23]

The fragmentation of power resulting from the dissolution of the old authority structure was indicative of Suharto's style of rule. Suharto had relied

on a strategy of division and fragmentation. He divided the state from the society, the military from civilians, and the bureaucracy from the legislature.
The linkages between institutions required for governing beyond his rule
were not in place. In fact, the institutions that made the New Order "work"
were precisely the ones that brought about its end. The extremely centralized
executive power, matched by weakness in every other part of the political
system, created economic benefits for the few, oppressed the political participation of the many, and sustained itself with the support of an accommodating army. The New Order state simply overpowered an underdeveloped civil
society. The fall of Suharto finally revealed the unsustainable nature of the
entire political system.

The collapse of a stable authoritarian government is not necessarily a slip-
pery slope to total anarchy, but it also does not mean a transition to democracy. The end of the Suharto regime indicated that Indonesia was in transition
from an authoritarian era, but whether it would make a transition to democracy was an open question.

REFORMASI IMPLEMENTED

Since the multiple crises of 1998, Indonesians have had the opportunity to begin to shape and reshape the political institutions that govern their lives. The
reformasi movement that emerged during the crisis period has continued to
be a force for political change. To many it has been an unsettling experience.
The dismantling of New Order institutions and their evolution in democratic
directions have exposed the society to an unfamiliar lack of predictability
about the future.

Yet the transition from Suharto was relatively nonviolent, compared with
the apocalyptic scenarios that many had expected and with respect to the actual number of deaths. Without discounting the trauma of the orchestrated attack on the Chinese Indonesian community, no one had predicted that the
New Order regime would come to such an abrupt and relatively peaceful end.
More surprisingly, the rapid removal of the veneer of political stability and
the unraveling of the regime of fear revealed a more mature opposition and a
greater readiness for contestation than had been expected.

The question on many people's minds was whether it was possible for Indonesia to become a democracy. Suharto was obviously the principal impediment to political liberalization, and his departure was essential to change.
But could his resignation be regarded as sufficient for the democratization of
Indonesia? Many doubted it. Immediately following his resignation, many assumed that he would continue to manipulate politics from behind the scenes.

Others feared that another authoritarian leader would emerge from the power vacuum left by his resignation.

The abrupt end of the Suharto presidency put Indonesia under the untested leadership of his vice president, B. J. Habibie. From the very beginning, Habibie was faced with many challenges. The economic crisis had to be stemmed. Students pressed for curbing corruption, collusion, and nepotism (the KKN mantra). Opponents to the new regime loudly demanded electoral reforms. Through the early months of the Habibie presidency, street protests persisted, the tough conditions of foreign aid did not abate, and calls for a transition to a truly new regime continued. Governing Indonesia under such conditions would have been difficult for anyone, but Habibie's narrow support base made him particularly ill-suited for the task. And yet his presidency made significant contributions to the prospects for democratization in Indonesia.

To the surprise of many observers, Habibie quickly and quietly shed his image as a holdover from the authoritarian New Order regime. He wanted his presidency, he said, to be known as the Reform Order, and in fact he oversaw some important reforms. Habibie even had the gloss of a democrat: releasing political prisoners such as the labor leader Mochtar Pakpahan and the youth activist Budiman Sudjatmiko, ending press censorship, tolerating the birth of new political parties, showing flexibility on the issue of East Timor, and overseeing the partial withdrawal of troops from East Timor and other troubled provinces such as Aceh and Papua (then known as Irian Jaya).

Changes were evident, but so were the continuities with Indonesia's authoritarian past. Especially damaging was the financial scandal the press called Baligate—the transfer of funds from Bank Bali, which was under special government supervision, to an account connected with figures closely associated with Habibie's political plans for the future. His presidency lasted seventeen months to October 1999; it might have been terminated even earlier, had it not been necessary to redesign the electoral process. But to the disappointment and surprise of many, Habibie's successor, Abdurrahman Wahid, severely damaged his reputation as a democratic intellectual and popular leader, and was reduced to struggling to sustain his hold on the presidency. Wahid managed to extend his presidency for only twenty months, before giving it up in July 2001 to Megawati Sukarnoputri, his vice president and the daughter of Sukarno, who, it was hoped, would last at least until the next scheduled elections in 2004.

The enduring elements and the evolving aspects of Indonesia's political institutions under these three successor presidencies are by now evident. One might ask, Do Indonesian political institutions today display more continuity with its authoritarian past, or more change to a potentially democratic future?

What forces are fueling the dynamics of the situation? And what issues promise to be significant for the future?

The following discussion provides a dissection of the institutional anatomy of Indonesian politics in order to begin to clarify these questions. I will examine several political institutions: the electoral process, the legislature, the judiciary, civil society, local government, and the military. These are not necessarily separate and distinct political arenas, but they will be dealt with separately for the purpose of analysis.

THE ELECTORAL PROCESS

Arguably the political institution that evolved the furthest during Habibie's presidency was the electoral process. Habibie himself was notable for his absence from the principal deliberations. The players who orchestrated these early changes were the members of the Tim Tujuh, or Team of Seven, headed by Ryaas Rasyid, who was director general of general administration and regional autonomy in the Ministry of the Interior. This group of political technocrats devised new laws regarding the formal institutions of democracy, namely, the eligibility of political parties, the rules of the electoral process, and the composition of representative legislative bodies. In November 1998, Parliamentary Decision no. XIV/1998 outlined what was envisioned. It declared that "elections should be conducted in a free and fair manner; the National Elections Commission shall be independent and consist of representatives from parties that are eligible to run in the elections plus representatives from the government; a nonpartisan agency will carry out election monitoring; independent organizations from civil society may also observe."[24] This parliamentary decision set in motion what was to be the biggest expression of popular opinion in the history of Indonesia.

The June 1999 parliamentary elections made several important breaks from the past with regard to political parties, the administration of the election itself, and the composition of the national and regional assemblies. Creating a truly multiparty system was the goal of the first law. Political parties were no longer required to have *pancasila* as their sole philosophical basis, although their platforms could not conflict with these five principles. It also became relatively easy to form a political party, requiring signatures of only fifty citizens who were at least twenty-one years old, as well as registration at a court of the Ministry of Justice. Eligibility to compete in elections, however, required the fulfillment of additional requirements. Political parties had to have some kind of local organization (*pengurus*) in one-third or nine of Indonesia's then twenty-seven provinces as well as in half of the districts in each of those provinces.[25]

To participate in future elections, political parties would have to obtain at least either 2 percent of the seats in the DPR or 3 percent of the seats in the regional legislatures in at least half of the provinces and half of the districts in those provinces in the June 1999 elections. Party activities were permitted all the way down to the village level, encouraging greater integration of societal interests into the electoral process and greater political interaction between voters and their potential legislators. An unprecedented forty-eight political parties became eligible to compete, including the Democratic People's Party, whose leader, Budiman Sudjatmiko, had been a political prisoner during the Suharto regime. This was a dramatic change in the number of political parties that were permitted in the elections during the New Order regime, and in the variety of the ideologies they represented.

Representatives of all forty-eight political parties, together with five government representatives, became the members of a newly independent General Elections Commission. The commission took over the responsibilities of the General Elections Institute, which had been a government-run authority. The commission had many important responsibilities related to planning and implementing the elections, including: ruling on the eligibility of political parties; establishing the National Election Committee and coordinating its activities at all levels; determining the number of seats in the national parliament, provincial parliaments, and district parliaments; collecting and processing the election results; and revising the electoral system.[26]

Political campaigning marked another significant break from elections under New Order rules. Rather than the stiff and predictable "festivals of democracy" of past decades, the campaign period became a truly popular celebration of political participation. In Jakarta, the traffic circle in front of Hotel Indonesia became the focus of most of the campaigning. Since it lies at the heart of Jakarta's traffic flow, the congestion there reached nightmare proportions. But no one seemed to mind; there was a sense that this was a transformative moment for Indonesia. Each political party was assigned days for campaigning. Party paraphernalia were widely available, and party supporters colored the entire city with their party's colors on their campaign days: red for the Indonesia Democratic Party of Struggle (PDI-P), green for the Development Unity Party (PPP), blue for the National Mandate Party (PAN), and so on. PDI-P became a model of popular support; in towns throughout Bali, villages pooled money to buy the red party paraphernalia to decorate their streets and buildings. For obvious reasons, the yellow days of the incumbent Golkar were rather subdued. Even so, Golkar tried to get into the new spirit by renaming itself Golkar Baru or New Golkar. But a large banner at the Hotel Indonesia traffic circle summed up the ambiguity of its transformation. It read: *Golkar Baru Cinta Indonesia*. This slogan could mean either "the New

Golkar loves Indonesia" or critics suggested, "Golkar has just started loving Indonesia," implying that it hadn't before.

In another break from the past, public servants were no longer required to vote for the government's pseudo-party, Golkar. Although they were not allowed to join a political party, they could vote as they pleased. Moreover, if they were interested in participating in party activities, they could take a leave of absence with pay. To reinforce the new rule of public service neutrality, election day became a public holiday so that everyone could vote in their own home neighborhoods and not at their place of work, thus releasing workers from the watchful eyes of their bosses.

Several measures were taken to combat the fraudulent voting practices of the New Order years. There was an active process of voter registration. On election day, special ink was put on voters' fingers to ensure that each voter cast only one ballot. All forty-eight political parties were permitted to send a representative to each of the polling stations to monitor the preparation, voting, and vote counting. Both domestic monitoring and international observation became fully integrated components of the process. The Indonesian election monitoring organizations (EMOs) were the Independent Election Monitoring Committee, the University Network for a Free and Fair Election, the Rectors Forum, the Societal Network for Election Monitoring, and the All-Indonesia Labor Union (SBSI). International observers did not have the same reach as the Indonesian EMOs, but they provided an important supplemental presence. International teams included one from the Australian Council for Overseas Aid, a regional team from the European Union, a Japanese governmental delegation, and a team from the United States formed jointly by the National Democratic Institute and the Carter Center.[27] Finally, the actual vote tabulation was open not only to monitors and observers, but also to ordinary citizens. The transparency of the process was impressive. The ballots were opened publicly at each and every polling station throughout the country in the first stage of an elaborate tabulation process. These results were validated by a parallel tabulation system administered by the Indonesian EMOs.

Election Results

Ultimately most Indonesian citizens cast their votes for non-Golkar parties. Megawati Sukarnoputri's PDI-P won a plurality with 33.7 percent of all votes cast; Golkar was in second place with 22.4 percent; Abdurrahman Wahid's Nation's Revival Party (PKB) came in third with 12.6 percent; the merged Islamic party from the Suharto days (PPP) attracted 10.7 percent; and Amien Rais's PAN finished fifth with 7.12 percent, the highest finish of a new political party.[28] The remaining forty-three parties captured the remaining 9 percent of the vote, making it impossible for most to qualify to compete in the next general elections.

The Indonesians had written their own new political and electoral laws, but assistance from the international community helped them to implement the new laws and administer the June 1999 elections. Without the logistical and technical assistance coordinated through the United Nations Development Program (UNDP), it is unlikely that the elections would have run as smoothly as they did. The numbers were truly staggering. This UNDP description of the Indonesian elections puts it succinctly: "No other country has had an election on the same scale as Indonesia. With 17,000 islands, 120 million voters, three concurrent elections, 48 parties, over 320,000 polling stations, over 600,000 national monitors, 600 international monitors, and thousands of local and international media representatives, the 1999 election was in a class of its own."[29] Not only were the numbers startling, but also the speed with which the technical assistance program was pulled together to support the elections was very impressive.

The June 1999 elections were an important first step in the evolution of Indonesia's political institutions, but they left unresolved the manner of electing the president. The MPR agreed, at a meeting in November 2001, that the president and vice president should be elected directly. But how to deal with the lack of a clear majority in the first round was not agreed on. A second round was virtually ensured by the likely number of contending parties. The larger political parties, however, wanted the MPR to retain the right to select the president and vice president in a second round of voting so that the leaders of these parties could continue to hold the presidency and vice presidency in their own hands, putting them in a position to negotiate terms with the leading candidates.

An opinion survey in May 2002 found that 74 percent of prospective voters preferred direct election of the president and vice president, and 55 percent supported direct election in a second round if one were needed; only 28 percent thought the MPR should select them in a second round.[30] This evidence of popular support for direct elections began to make an impression on the major parties. Golkar, PPP, and PKB spoke out in support of direct elections in a second round. Megawati demurred. She said direct elections should be deferred to 2009 because Indonesians were not ready for them, citing clashes among demonstrators as evidence of "immaturity."[31] But members of the legislature evidently were not willing to suggest in public that they thought the population was too immature to vote. In August 2002, the MPR resolved the matter in a consensus agreement that provided for direct presidential elections in the 2004 elections.

Further Electoral Reform

The Indonesian voter now faced a much more complex electoral process. The voting in April 2004 resembled the June 1999 parliamentary elections with contests at the national, provincial, and district levels, but with only half the number of political parties. In these elections, the political parties were required to switch from a closed list to an open proportional list, so rather than voting only for a political party, voters were able to vote for a particular candidate within a political party.

Political party eligibility arose as an issue because more than 230 political parties registered for the 2004 elections, threatening a logistical nightmare.[32] Some politicians, especially those whose parties were already qualified to compete, argued that these restraints were necessary to make an orderly electoral process possible. Other politicians, and some observers, countered that disqualifying smaller, nascent parties was not only undemocratic but also gave an unfair advantage to larger parties that were, after all, remnants of the New Order.[33] The critics were undoubtedly right, but creating new political parties that had some scale to them, so as to help build broader coalitions, seemed beyond the power of the legal process. Indonesian voters had little faith in the political parties. In a poll conducted by the Institute for Economic and Social Research, Education, and Information (LP3ES), 64 percent of the respondents said that the existing parties would not live up to their aspirations.[34]

To begin the process of reducing the number of parties to a manageable number, several layers of vetting have been put into place. In order to qualify for a license from the Ministry of Justice, a political party needed to have branches in half the provinces, and then branches in half of the districts in those provinces. Moreover, according to another law, in order to be eligible to compete in elections, a political party was required to have an executive board in at least two-thirds of the provinces, in at least two-thirds of the districts in those provinces, and 1,000 members in each of those districts. Finally, a general elections law also would require a political party either to win at least 3 percent of the DPR seats and 4 percent of the seats in the DPRDs (local legislatures) in at least one-half of the provinces and one-half of the districts in the 2004 elections, or form a coalition with other parties in order to be eligible to compete in subsequent elections.[35]

These measures, however, did not reduce the number of political parties competing in the 2004 elections to a level desired by the Indonesian public: 28 percent of respondents in the LP3ES survey felt that six to ten eligible parties would be ideal, and 55 percent believed that the electoral competition should be limited even further to fewer than six eligible parties. Instead, twenty-four political parties were deemed eligible to compete in the 2004 elections. Such voter opinion reflected a reasonable concern that the newly constituted legislature should be functional as well as representative.

A more innovative reform of the electoral process was evident in the first direct presidential election via a majoritarian two-round system (TRS). In the first round of the new direct presidential elections on July 5, 2004, voters cast their votes for the "candidate pairs" (president and vice president together on a ticket) of qualifying parties. A political party was qualified to submit such a ticket if it had won at least 5 percent of all the votes cast for the DPR in the April parliamentary elections or at least 3 percent of the DPR seats. In order for a ticket to win in the first round, it needed to receive a majority of all the votes, as well as at least 20 percent of all the votes in at least half the country's provinces. Predictably, no candidate pair won a majority, therefore a second round, or runoff election, was held between the top two finishers, the incumbent president Megawati and the retired general Susilo Bambang Yudhoyono, on September 20.

Other measures for electoral reform that had been left unresolved in the 1999 elections were dealt with in time for these 2004 elections.[36] To ensure the independence of the General Elections Committee (KPU), all of its members were permanent and nonpartisan. Also, the newly created Constitutional Court was responsible for adjudicating the dissolution of a political party as well as hearing disputes regarding electoral results. Combating corrupt practices in campaign funding, however, remains a challenge for the political system. The passage of political laws and constitutional amendments was a first step in addressing these issues, and some were effectively implemented in the 2004 elections. But further reforms, particularly in campaign financing as well as in certain geographic areas, are necessary for achieving the democratic vision of the *reformasi* movement.

Thus the pace of reform of the electoral process and party laws initiated during the Habibie presidency slowed significantly with each successive presidency, until the very end of Megawati's presidency. Party leaders of every stripe sought refuge in the old way of doing things, which was deal making in secret. Even though the 1999 parliamentary elections were heralded as the freest, most democratic elections since 1955, the euphoria among Indonesian voters evaporated quickly. However, their disillusionment with the political parties did not lead to voter apathy in any of the successive rounds of the 2004 elections, which would have been a major setback to Indonesia's *reformasi* process.

More troubling for the possibility of ongoing political reforms was the astonishing victory of Golkar in the 2004 parliamentary elections. Golkar recaptured first place with 21.6 percent of the vote, PDI-P moved into second place with 18.5 percent. PKB attracted 10.57 percent for third place, PPP, 8.15 percent for fourth place, and PAN, only 6.44 percent, trailing in seventh place. Golkar's win, however, was not the result of its own rising star, but rather the public's disillusionment with PDI-P. Golkar's support base remained relatively stable from the first post-Suharto election to this more recent one, but PDI-P's support dropped from nearly 34 percent to almost half that. Because of the strong identification of political parties with their leaders, PDI-P suffered from the disillusionment with Megawati's performance as president. By the same token, a new political party, Partai Democratik (PD), rose with Susilo Bambang Yudhoyono, who went on to win the presidential ticket over Megawati with 61 percent of the popular vote in the second round of voting.

THE LEGISLATURE

The June 1999 elections brought into the parliament a population of newly elected legislators who, given their route to power, were bound to change the nature of relations with the presidential office. On one level, basic changes were written into law and immediately implemented that gave the legislature greatly expanded powers vis-à-vis the executive branch. What have been more difficult to evaluate are the more subtle ways in which the relationship continues to evolve in practice. The power balance at any point in time depends in part on the particular person who is serving as president. But a process of institutionalization is taking place, and the weight of the legislature in the relationship continues to increase significantly.

During Habibie's sixteen-month presidency, the legislature passed fifty bills into law. One of the most visible in its outcome was the January 1999 law that revised the composition of the People's Representative Council (DPR) and the People's Consultative Assembly (MPR). Beginning with the June 1999 elections, a total of 462 of the 500 DPR seats were determined through proportional voting. The remaining thirty-eight seats, reduced from seventy-five seats, were reserved for the Indonesian military, with the understanding that these would eventually be eliminated altogether. The number of seats in the MPR was reduced from 1,000 to 700, of which 500 were still filled by the 500 members of the DPR, and the number of exclusively MPR members was reduced from 500 to only 200. Of these 200 exclusively MPR members, 135 were regional representatives (*utusan daerah*), made up of five representatives from each of the (then) twenty-seven provinces. The remaining sixty-five were group representatives (*utusan golongan*), selected by the newly elected DPR members based on their determination of the societal groups that were not sufficiently represented, a holdover from Suharto's corporatist political structure. For the 1999–2004 MPR, these groups and their number were religious (20), economic (9), academics and intellectuals (9), women (5), ethnic minorities (5), civil servants (5), youth, students, and NGOs (5), and the handicapped (2).

Following the parliamentary elections, the MPR was called into session in October 1999 to select Indonesia's new president and vice president. PDI-P and its leader, Megawati Sukarnoputri, obviously enjoyed the greatest popular support, but she and her close associates proved to be incompetent at building coalitions with the leaders of other political parties. As a result, she was not able to garner enough votes to capture the presidency in the vote in the MPR. Instead, Abdurrahman Wahid became president, and Megawati's consolation prize was the vice presidency. It is important to note that Wahid was not an elected member of the DPR, but an appointed member of the MPR through the corporatist *utusan golongan* because he was the head of Indonesia's largest Muslim organization, the Nahdlatul Ulama (NU). Through clever coalition building and backroom maneuvering, he had managed to capture the presidency from Megawati. Many reformers were not as critical of this process as they might have been because they were concerned that Megawati, given her strong nationalist orientation, would rely heavily on the military to keep the country together.

Decline of the Presidency

The brief presidency of Abdurrahman Wahid illustrates how far the presidency had declined since the end of the New Order and how much political power had shifted laterally from that office to the legislature. Both legislative bodies were given new powers that marked their evolution away from their institutional past as rubber stamps. The DPR could now demand information from the president, conduct investigations, initiate legislation, and determine its own budget. In the standoff between the DPR lawmakers and an embattled President Wahid, the power balance shifted sharply from the presidency to the legislature. Wahid's experience as a wily opponent of the New Order regime did not sufficiently prepare him to be president of a country with such a variety of urgent needs. The fact that he was legally blind and had recently suffered two strokes made his already challenging position nearly impossible. The DPR first censured him for his poor performance and sought a compromise by reducing his presidential powers. By presidential decree Wahid delegated some responsibilities to Vice President Megawati. But the gesture proved to be more symbolic than substantive, and Megawati appeared to lack the initiative to take full advantage of the presidential decree.

Not only did the DPR begin to flex its muscles vis-à-vis the president, but the MPR also stepped in to curb presidential powers. The assembly demanded an accountability speech from Gus Dur at the end of April 2001, but Wahid refused to oblige, arguing that it was unconstitutional for the MPR to make such a demand. If he had given the speech and the MPR rejected it, that would amount to a no-confidence vote, something that was not conceivable during the New Order years. In a desperate attempt to save his presidency, Wahid threatened to declare martial law on Friday, July 20, 2001, thereby dissolving parliament and preventing it from censuring him. But the Indonesian military refused to accept such a Wahid decree, asserting that it was unconstitutional. His actions prompted the DPR to call a special session of the MPR. Wahid then reacted by demanding that the military faction not attend because constitutionally the MPR required the presence of all factions. However, the MPR session was convened on July 23 with the military faction in attendance. With nearly all members of his own political party, the PKB, boycotting the special session of the MPR, Abdurrahman Wahid was voted out of office almost unanimously. Although just about everyone was playing by the rules of the game, the rules were ambiguous, and in many particulars they permitted interpretations that were anything but democratic.

Ultimately Gus Dur was ousted from his presidency prematurely because his base of support proved too small, because his personal resources were insufficient to make up for this, and because he had been linked to corruption surrounding the Bulogate scandal (see below). While Habibie was perceived to be too close to the Suharto regime and not effective in combating corruption and other New Order ills, arguably one of the reasons for Wahid's inability to make more progress was that he was too removed from the old New Order, and was therefore not powerful enough to bring about the desired but painful changes. In particular, his lack of support from the military caused many Indonesians to accept Megawati's rise to the presidency as necessary for political and economic stability.

The first year of Megawati's presidency slowed the pace of evolution of the legislature considerably, and made one of the enduring features of the Suharto era increasingly apparent. During Habibie's presidency, fifty bills were passed, whereas during Megawati's first year, only five were passed. In its session from January 7 to March 28, 2002, the DPR passed only three of its twenty-four targeted bills, and in its session from May 13 to July 19, 2002, passed only two, one on copyrights and a second on science and technology. DPR members cited a lack of adequate funds for the costs of deliberations, including their own salaries.[37] Clearly the institutional resources available to members of the legislature were another impediment to the Indonesian state's effectively representing the interests of the people who elected them.

Further Legislature Reform

Nevertheless, both the August 2002 meeting of the MPR and the final days of the DPR session in November 2002 brought about significant changes. Chastened by the popular dissatisfaction with politics and politicians, the MPR took the unusual step of reinventing itself. Appointed seats for representatives of underrepresented groups in society were abolished. Appointed seats for the armed forces, which had been overrepresented in the political system, were also abolished. Instead, the MPR would be entirely elected through its two constitutive legislative bodies, the DPR and a new Council of Provincial Representatives (Dewan Perwakilan Daerah, or DPD), or so-called Senate. For the DPD, each province would elect four representatives, all of whom were to have no political party affiliation.[38] The DPD would propose, discuss, and monitor any law relating to regional autonomy, or center-region relations more broadly construed, and make recommendations to the DPR on these issues.

Shorn of its power to elect the president and demand presidential accountability, the new MPR would be limited to approving constitutional amendments. A source of powerful leverage over the presidency was being replaced by a system of potentially more credible representation. The legislature was in transition, untested, unpredictable, but moving in a broadly reformist direction.

THE JUDICIARY

Another New Order institution that began to evolve following Suharto's resignation, but much more gradually than those so far surveyed, was the judiciary. Of course a judiciary is less susceptible to societal input than representative institutions such as political parties and legislatures, so a slower pace of reform was to be expected. Perhaps the two most prominent sorts of political issues in post-Suharto Indonesia that challenged the judicial system were human rights abuses and corruption. The New Order judiciary proved to be so well entrenched that very little appeared to change in its affairs during the Habibie and Wahid presidencies. Only by the time Megawati was president did earlier societal pressures come to fruition in a few high-profile cases.

The end of the Suharto regime brought about a significant diminution of human rights abuses perpetrated or condoned by the state. Disappearances or unlawful detentions of student and labor activists were now almost unheard of in Java. But in parts of the country where secessionist movements were a threat to the nation's physical integrity, disappearances and violence continued unabated. Moreover, investigations and prosecutions of past human rights violations were making little headway. During the Habibie presidency, the National Human Rights Commission, a government-sponsored body, established a special inquiry into charges of human rights crimes committed in East Timor following the U.N.-administered ballot. In a report released in January 2000, the inquiry team reported its findings of violations, including the names of thirty-two Indonesian officials, military men, and militia leaders it found responsible. A year later eighteen were indicted, most of them junior military officers, and in March 2002 the first trials began. The outcomes were extremely disappointing to U.N. and other observers. A former civilian governor of East Timor was found guilty and sentenced to three years. Another year later, of the sixteen completed cases, eleven were acquitted. Brigadier General Noer Muis, a former military chief in East Timor, was sentenced to five years in prison for failing to prevent the violence committed by pro-Indonesia militias but remained free pending an appeal. The pressure for the trials had been almost entirely international in origin; almost none was generated by Indonesian civil society.

This history was repeated during the Wahid presidency. The National Human Rights Commission established two more special inquiries, one into the violence in Aceh and the other into (then) Irian Jaya. These cases led to still less official action. The three taken together indicate that there is little interest in possible human rights violations committed by the Indonesian armed forces in remote areas of the archipelago threatening to secede. Moreover, human rights cases that have been the object of significant domestic interest but little international attention, such as the killings of the Trisakti students and the Tanjung Priok killings from the Suharto era, have made limited or no progress. Having international scrutiny as a critical variable does not indicate either a healthy judicial system or much promise for fundamental reform.

Charges of Corruption

The handling of cases involving charges of corruption, collusion, and nepotism has been somewhat better, but only relatively so. Despite the advances in political laws made during Habibie's presidency, he did not effectively address issues of KKN. For many Indonesians, Habibie himself symbolized New Order KKN because of the extraordinary treatment of his favorite projects, such as the IPTN aircraft enterprise, which was heavily subsidized. Nevertheless, the political liberalization that characterized his presidency did make possible the emergence of new NGOs responsive to the new situation, such as Indonesia Corruption Watch, which became a prominent domestic critic of questionable official behavior.

The progress made during the Wahid presidency was only relative. The most prominent case saw the trial and imprisonment of Suharto confidant and timber tycoon Bob Hasan on charges of misuse of government forestry funds. But not all government initiatives were successful. An attempt was made to prosecute Ginandjar Kartasasmita, former coordinating minister for the economy, finance, and industry, on charges of corruption. While undergoing investigation, Ginandjar was detained until he conveniently became ill. With the rise in the number of investigations, interrogations, and indictments, people joked that suddenly everybody in Jakarta seemed to be getting sick and going to the hospital.

In the end, Wahid was greatly weakened in his role as a crusader against corruption by his own behavior and that of people close to him. Two major scandals contributed to the early end of his presidency. In one of these scandals, dubbed Bulogate by the press, Wahid's masseur, using the president's name, demanded 35 billion rupiah (about $4 million at the time) from the National Logistics Agency (Badan Urusan Logistik or Bulog), the state food monopoly. Many believed it was improbable that these funds changed hands without Wahid's knowledge. In the second scandal, known as Bruneigate, Wahid received a $2 million personal donation from the Sultan of Brunei to help people victimized by the communal violence in Aceh, but never disbursed the funds to victims. The two cases were investigated by a special committee of the DPR but not the police or the public prosecutor; evidently the parliament did not have adequate faith in the integrity of these institutions to entrust the handling of these cases to their care.

The public prosecutors finally brought a spate of high-profile cases to trial during Megawati's first year as president. The cases of DPR speaker and Golkar Party chairman Akbar Tandjung and former President Suharto's son, Hutomo (Tommy) Mandala Putra, captured by far the most national attention. Because Akbar's case again involved funds from Bulog, it was dubbed Bulogate II. Akbar was suspected of using 40 billion rupiah of Bulog funds for Golkar's campaign prior to the 1999 elections. In a bizarre twist, after Akbar had been detained by the attorney general for four days, two other suspects returned 32.5 billion rupiah to Bulog. With the return of the funds, the DPR vetoed establishing a special committee to investigate Akbar, thus protecting one of its own. The Jakarta Central District Court, however, sentenced him to three years in prison for corruption in September 2002; the High Court upheld the decision in January 2003. Nonetheless, not only did Akbar insist on not serving the sentence pending appeal to the Supreme Court, but also he refused to surrender his position as speaker of the House of Representatives.

The case against Tommy Suharto made rapid progress by comparison. Initially sentenced to jail for corruption in September 2000, Tommy was subsequently charged with paying two "hit men" to kill Supreme Court Justice

Syafiuddin Kartasasmita, who had sentenced him. In July 2002, the court found Tommy guilty in the murder case and sentenced him to fifteen years in jail. Stung by press reports of the lenient treatment Tommy received while confined in Jakarta, the government subsequently moved him to an island prison. The case did not signify that anything fundamental had occurred in the judicial system, however. Rather, Tommy was a notorious member of the former president's family, the evidence against him was strong, and the judiciary felt obliged to respond to the killing of one of its own members.

These high-profile convictions aside, according to a survey conducted by the Political and Economic Consultancy (PERC) in 2002, Indonesia was revealed to be the most corrupt economy in Asia, with the worst score of any country since the start of the survey in 1995. PERC added, "It is hard to believe that the problem of corruption in Indonesia could grow worse (since the fall of Suharto), but that is what is happening."[39] Moreover, Indonesian Corruption Watch published a report at about the same time, *Unveiling Court Mafia*, maintaining that corruption within Indonesia's judiciary was not only glaring but well organized.[40] Confirming these charges, a U.N. special rapporteur for judicial independence, Param Cumaraswamy, in a visit in mid-2002, came to the conclusion that corruption in the Indonesian legal system was "endemic."[41]

Evidence so far available thus suggests that the principal characteristics of the Indonesian judiciary of the Suharto era continue to endure. There have been few signs of evolution of the judicial system into an independent protector of human rights or into anything like an impartial and incorruptible source of the application of commercial or criminal law.

Perhaps a few possibilities for positive reform have emerged. The first is the creation of the Constitutional Court. This newly established court can, for the first time in Indonesia's history, determine the constitutionality of a law. Also, it is responsible for resolving disputes over the political authority of state institutions, as well as the responsibilities for adjudicating disputes within the electoral process, as listed above. The second harbinger of greater reform to come is President Yudhoyono's appointment of former Supreme Court judge Abdurrahman Saleh, who is perceived as incorruptible, as attorney general. A coalition of Indonesian NGOs led by Teten Masduki have vowed to support him in his crusade against the corrupt practices that pervaded the New Order regime. Finally, the current Chief Justice Bagir Manan has proposed a program of judicial reform for the next twenty-five years. Although it remains to be seen whether the plan can be effectively implemented, at the very least there exists a specific plan that was produced by a state official who conceivably has the authority to push for its implementation.

CIVIL SOCIETY

Supplementing the early lateral shifts in power away from the presidency were vertical shifts that began to open up the Indonesian political system to greater social participation. Indeed, civil society's attention to issues of economic incompetence, corruption, human rights, and justice contributed to Suharto's resignation in May 1998. How civil society institutions, such as NGOs and the mass media, have fared in successive presidencies, however, signifies that New Order institutions remain resistant to societal pressures for reform. The challenges facing the institutionalization of a vibrant, effectively incorporated civil society outnumbered the minor successes of Indonesian civil society in the early post-Suharto years.

Early in the *reformasi* phase, one significant means of civil society participation was gathering information about Indonesian politics and providing policy alternatives through nongovernmental channels. Research was conducted professionally in research institutes and by the media, and more informally on campuses, in other meeting places, and via the Internet. A renewed international interest in the Indonesian polity and economy prompted international donors to fund many research projects conducted by Indonesian institutions. Donors no longer were concerned about antagonizing the government, as they were in the Suharto era.

As ideas about specific political reforms began to emerge, it became more evident that Indonesian NGOs were a significant source and support of these new ideas. Indonesian Corruption Watch (ICW) and its head Teten Masduki kept public attention on issues of corruption, collusion, and nepotism that continued to plague Indonesian politics in the post-Suharto period. Another important example was Smita Notosusanto and her organization, the Center for Electoral Reform (CETRO); she was perhaps single-handedly responsible for promoting and pursuing to fruition the idea of direct presidential elections. These individuals and their organizations, as well as a variety of NGO coalitions, have been prominent players in the post-Suharto reforms.

During the Habibie presidency, significant liberalization measures supported the growth of Indonesian civil society, including the release of political prisoners, the relaxation of laws that had limited the freedom of association, and the passage of the 1999 press law that granted freedom from censorship for the Indonesian media. Habibie's information minister, Mohammed Yunus Yosfiah, issued more than 1,200 publication licenses, 912 radio licenses, and five television broadcast licenses.[42] Furthermore, the Indonesian Journalists Association was no longer the sole officially sanctioned association for journalists, and alternative groups, such as the Alliance for Independent Journalists and the Press Council, were increasingly seen as legitimate representatives of the profession. Habibie's willingness to engage the domestic and international press was perhaps the most obvious break with the New Order regime. While his chattiness was frequently ridiculed, it set the important precedent of communicating with the Indonesian public through the press and contributed to the sense of greater transparency in the political process.

Under President Wahid, Indonesian civil society as a whole fared well, but his record with the press was mixed. Wahid brought several civic leaders and academics into his cabinet, ensuring the incorporation of societal interests in the policymaking process. They included Marzuki Darusman as attorney general, Erna Witoelar as minister for settlement and regional development, and Mohammed A. S. Hikam, who has written extensively on Indonesian civil society, as state minister for research and technology, a position once held by Habibie. Moreover, Wahid created the position of state minister of human rights and abolished the Ministry of Information. In place of the latter he established the National Information Agency, which was limited to disseminating official information to the Indonesian public. Despite these early indications that the relationship between the Indonesian state and its society was beginning to evolve in a more democratic direction, Wahid, struggling to protect his crumbling presidency, often lashed out at the press for misquoting him and continually threatened to sue the media.[43]

The Wahid presidency was followed by rising challenges to press freedoms. In her cabinet lineup of August 2001, Megawati named Syamsul Muarif as state minister for communications and information. Syamsul's decision to house his new office in the old ministry's building countered his efforts to dismiss any similarity with the New Order institution. Furthermore, at the end of the year, he said that the government would reinstate some measures to rein in the Indonesian press. He justified this move as a response to requests by DPR members, who maintained that reporters had become *kebablasan*, or out of control.[44] One critic blasted the new broadcasting bill because, of its sixty-three articles, twenty-one were judged repressive, whereas the comparable Suharto-era law contained only eleven repressive articles.[45] Indonesian journalists admitted that problems of professionalism and ethics existed in the media, but argued that the new press bill denied them freedom of expression without effectively addressing these weaknesses.[46] Moreover, the economic and political elite displayed a growing tendency in post-Suharto years to stifle criticism in the media by bringing libel suits against the journalists and editors of prominent publications in the courts.

The Indonesian media were not only threatened by a rise in repressive government measures; they were also experiencing a decline in access to government sources. If excessive chattiness characterized Habibie's manner with the press, then an aloof silence described Megawati's. Even at the height of her popularity during the 1999 political campaign, she showed a considerable reluctance to engage the press. As president, she banned "doorstop" or impromptu press conferences for herself and Vice President Hamzah Haz.[47] An editorial in the English-language daily newspaper *Jakarta Post* concluded, "President Megawati has shown increasingly the traits of a leader who is not accommodative, if not intolerant, of the press."[48] Without ready access to elected officials and without freedom of expression, Indonesian civil society would be severely handicapped in its ability to participate as a legitimate player in the policy-making process.

REGIONAL AUTONOMY

The attempt by the Netherlands in the late 1940s to reestablish its rule in Indonesia had one lasting impact on the Indonesian political structure that remains to be considered: it proposed the creation of a federal system that would divide its former colony into separately governed parts, hoping to appeal to the leaders of smaller populations on islands other than Java and thus divide the independence movement. That Dutch attempt failed but left the Indonesian national political elite with a profound fear of centrifugal politics that remains to this day. Sukarno and the other national leaders of the time focused their efforts on devising a strong unitary state that would bring the disparate parts of the independence movement ever more closely together. Given the diversity of the society, this process of state formation or nation building was a considerable undertaking. More than half a century later, the issue of center–region relations remains one of Indonesia's most fundamental political problems.

A shift in power has nevertheless been taking place from the central government in Jakarta to local governments in cities and towns throughout the country.[49] In response to local demands for greater autonomy and economic independence, the Habibie government began a process of decentralizing a substantial share of its authority with the promulgation in 1999 of Law no. 22, which provides for the devolution of administrative authority, and Law no. 25, which provides for fiscal redistribution to the district (*kebupaten*) or city (*kota*) level. The laws were the product of a group of young political experts to whom Habibie granted exceptional authority. Known collectively as the De Kalb mafia, many members of the group had studied political science with Dwight King at Northern Illinois University in De Kalb.

While the regional autonomy program was designed to provide incentives for regional areas to remain in the republic, armed secessionist movements and the historic fear of centrifugal forces complicated the picture. Most of Indonesia's natural resources are found in areas beyond Java. If one or more of the better endowed of these areas were to secede from Indonesia, the central government would lose substantial revenues. Worse still, some feared, the whole territorial structure of the Indonesian state might begin to fragment. The political elite in the capital felt vulnerable to these local independence movements.

The Case of East Timor

Recent developments in East Timor only confirmed the fears of internal threats to national unity. From the early sixteenth century until 1975, East Timor had been a Portuguese colony, with only a brief interruption in the Portuguese rule by the Japanese occupation during World War II. In 1974, three weeks after the downfall of the Caetano regime in Lisbon, East Timor was decolonized, and nascent political associations began to appear. Driven by a fear of a communist East Timor, the Indonesian military seized the opportunity presented by the political confusion and invaded East Timor on December 7, 1975.[50] The U.N. Security Council called on Indonesia to remove its troops, and in a slight bow to international opinion, the Indonesian government staged an act of integration on May 31, 1976. In this ceremony, twenty-eight "prominent citizens of East Timor," handpicked by Indonesian intelligence officers, voted to approve integration into Indonesia. The Indonesian DPR and MPR subsequently passed bills formally annexing East Timor as Indonesia's twenty-seventh province. The Indonesian military then set up an administrative structure that was closed to all outsiders, Indonesian and foreign alike, and took responsibility for all sociopolitical and economic affairs in East Timor. The East Timorese response to Indonesian rule was the rise of armed resistance by Fretilin, and the international community, particularly the United Nations and the Catholic Church, was persistent in its campaign to defend East Timor's right to self-determination.

On January 27, 1999, President Habibie announced that Indonesia was ready to offer a special autonomy package to the East Timorese people, after a twenty-three-year military occupation. The United Nations established the U.N. Transitional Administration in East Timor in May and administered the ballot at the end of August.[51] Following the announcement that an overwhelming 78.5 percent of East Timorese voters rejected Indonesian rule, a "scorched earth" campaign erupted.[52] Pro-Indonesian militias destroyed public buildings, private homes, and other infrastructure, killed an estimated 1,000 people, and obliged as many as 400,000 people (almost half the population) to flee their homes.

At the same MPR session at which Indonesia accepted the results of the East Timorese ballot, Wahid succeeded Habibie as president. Having reluctantly watched East Timor depart from the formal fabric of the nation, Wahid supported the policy of decentralization as a potential means of keeping other regions from following East Timor's example and established a Ministry for Regional Autonomy. Moreover, during his presidency, the number of government directives regarding regional autonomy—at least twenty government decrees, thirteen presidential instructions, six ministerial decrees, as well as dozens of regional decrees—would have been impressive, had they not sometimes been mutually contradictory.[53]

That was only one sign of Jakarta's ambiguity regarding the regional autonomy plan. The principal justification for granting regional autonomy in the first place for some had been to prevent the loss of East Timor. With that possibility gone, Jakarta was less than confident that the decentralization program would head off the secession of the provinces of Aceh and (then) Irian Jaya, where armed independence movements were under way.[54] The domestic dimensions of these cases are addressed in chapter 1 and their international dimensions in chapter 5.

Measures to decentralize authority in the rest of the country proceeded amid massive confusion. Local governments overstepped their authority in all directions, levying unauthorized taxes, revoking licenses granted by the national government, and trying to take over enterprises owned jointly by foreign investors. The Megawati government indicated its intention to review the legislation and encountered a furious reaction from the regions.[55] Associations of local governments accused Jakarta of trying to recentralize political power, and the Megawati cabinet agreed to desist.

In spite of the uncertainties regarding Jakarta's long-term intentions, regional autonomy legislation has led to a considerable proliferation of sites of political authority in Indonesia. Two million government officials have been transferred from the central government rolls to those of local governments. Whereas less than 12 percent of revenues had been spent by local governments before, approximately 30–35 percent was being spent by them now with the passage and implementation of the regional autonomy program.[56]

As a practical political matter, the new relationship between the center and the regions appeared to be fundamentally irreversible. Nevertheless, decentralization falls far short of federalism; it lacks a constitutional basis. Furthermore, there was no assurance that local governments would be any more democratic in their behavior than the national government had been. On the contrary, most localities lacked mass media and NGOs with the independence to monitor their government officials effectively. The danger, and perhaps even tendency, of regional autonomy was a parallel decentralization of official corruption and criminal activity to many of these new sites of political authority.

THE MILITARY

Since the onset of the economic and political crises of the late 1990s, no political institution in Indonesia has suffered a greater crisis of legitimacy than the military. Theorists argue that civil–military reform is a critical component of democratization, but many Indonesians credit the military with a role in the founding of Indonesia and tolerate its often violent approach to quelling conflict in *daerah rawan*, or troubled areas. At the same time, the deaths of students and other civilians in Jakarta—at the elite Trisakti University on May 12, 1998; at Catholic Atmajaya University on November 13 (this event nicknamed "Semanggi I"); and during an antimilitary, anti-Habibie rally on September 18 of the following year (dubbed "Semanggi II")—was the proverbial straw that broke the camel's back. These students were the children of the urban middle class that had been created by the New Order policies and had supported the regime, albeit some wholeheartedly, others more reluctantly. These events in Jakarta, coming after years of corruption and misuse of power, caused the military's credibility to collapse in the eyes of many in the capital.

Critics argued that the *dwi-fungsi* doctrine had become the military's justification for involving itself in every aspect of running the country: politics, social control, economics, and security, both internal and external. One Indonesian opinion leader grumbled, "Unlike in most countries, the Indonesian military, with its peculiar dual function (holding both the sword and the plowshare), evolved from being the saviour to becoming the scourge of the nation."[57] Demands for military reform became routine, including demands that it withdraw from formal politics by ending its dual-function doctrine, dismantling its territorial command structure, accepting civilian control, and introducing transparency into its budget process.

During the Habibie administration, the military undertook several reforms in response to such criticism. In April 1999, the armed forces announced a "new paradigm" and, in an attempt to signal reform, changed their name from the Angkatan Bersenjata Republic Indonesia (ABRI) (Armed Forces of the Republic of Indonesia) back to their original name during the revolutionary period, Tentara Nasional Indonesia (TNI). This name was a source of pride and in a sense reclaimed their past glory. In February 1999, the law regarding the composition of the legislatures reduced the seats reserved for the military at all levels by 50 percent in the bodies to be formed by the 1999 elections.[58]

The TNI readily accepted the end of the *kekaryaan*, or secondment, system that placed military officers in civil posts; in fact, many within the armed forces were proposing this step in the interest of professionalizing the services. Another early step, taken by the military on its own initiative, was to cut its formal ties with Golkar and adopt a strictly neutral position in elections.[59] To its credit, the TNI did not intervene in the administration of the June 1999 parliamentary elections.

With Wahid in the presidency, civil–military relations experienced some dramatic developments, but drama did not translate into fundamental reform. A potentially significant change was the separation of the Indonesian police (Polisi Republik Indonesia, or POLRI) from the armed services of army, navy, and air force, ostensibly to divide responsibility for internal security and external defense between them through the MPR Decrees no. 6/2000 and no. 7/2000.[60] The international community has paid considerable attention to this division. International funding for security-building measures initially targeted police training programs, avoiding direct association with the three armed services. In spite of this international support, the division between the POLRI and TNI was not as effective as had been hoped because the TNI continued to focus on internal threats to Indonesian security.[61] Indeed, because of the overlap in jurisdiction, some of the fighting in trouble spots such as Maluku was between the police and the armed forces.[62]

In an attempt to assert some civilian control over the military and reduce the power of the army in particular, President Wahid appointed Juwono Sudarsono, a professor and former dean at the University of Indonesia, as the first civilian minister of defense since the 1950s, and Admiral Widodo Adi Sucipto as the first-ever nonarmy TNI commander.[63] About a year later, in a cabinet reshuffle, Wahid replaced Sudarsono with a constitutional law scholar, Mohammed Mahfud Mahmudin, from Gadjah Mada University. Though they were symbolic steps in a democratic direction, these appointments did not amount to any notable civilian *control* over the Indonesian military.

Meanwhile there was a continuing seesawing of policy on the military's withdrawal from formal politics. The MPR in 2000 extended the time frame for reserved seats for TNI and POLRI—in the DPR until 2004 and in the MPR until 2009. In August 2002, the MPR voted to eliminate reserved seats for the military in all the legislative bodies following the 2004 elections.[64]

The drama, in any case, was not owing to these events but to Wahid's effort to impose emergency law toward the end of his bitter struggle with the legislature for dominance. Both the police chief and the armed forces leadership refused to support Wahid's declaration of civil emergency. Retired three-star general Agus Widjojo insisted that there was a constitutional process for such a declaration, and that the military would analyze the situation and confer with Indonesia's legislators about whether such a declaration was warranted. Although this military defiance was seemingly democratic, more cynical observers pointed out that, if Wahid were forced out of office, then Vice President Megawati would automatically become president. Given Megawati's agreement with the military on many issues of governance, this would enable the military to regain some political power.

The cynics appeared to be correct. Under Megawati the armed forces regained some political power, and key democratic reforms they had opposed were rolled back. She encouraged the military to resolve the conflicts taking place around the archipelago by whatever means were at their disposal. In a speech marking Army Day 2001, Megawati called on the troops to "carry out your duties and responsibilities in the best possible manner without having to worry about human rights abuses."[65] In addition, past abuses were swept under the rug through a variety of measures. A constitutional amendment barred retroactive legislation. From a legal perspective, prohibiting retroactivity actually protects human rights, since a person's legal action cannot in the future become illegal. However, this legal measure also became a source of frustration and an impediment for those who sought to prosecute Suharto-era human rights violations. Moreover, the DPR approved a resolution on March 27, 2002, to the effect that the Trisakti, Semanggi I, and Semanggi II killings should not be classified as gross violations of human rights.[66] Coupled with the outcomes of the first East Timor trials, the Megawati administration appeared to be giving the TNI carte blanche to do as it saw fit.

Military appointments and restructuring of its command structure only reinforced this perception. Megawati agreed to the reestablishment of the Iskandar Muda Regional Military Command in Aceh, which had been eliminated in 1985, a strong indication of how far her government was prepared to go to force an end to the separatist movement there. Megawati returned the TNI leadership to the army when she appointed army chief of staff General Endriartono Sutarto to that position in May 2001. Endriartono's long association with the army strategic reserve command, which Suharto once headed, and his service as chief of the presidential guard during Suharto's final year, signaled the resurgence of military figures prominent in the New Order. Also, with Endriartono's rise to TNI chief, a military hard-liner on separatism, General Ryamizard Ryacudu, became the new army chief of staff. He categorically rejected calls for the elimination of the territorial command structure.[67] His stance dismayed critics who viewed this security structure as the central means for preserving the military's role in political and economic affairs at the local level.

Indonesia's reaction to the terrorist attacks of September 11, 2001, in the United States lent some hope for the possibility of civil–military reform in

Indonesia. While many other democratizing countries used the war on terror as a justification for rolling back critical reforms and reinstituting authoritarian measures, Indonesia, much to the frustration of the Bush administration, dragged its feet on passing an antiterrorism law. While many U.S. lawmakers perceived this delay as a lack of support and sympathy for American terror victims, many Indonesians, especially civil society leaders, were more concerned about the dangers of an antiterror law being manipulated to intimidate or even prohibit political opposition to the regime, much as the subversion law had been used during the New Order period. Following the Bali bombings, Indonesia passed a relatively weak set of government regulations to combat terrorism in October 2002, and the antiterror bill was eventually passed by the DPR in March 2003. Another promising development was the investigation by the Indonesian police of the Bali bombings. Inspector General I Made Mangku Pastika was acclaimed both domestically and internationally for his job in identifying the alleged perpetrators of the bombings. It is also noteworthy that in this instance the military respected the distinction between itself and the police.

The global war on terror has given the Indonesian military an opportunity to attempt to roll back some of the earlier 1999 reforms. On February 20, 2003, hundreds of active and retired senior army officers held a closed-door meeting at army headquarters to discuss the military's role in Indonesian security.[68] This meeting was the prelude to the public disclosure of a controversial new draft of proposed legislation based on a Department of Defense white paper entitled, Defending the Homeland at the Start of the Twenty-first Century (*Mempertahankan tanah air memasuki abad 21*). The controversy was focused on the bill's article 19, which the Indonesian press quickly dubbed the "coup d'état article" because it would allow the TNI commander to take military action and deploy troops without having to inform the president for twenty-four hours if he determined that there was any kind of threat to Indonesia's security. This provision would contravene not only the MPR decision to give responsibility for internal security to the national police but also article 14 of the national defense law, which vests the authority to use military force in the president, effectively reversing efforts to establish civilian control over the military, as well as those to limit the military's role to external security.[69] Granted, as detailed in the white paper, Indonesia was facing "nontraditional threats," such as terrorism, separatism, communal conflict, piracy, and human smuggling. But, as an editorial in the *Jakarta Post* rightly argued, these new challenges required strengthening the Indonesian police, rather than reversing the civil–military reforms that had taken place and permitting the Indonesian military to revert to their former authoritarian practices.[70]

In a more positive development for civil–military reform, Juwono Sudar-sono, before being named defense minister in Susilo Bambang Yudhoyono's United Indonesia cabinet, proposed his own plan for military reform, much along the same lines as Chief Justice Bagir Manan's twenty-five-year judicial reform document. He recommends a number of reforms, including: convert-ing all military-owned companies into state-owned enterprises and having them audited by independent auditors; strengthening the political party sys-tem and the civilian political institutions; reviewing and revamping all legis-lation "condoning halfhearted civilian control over the TNI"; revising the se-curity doctrine that governs the military; among other key reforms.[71] He argues that for too long Indonesia's military doctrine has reflected "a ten-dency in Indonesian political culture to compensate for the lack of effective ability with an excess of declaratory dogma."[72] This reform is a plan that has been created by a state official who conceivably has the authority and com-mitment to push for its effective implementation.

Despite some early promising developments, then, the role of the military in Indonesian politics and internal security continued to be the greatest obstacle to democratic reform in Indonesia. On the one hand, one might argue that the fast pace of change in civil–military relations during the Habibie and Wahid presidencies was destabilizing for the Indonesian military, and that the restora-tion of some of TNI's authority was needed to help address its crisis of legiti-macy. After all, the TNI had only 337,000 troops and a defense budget of just over $1 billion—relatively low numbers for such a large and diverse archipel-ago. On the other hand, reformist elements were alarmed at the cost of resus-citating the morale of a military that had brutalized its own society. Certainly the TNI accepted some civil–military reform, particularly in Jakarta, and in that respect it was no longer the same New Order institution.[73] However, beyond Jakarta, the military continued to rely on the same New Order values and tools, indicating that it hadn't sufficiently learned any lessons from its past mistakes.

CONTINUING EVOLUTION?

Many people in Indonesia were discussing and debating what sort of state they wanted governing their lives and how to reform the current state to achieve those goals of *reformasi*. The overwhelming power of the central ex-ecutive had been reduced by strengthening the DPR and creating the DPD, and by creating the constitutional possibility of impeaching a president. The freedom of association that was introduced by Habibie had not been chal-lenged and was leading to a proliferation of political parties. The mass media—press, radio, and television alike—were functioning as vehicles that were enabling the civil society to express its views, offering alternative policy ideas regarding issues of governance. These institutions were fragile. The parties were focused on personalities rather than on programs, and the mass media were often sources of misinformation. But they were functioning very much as was to be expected at this early stage of reform.

Looking at the major national consensus reached by the People's Consultative Assembly in August 2002, there seems to be widespread agreement about what the Indonesian people do and do not want of their state. They do not want to be governed by a small group of party leaders who can select the nation's chief executive. And they do not want a state in which any one tradition of religious thought is allowed to dominate all others. A resolution to establish *shari'a* law was withdrawn in the face of massive opposition. In short, Indonesians want a state in which there are checks and balances among institutions of strength. And they want a state in which religious pluralism is the guiding spirit.

Also visible are the principles according to which it is to be reformed. The constitution now calls for the direct election of the president and the vice president. And the lower house (the DPR) is to be joined by an upper house or Senate composed solely of representatives of the provinces of Indonesia (the DPD). Together they would form the new MPR, with the power to further amend the constitution. These provisions needed to be translated into detailed legislation, and there was concern that not all the needed work could be accomplished before the elections of 2004, and that not all points in the consensus would necessarily be honored in that process. And yet the legislative process was completed and most if not all of the major points of the consensus were honored in the 2004 elections. This all indicated a significant development in Indonesia's evolution toward a more democratic state.

There also were other signs of this evolution. The decentralization of funds and functions to provincial and local governments was holding fast, so that the gap between government and people was much reduced in many sectors of social and economic life. The electoral law reforms established a mixed system of the proportional representation used in the past (in which voters choose among parties) and the single member constituencies desired by reformers (in which voters choose among candidates).

At the same time, the positive signs were nearly matched by the endurance of institutions from the authoritarian period. Local government remained at risk of being dominated by a hundred "little Suhartos," with ties to the armed forces, paramilitaries, and criminal elements that survive from place to place. The mass media needed constitutional and political protection in order to function freely. This is not even to mention the development of habits of compromise and accommodation across ethnic and religious divisions. Perhaps more problematically, the national parties and their leaders were holdovers from the New Order era: survivors with a stake in continuity rather than new parties and leaders without the taint of complicity with the past. Golkar's first place finish in the April parliamentary elections was a stunning reflection of not only that. The winning candidate pair included the retired general Susilo Bambang Yudhoyono. Although he was using a new political party as his vehicle to the presidency, he had been part of Golkar through his long army career. His running mate, Jusuf Kalla, became head of the Suharto-era political machine Golkar in December 2003, just a few short months after becoming vice president. The rivalry between these two top state officials, as evidenced in their public dispute over tsunami relief efforts in Aceh, suggested that a Golkar-led government might not be monolithic.

Indonesia is finally addressing the issue of relations between the state and its component island parts, especially between the capital on Java and regions of the outer islands that are rich in tropical forests, fossil fuels, and precious minerals. It is probable that the devolution of power can be halted short of weakening the democratic institutions of the Indonesia state. It is possible that sufficient autonomy can be negotiated with breakaway provinces to retain the territorial integrity of the state. But these are not assured. Whether the lessons of history have been learned is still in question.

What weighs heavily on the endurance side of the balance sheet is primarily the continued absence of accountability by the armed forces for their actions. They continue to be financed principally outside the government budget and without public scrutiny. The army continues to maintain a territorial command structure that reaches into every community in the country and involves it in any political or economic matter of interest to it. The newly elected president is a retired army general, albeit one committed to political reform, as is his defense minister. Given this political structure, Indonesia still needs reforms before either its own reformists or the international community would consider it substantively democratic.

The task of removing this last obstacle to the country's political evolution must be reckoned as substantial. Financing the armed forces from the public budget would require a vastly larger budget than the one that already presents the government with sizable difficulties. Not least among the facets of the task that make it difficult is the lack of accountability for off-budget funds within the armed forces, with the result that individual officers have become extremely wealthy. The senior leadership of the Indonesian army, in particular, is a law unto itself. It is no wonder that the president needs the political support of army leaders in order to govern.

On this issue alone, the future of Indonesian politics can be said to hang in the balance. One can only speculate as to how the Indonesian military can be brought under the control of civil society. The years of corruption and abuse of power, coupled with its history of abuse in East Timor, and its ongoing violent approaches to the conflicts in Aceh and Papua, were evidently not enough. That is a grim reminder of what continues to be the dark underbelly of politics in Indonesia and will probably continue to be for some time to come.

NOTES

1. Peter Hall, *Governing the Economy: The Politics of State Intervention in Britain and France* (Oxford: Oxford University Press, 1986), 19.

2. Herbert Feith, *The Decline of Constitutional Democracy in Indonesia* (Ithaca, N.Y.: Cornell University Press, 1962), xi.

3. David Bouchier and John Legge, eds., *Democracy in Indonesia: 1950s and 1990s* (Clayton, Australia: Monash Asia Institute, Monash University, 1994).

4. Harry Benda, "Democracy in Indonesia," *Journal of Asian Studies*, March 1964, 449–56.

5. David Reeve, "The Corporatist State: The Case of Golkar," in Arief Budiman, ed., *State and Civil Society in Indonesia* (Clayton, Australia: Monash Papers on Southeast Asia, No. 22, 1990), 151–76.

6. Body for the Protection of the People's Political Rights Facing the 1992 General Election (BPHPR), translated with Introduction by Dwight Y. King, *"White Book" on the 1992 General Election in Indonesia* (Ithaca, N.Y.: Cornell Modern Indonesia Project, 1994), chap. 2.

7. Ichlasul Amal, "The Dilemmas of Decentralisation and Democratisation," in Bourchier and Legge, *Democracy*, 218.

8. The number of elected and appointed DPR members varied over the years, but the total number of DPR members remained the same. The final MPR of Suharto's presidency had 425 elected members and 75 appointed military officers.

9. R. E. Elson, *Suharto: A Political Biography* (Cambridge: Cambridge University Press, 2001), 239.

10. Philip J. Eldridge, *Non-Government Organization and Democratic Participation in Indonesia* (New York: Oxford University Press, 1995); Jan-Paul Dikse, Frans Husken, and Mario Rutten, eds., *Development and Social Welfare: Indonesia's Experiences under the New Order* (Leiden: KITLV Press, 1993); and Fred Bunnell, "Community Participation, Indigenous Ideology, Activist Politics: Indonesian NGOs in the 1990s," in Daniel S. Lev and Ruth McVey, eds., *Making Indonesia: Essays on Modern Indonesia in Honor of George McT. Kahin* (Ithaca, N.Y.: Modern Indonesia Project: Southeast Asia Program, Cornell University, 1996), 180–201.

11. "Current Data on the Indonesian Military Elite January 1, 1998–January 31, 1999," *Indonesia*, April 1999, 147.

12. "Current Data," 147.

13. For further details, see Salim Said, *Genesis of Power: General Sudirman and the Indonesian Military in Politics 1945–1949* (Singapore: Institute of Southeast Asian Studies, 1991), 137–40.

14. Agus Widjojo, "Repositioning of the Indonesian Military: A Process of Reform Necessity or a Political Issue?" in Uwe Johnson and James Gomez, eds., *Democratic Transitions in Asia* (Singapore: Selection Publishing/Friedrich Naumann Foundation, 2001), 163.

15. For a discussion of these shifts, see Doug Kammen, "Akhir 'Kedigdayaan' ABRI?" [The End of the Indonesian Military's 'Invulnerability'?] (prepared for the Twelfth INFID conference, September 14–17, 1999), 13–14.

16. Widjojo, "Repositioning," 175.

17. Benedict R. O'G. Anderson, ed., *Violence and the State in Suharto's Indonesia* (Ithaca, N.Y.: Southeast Asia Program Publications, Cornell University, 2001).

18. Hal Hill, *The Indonesian Economy since 1966: Southeast Asia's Emerging Giant* (Cambridge: Cambridge University Press, 1996), 47.

19. Jeffrey A. Winters, "Criminal Debt," in Jonathan R. Pincus and Jeffrey A. Winters, eds., *Reinventing the World Bank* (Ithaca, N.Y.: Cornell University Press, 2002), 101–30.

20. This photo is reminiscent of a photo taken of Jan Pronk when he was dressed in safari garb looking very imperialistic, just before Suharto's rejection of Dutch aid in March 1992.

21. Hal Hill, *The Indonesian Economy in Crisis: Causes, Consequences, and Lessons* (Singapore: Institute of Southeast Asia Studies, 1999), 31. This book is a highly readable analysis of the Indonesia economic crisis.

22. Because of the difficulty in recording this kind of sexual violence, the number of rapes is contested. For instance, in the case of gang rape, should it be counted as one case or multiple cases? The personal trauma and social shame of rape also makes it more unlikely that victims would speak up. These methodological challenges lead to the discrepancy of numbers, as evidenced in this chapter and Hefner's. According to Ariel Heryanto, the number of confirmed rapes is about 120. See his "Rape, Race, and Reporting" in Arief Budiman, Barbara Hatley, and Damien Kingsbury, eds., *Reformasi: Crisis and Change in Indonesia?* (Clayton, Australia: Monash Asia Institute, 1999), 299–334.

23. Thomas L. Friedman, "What a Mess!" *New York Times*, October 3, 2000.

24. UNDP Program Support Document, Technical Assistance Program for the 1999 General Elections in Indonesia, Project of the Government of Indonesia, Project no. INS/99/001/A/01/NEX, February 4, 1999, 26. Because of the fast pace with which the UNDP set up this program, some of its translations of the names of Indonesian organizations into English were inaccurate. In this case, what it termed the National Elections Commission was probably the General Election Committee.

25. At the time of the parliamentary elections, the United Nations was beginning to prepare for and administer the "political consultation" that could potentially change the sovereign status of East Timor. Nonetheless, representatives from East Timor were still included in the DPR, and therefore the number of provinces was still twenty-seven.

26. "The KPU at a Glance," *Election Update*, April 23, 1999, 2.

27. I monitored the election in Yogyakarta as a member of the New York–based Indonesian Election Watch.

28. Technically, PDI-P and PKB were also new parties, but they had historic antecedents, PDI and NU respectively, which cast them as revamped political parties.

29. "AEC: Vote Count on Schedule," *Election Update*, June 18, 1999, 1.

30. "Let the people elect their president: Survey," *Jakarta Post*, June 25, 2002. The survey was conducted by Taylor Nelson Sofres Indonesia in cooperation with the International Foundation for Electoral Systems.

31. Dean Yates, "Megawati Unsure If Indonesia Ready to Vote," Reuters, Jakarta, July 3, 2002.

32. Arya Abhiseka, "General Election to Be on April 5 Next Year: KPU," *Jakarta Post*, March 15, 2003.

33. Kurniawan Hari, "Political Draft Law Deemed Unrealistic, Unfair," *Jakarta Post*, July 8, 2002.

34. "People Distrust Political Parties: LP3ES Survey," *Jakarta Post*, June 14, 2003.

35. Berni K. Moestafa and Debbie A. Lubies, "Parties Told to Meet Tough Terms," *Jakarta Post*, December 14, 2002.

36. Annastashya Emmanuelle and Kurniawan Hari, "Loopholes in Draft Law Haunt 2004 Elections," *Jakarta Post*, May 31, 2002.

37. Fabiola Desy Unidjaja and Kurniawan Hari, "House Leaders Ask for More Funds for Passage of Bills," *Jakarta Post*, July 17, 2002; Kurniawan Hari, "Legislators Do Not Deserve More Money: Activists," *Jakarta Post*, July 18, 2002. Legislators received Rp. 12.4 million (US$1,370) a month in salary and allowances, as well as Rp. 300,000 for each hearing and Rp. 750,000 for each law passed.

38. Andrew Ellis, "Constitutional Reform and the 2004 Election Cycle," *USINDO*, October 8, 2002.

39. "Singapore, Japan, Hong Kong Judged Asia's Least Corrupt Economies," Agence France-Presse, March 10, 2002.

40. Berni K. Moestafa, "Report Reveals Corruption in Court Is Organized," *Jakarta Post*, July 23, 2002.

41. Shanthy Nambiar, "UN Envoy Says 'Endemic' Corruption Hurts Indonesia Investment," Bloomberg, July 25, 2002.

42. Philip Kitley, "After the Bans: Modelling Indonesian Communications for the Future," in Grayson Lloyd and Shannon Smith, eds., *Indonesia Today: Challenges of History* (Singapore: Institute of Southeast Asian Studies, 2001), 256.

43. "Indonesia's Media: Freedom or Professionalism?" Laksamana.net, December 30, 2001, http//www.laksamana.net/vnews.cfm?news_id=1626.

44. "Information Minister Ponders New Ways to Rein In Media," *Jakarta Post*, December 29, 2001.

45. Muhammad Nafik, "Opposition Mounts against New Broadcasting Bill," *Jakarta Post*, May 17, 2002.

46. The problems of the press and possible democratic solutions are explored in Claire Harvey, "World Press Freedom Day 2002: The Face of RI Media," May 3, 2002; Ati Nurbaiti, "Media Union Need Not Be Seen as Confrontational," *Jakarta Post*, May 3, 2002; "The Envelope Is Mightier than the Sword," Laksamana.net, May 4, 2002, http//www.laksamana.net/vnews.cfm?news_id=2647; and A'an Suyana and

Berni K. Moestafa, "Press and Public Go Their Separate Ways after 1998," *Jakarta Post*, May 18, 2002.

47. Ati Nurbaiti, Chairperson, Alliance of Independent Journalists, "Press Faces Growing Threats to Its Freedom," *Jakarta Post*, February 15, 2002.

48. "Good Press, Bad Press," editorial, *Jakarta Post*, January 7, 2002.

49. For a review of historical attempts at regional autonomy, see Wiahan Kirana Jaya and Howard Dick, "The Latest Crisis of Regional Autonomy in Historical Perspective," in Grayson Lloyd and Shannon Smith, eds., *Indonesia Today: Challenges of History* (Singapore: Institute of Southeast Asian Studies, 2001), 216–28. For an analysis of regional autonomy from various regional and local perspectives, see Michael Malley, "Regions, Centralization, and Resistance," in Donald K. Emmerson, ed., *Indonesia Beyond Suharto: Polity, Economy, Society, Transition* (London: M. E. Sharpe/Asia Society, 1999), 71–105.

50. Peter Carey and G. Carter Bentley, eds., *East Timor at the Crossroads: The Forging of a Nation* (London: Cassell/Social Science Research Council, 1995); M. Hadi Soesastro, "East Timor: Questions of Economic Viability," in Hal Hill, ed., *Unity and Diversity: Regional Economic Development in Indonesia since 1970* (Singapore: Oxford University Press, 1991); Arnold S. Kohen, *From the Place of the Dead: The Epic Struggles of Bishop Belo in East Timor* (New York: St. Martin's, 1999); John Taylor, *East Timor: The Price of Freedom* (New York: Zed, 1999); and Constancio Pinto and Matthew Jardine, *East Timor's Unfinished Struggle: Inside the Timorese Resistance—A Testimony* (Boston: South End, 1997).

51. Ian Martin, *Self-Determination in East Timor: The United Nations, the Ballot, and International Intervention*, International Peace Academy Occasional Paper Series (Boulder: Lynne Rienner, 2001); Hal Hill and Joao M. Saldanha, eds., *East Timor: Development Challenges for the World's Newest Nation* (Canberra: Asia Pacific Press/Australian National University, 2001).

52. I witnessed this campaign in the eastern districts of East Timor, based in Bacau as a long-term observer with the Carter Center.

53. Santi EW Soekanto, "Regional Autonomy: A Double Standard Set in Motion?" *Jakarta Post*, December 27, 2001.

54. "Hard Lessons to Be Learned from East Timor," *Jakarta Post*, December 7, 2000.

55. Ainur A. Sophiaan, "Opposition Grows against Autonomy Law Review," *Jakarta Post*, February 6, 2002.

56. Terry Myers, "Decentralization Revisited: Indonesia's Experience in Regional Autonomy," USINDO brief, July 10, 2002.

57. Desi Anwar, "Soldiers Jeopardize Democracy," *Jakarta Post*, September 13, 1999.

58. *Undang-Undang Republic Indonesia Nomor 4 Tahun 1999 Tentang Susunan dan Kedudukan Majelis Permusyawaratan Rakyat, Dewan Perwakilan Rakyat, dan Dewan Perwakilan Daerah. Disahkan pada tanggal 1 Pebruari 1999.* (Republic of Indonesia Law No. 4 of 1999 Regarding the Structure and Position of the People's Consultative Assembly, People's Representative Council, and Regions' Representative Council. Approved February 1, 1999.)

59. Widjojo, "Repositioning," 178.

60. Dini Djalal, "Front-Line Friction: Conflict between Army and Police Spurs Separation," *Far Eastern Economic Review*, April 22, 1999.

61. Tiarma Siboro, "TNI to Continue Focusing on Internal Security," *Jakarta Post*, June 11, 2002.

62. International Crisis Group, "Resuming US–Indonesia Military Ties," Indonesia briefing, May 21, 2002.

63. "Changes in Civil–Military Relations Since the Fall of Suharto," *Indonesia*, October 2000, 126.

64. Geoffrey Robinson, "Indonesia: On a New Course?" in Muthiah Alagappa, ed., *Coercion and Governance: The Declining Political Role of the Military in Asia* (Stanford, Calif.: Stanford University Press, 2001), 226–55.

65. "Indonesia's Megawati Tells Troops Not to Worry about Rights Abuses," Agence France-Presse, December 29, 2001.

66. "House Backs Military over Slaughters," Laksamana.net, March 29, 2002. http//www.laksamana.net/vnews.cfm?news_id=2354.

67. Jupriadi, "Army to Keep Network in Regions: Ryamizard," *Jakarta Post*, July 14, 2002.

68. Tiarma Siboro, "Army Wants Power Again," *Jakarta Post*, February 21, 2003.

69. "TNI: The Quiet Indonesians?" *Tempo*, March 11–17, 2003.

70. "TNI's Half-hearted Reform," editorial, *Jakarta Post*, April 15, 2003.

71. Juwono Sudarsono, "Military Reform and Defense Planning: A Top Priority for Indonesia's Next Administration," in Allene Masters, ed., *Indonesian Voices: Hopes and Concerns for the Future* (Washington, D.C.: United States–Indonesia Society, 2004), 26.

72. Sudarsono, "Military Reform," 27.

73. Geoffrey Robinson, "Indonesia: On a New Course?" in Muthiah Alagappa, ed., *Coercion and Governance: The Declining Political Role of the Military in Asia* (Stanford, Calif.: Stanford University Press, 2001), 226–56.

4

Economic Recovery and Reform

John Bresnan

The social and political crisis that gripped Indonesia in the last years of the twentieth century came on the heels of an economic collapse of massive proportions. The economy of Indonesia was the largest in Southeast Asia, and it is not surprising that its losses were the most sizable in the region. But the Indonesian economy also experienced losses that were large in relation to its size; the percentage decline in its gross domestic product per capita was much greater than that of any other economy in East Asia. In addition, the social and political aspects of the crisis were much more significant in Indonesia than in neighboring countries, to the point that even the continued existence of Indonesia as a nation-state came into question. The tsunami of 2004 occurred just as Indonesia was beginning to recover from the 1998 crisis, and it added the burden of reconstruction in a province that was already in a state of rebellion. These observations suggest that a way out of the troubles experienced by the economy is not to be sought solely in terms of the economy itself but also in terms of the dynamics of its relations with Indonesia's society and polity.

I will take these dynamics as the starting point for an inquiry into the progress of and prospects for economic recovery and reform. By economic recovery I mean a return to precrisis levels of economic performance. By economic reform I mean changes in economic institutions to improve efficiency and the equitable distribution of benefits.

In this chapter I argue that the speed and durability of recovery depend on the degree of reform that accompanies it. In the last precrisis year of 1996, the bulk of the major banks and corporations were owned and operated by members of the small Chinese minority, by members of the presidential family, and by the Indonesian state. The crisis led to the takeover by the state of a very large share of the banks and corporations owned by the Chinese and the former first family. Added to what was already a sizable state-owned sector, these new acquisitions gave Indonesia one of the most highly nationalized economies in the world.

To the extent that this state dominance of the economy continues, I argue, it will have a negative impact on a return to rapid economic growth and on hopes for rapid movement toward more transparent and accountable governance. On the other hand, to the extent that the former pattern of ownership is restored, its political durability is likely to last only until the next major crisis occurs. If growth is to return in a way that is durable, then a new structure of ownership needs to be arrived at. Although theoretical alternatives exist, the only available alternative is to give a larger place to foreign investors. In light of Indonesia's well-known history of nationalism, this is not a politically attractive pathway to a prosperous economic future. That is the strategic dilemma that Indonesian leaders face.

Some restructuring of the Indonesian economy had been accomplished by late 2004, but much remained to be done to complete the reforms that post-crisis governments set for the country. The fragility of new or reformed political institutions, as described in the previous chapter, means that much depends on the imagination and strength of will of individual leaders, at both national and local levels. I aim in this chapter to provide a comprehensive analysis of the challenges these leaders will face if reform is to continue and rapid growth is to return, along with a clear sense of the cost of failure to the society and body politic.

RISE AND FALL OF A "MIRACLE" ECONOMY

To put the case in context: Indonesia was part of the economic boom that swept East Asia in the years before the crisis broke out in 1997. Table 4.1 shows how the gross domestic product (GDP) of the five economies most heavily impacted by the crisis—Indonesia, Korea, Malaysia, Philippines, and Thailand—grew between 1965 and 1995. The GDP of Indonesia grew 7.7

Table 4.1.   GDP in Constant 1995 US$ (billions) 1965–1996

	1965	1970	1975	1980	1985	1990	1995	1996
Indonesia	26	35	51	75	98	138	202	218
Korea	44	73	107	149	217	342	489	522
Malaysia	11	15	21	32	41	56	89	98
Philippines	25	32	42	56	53?	67	74	78
Thailand	17	27	36	52	68	111	168	178

Source: World Bank, *World Development Indicators*, CD-ROM, 2002.

times from $26 billion in 1965 to $202 billion in 1995. The GDPs of Korea, Malaysia, and Thailand all grew more rapidly. The GDPs of the Philippines and all other economies in Southeast Asia—Cambodia, Laos, Myanmar (Burma), and Vietnam—grew more slowly.

The rate of growth of the Indonesian economy was remarkable in all three decades. As seen in table 4.2, Indonesia grew at an annual average of 7.8 percent during the 1970s, an average of 7.0 percent during the 1980s, and an average of 8.0 percent during the 1990s up to and including 1996, the last "normal" year before the crisis began. The rates of growth of the economies of Malaysia and Korea were higher in two of the three time periods, and Thailand's was higher in the early 1990s. The Philippines and all other economies of Southeast Asia grew more slowly in every one of these decades.

As these data demonstrate, Indonesia was part of the East Asian economic "miracle." The rapid growth of the region was attributed in the well-known World Bank study, *The East Asian Miracle*, to a complex array of conditions: conservative fiscal policies, prudent monetary policies, flexible exchange rate management, investment in human capital, high savings rates, relatively limited price distortions, an openness to foreign technology, high investment in rural infrastructure, a secure institutional environment for private investment, government intervention to encourage rapid export growth, and insulation of a technocratic elite from excessive political pressure.[1] The description is broadly applicable to the Indonesian political economy during the three decades from 1966 to 1996.[2] It is evident from simply recounting these conditions that they are not likely to be replicated at any time soon.

The Asian financial crisis saw the GDP of each of the crisis economies of East Asia peak in 1996 or 1997, then fall sharply in the following two years, before beginning slowly to recover, as seen in table 4.3.

Indonesia suffered the greatest loss. As seen in table 4.4, the GDP of Indonesia fell in 1998 by 13 percent. The GDP of Thailand fell 11 percent, and that of Korea and Malaysia fell 7 percent. The Philippines fell 1 percent.

Indonesia's losses were much more severe in per capita terms. As seen in table 4.5, Indonesia's GDP per capita, measured in international dollars, peaked in 1997 at 3,217 and bottomed out in 1999 at 2,092, a loss of 34 percent in two years. Thailand's GDP per capita lost 13 percent over two years; Korea, Malaysia, the Philippines, and the rest of the region registered losses in single digits. After Thailand, Indonesia also was furthest from recovering to its precrisis level of GDP per capita at the end of the year 2000.

Thus the Indonesian economy suffered greater losses than any of the other "miracle" economies of the region. Why was this so? I have suggested that the answer to this question lies not in the economy itself but in the dynamic relations of the economy with the society and polity. I now turn to the nature of these relationships.

Table 4.2.   Average Annual Rates of Growth (%)

	1970s	1980s	1990–1996
Indonesia	7.8	7.0	8.0
Korea	8.5	7.4	7.4
Malaysia	8.0	5.8	9.5
Philippines	5.9	2.8	2.7
Thailand	7.3	7.4	8.5

Source: Calculated by author from World Bank, *World Development Indicators,* CD-ROM, 2002.

Table 4.3.   GDP in Constant 1995 US$ (billions) 1996–2000

	1996	1997	1998	1999	2000
Indonesia	218	228	198	200	209
Korea	522	548	512	568	618
Malaysia	98	105	97	103	112
Philippines	78	83	82	85	88
Thailand	178	176	157	160	170

Source: World Bank, *World Development Indicators*, CD-ROM, 2002.

Table 4.4.   GDP Growth (annual %)

	1996	1997	1998	1999	2000
Indonesia	9	5	−13	1	5
Korea	7	5	−7	11	9
Malaysia	10	7	−7	6	8
Philippines	6	5	−1	3	4
Thailand	6	−1	−11	4	4

Source: World Bank, *World Development Indicators*, CD-ROM, 2002.

Table 4.5.   GDP Per Capita PPP (current international $)

	1996	1997	1998	1999	2000
Indonesia	3,125	3,217	2,806	2,092	3,093
Korea	14,731	15,295	14,204	15,878	17,380
Malaysia	8,146	8,582	7,608	8,107	9,068
Philippines	3,785	3,872	3,603	3,806	3,971
Thailand	6,727	6,591	5,843	6,135	6,402

Source: World Bank, *World Development Indicators,* 2002, CD-ROM.

POLITICAL DYNAMICS OF THE CRISIS

Suharto has rightly been credited with a key role in the achievements that made Indonesia part of the East Asian "miracle." By the late 1990s, however, as described in the previous chapter, he was elderly, in ill health, and since the death of his wife, dependent on the companionship of his children and a few close friends. He also was dependent, from November 1997, on the International Monetary Fund (IMF), to which his advisers had turned when the rupiah came under pressure following the fall of the Thai baht the previous July. Suharto agreed in writing to take actions demanded by the Fund, but he delayed actually taking them. He even countermanded a number of decisions that had already been made, each of them linked to interests of his family or friends. In January 1998, with elections in the offing, he arranged for his political organization, Golkar, to nominate as its vice presidential candidate B. J. Habibie, a man with limited political experience, thus confirming that Suharto intended to remain in the presidency for another five-year term. The rupiah, which was trading in the vicinity of 2,500 to the U.S. dollar before the onset of the crisis, hit an all-time low, briefly reaching 17,000 to the dollar.[3]

By early March 1998, student groups were demonstrating in the streets of the capital city of Jakarta, and they were demanding political as well as economic reforms. On May 4, with the International Monetary Fund protesting noncompliance with its agreements and withholding funds, Suharto abruptly approved a 71 percent increase in the price of gasoline and a 20 percent increase in electricity prices. The public was unprepared for this jolt. Student protests grew. On May 12, four students demonstrating near a university campus in Jakarta were shot dead, apparently by snipers, and the next two nights saw rioting, looting, and arson in the capital city that resulted in the estimated 1,000 deaths mentioned in earlier chapters, as well as some 5,000 commercial buildings and 1,000 homes damaged or looted, and more than 1,000 automobiles and almost as many motorbikes set ablaze. Chinese-owned shops and homes were particular targets of looters and arsonists, and Chinese women were particular victims of rape. On May 20, huge anti-Suharto demonstrations occurred across Indonesia, and the economic ministers in the cabinet resigned en masse.[4]

On May 21, 1998, Suharto himself resigned, leaving Habibie nominally president but without legitimacy in the eyes of the students and the many others who now began to express their opinions of the regime openly. Habibie's transitional presidency was significant, however, in restoring freedom of speech and association, and in organizing fresh elections to parliament, which were held in June 1999. A new president was chosen by party leaders in October 1999. Given the lengthy Suharto reign of power, the level of violence that preceded its end, and the lengthy transition to new leadership, it is hardly too much to say that the political dimensions of the crisis in Indonesia were unmatched in any other country.[5]

The crisis was profound in the Indonesian case for the additional reason that the banking system was deeply corrupt. Banks were the principal source of funds for corporate expansion, and Suharto personally approved the largest loans of the state banks, which were at the core of a vast system of corruption. Chinese owners of the biggest private banks channeled depositors' money to their own corporations more or less as they pleased. Banks and corporations, both publicly and privately owned, also borrowed heavily abroad, where interest rates were lower, relying on the government to keep the exchange rate stable. They also imprudently responded to the eagerness of foreign investment houses to participate in the rapid growth that was taking place in East Asia, borrowing short-term capital for long-term purposes, and thus gambling on the continued willingness of foreign creditors to "roll over" their loans when they became due.

The financial crisis that was reaching its peak in Jakarta by January 1998 caused Indonesian business owners and foreign investors alike to panic. Capital flight kept the exchange rate in the vicinity of 10,000 rupiah to the dollar, or up to four times what it had been, and most banks and corporations could not meet their obligations to foreign creditors. With depositors withdrawing their funds, Indonesian banks threatened to go under, and the government flooded them with liquidity in return for pledges of collateral. In time, many borrowers proved unable or unwilling to repay the government, and ownership of a large portion of the country's modern private banks and corporations fell into the hands of the state.

SOCIAL DYNAMICS OF THE CRISIS

The crisis hit all classes of society. Most wealthy Indonesians were minority Chinese, who bore the brunt of popular anger let loose in the 1998 riots. Much of the residential and commercial real estate in Glodok, the old Chinese part of Jakarta, was reduced to burned-out shells. Traumatized Chinese tycoons transferred large sums abroad, including liquidity funds paid out to stem the runs on their banks, and, as reported in chapter 2 of this volume, as many as 100,000 businessmen and members of their families fled the country as well. The government faced a major dilemma in trying to get the economy growing again and at the same time bring an end to the dominance of the private sector by this small ethnic minority. (I will refer to the members of this minority as "Chinese Indonesians" or simply "Chinese" in the pages that follow;

what is meant in all cases is Indonesian citizens of full or partial Chinese descent. They are usually estimated to be 3 percent of the total population.)

The Indonesian middle class, the principal social product of the policies of the Suharto years, owned the savings deposits in the local banks. They were the people who started the run on the banks that led to the system's collapse. They also were the parents of the students demonstrating in the streets. These associations gave the new middle class a unique role in the economic and political debacle that was the end of the Suharto regime. It was the only large social group in the population to be protected financially by government action in the wake of the crisis.

The impact of the crisis was greatest on the most vulnerable, those living below the poverty level or close to it. The percentage of poor households went from 11 percent in 1996 to 20 percent in 1999, meaning that an additional 19 to 20 million people fell into poverty. Urban areas and rural Java (which was experiencing a drought) were hit much harder than other parts of the country. Formal wages fell 34 percent in real terms between 1997 and 1998; agricultural wages fell 40 percent. Inflation, which had been running at 8.8 percent per annum between 1990 and 1996, jumped to 57.6 percent in 1998—almost 100 percent if put on an annualized basis from late 1997 to mid-1998. One indication that the crisis overwhelmed informal safety nets was the labor participation rate for women; only 55 percent of women twenty-five and older were in the labor force in 1996, but 72 percent were there in 1998.[6]

Why Corruption Matters

Could this state of affairs have been avoided? Might Indonesia have suffered no more seriously than the rest of East Asia? That is indeed possible. But by the mid-1990s, Indonesian policy was being driven by the interests of the Suharto family. There had been corruption before in Indonesian history; corruption even played a role in the demise of the Dutch East Indies Company. Moreover, there was much evidence of widespread corporate corruption in any number of other economies in the late twentieth century, including that of the United States. But the Suharto case was one of a kind: he was president of the country, and his corruption had become monumental in scale. Transparency International rated him in 2004 as the biggest embezzler of public funds in the world in the previous twenty years; the organization put his total misappropriations at somewhere between $15 billion and $35 billion.[7] Indonesia had to deal with the same international forces as the rest of the region in 1997 and 1998, but it did so from a position of considerable institutional weakness.

Any corruption on the part of a nation's political leadership matters in two respects. In the first place, corruption introduces misallocation of resources, protection of high-cost producers, and price distortions that constitute a drag on the economy and will delay a return to rapid growth. Linda Y. C. Lim and Aaron Stern found no clear evidence in studies of Southeast Asian countries that corruption necessarily leads to lower economic growth; as they point out, "a very corrupt country like Indonesia experienced rapid economic growth for three decades."[8] It also is sometimes argued that corruption has been critical to capital accumulation in other economies in the past. But corruption was decidedly on the rise in notoriety if not scale in Indonesia in the 1990s, when foreign funds were flowing into the country at record levels and the holdings of Suharto's children seemed to be expanding with equal rapidity. Moreover, the circumstances that gave rise to the East Asian "miracle" cannot be repeated; the years ahead will be ones of much more intense competition for capital and markets, especially for countries like Indonesia in East Asia, where China has become a major destination of foreign investment and a major producer for export.

Less commonly taken into account is the demoralization that occurs among a people when rampant corruption involves their head of state. Suharto fell in 1998 for a complex of reasons, but the outrage of the middle class over his corrupt behavior was certainly prominent among them. His first two successors, B. J. Habibie and Abdurrahman Wahid, both experienced shortened tenures in the presidency as a direct result of acts of financial corruption committed in their names. Megawati Sukarnoputri, who succeeded Wahid in the presidency, promised to rein in corruption but failed to do so, and lost her bid for reelection. Susilo Bambang Yudhoyono was making a similar promise as he took office in October 2004.

Corruption of the system of governance also was among the causes of the interethnic and interreligious violence that broke out across the archipelago about the time Suharto fell. Having lost confidence in officialdom, people began taking the law in their own hands. The violence in turn was a major cause of severe decline in the level of foreign capital invested in the country and therefore was an added obstacle to economic recovery.

Official corruption in Indonesia was thus a source of economic inefficiency and political instability that had a powerful influence, not only on the speed of recovery of the economy but also on the ability of the polity to avoid laying the ground for another crisis in the years ahead. Indonesians were to find that removing a feature rooted so firmly in their social, political, and economic structure would not be easy. Almost all the old players remained on the scene, commanded significant resources, and did everything possible to protect their interests. Yet a return to anything like the status quo ante would not satisfy either the domestic forces of reformist sentiment or the external forces of rational choice, both of which were beyond the ability of the elected government in Jakarta to ignore with impunity.

It is thus desirable to identify the principal means by which corruption is taking place in Indonesia and the choices the society faces in bringing it under control. This observation leads to the plan for the remainder of this chapter. The discussion is divided into the following sections: efficiency, corruption and the role of the state in the economy; ethnicity and corruption in the private sector; the multiple tasks of restructuring the banking system, balancing the budget, and paying for the bailout; and coping with the global movement of capital. These sections will be followed by a concluding section on the prospects for recovery and reform.

EFFICIENCY, CORRUPTION, AND THE STATE

The principal models of public economic policy familiar to the Indonesians as they achieved independence at the end of World War II were the colonial government's deep intervention in the economy during the depression of the 1930s and the Japanese military's control of the economy during its occupation from 1942 to 1945.[9] Thus a major role for the state in the economy was assumed. Article 35 of the 1945 Constitution reads:

> The economy shall be organized as a common endeavor based on the principle of the family. Branches of production which are important for the state and which control the lives of large numbers of the people shall be controlled by the state. The land and water and the natural resources therein shall be controlled by the state and utilized for the maximum prosperity of the people.[10]

Some held that the forms of "common endeavor" meant by the constitution were either state ownership or cooperatives. But cooperatives were more talked about than experimented with; in practice, given the opportunity, Indonesian leaders consistently favored ownership by the state. Thus, when impatience with the Netherlands over the delayed return of the western half of New Guinea erupted in 1957, all Dutch-owned enterprises in Indonesia were nationalized, including banks, mines, shipping lines, and plantations. When the value of the country's exports of oil and natural gas rose dramatically in the 1970s, the government acted like the governments of communist China and socialist India in earlier decades: it invested in state-owned heavy industry, in plants refining petroleum and producing steel, aluminum, cement, fertilizer, and basic chemicals. In 1996, Hal Hill found 164 state enterprises occupying a prominent place in the economy and contributing about 30 percent of GDP.[11] But there was no ambiguity about mineral resources on land or under the sea. The constitutional provision that these be controlled by the state was taken to mean they would be owned by the state.

State Ownership and Corruption

Government corporations were major players in oil and gas, trade, manufacturing, transportation, plantation agriculture, utilities, communications, and finance.[12] To this sizable state sector were added, as a consequence of the financial crisis, most of the country's largest private banks, hundreds of its largest private corporations, and a very great deal of real estate in which these entities had invested, ranging from beach resorts to urban skyscrapers, oil palm plantations to auto assembly plants.

This structure of ownership presented countless opportunities for corruption, and the lack of transparency in governance helped ensure that the opportunities would be seized. A presidential commission as early as 1970 had warned Suharto that corruption was "running unchecked" in his government and that the cleanup "must begin at the top."[13] Indonesian corruption resulted in the first instance from the behavior of the president himself, who began using state enterprises as sources of extrabudgetary funds for regime maintenance and ended acting like any overly fond Javanese father who could not resist spoiling his children. Government contracts and licenses found their way to Suharto's children's firms. Monopolies were created expressly for their profit. As foreign funds came flooding into Indonesia in the 1990s, it became common for a Suharto family member to accept 10 or 15 percent of the shares in a joint venture with the foreign investor at no cost, in return for serving as the Indonesian "partner" in the enterprise, which was required by law.[14] Whether the scale of corruption relative to the size of the economy remained constant or grew larger is not known, but in Indonesia in the 1990s it became publicly centered on the president and his family and affected the very framework of public policy.

The most notorious case, mentioned in the previous chapter, was a provision that built-up automobiles imported by a company owned by a Suharto son, Hutomo "Tommy" Mandala Putra, would be deemed to have been assembled in Indonesia, protecting them from payment of customs duties and thus lowering their cost. Public distaste caused the vehicles to languish unsold in a large parking lot, providing a public symbol of the conflict that was developing between Suharto and his children on the one hand and the automobile-buying middle class on the other.

Dynamics of Competitive Politics

To these conditions were added, with the fall of Suharto, the dynamics of competitive politics. The need to compete in elections across Indonesia's wide and variegated landscape required funding on a large scale, and a way has yet to be found to meet this requirement that is broadly effective and acceptable to informed opinion. Of course, financing political activity is a problem the world over. But the continued prevalence of blatant financial corruption at the apex of the political system in the midst of a national crisis was seen by many Indonesians—students and intellectuals prominent among them—as particularly unseemly.

The ubiquity of corruption in the Habibie, Wahid, and Megawati presidencies added to the notoriety of what Indonesians were now calling KKN (*korupsi, kolusi, nepotisme*). World Bank staff in 1998 and 1999 rated Indonesia the most corrupt economy in East Asia.[15] A study by PricewaterhouseCoopers on global business transparency concluded that by the year 2000 Indonesia was one of the most corrupt economies in the world.[16] The 2002 annual survey of worldwide corruption by Transparency International, based on fifteen polls and surveys from nine independent institutions, showed Indonesia near the global bottom along with Uganda, Azerbaijan, Nigeria, and Bangladesh.[17]

Suharto and Corruption

Suharto said consistently that he had few material possessions in his own name. This may have been accurate in the sense that he had little of which there was a written record. A prominent Chinese Indonesian businessman once told me that Suharto had come to him soon after arriving in Jakarta as an army general, handed him a sum of money to invest, and never asked for so much as a receipt. Suharto did not order his government ministers to give preferential treatment to enterprises in which his children had an interest. Any senior bureaucrat knew what was expected of them. Investors also understood that, in order to gain bureaucratic approval of a new venture, a partnership with a Suharto crony or child was a sine qua non. As early as 1989 an expatriate in the oil industry complained to me that "the family" had become so rapacious that, whereas at one time they wanted a share in all the big projects, now they were demanding a share in small ones as well.

Whatever the scale of the Suharto family's wealth, it was greatly reduced as a result of the crisis and Suharto's resignation. In U.S. dollar terms, of course, all Indonesian assets were drastically reduced in value; the Indonesian rupiah lost 80 percent of its dollar value between mid-1997 and early 2001.

Also, with Suharto out of the presidency, the law seemed at times ready to catch up with him and his circle, which would have further reduced the value of his children's holdings. Students mounted daily demonstrations demanding that he be taken to court. Wahid attempted to negotiate a settlement but failed. The attorney general drew up charges that Suharto misused $571 million of government funds paid into private foundations over which he presumably had control; a Jakarta district court found the former president too ill to stand trial, and the Supreme Court, although in a position to overturn this ruling, did not do so. That performance by the courts, which were filled with justices who owed their careers to Suharto, confirmed the common image of the judiciary as mired in corruption itself. There was an element of regret in some of the commentary about the Suharto case; it was recalled, for example, that he had kept Sukarno out of court, contrary to what some of his fellow army generals would have liked, after 1965. But when it came to Suharto's children, the prevailing public attitude might have been supposed to yield more action.

Dealing with the Family

The only serious court case involving the Suharto family centered on the youngest son, Tommy, who reputedly had a taste for fast cars and fast women. He was sentenced to a jail term in 2000 for corruption in a land deal that lost the government $8 million. He disappeared while an appeal was pending and led the Jakarta police on a chase for more than a year, causing critics to charge that the police were afraid to take him in. While he was on the run, the court reversed itself and threw out the conviction. Meanwhile, a judge who presided over his trial and sentencing was assassinated in a drive-by shooting in broad daylight. Tommy eventually was found, arrested, and accused of having ordered the judge's killing. In May 2002, three men were found guilty in the killing of the judge. In July 2002 Tommy was found guilty of paying the hit men to murder the judge and was sentenced to the relatively light term of fifteen years in prison.

At about this same time, Siti "Tutut" Hardiyanti Rukmana, Suharto's eldest daughter, was accused of lying about the value of assets she put up as guarantees of repayment to the central bank for liquidity it advanced to a bank she owned during the banking crisis. A legal team recommended criminal as well as civil charges against her. Tutut was one of a number of errant bankers whose fate was finally determined by the cabinet. Earlier she was identified by prosecutors as a suspect in an oil pipeline case that allegedly cost the government $22 million in losses, and was ordered not to leave the country. In December 2004, a British court released documents showing testimony by executives of Alvis, a British manufacturer, that they had sold fifty Scorpion light tanks to the Indonesian army—and gave Tutut a fee of 10 percent for arranging the purchase.[18]

In April 2003, Suharto's half brother Probosutedjo was convicted of embezzlement and fraud for taking the equivalent of $11.2 million from a state reforestation fund by overstating the size of his timber estate and the number of new trees he had planted. He remained free pending an appeal. At least two other Suharto children were still being investigated for corruption in early 2003. None of these cases of alleged corruption resulted in any first family member other than Tommy going to jail.

Dealing with the Cronies

By late 2004, more than six years after Suharto's resignation, only one of his cronies had been tried, convicted, and jailed for corruption. Mohammed "Bob" Hasan, Suharto's Chinese golf partner, was found guilty of misusing $75 million in funds belonging to the Ministry of Forestry. Hasan became a tycoon in the timber and plywood industries and chairman of the Indonesian Forest Concessionaires Association. He was initially fined and ordered to spend two years under house arrest. Following a public outcry over the light sentence, a Jakarta high court ordered him to spend two years in jail, and later increased the term to six years. Hasan was placed in an island penitentiary in March 2001.

In addition to Suharto's daughter Tutut, some thirty-five bankers faced court proceedings for illegal use of liquidity credits paid out between August 1997 and early 1999. Credits totaling $14.5 billion were extended to forty-eight private banks by Bank Indonesia in the early stages of the monetary crisis. But most of the funds went to a few Suharto friends. And rather than using the funds for normal bank operations, most traded them for foreign currency and sent it abroad. In March 2002, Megawati, as president, decreed that criminal charges would be waved if "good faith" efforts were made to repay the central bank. That sounded like an invitation to negotiations, and so it was.

An Indonesian government might eventually exact a price for the ill-gotten gains of the Suharto family and friends sufficient to deter future power holders. But this was not assured. Not only were the members of this circle personally wealthy but also able to benefit from the prevailing corruption of the judiciary. And the justices weren't the only ones who stood to gain. Public prosecutors, court clerks, and private attorneys also profited by delivering justice to the highest bidder. The failure to deal with such rampant corruption from the late Suharto years was to have a baleful effect on the presidencies of all three of his immediate successors.

Habibie and Corruption

Two events that occurred in August and September 1999 cost B. J. Habibie election to the presidency. One of these was the referendum in East Timor that was followed by violence and destruction wrought by pro-Indonesian militias; that event captured headlines in the international press. The Jakarta press gave much more attention to the second event—the scandal that became known as Baligate.

In early August 1999, reports began to circulate about serious irregularities at Bank Bali, a private Indonesian bank in which Standard Chartered Bank of the United Kingdom was intending to acquire a minority stake. The sale was in the hands of the Indonesian Bank Restructuring Agency (IBRA), a new agency designed to restructure the banking industry; Bank Bali had been effectively, if temporarily, nationalized. An audit on behalf of the prospective buyer revealed that the equivalent of $80 million had been paid by Bank Bali as a "facilitation fee" to a company controlled by, among others, the deputy treasurer of Golkar, the government party; it was not clear what services the company had performed for this payment. Before the month was out, officials at Bank Indonesia, the Ministry of Finance, and the IBRA were implicated, as were Habibie's younger brother and the head of the Supreme Advisory Council, a Habibie intimate. The international accounting firm of PricewaterhouseCoopers was hired to make an independent audit of all transactions related to the affair. Their report pointed to "irregularities, bribery, corruption, and mismanagement by key individuals involved." Those implicated included "ministers, political personalities, and senior officials."[19] The World Bank, the International Monetary Fund, and the Asian Development Bank froze relations with the Habibie government over "Baligate" for a time while the controversy raged.[20]

Two officials were taken to court to face charges, but the case was thrown out—many believe as a result of judicial corruption. By then, however, the damage to Habibie's presidential future had been done. On October 14, 1999, Habibie gave an "accountability" speech to the People's Consultative Assembly (Madjelis Permusyawaratan Nasional, or MPR), which was convening to elect a president and vice president. A Suharto-controlled assembly had obliged President Sukarno to account for his leadership of the nation in 1966. Suharto maintained the practice, every five years, just before his reelection to another term. Sukarno's speech was rejected by the assembly, but of course those by Suharto never were. On October 19, 1999, Habibie's speech was rejected by a vote of 355 to 322, effectively ending his political career.[21]

Much later, in March 2002, Syahril Sabirin, the governor of the central bank when the Bank Bali scandal erupted, was sentenced to three years in jail in the case. He was found guilty of approving the disbursement of funds to Bank Bali in the affair after attending a meeting in a hotel with a group of Golkar fund-raisers. Sabirin remained in office pending an appeal; the appellate court overturned the conviction.

At the turn of 2002, reports also surfaced alleging that Akbar Tanjung, the head of Golkar and the speaker of parliament, was involved in the transfer of some $4 million in government funds for use in financing Golkar's campaign in the 1999 elections. According to a former official, the funds were drawn from Bulog, the state food monopoly, which was a notorious source of off-budget funds in the Suharto era.[22] Tanjung denied the allegations but was tried in the case, convicted of graft and corruption, and sentenced to three years in prison. He also remained in office pending appeal, and the earlier court decisions in his case were overturned. He was to be a powerful ally of Megawati in the 2004 election, moving his party to her support, in spite of much opposition from within Golkar ranks.

Thus Golkar and its leading figures escaped paying any price for their illegal behavior. Financial corruption was eating away at Indonesia's image at home and abroad, and yet it could not be stopped. For a nation already in political disarray, this condition was seriously limiting. By default, the International Monetary Fund increasingly found itself championing reforms that Indonesians ought to have been championing themselves. It was not a formula that could be sustained indefinitely.

Wahid and Corruption

Although the amount of money involved was small by comparison with the Bank Bali case, a scandal that erupted in May 2000 triggered the fall of the Wahid presidency just as surely as Baligate had triggered the fall of Habibie.

Wahid was, early in his time in office, seriously in search of money from outside the government budget for one or more purposes. One of the possible sources he mentioned to an aide was Bulog, the same state agency that was to figure in the Akbar Tanjung case. The official version of what happened is that Wahid was told that no special funds existed at Bulog that he could tap, and Wahid turned instead to the sultan of neighboring Brunei, one of the world's richest individuals, who gave him $2 million for "humanitarian relief."

The Jakarta press told a different story. The deputy head of Bulog said he had paid out the equivalent of about $4 million from the staff pension fund under pressure from President Wahid. The go-between in the case was the president's masseur. The Bulog bureaucrat was arrested, tried, and jailed. The masseur disappeared for a time but was later taken to court. The state secretary,

Bondan Gunawan, resigned. Portions of the Bulog money were later reportedly traced to the bank accounts of a variety of individuals, including a staff member of a new airline established by Wahid and the masseur; the airline staff member disappeared.

Not surprisingly the newly independent parliament reacted to these press reports by establishing a special commission to investigate the allegations. The commission in due course concluded that Wahid was involved in what was now known as Bulogate more deeply than he had acknowledged, and that he had improperly used the funds from the sultan of Brunei by failing to turn them over to the state treasury. Parliament voted 393 to 4 to accept the commission report and on February 5, 2001, issued a formal censure. This began the process that led to the special session of the People's Consultative Assembly that removed Wahid from office on July 23, 2001.

Financial corruption was not the only reason for Wahid's premature departure from office. He was widely seen as physically and perhaps psychologically unfit, but these shortcomings were not sufficient for impeachment. The taint of financial corruption set in motion the shift in opinion that brought him down. That this should be the fate of the first Indonesian president installed as a result of a free and fair election was a body blow to the democratic process, as well as to economic recovery.

Megawati and Corruption

Many observers, at the time of Megawati's arrival in the office of the president, believed that her vulnerability lay with her third husband, Taufik Kiemas, the owner of a string of gasoline stations, and an elected member of parliament who controlled her party's executive committee. It was rumored that payments were made to the 2004 election campaign fund of Megawati's party by applicants for government favor, especially in cases of major sales by the bank restructuring agency, IBRA.

The most damaging evidence of corruption in the Megawati government was provided not by political opponents but by officials of her own party. In late December 2002, the research and development unit of the Indonesian Democratic Party of Struggle (PDI-P) blamed the government's "bad performance" during the previous year in part on "the prevalent corruption in the executive and legislative bodies, as well as the judiciary." Subagyo Anam, secretary of the party research center, said, "Frankly speaking, almost all state officials and public servants are corrupt, but Attorney General M. A. Rachman has an even worse situation because his (corruption) case has been exposed to the public." The attorney general, the most senior official responsible for prosecuting cases of corruption in the courts, was accused of amassing a large amount of money from unknown sources, with which he bought a house after less than two years in office.[23] The party analysts had clear advice to offer the president: get rid of high-level troublemakers and replace them with professional people from outside the bureaucracy. But Megawati did not replace her attorney general, and people were left to wonder at this instance—one of many—of presidential inaction. When Megawati lost the runoff presidential election in 2004, many thought one of the principal reasons was her failure to make a dent in political and bureaucratic corruption during her several years in office.

Susilo and Corruption

President Susilo went further than any of his predecessors in committing his administration to attacking corruption. On many occasions during his campaign for election, he promised to clean up the government, starting with the judicial system. In his first interview after taking office, he told *Time Asia*:

> We have to eradicate corruption structurally and culturally. I've told the police and Attorney General that any corruption cases once held up should be started again. My own office and those of the Vice President, the ministers and the provincial governors need to be seen as clean and corruption-free. I've asked that the same steps be taken at the provincial government level. I've also asked the Attorney General to take legal action against any banks that are unhealthy, or where there are indications of corruption, regardless of who is behind them. This country will be destroyed if we do not stop the growth of corruption. There needs to be some shock therapy so that the people know that this government is serious about corruption. We want to improve the investment climate, starting with political stability, improved security, good taxation and economic policies, and legal certainty—sanctity of contracts, and that all dispute-settlement systems are fair.[24]

The reference to structural corruption was a new and significant note. Pursuing violators of the law is only one approach to the problem of corruption. The institutional conditions in which corruption flourishes also need to be reassessed. On the basis of the experience of the past presidents of Indonesia, one is obliged to conclude that official financial corruption is not going to go away without structural change. As long as the state owns a large portion of the productive forces in the economy, leaders and others in high places will look for ways to tap this state sector for their own purposes. IMF letters of intent and World Bank reports were full of ideas that, if effectively implemented, could help reduce the incidence of corruption. But it was easier to recommend such qualitative improvements than to make them happen.

Reforming the State Sector

A significant body of opinion in Indonesia holds that state-owned economic enterprises serve the national interest and should be preserved as agents of the state. This is partly a heritage of the Sukarno era, when socialist ideologies were sweeping the newly independent states that were coming into existence out of the ruins of the colonial system. Not coincidentally, state ownership also means that some of the country's biggest enterprises will be managed by indigenous Indonesians and provide a balance to the Chinese dominance of the modern private sector. In addition, state ownership worked in the interest of the civilian and military bureaucracies that held power during the late Sukarno years and throughout the Suharto presidency, providing them with sources of income, both personal and institutional, that helped hold the political regime together. After Suharto fell, it was not only the International Monetary Fund that made the state sector a prime target. Reformist opinion in Indonesia also ran strongly against state ownership.

The central bank, Bank Indonesia, was described by one of its incoming governors as a den of thieves. The state oil company, Pertamina, which was involved in one of the Suharto sons' cases, and the state food monopoly, Bulog, which was involved in the Wahid and Tanjung cases, were notorious from early on in the Suharto era as off-budget sources of funds for political purposes. A cluster of ten enterprises identified as "strategic" industries were subordinate to Habibie during the period in which he functioned as minister of research and Suharto's heir apparent, and were free to ignore efforts to subject them to audits of their finances.

Most state enterprises were overseen by the ministries responsible for the technical fields concerned. Thus state-owned plantations reported to the minister of agriculture, telecommunications enterprises to the minister of communications, and so on. The enterprises provided generous honoraria and other perquisites to government officials appointed to their boards, and postretirement employment to top officials of their supervising ministries. As a result, state enterprises functioned in a world protected from public scrutiny. They did not issue public financial reports. Confidential assessments over the years found them poorly managed, burdened with contradictory objectives, providing subsidies to their employees and clients, and registering poor returns on the public funds invested in them. In the wake of the monetary crisis, most were believed to be heavily in debt.

The first line of action agreed on with the International Monetary Fund was to reduce the scope and increase the surveillance of some of the worst offenders. Pertamina, the country's largest state enterprise, was a longtime center of inefficiency and corruption; according to one audit, it "lost" $5 billion in a two-year period in the mid-1990s.[25] Pertamina was directed to sell off its network of retail gasoline stations, and in October 2001 the Indonesian parliament passed a landmark bill ending its thirty-year monopoly of the domestic fuel market.[26] The Bulog monopolies in the import of rice, wheat, sugar, and soybeans were eliminated. Both Pertamina and Bulog were to be subjected to international audits of their finances. The state-owned aircraft building firm that was a favorite of Habibie was denied further subsidy from any source. But the International Monetary Fund would be around as a source of pressure for selected actions like these only for so long. More fundamental steps were required as well.

The main line of attack was to place all state-owned enterprises under a new Ministry of State Enterprises in March 1998, created by agreement with the Fund in order to increase budget revenues and achieve efficiencies. Over time, enterprises operating in competitive markets were to be privatized. In the short term, state firms with some shares already listed on the stock exchange were to sell additional shares on the market.

A first effort to professionalize the management of the state sector was undertaken by Laksamana Sukardi, a former banker and an adviser to Megawati, as minister of state enterprises in the Wahid cabinet. But Wahid wanted to use the state enterprises to help build a war chest for the 2004 elections, and Sukardi was soon replaced by a leader of the Nahdlatul Ulama. The first serious effort at state enterprise reform thus collapsed before it got started.

Privatizing the State Sector

President Megawati reinstated Sukardi as minister for state enterprises in 2001, indicating that she was prepared to permit an effort to reduce the role of state ownership through a program of privatization. That he was as much in need of presidential support as before was soon evident. The vice president, Hamzah Haz, campaigned for improving the state enterprises rather than selling them. Megawati's cabinet minister for development planning, Kwik Gian Kie, a man given to harsh criticism, publicly excoriated the very idea of privatization. The chairman of the People's Consultative Assembly, Amien Rais, lobbied against it also, saying it amounted to selling the country to foreigners. "Indonesia will become a nation of coolies," was how he put it.[27]

The first major case of privatization was planned to be the sale in 1998 of a majority stake in Indonesia's state-owned cement company, Semen Gresik. The company was well chosen. Semen Gresik had been built with American aid, and its management was well regarded in professional circles. A number of shares in the firm were already being traded on the Jakarta stock exchange, and Cemex, a Mexico-based firm and the world's third largest cement producer, offered to pay double the market price for 51 percent of Semen Gresik—35 percent to be bought from the government and 16 percent from the public. Workers at the plant near Surabaya in eastern Java and at Gresik subsidiaries in western Sumatra and southern Sulawesi protested vigorously against the prospect of a foreign takeover, and the government retreated. Cemex was able to buy only 14 percent of the firm from the government and 11 percent from the public. It also obtained a promise that it would be allowed to pursue a majority holding at a later date.

By late 2001, Cemex was still waiting, and the clouds hovering over the sale had darkened; the rapid decentralization of fiscal authority, and with it political power, was looming as a new obstacle to the Gresik sale. The governor and provincial council of West Sumatra protested the sale by issuing a statement that Semen Padang, the local Gresik subsidiary, was being placed temporarily "under the control of the people of West Sumatra." Authorities in South Sulawesi said they were giving the central government six months to spin off the Gresik subsidiary in their province, Semen Tonasa, to local owners before the sale to Cemex or "steps will be taken."[28] The local interest was clear. The subsidiaries were major employers in their localities. In at least one of the provinces, the speaker of the legislature was reputedly the supplier of coal to the local cement plant. Megawati bowed to the newly powerful force of localism, and Laksamana Sukardi had to back down. The Cemex–Gresik deal was canceled, and Cemex took the government of Indonesia to court to recover damages.

Another major case of privatization was not attempted until, in December 2002, a large government stake in the long-distance telephone company, Indosat, was sold to Singapore Technologies Telemedia. This was the telecommunications company owned by the government of neighboring Singapore. Telemedia paid US$632 million for a 41.94 percent stake in, and management control of, PT Indonesia Satellite Corporation, or Indosat. The Indonesian government retained a 15 percent stake in the company. The sale was the largest of an Indonesian asset to a foreign investor since the financial crisis began. The sale had been delayed by labor union threats to strike, fearing mass layoffs.[29] It was a major triumph for Laksamana Sukardi, although a politically controversial one, as Singapore had few political allies in Jakarta, and Sukardi was immediately accused of having decided the case in return for campaign contributions to Megawati's party.

It was suggested in Singapore that the government there saw investing in Indonesia as a way of helping maintain its political stability. Singapore initially committed $5 billion to the IMF bailout, but after Suharto fell the government of the city-state lacked the confidence in his successor to stay the course. Then President Habibie reacted in a famously angry outburst, referring to Singapore as just "a red dot" on the map. Prime Minister Goh Chok Tong later committed $2 billion to the purchase of stakes in Indonesian state-owned enterprises as an alterative way of being helpful. The governments of Singapore and its giant neighbor were entering a new era of more intimate relations, and much would depend on how carefully both sides managed the problems that were bound to arise.

The Indonesian Dilemma

The Indonesians clearly face a dilemma. The sale of state assets is needed to reduce the opportunities for corruption and, as I shall show later, to help repay the national debt. In addition, shareholders other than Indonesian bureaucrats could be expected to insist that the enterprises be managed more efficiently, without the price distortions that reduced the companies' return on the capital invested in them. Given the attenuated condition of the Indonesian business community, however, the likely buyers were mostly foreigners. And foreigners were likely buyers only if they could obtain majority control; the attraction of holding a minority stake in an Indonesian enterprise controlled by Indonesian bureaucrats was distinctly limited.

Sentiment was easily generated against the sale of majority stakes to foreign interests. Workers feared the loss of jobs. Parliamentarians feared being accused of allowing foreigners to profit from Indonesia's straightened circumstances. Policy makers worried whether it was prudent to sell off the efficient enterprises and be left with the inefficient ones. One of the appeals of state ownership, after all, was that it gave Indonesians a part of the modern economy they could call their own, and a means of opening senior management ranks to indigenous personnel. Any president of Indonesia would face a major challenge in attempting to privatize the public sector.

In March 2003, it was reported that the sale of state assets might be put off indefinitely because of poor market conditions. In October 2004, Jusuf Kalla, SBY's vice president, announced that the sale of state enterprises would be reviewed. Such statements made it probable that the state sector would continue to be a prominent feature of the Indonesian economy, and that the inefficiencies and corruption associated with it would continue.

ETHNICITY AND PRIVATE SECTOR CORRUPTION

Just before the financial crisis broke in 1997, it was possible to describe the upper reaches of the Indonesian economy as privately owned. This was a recent development. Foreign (mainly Dutch) owners had dominated the heights of the economy at independence, but the Indonesian state was dominant after Sukarno nationalized Dutch properties in 1957. The oil boom years from 1973 on saw the state's dominance increase annually until 1985, when it peaked owing to a number of global developments, including the dramatic collapse of oil prices. By 1986, Indonesia was experiencing a severe economic slowdown, and its balance of payments was deteriorating at an alarming rate. Economic necessity demanded a change of policy, and it was decided that the private sector should be deregulated with the aim of increasing nonoil exports.[30]

This "strategic retreat of the state," to use Andrew MacIntyre's phrase, had a rapid and dramatic impact on the private sector.[31] Most dramatic was the rapid expansion of business groups owned and operated by Indonesians of Chinese descent and containing within them large numbers of diversified enterprises. (I avoid use of the term "conglomerate" in referring to these groups, as the term has acquired a pejorative meaning; in fact, similar groups are prominent in other countries of Southeast Asia and elsewhere in the developing world.) In 1985, just before the change in public policy, Richard Robison found that groups composed of large numbers of companies but owned by a single individual or family were already widespread.[32] In 1994, Hal Hill and Thee Kian Wie found that of the twenty-five largest family business groups in Indonesia, twenty-one were in the hands of Chinese Indonesian individuals and their families. Only four indigenously owned groups made it into the list of twenty-five, and two of these were owned by sons of Suharto; the other two were at the very bottom of the ranking.[33] In the years following the crisis, World Bank staff judged Indonesia to have the highest concentration of ownership control among its top fifteen families of any country in East Asia.[34] Besides the Suharto family, these wealthy owners were presumably all Chinese. This was a remarkable position in which the small Chinese Indonesian minority found itself.

Communities of Chinese traders have been reported in the entrepôts of Southeast Asia since the early 1400s.[35] Most of the Chinese of Indonesia are, however, descendants of migrants who came to the islands in more recent times. A wave of Chinese laborers came during the last half of the nineteenth century to work in Dutch-owned plantations in northern Sumatra and the tin mines of nearby islands. Much larger numbers came after 1900, reaching a peak of 40,000 a year in the 1920s. Many of these immigrants fanned out across the archipelago to work as traders and moneylenders.[36] The phenomenon was not unique to Indonesia. Much of Southeast Asia had similar experiences.[37]

The Big Chinese Entrepreneurs

The top Chinese Indonesian owners identified by Robison in the 1980s and by Hill and Thee in the early 1990s were a varied group. Some had been born in China, but many in Indonesia. Some were members of families with business histories dating from the 1930s, some only from the late 1960s. All had had ties to the Indonesian army at one time or another, a few dating from the struggle for independence in the late 1940s, and others with ties to Suharto and other army leaders only after 1965. Some retained close ties to Suharto, while others did not. Their holdings were highly diversified as a means of risk avoidance, many with investments in finance, manufacturing, plantations, real estate, and other fields. Like Chinese minorities elsewhere, they had access to well-established networks of credit, market information, and domestic and overseas trading contacts. In addition, they understood the Indonesian bureaucracy and the prevailing system of patronage. They were not adept at doing business only in Indonesia, however. Quite a few were by the mid-1990s operating in other countries of Southeast Asia, and some in China, the United States, and Europe.[38]

Suharto believed that the Chinese were especially capable in business and that other Indonesians would have to learn from them. He also must have been well aware of the fact that the Chinese, being a highly vulnerable minority, constituted no potential political threat to himself. And his patronage was highly significant. A study conducted for the World Bank found that as much as one-quarter of the value of firms politically connected with Suharto was attributable to this connection.[39]

Not surprisingly, Suharto's oldest and closest associate in business was far and away the most successful of all. Soedono Salim (formerly Liem Sioe Liong) was in a class by himself. The Salim Group was large even in regional terms; the turnover in 1994 of its 450 companies was believed to be greater than that of any other business group in Southeast Asia, Taiwan, or Hong Kong.

Born in China, Salim sold supplies to the Indonesian army from the independence struggle of the late 1940s onward, and by the 1950s was personally acquainted with Suharto. In 1968, with Suharto in the presidency, Salim's firm was one of two given control of the import of cloves, which were used in the making of spiced *kretek* cigarettes, especially favored in Java. By the early 1990s, his group included the world's largest noodle factory, the country's largest private bank, its largest flourmill, and a giant cement plant. The Salim Group was earning about 35 percent of its revenues abroad, thus becoming more independent of the Indonesian government at the same time that it was becoming more powerful. Salim was a prime example of the manner in which the process of globalization of trade and finance was weakening the power of the state and increasing the freedom of the private sector in Indonesia's economy.[40]

The Chinese and the Foreign Debt

Salim and the other owners of large corporate groups also were primarily responsible for the borrowing of short-term capital abroad that contributed to the spread of the currency crisis from Thailand. Estimates reported by the World Bank in 2000 were that large private corporations were responsible for $85 billion of debt, out of a total for all Indonesian business, including state enterprises, of $119.7 billion.[41]

The government faced a thorny issue in how to deal with these corporate groups and their owners. There was a history of the Chinese being set apart since colonial times, when they had separate civil status, more privileged than all but a few Indonesians. Their competition with native Muslims in business helped give rise to the nationalist movement in the early part of the twentieth century.[42] Unlike the Chinese of Thailand and the Philippines, they resisted assimilation into the majority culture. And for most of the time since independence, they have been denied a role in national politics or government. Thus confined to private business, they excelled there, but at a price. In the judgment of historian Wang Gung Wu, the Chinese of Indonesia have experienced more racist violence than those of any other country in Southeast Asia.[43]

It was thus not a straightforward matter of how to get the country's big corporations back on their feet, as desirable as that might have been in terms of production of goods and services, employment, exports, and tax receipts. On the contrary, the big Chinese business owners were perceived by many non-Chinese Indonesians as having been successful, not because of any special merit of their own, but because Suharto favored them. Many Chinese had indeed been favored by loans at preferential rates from the state banks and had prospered behind walls of protection from competition. With the fall of Suharto, the big Chinese owners were in need of political allies.

It might therefore be thought that the government was in a position to impose its will on the erring owners. But these same owners now held substantial assets abroad that, if brought back to Indonesia, could help stimulate economic growth, and if not brought back, could greatly delay recovery. The financial crisis of 1997–1998 did, however, increase the government's leverage over some of the biggest of the Chinese groups. The government could, if it chose, retain a significant private sector in the banking industry by internationalizing its ownership rather than preserving the resident Chinese as major bank owners. The crisis gave the government an extraordinary opportunity to reform the structure of corporate ownership as well by selling off shares regardless of the nationality of the purchasers. Many economists in the government favored both these lines of action, but a few did not, and they were echoed by a great many members of the legislature. In the sections that follow, I shall explore the progress of and prospects for action in regard to both banks and corporations.

RESTRUCTURING THE BANKS

Indonesia's banks were a concern from the beginning of talks with the International Monetary Fund. On November 1, 1997, the day after the first IMF agreement was signed, the government closed sixteen banks, all small institutions. The aim apparently was to strengthen confidence in the banking system, but the closures had the opposite effect. Many depositors feared that additional banks might be closed. Indonesia had no deposit insurance system, and depositors began to withdraw funds from the remaining private banks at a rapid rate. Some moved their funds to state banks and foreign banks, which were seen as safer. But there also was a net outflow of money from the banking system as a whole, some of which took the form of capital flight out of the country. The damage caused by the bank closures may have been the most costly error of judgment made in the entire IMF program.[44]

Private banks had grown in significance after the sector was deregulated in 1988; within five years private banks held more than half of all bank deposits. The largest of these banks were major sources of capital for corporate purposes. Indonesia had only limited experience in raising capital through the sale of equity; business expansion traditionally was financed principally by borrowing from banks, as was common elsewhere in the region. Not surprisingly, the largest private banks were those founded by the owners of the biggest Chinese Indonesian family groupings.

Owing to the public reaction to closure of the sixteen banks, the government was reluctant to close more, and had no other option but to provide emergency funding to the rest in an effort to keep them functioning. In January 1998, when the rupiah hit 17,000 per U.S. dollar, there were concerns about the ability of the banking system to meet the mushrooming withdrawals. This in turn prompted further withdrawals. "The crisis," a later IMF report observed, "had become fully systemic."[45]

Loans without Collateral

At this point, on IMF advice that has since been faulted, the government guaranteed all deposits and credits of all domestic banks with no limit as to amount.[46] The central bank also continued to make emergency loans. Conventional practice was to extend this support in exchange for collateral, but the banks by now had little useable collateral left. Bank Indonesia therefore "extended liquidity on the basis of personal guarantees that the money would be used to meet deposit withdrawals and that the bank was in compliance with all prudential requirements."[47]

Several aspects of this process were found, upon inspection, to be unsettling. One was that the liquidity support was concentrated in a small number of banks. Out of more than 200 banks in the country at the time, more than 60 percent of the total liquidity up to June 1998 was paid out to only three banks, and 80 percent to only five banks. The largest borrower was Salim's Bank Central Asia, which borrowed 31 trillion rupiah between May 15 and June 5, 1998. Little or no attempt was made to match the support to deposit withdrawals. Later audits also revealed many prudential violations, chiefly breaches of the legal limit on lending to related parties.[48]

The Indonesian Bank Restructuring Agency

The Indonesian Bank Restructuring Agency (IBRA) was established at a high point of the crisis in January 1998. In effect it took over a nationalized banking system. IBRA was to oversee the restructuring or liquidation of weak banks, both private and state-owned, so as to limit the costs to the public budget of the government's blanket guarantees. It was to take responsibility for troubled private banks that the authorities took over but did not close down out of a desire to retain a private element in the banking sector. IBRA also had to dispose of substantial shares in hundreds of the country's best-known companies, which had been pledged as collateral for emergency liquidity support in 1997–1998 or were turned in by their owners to escape prosecution and possible prison terms.[49] Nonperforming loans by the banks were to be offered for sale.

So massive were the assets that fell under IBRA's control that the agency was soon at the center of a struggle for the nation's economic soul. On the one hand were the former owners of the banks and corporations, who were still very wealthy individuals and had an interest in retaining control of as many of their companies as possible. On the other hand were politicians, who saw IBRA as a prize cash cow. In the middle were IBRA officials assigned to dispose of its holdings in a rational manner.

From the start of the crisis until late 2001, out of 237 banks, 68 were closed, those already owned by the state were merged into four, and seven of the largest surviving private banks were under the supervision of IBRA. In the course of these changes, deposits "migrated" from private banks to the state banking system. These developments put the government directly in control of fully 70 percent of the deposits in the banking system, compared to 40 percent in Korea and 23 percent in Thailand. In addition, the government also held significant stakes in the private recapitalized banks. The process was extremely costly. The government estimated that the total cost of recapitalizing troubled banks that had not been closed, and of meeting its deposit guarantee for private banks being liquidated, would amount to 406 trillion rupiah, or the equivalent of $50 billion. By October 2000 the cost of recapitalization alone was revised to 650 trillion *rupiah*, or the equivalent of more than $90 billion.[50] It was becoming increasingly urgent to balance these rising costs with revenue from selling off the banks that were still marketable.

Selling the Banks

The single most attractive bank was Bank Central Asia (BCA), Indonesia's largest private bank with 767 branches. Bank Central Asia had been owned by Soedono Salim and members of the Suharto family. It survived the first run on private banks, depositors evidently reckoning that Suharto would not let that one bank fail. But after Suharto fell from power, Bank Central Asia experienced a heavy run on its deposits, and Bank Indonesia provided 32 trillion rupiah in liquidity support—a staggering $4 billion at the then prevailing rate of exchange. Government auditors subsequently discovered that nearly 70 percent of the bank's loans had gone to other Salim Group companies; the limit permitted under Indonesian law was 20 percent. The BCA owners eventually were found to owe the government 52 trillion rupiah, or the equivalent of $7.2 billion at the time.

Under threat of criminal prosecution, the owners signed over to an IBRA holding company shares in 104 companies, including Bank Central Asia itself. In agreement with the International Monetary Fund, the government first committed itself to selling the BCA shares during the first quarter of 1999, but this was delayed by parliamentary interference. A sale finally came off in May 2000, but only 22.5 percent of BCA shares were part of the public offering. Clearly the government was reluctant to allow too many of IBRA's once private assets to be sold under what were seen as fire sale conditions. The amount raised by the sale was deeply disappointing; the shares yielded a mere 13 percent of their book value.[51]

Nevertheless, the budget pressure could not be ignored. In July 2001, IBRA announced a plan to sell a further 40 percent stake in BCA, including 10 percent to the public and 30 percent to an unnamed strategic investor. The press expressed the fear that only a front for the Salim family could be expected to buy Bank Central Asia in the political and economic circumstances prevailing at the time. This was enough for IBRA to cancel its review of the bids and to restart the whole process.

In September 2001, the Indonesian parliament finally approved the concept of the sale of 51 percent of Bank Central Asia to a single strategic investor. And in March 2002, three years later than initially intended, Laksamana Sukardi announced the sale of 51 percent of BCA to a consortium led by a small San Francisco hedge fund, Farallon Capital Management, for $541.6 million. Farallon had never run a bank before. The consortium included a local partner, the Hartono family, owners of PT Djarum, a manufacturer of cigarettes, the sales of which were untouched by the prevailing slowdown in business. The absence of a major foreign bank among the purchasers was a big disappointment to many reform-minded observers.

In September 2002, the parliament approved the twice-delayed sale of 51 percent of Bank Niaga, the country's tenth largest bank, and the next month the government announced Niaga's sale to a Malaysian firm. In May 2003, the government sold a 51 percent stake in Bank Danamon, into which several private banks had been merged, to a consortium led by Temasek Holdings, the investment arm of the Singapore government; Deutsche Bank was part of the consortium. The government still had banks to sell when IBRA's mandate ran out in February 2004. Among them was Bank Mandiri, the country's largest financial institution, created by the merger of four state banks, which was to be sold via shares on the stock market. When the first shares of Bank Mandiri were marketed in mid-2003, foreign investors made bids that were 10 times the number of shares that were up for sale. The government was coming close to completing the privatization via internationalization of the country's banking industry.

Dealing with Errant Bankers

A remaining issue was how to deal with bank owners charged with violating banking regulations, lying about the value of their collateral, or resisting repayment of debts they owed the central bank. A cabinet-level Financial Sector Policy Committee proposed that problem bankers who violated maximum lending limits or lied in surrendering assets should be subject to criminal charges. The committee also proposed civil actions such as forced takeovers of firms and forced sale of personal assets. A team of six prominent lawyers was appointed to review the record, case by case, and recommend action. Final decisions were to be made by the cabinet.

Perhaps the most egregious case was that of Nirwan Dermawan Bakrie, who seemed to have broken all the banking rules and then put off turning over shares that he had offered as collateral. Yet he could well afford to pay what he owed. The Bakrie Group was reported to have funds invested in telecommunications in Vietnam; mines in Kazakhstan, Uzbekistan, and Iran; and an oil field in Yemen. Its oil business alone was estimated to be worth $1 billion.[52]

IBRA had a mandate to settle the civil charges, and was doing so, but it had no mandate with regard to the criminal charges. The government faced a strategic question: should it pursue the criminal charges and thus make permanent the flight of crony billions being held offshore—the total was estimated at $25 to $30 billion—or offer an amnesty to some number of the entrepreneurs concerned in return for their repatriating their money?

Foreign government donors and international agencies urged strict enforcement of the law. Indonesian officials with responsibility for the economy were inclined to be more flexible. They reasoned that the Suharto political regime had created the cronies, not the other way around; yet the leading figures of the political regime were not being prosecuted. In addition, the exile capital might be the last large resource still available to the government of Indonesia, if, as seemed inevitable, IBRA asset sales and privatization of state enterprises proved impossible to pursue to their targeted levels. Only a handful of bankers had been prosecuted under criminal law. Five were given sentences of twenty years to life, but they were tried in absentia and were not expected to serve any time at all. Another twelve received much lighter terms of ten months to five years. In civil suits, only 2.8 trillion rupiah had so far been ordered repaid out of 138 trillion paid out by the central bank at the height of the crisis. As of late 2004, not a single major banker had spent a night in jail.

By the end of June 2003, IBRA had recouped a total of only 146 trillion rupiah, or $17.4 billion, of the 650 trillion rupiah ($77.5 billion) spent on resuscitating the banking system. Critics believed the agency's staff, which at its peak numbered 5,000, had "slowly surrendered (in) its battle of attrition with the country's richest, most powerful people."[53] John McBeth, the long-time bureau chief in Jakarta for the *Far Eastern Economic Review*, observed that, with such limited returns, the banking scandal might amount to "the biggest bank heist in history," and added that it left the government "with little choice but to divert money away from such important areas as health and education to pay for the damage."[54]

The Quality of Banking

The quality of the bank sell-off was thus decidedly mixed. Clearly the process had been highly politicized; IBRA had seven chairmen in only four years. That the sell-off earned the government much less than had been hoped was also clear. At the same time, it was now certain that the outcome would be a more diverse ownership in the banking sector, including a variety of entities, governmental and private, domestic and foreign. If this prospect were accompanied by strengthened supervision, the resulting system promised to be politically more durable than the one it was replacing, as well as economically more efficient.

Improving bank supervision was now a high priority. In October 2002, Syahfruddin Temenggung, appointed chairman of IBRA the previous April, said that Indonesia's banks remained vulnerable to another financial crisis as too little had been done to improve their governance. The government was only then beginning to set up the Financial Services Authority that was to take over the supervisory role of Bank Indonesia, which had failed to halt the profligate channeling of bank funds to affiliated companies. The government was only just moving to establish the Deposit Insurance Corporation, which would guarantee the public's bank deposits, the absence of which had helped fuel the bank runs in 1997–1998.[55]

Thus, at enormous cost, the banking system of Indonesia was restructured. Through several presidencies, a tortuous process gave somewhat coherent shape to a banking system that would have to see the economy well into the twenty-first century. Many of the problem banks were still passively subsisting on dividends paid out on government bonds, and not yet engaging in the active lending that recovery required. The transition of banking away from the financial crisis stretched out further and further into the future.

BALANCING THE BUDGET

The financial crisis and the cost of paying for the bank bailout caused considerable "fiscal distress" in Indonesia, to use the words of Anwar Nasution, senior deputy governor of Bank Indonesia.[56]

Indonesia had followed a conservative fiscal policy based on a roughly balanced budget for many years, but this policy was abandoned early in the crisis. Sovereign debt jumped from 24 percent of GDP in 1997 to 100 percent of GDP in the three years from 1997 to 2000, owing largely to the bank bailout; it was expected to be down to 68 percent of GDP in 2004, which was still high by regional standards. Interest paid on the public debt increased from 1.8 percent of GDP in fiscal 1997–1998 to 5.7 percent in fiscal 2000, and increased from 15 percent of government expenditures to 23 percent in those same years. Repayments of principal became significant in 2003, jumped to a much higher level in 2004, and were to continue increasing in each of the three years thereafter. In response to the rising burden of debt service obligations, the Megawati government cut nondebt expenditures, but meeting the growing cost was a matter of mounting concern.

The country's external debt increased from $66.9 billion in 1990 to $141 billion in December 2000, making it the largest in East Asia. The government's share of this external debt was $73.5 billion as of July 2002, and the cash flow needed to finance it constituted a heavy drain on budget resources, as well as on the balance of payments. To ease the pressure, the Paris Club of creditor nations had agreed to a series of delays in principal repayments of Indonesia's public external debt, and even, on one occasion, a delay in payment of interest. But this did not solve any problems; it only transferred the task of repayment to future years. And there was no way to ensure that external creditors would be willing to postpone repayment indefinitely.

The burden of debt service obligations was expected to remain high, particularly if economic growth were to remain low. President Susilo promised to raise annual growth to around 6.6 percent from levels of around 4.5 percent when he entered office in 2004, but it was not known how he proposed to accomplish this. Together with the rising international price of oil (of which Indonesia was by 2004 a net importer), this left no alternative, in the opinion of central bankers, except for the government to speed the sale of nationalized corporate assets, which was problematic, or raise more revenue from taxes, which a corrupt tax service could not be counted on to accomplish. That left continued reductions in social services, which would hurt the lower income levels of society, meaning that a further cost of the bank bailout would be a worsening of the pattern of income distribution. Preserving the assets of a few wealthy bank owners and the savings of middle-class bank depositors at such a cost seemed unconscionable to at least some in Jakarta, and the issue seemed bound to become a major issue for public policy sooner or later.

Selling Corporate Assets

As of March 2001, the corporate assets taken over by IBRA from failed banks were valued at $50 billion, equal to 57 percent of GDP, of which only 7 percent had been sold. The performance of other countries of the region was strikingly different: Korea had taken over assets valued at $84 billion, equal to 11 percent of GDP, of which 48 percent were sold; Thailand had taken over assets of $13 billion, equal to 11 percent of GDP, of which 70 percent were sold; and Malaysia, assets of $10.3 billion, equal to 12 percent of GDP, of which 61 percent were sold.[57] Indonesia had taken over a larger volume of assets relative to the size of its economy, and yet was far behind the others in reselling them. Why was it so much more difficult for the government of Indonesia to sell these assets?

By January 2001, IBRA was negotiating the future of some 1,000 corporations. The true value of many of these firms could not easily be determined.

Shares of many of them had never been sold on the public market. Most had no history of releasing financial information to the public. Moreover, the nature of the connections the firms had with others in the same group was opaque. The situation was ready-made for controversy and delay.

Selling Astra Motors

One of the first corporations marked for sale was PT Astra International, an assembler and distributor of motor vehicles, and often rated as the best-managed company in the Indonesian private sector. The firm had been founded by William Soeryadjaya, an Indonesian-born Chinese entrepreneur who had received some business training in the Netherlands. Astra controlled half the country's motor vehicle market, thanks to government protection and a strong management team. But Soeryadjaya was never close to Suharto, and when the Soeryadjaya-owned Bank Summa collapsed in 1992, the government did not offer to bail it out. Soeryadjaya put his holdings in Astra up for sale in order to repay Bank Summa depositors, and relatives and friends of Suharto bought most of the shares. Several of these new shareholders later pledged their Astra shares in return for liquidity support to their banks from Bank Indonesia during the crisis; others surrendered Astra shares in partial settlement of fines for violating legal lending limits. As a result, about 30 percent of Astra shares came to be held by IBRA. Interest in the sale of the Astra shares was intense. For IBRA too the sale was critical. IBRA had yet to make a major sale of once private assets.

   A first effort to sell Astra ran afoul of domestic politics. In the end, the Astra stake was sold in March 2000 for $500 million to a Singaporean automobile distributor, Cycle and Carriage, which was desperately trying to break out of its small home market. The Government of Singapore Investment Corp. played a key role in convincing a competing group, made up of Lazard Freres & Co. and a bank part-owned by George Soros, to drop their bid and join forces. Two U.S. investment firms, Newbridge and Gilbert, had pulled out two days before the bidding deadline, and President Wahid had advised the Soeryadjaya family to withdraw. The Astra deal was thus riven with politics, but this did not save its shares from falling into foreign, largely Singaporean government, hands.

Selling Salim Plantations

The next major sale was completed only a year later, when IBRA sold 180,000 hectares of palm oil plantations, mainly on the islands of Sumatra and Kalimantan (Indonesian Borneo), for $368 million to Kumpulan Guthrie

Bhd., a Malaysian firm. The Malaysian plantation industry had been caught in a price squeeze and was seen as increasingly uncompetitive. International palm oil prices were depressed, high land costs were already causing producers to relocate from the peninsula to the north coast of Borneo, and high labor costs were causing them to rely on migrants from Indonesia for 60 percent of their workforce. The plantations sold to Guthrie were among the assets turned over to IBRA by the Salim Group, which remained a powerful force in the Indonesian plantation industry, controlling most of the marketing of refined palm oil. Political developments delayed the signing of the deal, originally announced in November 2000.

Parliamentary members of then Vice President Megawati's party objected strenuously that Malaysia would be in a position to dominate the international palm oil market, and farmers claimed they had not been compensated adequately for land used to establish the plantations. After the deal was closed, farmers' groups demanded the right to farm plantation land themselves and sell their produce to Guthrie. Megawati, responding to these nationalist and populist appeals, called for the agreement to be reviewed again. Guthrie's money was held in escrow until the DPR (Dewan Perwakilan Rakyat or Council of People's Representatives) approved the sale in early 2002, amid rumors that bribes were paid to DPR members and that the objections had been designed to squeeze the investors to pay up.

The Future of Asset Sales

These cases raised serious questions about how effective IBRA could be in rescuing the government budget by selling off former assets of the wealthiest business houses. The purchasers were under considerable competitive pressure to expand into Indonesia, where the auto market was large and palm oil production costs were low. Such conditions could not be replicated in many other cases. The Astra and Guthrie deals did provide one clue as to how IBRA might fare down the line: nationalist political sentiment and the valuations issue seemed likely to scare off all but the most hardy of investors, making it virtually impossible to realize "market values" for the assets.

IBRA sales also faced an uncertain future because of the prominence of the owners. Members of the Suharto family and the wealthiest Chinese businessmen in the country faced the prospect of being removed from the ownership of some of the nation's largest corporate assets. There was a high probability that former owners were using IBRA sales to buy back their former corporate assets through third parties at bargain prices, and leaving the state to deal with the banks, in which much less of their own money was involved. With their longstanding knowledge of the corporations, continuing personal ties to corporate managers, and working through front companies, former owners were thought to have a considerable advantage in IBRA auctions or negotiations.

When the possibility was broached in March 2003 of delaying the sale of IBRA assets altogether, pending better market conditions, it was not as though a vigorous program was in danger of being halted. The large, diversified Chinese Indonesian family-owned groups were not about to disappear. Many were likely to survive into a future in which they might be less diversified and more focused on their core assets. The corporate structure of the Suharto era, with families owning highly diversified holdings, dependent on personal access to the president of the country and on presidential control of state banks, seemed an anachronism in the twenty-first century. Yet family-owned corporate groups are common in many emerging markets around the world, and "relationship banking" is common throughout East Asia. It is therefore not likely that the family-owned business groups of Indonesia will give way to Western-style, professionally managed corporations with diversified ownership at any time soon.[58]

IBRA closed down in 2004 with part of its agenda unfinished, and the Ministry of Finance became responsible for completing the sales of banks and other corporate assets that were still in government hands. A special unit was created to meet this responsibility. Whether it would be anything other than a scaled-down IBRA, perhaps subject to less intense public attention, was uncertain. The original IBRA had a reputation as a corrupt instrumentality that failed to meet many of the objectives for which it had been created.

The Foreign Debt

The foreign debt was equally problematic. The Paris Club of foreign bilateral donors had rescheduled Indonesia's foreign public debt three times since the crisis began. This was in the context of an IMF program in place. But the political elite of Indonesia was growing increasingly restive under IMF supervision, and in August 2002 the MPR approved a resolution providing for an end of the IMF program when the current agreement would terminate in November 2002. In the absence of an IMF program, it was expected that there would be no Paris Club 4. This left no clear sense of how the problem of repaying the foreign public debt was going to be resolved.

Foreign private debt problems also remained. The most spectacular case was that of Asia Pulp and Paper, owned by the Widjaja family, which owed $13.9 billion to scores of international bondholders, banks, and trading companies, as well as foreign government agencies. Ambassadors representing the home countries of eleven export credit agencies, which were owed $6.7 billion of the total, sent a letter to President Megawati in March 2003, protesting a restructuring plan approved by IBRA as too lenient. The *Far Eastern Economic Review* commented at about that time that, as Indonesia headed toward presidential elections in 2004, "wealthy owners of indebted conglomerates may be able to increase their leverage with politicians seeking campaign funding, making it harder for state agencies like IBRA to pressure debtors like APP."[59]

COPING WITH GLOBAL FORCES

The crisis that began in 1997 owed more than a little of its severity in Indonesia to the weakness of domestic institutions of governance. Suharto's own failings and the legacies of his long authoritarian rule left the nation ill prepared to deal effectively with the forces of economic globalization. At the same time, foreign governments and international institutions contributed their share to the widespread repercussions of the Indonesian debacle.

The central international player was the International Monetary Fund, members of whose staff made front-page news in Jakarta with their frequent comings and goings. Less visible but ultimately more powerful were the international financial markets and the corporations that, as direct investors, brought capital, technology, management skills, and market access to the Indonesian economy. The perceptions and behavior of these forces constituted major challenges for the first governments that followed Suharto and promised to do so for successors yet to come.

The Fund announced on October 31, 1997, that it would provide Indonesia with $10 billion as a first line of defense of the rupiah over three years, provided Indonesia met the terms of a reform program agreed on with IMF officials. Pledges and promises from other international agencies and member governments brought the total to approximately $40 billion. It was said to be the second largest financial bailout in history, outsized only by the Mexican bailout of 1995.[60] After the three years of the program ran out, the Fund agreed to a further $5 billion over three years, again provided that specified reforms were carried out.

The IMF Performance

The Indonesian bailout took place in an atmosphere of controversy from the very outset. The future of the Fund itself was being debated in the United States, where prominent conservatives were arguing that the Fund encouraged governments to run imprudent risks.[61] The Fund ought to be closed down and governments left to deal with the financial marketplace on their own, it was argued, as this was the only way they would learn self-discipline. Liberals, on the other hand, argued that the Fund should consider the quality of governance in its assessments and not limit itself to monetary issues alone, as bad governance was often at the heart of financial crises in the first place. This debate caused the performance of the Fund itself and the quality of governance in Indonesia to become issues in the bailout from the very outset. At the time, the government of Japan, highly critical of the depth of Fund intrusion in Indonesia, began soliciting views on a possible Asian Monetary Fund.[62]

The initial agreement between the Fund and the government of Indonesia, signed on November 1, 1997, was promptly criticized for requiring the Indonesian government to reduce its spending. Jeffrey D. Sachs, whose Harvard institute was advising the Indonesians on a range of economic policy matters, argued that the Fund was applying the wrong medicine, a lesson drawn from the Fund's experience in Latin America, where governments frequently engaged in spending beyond their resources. Sachs pointed out that the government of Indonesia was already running a surplus, not a deficit.[63] The Fund acknowledged the accuracy of this criticism implicitly by reversing itself in a greatly revised agreement in January 1998, which permitted the government to run a modest deficit in hopes of stimulating a return to growth. But critical momentum had been lost.

The closing of sixteen banks mandated by the Fund in the November agreement backfired, as already noted, leading to the run on private domestic banks that began the breakdown of the banking system. Another point of controversy regarding IMF advice in the banking sector was the delayed timing and unlimited terms of the government's guarantee to depositors. Some economists among the critics, including Nobel Prize winner Joseph Stiglitz, judged the Fund to have failed in Indonesia on the basis of these events alone.[64] An internal IMF evaluation later acknowledged that the initial strategy of the Fund in October 1997 failed because its staff "underestimated the severity and the potential macroeconomic risks" posed by the vulnerabilities of the Indonesian banking sector and "misjudged the extent of ownership (of the strategy) at the highest political level."[65]

Later Criticisms of the Fund

Much later the Fund was criticized for overreaching in Indonesia, calling for too many reforms, delving into matters that went beyond the experience of its staff, and failing to establish clear priorities for government attention. The Fund did reach deeply into the governance of Indonesia. It insisted on changes in draft legislation concerning the independence of the central bank;

on being consulted about interest rates, the money supply, and inflation; and on revisions being made in the budget to avoid an excessive deficit. It pressed constantly for faster restructuring of the banks and faster disposition of assets by IBRA. It actively supported the ban to keep former owners from buying back their old companies at bargain prices. It also set targets for court reform, and warned of dangers to be avoided in the process of decentralization. The number of its conditions, at their peak, ran to 130.

Robert E. Ruben, U.S. Secretary of the Treasury during this period, later observed:

> Many of the changes that the IMF pushed were outside its usual realm of ex- pertise on exchange rates, interest rates, and government finances. And in hind- sight, many people involved agree that there were too many conditions spread across many different areas. Expecting the government to fix so many problems at once just wasn't realistic and probably blurred focus on the most urgent ones. The most controversial measures, however, were not dreamed up by the IMF, the U.S. Treasury, or other outsiders. . . . In this case, the Fund's policy condi- tions were informed by the views of a number of Indonesian officials . . . as well as by the World Bank.[66]

Most seriously, the Fund was charged with hastening the departure of Pres- idents Suharto, Habibie, and Wahid from public office. The Fund suspended payments to Indonesia at key points in the presidencies of all three. The first suspension occurred in the early months of 1998, when Suharto failed to carry out reforms that he had personally agreed to undertake; with his government starved for cash, Suharto relented, removed the subsidies holding down gaso- line and electricity prices, and set loose a chain of events that led to his fall from power. The second suspension occurred when the Bank Bali scandal broke in September 1999, adding to perceptions of its seriousness and help- ing to end the Habibie presidency. The third suspension ran through the first eight months of 2001, during which the Wahid government was under such political pressure from parliament that its ability to meet commitments of any kind was in serious doubt. The criticism of the Fund was thus valid, but it did not negate the fact that the three Indonesian presidents were equally to blame for the breakdowns that occurred in the relationship.[67]

Ending the IMF Program

Irritated by the constant need to submit to IMF policy prescriptions, many Indonesian politicians and some Indonesian economists pressed the Megawati government to break relations with the Fund before the scheduled end of its program in November 2003. Rizal Ramli, who had been Wahid's senior economics minister during the eight months during which the Fund suspended payments, accused the Fund of incompetence and of destabilizing Indonesia politically. His assessment of IMF advice was blunt: "generic trash."[68] The frequently critical Kwik Kian Gie, who was Wahid's first senior minister for economic affairs and head of national planning in Megawati's cabinet, said that the IMF had not been relevant to Indonesia since the first quarter of 2001, when government repayments to the Fund exceeded the new funds being received from it. Those who thought the Fund was needed to boost world confidence in Indonesia were wrong, he said, as not a single foreign investor had come to the country since 1997. The IMF had "brought neither money nor good advice."[69]

The Fund's policy preferences were beginning to be questioned more widely as the monetary crisis in East Asia was followed by others in Russia, Brazil, and Argentina. Too many monetary crises were occurring around the world, and they were causing harm that was increasingly widespread, reaching deeply even into countries that were "doing everything right."[70] At the same time, as the Fund was the principal force for structural economic reform in Indonesia, many mainstream economists there believed that, after a poor start, it had made the best of a bad situation. The Megawati government agreed to a postprogram monitoring agreement under which its economic officials would meet with IMF staff periodically for policy discussions. Letters of intent and further IMF fund transfers were not intended to flow from these discussions. Fund reports were, however, expected to carry weight in the private international markets where Indonesia hoped to raise funds to fill its gap in income. Thus, the tenure of Dorodjatun Kuntjoro-Jakti as senior economic minister brought Indonesia's often stormy relations with the IMF to a peaceful conclusion. The Fund and three Indonesian presidents together had created a costly way out of what initially had been just a case of monetary "contagion."

The performance of the Fund was still creating political ripples in Jakarta at the start of the Susilo presidency. He initially intended to appoint an Indonesian executive director of the IMF in Washington as his minister of finance, but nationalist-minded political figures whom Susilo was attempting to hold in his coalition objected strenuously. A former senior official of the ministry got the post instead.

Private Investment

Loans available through the International Monetary Fund, the World Bank, the Asian Development Bank, and the governments that finance them are not sufficient to meet the needs of the Indonesian economy. The funds are not sufficient in either quantity or quality. The total debt of Indonesia was put at $198 billion by the minister of finance in July 2001, of which $132 billion was government debt and $66 billion was private sector debt. Because much of the government debt was domestic, quite unlike the pre-1997 situation, the dollar equivalent varied from time to time, but it was clear that this debt far outran the scale of foreign aid available from all sources by a large margin. In fact, pledges to Indonesia by these sources were declining in scale. It is ironic that the industrial democracies were reducing their economic aid to Indonesia just as the country's reforms were in need of political space.

Investment is needed from private parties outside Indonesia also because it can bring with it new technology, improved management skills, and market intelligence. (One would have, until America's corporate scandals, added "better corporate governance" to the list.) As table 4.6 shows, net private capital flows into Indonesia were at the level of $16.1 billion in 1996, the last full year before the crisis, and net flows out of Indonesia reached $11.1 billion in the year 2000. It was subsequently reported that the net flow outward continued at the level of $4.3 billion in the first half of 2001 and $2.5 billion in the first half of 2002. Some of this outflow could be attributed to private debt repayment, but most of it was unadorned capital flight.

The Security of Investors

The security of foreign investors will remain a major test for any Indonesian government in the early twenty-first century. It was not only the giant multinational operations in Aceh and Papua that were in need of protection, although the size of these and the environment of separatism in which they were functioning meant that they tended to serve as symbols of the wider condition. Businessmen I talked with on my visits after 1998 said it was the continual harassment of businesses, large and small, in Java and in the outer islands, by daily acts of thievery, vandalism, and intimidation by local gangs, by the ambitions of newly empowered local politicians, the protection rackets run by unscrupulous police and military, and after October 2002 the threat of terrorist violence, that worked against the attractiveness of Indonesia to foreign investors. The restoration of law and order on the scale called for was a major challenge, although the police success in identifying and capturing

Table 4.6. Private Capital Flows, Net Total (US$) (billions)

	1990	1996	1997	1998	1999	2000
Indonesia	3.2	16.1	10.8	−3.3	−8.4	−11.2

Source: World Bank, *World Development Indicators*, CD-ROM, 2002.

many of those involved in the Bali bombings offered some hope that this challenge would eventually be met.

Still others pointed to more conventional sources of losses by foreign investors, such as union strikes, mandated wage increases, high taxes, and rampant smuggling of cheap goods made in China as grounds for shifting production to other countries. Whatever the motives, many foreign firms were reducing orders from Indonesian producers, as Reebok and Nike did in 2002, laying off between 5,000 and 10,000 workers, or closing down altogether, as a Sony audio equipment factory did, laying off 1,000. Government approvals of Japanese direct investment, prized because most of it was for manufacturing, were down for 2002 to about $390 million, or a mere 7 percent of the 1997 level. The Japanese External Trade Organization said publicly that Indonesia was no longer a preferred destination for investment, as the advantages of low costs of labor and energy had eroded in the previous two years.[71]

An equally demanding challenge was the need for legal security of assets. Many elements of the Indonesian economy were functioning without the rule of law. Contracts signed with the national government were ignored by local officials. State corporations reneged on deals, often years after they were signed. Allegations were widespread of bribery by all participants in the judicial system, which a U.N. rapporteur visiting Jakarta in July 2002 called one of the worst he had ever seen.

The dysfunctional state of the judicial system was epitomized by the case of Manulife Financial Corporation, a major Canadian insurance company and part owner of an Indonesian subsidiary, Manulife Indonesia. Harassment by a disgruntled former minority partner, which fell into bankruptcy and was taken over by IBRA, reached the point that several top executives of Manulife were jailed on bogus charges. The company also was presented with a claim that it was bankrupt on the ground that it did not declare a dividend in 1999, and a panel of three judges in Jakarta upheld the claim. The Supreme Court eventually overturned the decision, and the minister of justice asked the police to investigate allegations of judicial bribery. The unwarranted legal proceedings became a cause célèbre. For some investors, the political and legal conditions of operating in Indonesia had become a "nightmare," and they were pulling out.[72]

Yet this agenda only scratches the surface of what is involved in making Indonesia competitive in the new global economy. The *World Competitive Yearbook*, issued in April 2001, ranking 49 countries in terms of 286 criteria affecting their competitiveness, ranked Indonesia last. Many of the criteria used in the ranking are structural, such as government efficiency and quality of education, and thus any nation's ranking will evolve only slowly over time. These again are matters of perception as well as objective fact, but the finding needs to be taken as yet another sign, if one were needed, that Indonesia faces a host of challenges, some of them long-term in nature, that will have to be overcome if it is to face the next phase of global capital movements more successfully than it did those of the decade from 1988, when banking was deregulated, to 1998, when Suharto fell. That prospect argues for Indonesia's need to be ready to take defensive action the next time crisis looms up from abroad.

THE TASK AHEAD

"Recovery" and "reform" of the Indonesian economy have more than one possible meaning. If recovery is taken in its narrowest sense, it means the return of Indonesia's GDP to where it was in 1996 before the crisis began. In U.S. dollar terms, the economy was growing slowly in the early years of the twenty-first century—at more than 3 percent in 2001 to 2003, and at 4.5 percent in 2004. At these rates, according to a Morgan Stanley estimate, the GDP would return to its precrisis level only in 2004, and the GDP per capita would do so only in 2005.[73] Thus Indonesia was expected to experience almost a decade of limited growth and forgone income—a high price to pay for the failures that caused the crisis to hit Indonesia as hard as it did.

Economic recovery also might be taken to mean a recovery to the precrisis rate of growth of GDP: that rate was an annual average of 7 percent or better in every decade from 1965 to 1995. President Susilo promised to bring the rate of growth back up to 6.6 percent during his five-year term of office, but the circumstances invited caution. Too much accumulated wealth had been lost. Too many established corporations had gone bankrupt, de facto if not de jure; too many banks, public and private, had been closed or merged out of existence; too many domestic investors had moved too much of their capital out of the country; and too many foreign investors had been scared off altogether. Replacing these institutions to regain the capacity for 7 percent growth is a very considerable challenge. And even this would leave Indonesia far, far below the trend line of per capita income that had been established in earlier decades.

Stability with Low Growth

Coming into office, Susilo Bambang Yudhoyono found the economy in a state of macrostability. The exchange rate was more or less steady. Inflation was more or less under control. Foreign reserves were up. But this stability was not leading to growth at precrisis levels.[74] Nor was it producing jobs. It was urgent that a way be found to stimulate faster growth, and in the short term that meant running a deficit in the public budget; the issue was how large a deficit could be tolerated without causing too much damage to the stability that had been so hard earned. The government faced a need to charge the state budget with the rising cost of fuel subsidies while it prepared the public for their reduction. With oil at $50 a barrel, the cost of these subsidies was rising rapidly. The government also had to meet the rapidly rising cost of servicing the domestic debt. Solving the budget problem was certain to be a major challenge.[75]

This was so even before the tsunami destroyed tens of thousands of homes and workplaces and wiped out much of the physical infrastructure of Aceh. With the relief phase of the response still having some distance to go, the cost of reconstruction was yet to be estimated, but it might well cost more than the foreign assistance received for the purpose. Neither the government of Aceh nor the people of the province were in any position to finance much of this reconstruction. Except for reserves of oil and gas of uncertain dimensions, Aceh commands minimal resources and has a GDP that amounts to less than 2 percent of the national GDP.

Also hard to measure was the time it would take to restore banking, and thus domestic investment, to a robust state. It was urgent that the economy return to higher rates of growth of GDP. One was already hearing references to the "Filipinization" of the Indonesian economy, implying that Indonesia might have to be satisfied with average annual rates of growth in the vicinity of 3–4 percent. That was the average annual rate of growth of the Philippine economy all the way from 1965 to 1995, as a result of which the economy of the Philippines had been declining relative to the other market economies of the region at least since the mid-1960s. In the early years of this period, it was a close second in size to the economy of Indonesia; by the start of the new century, it was the smallest among the five major economies of the region.

The people of Indonesia, long accustomed to growth that was more than twice as rapid as that of the Philippines, were not likely to tolerate slow growth indefinitely. It was widely believed that an annual growth rate of 6 percent was needed just to produce new jobs for Indonesia's 2 million entrants into the labor force each year. The Philippine response to the lack of employment opportunity has been to export between 7 and 8 million workers to jobs abroad. A relatively high level of general education plus considerable facility with the English language are factors that have favored this response in the case of the Philippines. Indonesia does not have that option.

The Human Cost

Unemployment was perhaps the principal social cost of the crisis that began in 1997. Open unemployment was a mere 2.8 percent in 1993, rose to 4.7

percent by the onset of the crisis in 1997, and reached 8.1 percent in 2001. An estimated 8 million people out of a total workforce of 99 million were openly unemployed. But the number of the disguised unemployed, or underemployed, was three and a half times the open unemployed, or an additional 28 million, of whom three out of every four lived in rural areas, and two out of every three worked in agriculture and forestry. Creating full employment for these rural citizens is much less costly than creating full employment for urban dwellers, but private banks and corporations cannot do this job. Creating jobs for the bulk of the unemployed was a task for public authorities.[76] The urgency of the task was underscored by a government report that 61 percent of the unemployed were young men in the range of fifteen to twenty-four years of age, the age-group most liable to become involved in criminal activity.[77]

It is important to keep this human dimension in mind when we observe that Indonesia will have sustained very substantial losses in its wealth and forgone income by the time the economy gets back to precrisis levels of growth. And these losses will be experienced by Indonesians of all economic classes, including those who can least afford them. The World Bank estimated that in 1999, while 7.7 percent of the Indonesian population was living below the international poverty level of $1 a day, 55.3 percent of the population was living below the near poverty level of $2 per day.[78] The loss of social solidarity that these conditions imply for the future of class relations, interethnic relations, interreligious tolerance, and political accommodation can only be imagined. It is a prospect that places great responsibilities for the long-term future on the shoulders of the nation's leading public authorities in the years immediately ahead.

Reform as a Continuing Process

If newly generated growth is to be durable, then the reform of economic institutions will need to be seen as a continuing process. The nation will have gained little from its economic trauma if it is to witness a continuation of the state as a dominant owner in the real economy. I have shown why continued state ownership will result in the management of economic enterprises in ways that are less efficient than would be the case under private ownership and management, and will thus constitute a drag on economic growth. I have shown too why state ownership will provide an enticement to financial corruption and thus be a factor slowing the process of democratization. I also have argued that the continued ownership of a large number of the country's largest corporations by a small number of families, most of them minority Indonesian Chinese, is neither socially desirable nor politically durable.

I have focused on ownership. This should not be confused with the power to regulate. The regulation of the Indonesian economy is a given, and deregulation on the pattern of banking in 1988 seems highly unlikely to be repeated for any real sector of the economy at any time soon. The importance of preparing for deregulation is a lesson one hopes many Indonesians will draw from the 1998 crisis and its aftermath. Moreover, anyone familiar with the Javanese bureaucratic mind knows that the provision of official "guidance" is a function normally expected of government in regard to economic activity in Indonesia. This alone will provide ample opportunities for continued corruption, but the opportunities would be less readily available than in the case of continued state ownership and its corollary: a large political hand in enterprise micromanagement.

Much will depend on the lessons that are drawn from the post-1998 experience by the future leadership of Indonesia. If a future president or aspirant to the presidency were tempted to respond to the pressures of global change by calling for Indonesia to turn away from the rest of the world, wise counselors would be needed to save the leadership from imagining that safety is to be found in attempting to isolate the economy internationally. Indonesia has been part of the global economy since at least the fifteenth century. Moreover, the geography of Indonesia makes its borders highly permeable, so that it makes far more sense to tax international trade than to inhibit it and encourage smuggling. The Indonesian economy would function very poorly in a policy environment of isolation. The case of Myanmar (formerly Burma) is right there in Southeast Asia for anyone to see the cost.

The future of the Indonesian economy needs to be conceived as a part of the larger, changing world of which it has for centuries been a part. The Indonesian economy needs to be resilient enough to engage this larger world. In all honesty, one must say that this resilience calls for a rapid improvement in the level of social services, particularly education, that might not be possible without substantial outside help.

Is it too much to suggest that the international community might have a role to play? External economic institutions had some share of responsibility for the excesses that were part of the boom years of the 1990s and the errors of judgment that marked the early stages of recovery. Indonesian bank owners and depositors panicked, but so did the major international financial houses. Indonesian officials made mistakes, but so did officials of the IMF and the governments that dominated its decision making. There is much opinion in Indonesia that it is owed some compensation for the losses it suffered in accommodating itself to these institutions.

It is true that the history of financial crises is written by the creditors.[79] Yet to leave the cost of the crisis of 1998 to be borne solely by the taxpayers of

Indonesia seems no more defensible than it would have been to leave the response to the tsunami to local resources. The IMF and the governments that are its principal members did contribute to making the sovereign debt of Indonesia as large as it is, and perhaps they could under the right circumstances consider helping restructure and reduce it. Did the devastation wrought by the tsunami bring about the "right" circumstances? Could the IMF and its principal owners bail out the Indonesian economy more fully than they have already done while so many wealthy Indonesians continue to escape paying any price for their own contributions to the debacle? Thus the economy may continue to be held hostage to the social and political forces that made the crisis of 1998 so damaging in the first place and that make the future of its transition still so difficult to chart.

NOTES

The author would like to thank Christopher Dagg, Ann Marie Murphy, and Mohamad Sadli for their roles in keeping him abreast of developments in Indonesia during the period encompassed in this chapter; Hal Hill and Hugh Patrick for commenting on an early draft of the manuscript; and anonymous reviewers for commenting on a nearly final draft. Errors remaining are the author's alone.

1. World Bank, *The East Asian Miracle: Economic Growth and Public Policy* (Oxford: Oxford University Press, 1993), 348–60.

2. For a detailed account of the Indonesian experience in the 1970s and 1980s, see John Bresnan, *Managing Indonesia: The Modern Political Economy* (New York: Columbia University Press, 1993).

3. Hadi Soesastro and M. Chatib Basri, "Survey of Recent Developments," *Bulletin of Indonesian Economic Studies*, April 1998, 3–54.

4. Soesastro and Basri, "Survey," 3–54.

5. Donald Emmerson, "Exit and Aftermath: The Crisis of 1997–1998," in *Indonesia Beyond Suharto* (Armonk, N.Y.: M. E. Sharpe, 1999), 295–343; James Luhulima, *Hari-Hari Terpanjang: Menjelang Mundurnya President Soeharto* (Jakarta: Kompas, 2001).

6. World Bank, various reports.

7. *New York Times*, March 26, 2004.

8. Linda Y. C. Lim and Aaron Stern, "State Power and Private Profit," *Asian-Pacific Economic Literature*, November 2002, 47.

9. On the colonial period as a whole, see Anne Booth, W. I. O'Malley, and Anna Weidemann, eds., *Indonesian Economic History in the Dutch Colonial Era* (New Haven: Yale Southeast Asia Studies Monograph Series, 1988); on Dutch intervention in the Indies economy during the depression, see the extensive treatment in J. H. Boeke, *The Evolution of the Netherlands Indies Economy* (New York: Netherlands

and Netherlands Indies Council, Institute of Pacific Relations, 1946); on the Japanese occupation period, see George McTurnin Kahin, *Nationalism and Revolution in Indonesia* (Ithaca, N.Y.: Cornell University Press, 1952), 101–33.

10. Translation by the author.

11. Hal Hill, *The Indonesian Economy since 1966* (Cambridge: Cambridge University Press, 1996), 101–2.

12. Hill, *Indonesian Economy*, 101–2.

13. *Sinar Harapan*, July 24, 1970.

14. Adam Schwarz, *A Nation in Waiting: Indonesia's Search for Stability* (Boulder: Westview, 2000), 133–61.

15. World Bank, *Indonesia: Accelerating Recovery in Uncertain Times* (Washington, D.C.: World Bank, 2000), 68, table 4.1.

16. Warren Caragata, "One Lousy Job," *Asiaweek*, February 10, 2001.

17. Reuters, Paris, "Index Points to Worldwide Corruption Crisis," June 27, 2001.

18. *Guardian*, December 9, 2004.

19. World Bank, *Indonesia: Macroeconomic Update: Current Developments, Policy Implementation, and Assessment* (Washington, D.C., 1999), 5.

20. Anne Booth, "Survey of Recent Developments," *Bulletin of Indonesian Economic Studies*, December 1999, 3–38.

21. William Liddle, "Indonesia in 1999," *Asian Survey*, January–February 2000, 32–42.

22. *New York Times*, January 8, 2002.

23. *Jakarta Post*, December 22, 2002.

24. "We Need Shock Therapy: An Interview with Indonesia's New President," *Time Asia*, November 8, 2004.

25. "Pertamina's Power Play," *Far Eastern Economic Review*, May 30, 2002.

26. "Indonesia to End Energy Monopoly," *International Herald Tribune*, October 24, 2001.

27. "MPR Speaker Amien Rais: Indonesia Could Become Nation of Coolies," *Tempo Interactive*, October 3, 2002.

28. *Jakarta Post*, November 6 and December 1, 2001.

29. AP, Jakarta, "Indonesia Boosts Privatization with Sale of Telecommunications Company," December 15, 2002.

30. Andrew MacIntyre, "Power, Prosperity, and Patrimonialism: Business and Government in Indonesia," in Andrew MacIntyre, ed., *Business and Government in Industrializing Asia* (Ithaca, N.Y.: Cornell University Press, 1994), 255.

31. MacIntyre, *Business and Government*, 254.

32. Richard Robison, *Indonesia: The Rise of Capital* (Sydney: Allen & Unwin, 1986), 271–322.

33. Hill, *Indonesian Economy*, 111.

34. World Bank, 2000, 68, table 4.1.

35. Anthony Reid, *Southeast Asia in the Age of Commerce: 1450–1680* (New Haven: Yale University Press, 1993), 12.

36. J. A. C. Mackie, *The Chinese in Indonesia* (Honolulu: University Press of Hawai'i, 1976).

37. Ruth McVey, "The Materialization of the Southeast Asian Entrepreneur," in *Southeast Asian Capitalists* (Ithaca, N.Y.: Southeast Asia Program, Cornell University, 1992), 7–33.

38. Leo Suryadinata, *Prominent Indonesian Chinese: Biographical Sketches* (Singapore, 1991); Schwarz, *In Waiting*, 98–132.

39. World Bank, *World Development Report 2002* (Washington, D.C.: World Bank, 2002), box 5.3, 106.

40. Robison, *Indonesia*, 271–322; Jamie Mackie, "Changing Patterns of Chinese Big Business in Southeast Asia," in McVey, *Capitalists*, 161–90.

41. World Bank, *Accelerating*, 16.

42. M. R. Fernando and David Bulbeck, *Chinese Economic Activity in Netherlands India: Selected Translations from the Dutch* (Singapore: Institute of Southeast Asian Studies, 1992); James R. Rush, *Opium to Java: Revenue Farming and Chinese Enterprise in Colonial Indonesia, 1860–1910* (Ithaca: Cornell University Press, 1990).

43. Wang Gung Wu, "Are Indonesian Chinese Unique?" in Mackie, *Chinese*, 204.

44. Hadi Soesastro, *The IMF and the Political Economy of Indonesia's Economic Recovery*, CSIS Working Paper (Jakarta: CSIS, March 2003), 4.

45. Charles Enoch, Barbara Baldwin, Olivier Frecaut, and Arto Kovanen, *Indonesia: Anatomy of a Banking Crisis: Two Years of Living Dangerously: 1997–1998* (Washington: International Monetary Fund, 1999), 32.

46. See especially Ross H. McLeod, *Dealing with Bank System Failure: Indonesia: 1997–2002*, Working Paper no. 2003/05 (Working Papers in Trade and Development; Division of Economics, Research School of Pacific and Asian Studies, Australian National University).

47. Enoch, Baldwin, Frecaut, and Kovanen, *Anatomy*, 32.

48. Enoch, Baldwin, Frecaut, and Kovanen, *Anatomy*, 44–46.

49. George Fane and Ross H. McLeod, "Banking Collapse and Restructuring in Indonesia, 1997–2001" no. 2001/10 (Working Papers in Trade and Development Division of Economics, Australian National University, October 2001).

50. World Bank, *Accelerating*, 9; Anwar Nasution, "The Privatization of State Controlled Banks," *Jakarta Post*, December 22, 2001.

51. Howard Dick, "Survey of Recent Developments," *Bulletin of Indonesian Economic Studies*, April 2001, 21–26.

52. Setiyardi, "Bad Debtors," *Tempo Magazine*, June 4–10, 2002.

53. Wayne Arnold, "Indonesian Bank Agency Fading Out," *New York Times*, October 2, 2003.

54. John McBeth, "The Betrayal of Indonesia," *Far Eastern Economic Review*, June 26, 2003, 16.

55. "Condition of banks 'scares' IBRA," *Jakarta Post*, October 11, 2002.

56. Anwar Nasution, senior deputy governor, Bank Indonesia, "Fiscal Distress Following the 1997–1998 Crisis" (paper presented at the Fourteenth Pacific Economic Cooperation Council, Hong Kong, November 28–30, 2001). Excerpts appeared in *Jakarta Post*, December 13–14, 2001. The two paragraphs that follow are based in large part on this paper.

57. "In Indonesia, a Difficult Job," *International Herald Tribune*, April 21–22, 2001, 11.

58. Hugh Patrick, "Corporate Governance and the Indonesian Financial System: A Comparative Perspective" (paper prepared for the Columbia University-CSIS program in Indonesian Economic Institution Building in a Global Economy, August 2001).

59. Michael Vatikiotis and Sara Webb, "The Creditors Have a Plan," *FEER*, February 20, 2003.

60. "The IMF and Indonesia: Baleful Bonanza," *Economist*, November 8, 1997.

61. For example, Martin Feldman, "Refocusing the IMF," *Foreign Affairs*, March–April 1998, 20–33.

62. John Bresnan, "The United States, the IMF, and the Indonesian Financial Crisis," in Adam Schwarz and Jonathan Paris, eds., *The Politics of Post-Suharto Indonesia* (New York: Council on Foreign Relations, 1999), 87–112.

63. Jeffrey D. Sachs, "The Wrong Medicine for Asia," *New York Times*, November 3, 1997.

64. Joseph E. Stiglitz, *Globalization and Its Discontents* (New York: Norton, 2002), 96; Steven Radelet and Jeffrey Sachs, *The East Asian Financial Crisis: Diagnosis, Remedies, Prospects*, Brookings Papers on Economic Activity no. 2, 1998, 1–89; see also Paul Blustein, *The Chastening: Inside the Crisis That Rocked the Global Financial System and Humbled the IMF* (New York: Public Affairs, 2001).

65. Independent Evaluation Office, International Monetary Fund, *The IMF and Recent Capital Account Crises: Indonesia, Korea, Brazil* (Washington, D.C.: International Monetary Fund, 2003), 1.

66. Robert E. Rubin and Jacob Weisberg, *In an Uncertain World: Tough Choices from Wall Street to Washington* (New York: Random House, 2003), 246–47.

67. For a defense of the IMF, see Jack Boorman and Andrea Richter Hume, "Life with the IMF: Indonesia's Choices for the Future" (paper presented at the Fifth Congress of the Indonesian Economists Association, Malang, Indonesia, July 15, 2003).

68. BBC, *World Business Report*, August 15, 2002.

69. "RI no longer needs IMF loans, development minister says," *Jakarta Post*, October 10, 2002.

70. See, for example, "A Cruel Sea of Capital: A Survey of Global Finance," *Economist*, May 3, 2003.

71. "'Unfavourable Policies': Foreign Firms Pulling Out of Indonesia Due to Labour Woes," *Straits Times*, August 25, 2002; "Prized Investors Leaving Indonesia," *South China Morning Post*, November 29, 2002; "More Investors Flee," editorial, *Jakarta Post*, November 29, 2002; "Indonesia: SONY Signs Off," *Far Eastern Economic Review*, December 12, 2002.

72. *Business Week*, Asian edition, May 20, 2002.

73. Paul R. Deuster, "Survey of Recent Developments," *Bulletin of Indonesian Economic Studies, April 2002*, 6; Morgan Stanley estimates cited by Rendi A. Witular in *Jakarta Post*, April 28, 2004.

74. Anton H. Gunawan, "Indonesia Economics: 2004 Budget: Key Word Is Fiscal Consolidation," Jakarta, Citigroup, November 14, 2003.

75. M. Sadli, "Mencari Silver Lining," *Koran Tempo*, December 9, 2002; Reuters, Singapore, December 15, 2002.

76. Satish Misra, "On Unemployment: Squaring the Circle," *Jakarta Post*, December 4, 2002.

77. "Majority of the unemployed are young men: BPS," *Jakarta Post*, October 1, 2002.

78. World Bank, *World Development Report 2002* (Washington, D.C.: World Bank, 2002), 234, table 2.

79. Steven Radelet and Jeffrey Sachs, "The East Asian Financial Crisis: Diagnosis, Remedies, Prospects," Harvard Institute for International Development, April 20, 1998, 1.

5

Indonesia and the World

Ann Marie Murphy

Indonesia's size and status make it an important international actor. The largest state in Southeast Asia, the Indonesian archipelago stretches 3,000 miles from Sabang at the northwestern tip of the island of Sumatra to Merauke at the southern end of the eastern border that divides the island of New Guinea. The physical scale of the country becomes even more significant when the territorial waters claimed by Indonesia are taken into account, including the narrow sea-lanes that connect the Pacific and Indian Oceans. Its natural resources, which include large reserves of fossil fuels, hard minerals, and tropical forests, contribute to the largest economy in Southeast Asia. Indonesia is the fourth most populous state in the world after China, India, and the United States, ensuring that Indonesia will be counted in any reckoning of the welfare of the human race as a whole.

Indonesia has often been at the forefront of pivotal movements in international affairs. Its championing of anticolonialism in Asia and Africa during the 1950s helped create the nonaligned movement, which embodied the will of many newly independent states to avoid Cold War entanglements. Its dedication to regional stability and economic development after 1967 provided the environment in which Southeast Asian countries achieved such rapid economic development that they were lauded as "miracle" economies. Indonesia's economic collapse in 1997–1998 undermined that stability and was seized on by the antiglobalization movement as proof that increasingly tight international linkages entailed significant risks for developing economies. The success of the war on terrorism will be dictated in part by events in Indonesia, site of the October 2002 terrorist attack on Bali which killed 202 people and home to Jemaah Islamiyah, a local Islamic radical group responsible for the attack on Bali, among others. Debates over the compatibility between Islam and democracy will be strongly influenced by Indonesia, which is home to the world's largest community of Muslims and currently engaged in a great transition to democracy. Consequently it is of more than casual interest to other societies and their governments how Indonesians perceive the rest of the world and how they respond when the world outside impinges on them.

The key goals of Indonesian leaders have remained remarkably consistent across time: maintaining the integrity of its far-flung territory, ensuring the cohesion of its diverse society, and promoting the country's economic interests. Indonesia is relatively immune from external attack; its primary security threats have been internal ones. The heterogeneity of its population, divided along ethnic, religious, and political lines, has led to secessionist movements, regional rebellions, and ethnic and religious conflict. But these internal challenges have often been magnified by the support of outsiders. Preventing interference in its domestic affairs and securing external resources that can help promote the country's social cohesion have been key goals of Indonesian leaders since independence half a century ago. Indonesia's relationship with the outside world, therefore, is characterized by tight linkages with domestic politics.

Despite the continuity of key goals, Indonesian foreign policy has undergone dramatic swings. When Sukarno and Suharto dominated the domestic scene, the tenor and content of Indonesian foreign policy was shaped by the policy preferences and personalities of these leaders. Under Sukarno, Indonesia nationalized numerous foreign economic assets, launched a low-level war against Malaysia, and proclaimed an anti-imperialist axis of "Djakarta-Phnom Penh-Hanoi-Peking-Pyongyang."[1] Under Suharto, Indonesia opened up to direct foreign investment, took the lead in creating the Association of Southeast Asian Nations (ASEAN), and "froze" relations with China while working closely with the West. Sukarno's Indonesia was a source of instability for Indonesia's neighbors while Suharto's Indonesia provided the linchpin for regional stability. In the *reformasi* era that began in 1998, with parliament and party leaders assuming larger roles, foreign policy has become less discernible.

Sukarno's militancy and Suharto's pragmatism epitomize two different strategies that Indonesia has employed historically in pursuit of its interests: *diplomasi* and *perjuangan. Diplomasi*, or diplomacy, can be described as using traditional tools of statecraft to accomplish goals. It entails a commitment to the peaceful pursuit of national interests and a willingness to abide by the established norms and practices of international affairs. *Perjuangan*, which literally means "struggle," connotes a strategy in which Indonesia adopts a confrontational posture to achieve its goals. *Perjuangan* has involved using armed might, freezing assets, withdrawing from the United Nations, and opposing conditions imposed on external assistance. The belief that Indonesia is engaged in a struggle for greater justice and equity in world affairs infuses *perjuangan* with a sense of righteousness.

During the Sukarno era, the term *perjuangan* often indicated a leftist opposition to the West. This chapter does not use the term *perjuangan* ideologically. Instead, it employs it to capture an underdog's struggle against injustice. For example, after Suharto engineered her ouster from the presidency of the officially sanctioned PDI political party, Megawati Sukarnoputri founded an alternative political party and called it PDI-Perjuangan. Although the terms *diplomasi* and *perjuangan* refer to different international strategies, there are periods when Indonesian foreign policy displayed aspects of *diplomasi* and *perjuangan* toward different issues at the same time. This is particularly true of the *reformasi* era.

Indonesia faced continuing threats to its core national interests after 1998: the integrity of the Indonesian state, the cohesiveness of its society, and its hope for economic advancement. At opposite ends of the Indonesian archipelago, in Aceh and Papua, independence movements challenged the writ of rule from Jakarta. Throughout Indonesia, social violence threatened and often erupted. Indonesian economic growth was set back for years by financial crises in the emerging markets. Invariably Indonesians blamed these crises in part on foreign interests.

Indonesia meanwhile found itself the target of international criticism over a variety of issues: its delay in cracking down on terrorists, its lack of compliance with the International Monetary Fund, and its lack of progress in prosecuting those responsible for atrocities committed in East Timor, to name just the principal ones. During this period, calls for jihad against America, demands for termination of relations with the International Monetary Fund, and proclamations of the innocence of Indonesian soldiers accused of human rights abuses are examples of *perjuangan*. In contrast, Suharto's pragmatism echoed in the voices warning that the country could not afford to risk International Monetary Fund aid and should pursue *diplomasi* to help secure the foreign aid and investment that were considered crucial to hopes for economic recovery.

In this chapter I ask, What will be Indonesia's foreign policy stance in the first decades of the twenty-first century? Anticipating the stance Indonesia adopts toward the outside world is of considerable concern to other nations. Historically, *diplomasi* has been associated with periods when Indonesia played a constructive role in world affairs. In contrast, *perjuangan* typically has denoted periods when Indonesia posed a threat to its neighbors and their allies. History also shows, however, that *perjuangan* has usually been precipitated by Indonesian leaders' unsuccessful attempts to accomplish their goals through normal channels. History also supports the argument that the key variable determining whether Indonesia chooses *perjuangan* or *diplomasi* is the congruence between Indonesia's definition of its national interests and the prevailing norms of the international system. Inasmuch as the prevailing norms of the system often have reflected those of the great powers, in practice this means that Indonesia's foreign policy stance has often been shaped by its relationships with the great powers. In the same way, the stance that Indonesia adopts toward the outside world in the coming decades is likely to be heavily influenced by the degree of congruence of its interests with those of the United States.

In developing this argument, I will first explore the roots of the *perjuangan/diplomasi* dichotomy in Indonesia's revolutionary period. I will then illustrate how Indonesia has exhibited characteristics of both these stances at key points in its later history. I then move to the recent past, analyze Indonesia's post-Suharto definition of its national interests, and examine how congruent they are with those of its regional neighbors and the more distant United States. The chapter concludes with an assessment of the implications of Indonesia's foreign policy for these other states.

THE SUKARNO ERA

The Formative Years of Revolution

The four-year period between the declaration of Indonesian independence in 1945 and the transfer of sovereignty in 1949 was a formative one for Indonesian perceptions of the rest of the world and for its strategies in dealing with it. During this period, two different groups within the Indonesian nationalist movement adopted radically different means to the common goal of independence from the Dutch. Older, Western-educated nationalist leaders pursued a policy of *diplomasi*, while younger, less educated *pemuda*, or militias, advocated a physical strategy of *perjuangan*, or struggle.[2] The fact that both *diplomasi* and *perjuangan* played a part in achieving Indonesian independence served to legitimize both strategies, and advocates of each can be found in current policy debates.

Despite apprehension over how the Allies would respond, Sukarno declared the republic of Indonesia independent on August 17, 1945, two days after the Japanese surrender. An independence preparatory committee elected Sukarno and Mohammed Hatta president and vice president respectively.

The Dutch, intent on reestablishing colonial rule, refused to recognize Indonesian independence. As British troops entered Indonesia to take the Japanese surrender on behalf of the Allies, they made it clear to Sukarno and Hatta that wartime collaboration with the Japanese was an obstacle to their securing the Western support required to achieve independence. Believing that foreign support was the key to securing independence, Sukarno and Hatta ceded executive authority to Sutan Sjahrir, a leading intellectual whose imprisonment by the Dutch made him acceptable to the *pemuda*, while his refusal to cooperate with the Japanese made him acceptable to the West.

On becoming prime minister and foreign minister in November 1945, Sjahrir adopted a strategy of *diplomasi* toward the international community. He believed that if the Indonesian Republic could demonstrate a capacity to govern and project a responsible image to the rest of the world, it stood a good chance of having its independence recognized.[3] The *pemuda* argued that the Dutch would make concessions only in the face of physical opposition, and Sjahrir's government worked to strengthen the country's military capacity in case *diplomasi* failed. In November 1946, with the British poised to withdraw and 55,000 Dutch troops redeployed on Indonesian soil, nationalist leaders signed the Linggadjati Agreement. Sjahrir and his supporters viewed the agreement as securing de facto recognition of the republic from eight countries, including the United States, Britain, Australia, and China. But the agreement fell so far short of popular demands that Sjahrir was forced to resign.

Despite provisions in the Linggadjati Agreement that called for disputes to be settled by arbitration, the Dutch embarked on a military offensive in July 1947, provoking an international outcry. India and Australia brought the issue to the United Nations Security Council, where Indonesia pleaded for international arbitration in the dispute. Indonesia hoped that the American commitment to anticolonialism would lead it to support Indonesia's request. But the Americans refused to support the Indonesian cause, profoundly disillusioning nationalist leaders.[4]

On December 19, 1948, the Dutch embarked on a full-scale offensive. Militarily, it was a great success for the Dutch: most of the republic's territory was overrun and key nationalist leaders were captured. Diplomatically, it was a disaster because it tilted international opinion heavily in favor of the Indonesians. The United States now threatened to cut off Marshall Plan aid to the Dutch, and they went back to the negotiating table.[5] In the end, the Indonesians and the Dutch signed the Hague Agreement, which granted Indonesia independence after nationalist leaders made a number of concessions. Indonesia agreed to restore Dutch economic enterprises, assumed much of the debt of the Dutch colonial government, and acquiesced in the Dutch retention of West Irian subject to further negotiations. On December 27, 1949, sovereignty was transferred from the Dutch to the Indonesians. But the conditions attached to independence led Sjahrir to observe that the republic had secured independence "at the expense of economic and diplomatic liberty."[6]

The revolutionary period had a number of lasting impacts on Indonesian attitudes and policies with respect to foreign powers. The failure of the great powers to support Indonesia's initial bid for independence produced an abiding wariness of great power politics and a conviction among many Indonesian leaders that the world was a hostile place. Resentment over the concessions that accompanied independence, as well as the belief that they were unfairly foisted on Indonesia, marked the beginning of a strong sensitivity to both the concept and practice of conditionality, which remains to this day.

Parliamentary *Diplomasi*

Following independence, Indonesia initially adopted a strategy of *diplomasi*. In large part, this was a function of domestic politics. Like many postcolonial states, Indonesia adopted a system of parliamentary democracy upon independence. Indonesia's heterogeneous population subscribed to a wide range of political views that were reflected in the numerous political parties in the parliament. During this period a series of weak coalition governments struggled to build national institutions and rehabilitate the economy. Foreign policy was viewed largely as a means of securing external resources to meet those goals. And just as the need for consensus constrained the governments of this period from taking bold action domestically, the need to ensure the support of the disparate political forces represented in parliament also constrained Indonesia from bold international moves.

Indonesian foreign policy hewed closely to the *bebas dan aktif* or "free and active" principle that Hatta had first enunciated in 1948 at the dawn of the Cold War. Hatta believed that a strong commitment to the *bebas dan aktif* framework would best enable Indonesia to meet the three key challenges facing the country: safeguarding Indonesia's independence, sovereignty, and security; consolidating the country internally; and promoting the country's economic interests.[7] There is nothing inherent in the *bebas dan aktif* principle that dictates whether Indonesia should adopt a strategy of *diplomasi* or *perjuangan*. Advocates of both, therefore, could at times justify their choice of strategy by appealing to a foreign policy principle that was universally accepted within Indonesia.

The depth of Indonesia's commitment to the *bebas* component of the doctrine was demonstrated in 1952, when Foreign Minister A. Subardjo accepted a $50 million loan from the United States under the terms of the Mutual Security Act of 1951. This act stipulated that the recipient should make a full contribution "to the defensive strength of the free world."[8] When the condition attached to the loan became public, the outcry was so great that the Sukiman cabinet resigned in February 1952. This was the first time Indonesia's strong opposition to political conditions tied to economic assistance led it to forgo desperately needed material aid. It would do the same on future occasions.

The Bandung Conference

The most concrete manifestation of Indonesia's commitment to the *aktif* component of its foreign policy doctrine during the parliamentary period was the Bandung conference of Afro-Asian nations in 1955. The first major gathering of leaders from nonaligned countries, it was aimed at promoting an alternative or "third way" to the American-led and Soviet-led blocs. The Bandung conference underscored Indonesia's desire to play an international leadership role befitting its size and anticolonial history. In this, the conference was successful, for it greatly increased Indonesia's international standing. Furthermore, the conference transformed the charismatic Sukarno into an international statesman by providing him with a platform on which to demonstrate the fiery anticolonial rhetoric at which he excelled.

During this time, Indonesia pursued its key foreign policy goal, the recovery of Irian, through diplomatic means. When the Netherlands refused to enter into negotiations regarding Irian, Indonesia took the issue to the United Nations. Four times during the 1950s, Indonesia sought support in the General Assembly for the appointment of a good offices commission charged with assisting in negotiations between the Dutch and Indonesians. All four, including the last in November 1957, failed to achieve the necessary two-thirds majority.[9]

Having thus failed to recover Irian through *diplomasi*, Indonesia turned to *perjuangan* tactics. It expropriated all Dutch enterprises in Indonesia and expelled thousands of Dutch citizens. The army took control of most Dutch assets, giving it access to a large new pool of funds that strengthened its political position. The lack of Western support for its case in the United Nations once again confirmed the Indonesian belief that the international system and its organizations were rigged in favor of the more powerful nations. This belief was greatly strengthened by the support Western powers and their Southeast Asian allies gave to the rebels in the outer island rebellions.

The Outer Island Rebellions

In December 1956, military officers in Sumatra began taking over power from the local civilian governors, and similar actions began to occur in Sulawesi

soon thereafter. The dissident officers were rebelling out of economic and ideological concerns. Economically, they were protesting against what they perceived as the unfair distribution of revenue between the center and the outer
island provinces, which were the source of most commodity exports. Ideologically, the conservative Muslim populations of these areas resented the increasing role played by the Communist Party of Indonesia (Partai Komunis
Indonesia or PKI) in national politics and Sukarno's unwillingness to clamp
down on it. The rebellions were also triggered by the resentment of local military commanders at the increasing centralization of the army. In short, the
roots of these rebellions had less to do with a desire to secede from Indonesia
than to change the distribution of political and economic power within it. But
clandestine U.S. support for the rebellions increased the magnitude of the
challenge posed by the rebellions and the possibility of Indonesia's disintegration as a result.

Why did the United States intervene? In part, the intervention was triggered by a clash of ideologies that produced divergent interests. The Eisenhower administration believed that nonalignment was immoral as well as
antithetical to American interests. Furthermore, Secretary of State John
Foster Dulles was alarmed by the rise of the PKI and by Sukarno's attempt
to unify Indonesia's people through appeals to *nasakom*, a reference to
Sukarno's belief that the three main ideological currents then strong in
Indonesia—*nasionalisme*, *agama*, and *komunisme* (nationalism, religion,
and communism)—were mutually supportive and could be pursued jointly.
The Eisenhower administration felt it was only a matter of time before Indonesia succumbed to PKI control. Believing that a divided Indonesia, of
which at least some part was noncommunist, was a more desirable outcome
than a unified Indonesia that was communist, the United States provided
money, arms, and, in Sulawesi, air cover to the rebels.[10]

The outer island rebellions had far-reaching consequences for Indonesia's
politics at home and abroad. Domestically, they led Sukarno to declare martial law in March 1957, which consolidated his personal power and that of the
army at the expense of the political parties. Internationally, the rebellions confirmed that powerful countries like the United States and Britain would flout
basic international rules when it suited their purpose. This only added fuel to
the desire of Sukarno and many Indonesian nationalists to change the rules of
international politics to reflect more fully the aspirations of the newly independent countries.

The complicity of Malaya, the Philippines, and Singapore in the outer island rebellions also raised tensions with Indonesia's Southeast Asian neighbors. British and American support for the rebels was funneled through the
British naval base in Singapore while American bombing runs over Sulawesi

were conducted from bases in the Philippines. Such complicity underscored widely held Indonesian attitudes that Anglophile Malayan and Americanized Filipino leaders were nothing more than lackeys of the West. Malaya's decision to grant many of the rebel leaders asylum rather than repatriate them as Indonesia requested only confirmed Indonesian stereotypes.

Sukarno and Militancy

In 1959, Sukarno reinstated the 1945 constitution, which provided for a strong presidency. This marked the beginning of what Sukarno termed guided democracy, a six-year period in which he retained his political leadership by balancing the competing desires of the armed forces (Angkatan Bersenjata Republik Indonesia or ABRI) on the right and the PKI on the left. Since the domestic political agendas of these two were largely anathema to one another, Sukarno maintained his position by uniting them behind his foreign policy initiatives. As Sukarno grew more radical in his views, so too did Indonesian foreign policy.[11]

In December 1961, Sukarno openly threatened military action if the Dutch refused to negotiate the future of Irian. Sukarno's threat was made credible by Indonesia's growing military relationship with the Soviet Union. Indonesia turned to the Soviets when the West refused to provide military aid during the outer island rebellions. The delivery of advanced weapons from the Soviet Union during the 1950s and Khruschev's offer of a $1 billion loan for military purchases during a 1960 visit to Indonesia meant Jakarta finally had sufficient capability to pursue its claim to Irian by means other than *diplomasi*.

Sukarno's threat worked; the United States now pressured the Dutch to resolve the Irian issue. An agreement was brokered under U.N. auspices by retired American diplomat Ellsworth Bunker, under which Irian was transferred temporarily to the United Nations, after which full control was transferred to Indonesia. The Indonesians were committed to give the people of Irian an opportunity to exercise self-determination at a later date. In July and August 1969, Indonesia stage-managed an Act of Free Choice in which 1,025 village leaders, handpicked by Indonesian authorities, unanimously agreed to become part of Indonesia. Although U.N. observers duly noted that there had been little "choice" in the process, the United Nations took no remedial action. In September 1969, Suharto incorporated Irian as the country's twenty-sixth province. Once again, Indonesia had achieved a key national goal through a combination of *diplomasi* and *perjuangan*.

Some Indonesian officials hoped that the recovery of Irian would usher in a period of economic and political consolidation. An economic stabilization plan had been developed in conjunction with the International Monetary Fund in 1961, but the Irian campaign made it impossible to secure the foreign funding on which it depended. In the wake of the Irian settlement, Indonesian administrators moved cautiously to implement the Fund program. The West supported this move, hopeful that rising standards of living would reduce the appeal of communism in Indonesia, help persuade the country to move closer to the West, and reduce its dependence on the Soviet bloc. These hopes were dashed when Indonesia adopted *konfrontasi* against Malaysia.

KONFRONTASI AGAINST MALAYSIA

The leaders of Malaya, Singapore, and Britain had announced plans in 1961 to join Malaya, Singapore, and the British crown colonies of Brunei, Sabah, and Sarawak into a new state to be known as Malaysia. Indonesia, which would share the island of Borneo with the new state, had a number of reservations about the Malaysia plan. The fact that the decision was made in London without consultation with Indonesia; that the peoples of Borneo were given little say in the matter, and that the plan would create a common border with what many Indonesians viewed as a feudal Malay state were all cause for concern in Jakarta. These objections were initially tempered by the need for British support in the U.N. Security Council on the Irian issue. In December 1962, two months after the United Nations signed off on the Irian agreement, rebels in Brunei launched a revolt against the Malaysia plan, claiming that they had been denied their right to self-determination. The rebels appealed to Indonesia for support. By February 1963, Indonesia had declared support for the rebels and used the term *konfrontasi* to describe its policy toward the Malaysia plan. Given that *konfrontasi* was the same term Indonesia had used to describe its struggle against the Dutch over Irian, it rang alarm bells in Kuala Lumpur, Singapore, London, and Washington.

After a series of diplomatic initiatives failed, Indonesia refused to extend diplomatic recognition to Malaysia when it was created in September 1963. Sukarno also severed trade links with the new country, which now included the port of Singapore, through which nearly half of Indonesian trade passed. The decision to cut trade ties with Malaysia meant that Indonesia stood no chance of meeting its export targets under the International Monetary Fund plan. The United States suspended economic aid that had been contingent on Indonesia's compliance with the program. Sukarno responded by telling the United States to "go to hell with your aid."

Sukarno now pursued a broad strategy of *perjuangan* that increasingly isolated Indonesia from all but the most radical states. Indonesia's military aggression against Malaysia led that country's commonwealth allies to deploy 40,000 troops to protect the new state from its larger neighbor. When Malaysia was given a seat on the U.N. Security Council in 1965, Sukarno withdrew Indonesia from the United Nations, the only member ever to leave the organization. China supported Sukarno's moves. But many of Indonesia's traditional friends in the third world distanced themselves from Indonesia in response to its increasing radicalism and aggressive behavior against its much smaller neighbor.

The growing alignment with China culminated in Sukarno's announcement of a Jakarta-Phnom Penh-Hanoi-Peking-Pyongyang axis. Celebrating the tenth anniversary of the Bandung conference in April 1965, he gave a speech entitled "Storming the Last Bulwarks of Imperialism," in which he called on his supporters to "build the world anew."[12] The interests of Indonesia and the West were now diametrically opposed.

But within months, the precarious balance of power that Sukarno had attempted to maintain between the army and the PKI came apart. Indonesia's new leaders would build Indonesia anew in ways that were antithetical to the vision held by Indonesia's founding father. In the process, they would also abandon Sukarno's strategy of *perjuangan* for one of *diplomasi* in order to obtain the resources needed to rebuild Indonesia's economy.

SUHARTO AND PRAGMATISM

The standoff between the army and the PKI climaxed in the September 30, 1965 coup and countercoup, often referred to by its Indonesian acronym G30S (from Gerakan Tiga Puluh September, or September 30 movement). In its aftermath, the army and anticommunist groups unleashed an orgy of violence against suspected PKI members in which perhaps 500,000 were killed. When Suharto formally took power from Sukarno on March 11, 1966, Indonesia was a politically unstable, diplomatically isolated economic basket case.

Suharto was determined to reverse course. Naming itself the New Order, the new regime defined itself in contradistinction to the old: political order would replace political instability, left-wing forces would be replaced by more conservative ones, and economic autarky would be replaced by integration into the global economy. Lacking Sukarno's nationalist credentials, Suharto set out to legitimize his regime through economic development. The wholesale reorientation of Indonesia's domestic agenda implied a wholesale revamping of the country's foreign policy as well. Suharto's commitment to anticommunism and market economics meant the West replaced the Soviet bloc as Indonesia's key supplier of military and economic aid.

It also dictated a shift from confrontation to cooperation with its Southeast Asian neighbors. During the first twenty years of his rule, Suharto defined Indonesian interests in ways largely congruent with both the West and his Southeast Asian neighbors, enabling Indonesia to achieve its foreign policy goals largely through *diplomasi*.

Suharto's regime made its commitment to economic recovery clear by naming its first cabinet Ampera (or Message of the People's Suffering). Indonesia's economy was in a state of near collapse. Inflation had exceeded 500 percent during 1965 while rice prices had risen by 900 percent. Payments on the country's foreign debt of $2.3 billion exceeded projected foreign exchange earnings.[13] Indonesia needed to reschedule these debts and secure external sources of fresh economic assistance and investment capital. Indonesia turned to the West and Japan.

Despite the country's dire need for economic assistance, Indonesian sensitivity to the conditions that often accompany aid was made clear in the first press statement of the new economics czar, Sultan Hamengku Buwono: Indonesia would "welcome foreign economic aid without strings from all countries."[14] The United States, however, made economic aid conditional on Indonesia's termination of *konfrontasi* with Malaysia. David Bell, head of the United States Agency for International Development, argued that it was impossible for the United States to provide assistance until Indonesia "abandoned its foreign adventures."[15]

Indonesia officially ended *konfrontasi* with Malaysia in August 1966, but this action was not the result of American pressure alone. By 1964, the army's initial support for *konfrontasi* weakened as officers came to believe that it was providing greater advantages to its domestic adversary, the PKI. At that time, intelligence officers under Suharto's command who opposed Sukarno's policy began secret contacts with Malaysian leaders.[16] Once Suharto and his allies obtained full political authority, *konfrontasi* was soon ended, clearing the way for Indonesia to rejoin the United Nations in September 1966.

The ending of *konfrontasi* paved the way for Indonesia to become the beneficiary of large-scale Western aid. In September 1966, Japan hosted a meeting between Indonesia and its Western creditor nations, at which Indonesia received a commitment in principle to reschedule its outstanding debts. At subsequent meetings, it was decided to create the Intergovernmental Group on Indonesia (IGGI), which would become the vehicle through which the West and Japan extended grants and loans to Indonesia.[17] Indonesian technocrats worked closely with both the International Monetary Fund and the World Bank. The close relationship Suharto developed early in his tenure with international aid donors would remain largely intact for the next thirty years and help Indonesia achieve stunning economic results during this time.

The zero-sum nature of Cold War politics dictated that Indonesia's shift to *diplomasi* with the West and Japan entailed a concomitant shift to *perjuangan* with the Soviet Union and China. The Soviet Union, which had become Indonesia's largest creditor during the Sukarno era, halted aid to protest the decimation of the PKI. Many staunchly anticommunist military officers argued that Indonesia should repudiate its $990 million of Soviet debt. Foreign Minister Adam Malik argued against repudiation, won this debate, and went on to negotiate a debt-rescheduling agreement.

Malik lost the debate over maintaining diplomatic relations with China. Most army leaders were convinced that China was involved in G30S. They also feared subversion through the country's Sino-Indonesian population. In October 1967, Indonesia withdrew its embassy staff from Beijing and requested that the Chinese do the same. Despite the efforts of successive foreign ministers to seek a rapprochement with China, military opposition was so strong that Indonesia did not resume diplomatic ties with China until 1990.

Indonesia's emergence as a bastion of anticommunism was a clear boon to the West in terms of Cold War competition. But an argument can be made that the biggest beneficiaries were its Southeast Asian neighbors. Sukarno's Indonesia had been a source of regional instability but Suharto's Indonesia became a force for stability in the region. The New Order regime not only ended *konfrontasi* but also demonstrated its commitment to replacing *perjuangan* with *diplomasi* by taking the lead to create a new regional organization, the Association of Southeast Asian Nations (ASEAN). ASEAN was established in August 1967 by Indonesia, Malaysia, Thailand, Singapore, and the Philippines. ASEAN was ostensibly formed to promote regional cooperation in the economic and social spheres, but in fact, through the promulgation of a regional code of conduct, was designed to resolve regional disputes through consultation. In this manner, ASEAN helped ensure the stable regional environment necessary for Indonesia's economic growth. New Order leaders also hoped that ASEAN would provide a political counterweight against China.

Because ASEAN associated Indonesia with four Western-allied states that had often been the targets of Sukarno's disparaging remarks, Malik worked hard to ensure that ASEAN's goals were consistent with Indonesia's *bebas dan aktif* principle. Malik made trips to Cambodia and Burma in an unsuccessful attempt to convince another of the region's nonaligned countries to join the new organization. Over strenuous Philippine objections, ASEAN's founding document affirms that "all foreign bases are temporary and remain only with the expressed concurrence of the countries concerned and are not intended to be used directly or indirectly to subvert the national independence and freedom of states in the area or prejudice the orderly procedures of their national development."[18] Subsequent ASEAN policy was strongly influenced by Indonesian security concepts.

New Order leaders hoped that ASEAN would serve as a vehicle for regional leadership. Aware that leadership entailed responsibilities, Indonesia mediated numerous disputes between its fellow ASEAN members, and, when requested, offered its good offices in domestic disputes as well. Believing that Indonesia's struggle for independence and its history of nonalignment put it in a unique position to help resolve the conflicts in Indochina, Indonesia tried to extend its regional leadership to this part of Southeast Asia. But Vietnamese suspicions of Indonesia led to frictions instead. Vietnam's invasion of Cambodia in December 1978 violated the most basic of ASEAN rules, the prohibition against the use of force in resolving disputes. When Vietnam rejected ASEAN entreaties to withdraw from Cambodia in exchange for investigations into the events that Vietnam claimed justified the attacks—Khmer Rouge border incursions into Vietnam and atrocities against Cambodians of Vietnamese descent—ASEAN took the lead in forming an international effort to force a Vietnamese withdrawal.

During the next decade, ASEAN under Indonesia's leadership would play a highly visible role over Cambodia and would emerge as the focal point through which external actors sought to engage the noncommunist states of Southeast Asia. But there were differences of opinion among ASEAN members regarding how to respond to Vietnam and what role extraregional actors should play in resolving the Cambodian crisis. As the frontline state most threatened by Vietnam's refusal to withdraw from Cambodia, Thailand favored a policy of bleeding Vietnam white, and worked closely with China and the Khmer Rouge to do so. In contrast, Indonesia feared that China was using the Cambodia issue to enhance its presence in Southeast Asia, thereby threatening the autonomy of regional states that Indonesia viewed as critical to its security. Indonesia, therefore, took the lead in forging a diplomatic solution. After years of painstaking effort, Indonesia served with France as cochair of the 1991 Paris Peace Accords that ultimately brought an end to the Cambodian conflict.

The East Timor Disaster

Indonesia invaded the former Portuguese colony of East Timor in 1975 in what would prove to be a humanitarian disaster of epochal proportions for the people of East Timor and a foreign policy nightmare for Indonesian diplomats. Indonesia's actions in East Timor were a stark departure from the broad *diplomasi* stance it adopted during the first two decades of the New Order.

In the wake of Portugal's announcement that it intended to free its remaining colonies, Indonesia's initial policy toward East Timor reflected its traditional commitment to anticolonialism and self-determination. In a June 1974 letter to Fretilin member José Ramos Horta, Foreign Minister Adam Malik reaffirmed that "the independence of every country is the right of every nation, with no exception for the people in Timor."[19] But military leaders believed that an independent East Timor would "go communist" and become a "Cuba on its doorstep" or a base for foreign subversion of Indonesia.

Military leaders believed their fears were coming true when the leftist party Fretilin emerged as the strongest party in East Timor's civil war. Indonesia responded by invading East Timor on December 7, 1975, claiming that it was acting in support of the "majority" wish for integration. Indonesia proceeded with the invasion confident of support from key countries such as the United States and Australia. Indonesia delayed the invasion until after a visit to Jakarta by U.S. President Gerald Ford and Secretary of State Henry Kissinger. During that visit, Kissinger gave his blessing to the invasion, asking only that it be carried out "quickly, efficiently" and without the use of American military equipment.[20] Indonesia would fail to meet any of these requests.

Despite covert U.S. support, Indonesia was aware that it would face repercussions from the international community. On December 23, 1975, the U.N. Security Council passed a resolution calling for Indonesian withdrawal and a genuine act of self-determination. Indonesia refused and instead staged an "act of integration" on May 31, 1976. Reminiscent of the 1969 "act of free choice" in Irian, thirty-seven handpicked East Timorese delegates voted for integration with Indonesia.[21] On July 17, 1976, President Suharto formally declared East Timor Indonesia's twenty-seventh province. On November 19, 1976, the U.N. General Assembly rejected the annexation of East Timor and Indonesia's claims that "volunteers" had been invited to assist the anticommunist parties in East Timor. The world body would call for self-determination in East Timor annually until 1982.

The East Timorese suffered tremendously. Seeking to cut Fretilin off from supporters, the Indonesian military uprooted most of the Timorese and moved them into designated hamlets, often in areas ill suited to agricultural production. In 1979, Indonesian Foreign Minister Mochtar Kusumaatmadja admitted that at least 120,000 people had died since the beginning of East Timor's civil war.[22] Others estimate that up to 200,000 people, or approximately one-third of the territory's prewar population of 650,000, perished during the period of Indonesian rule.

Indonesia's ability to weather international opposition to its actions in East Timor was greatly facilitated by the support of key Western states. The Ford and Carter administrations helped bolster Indonesia by repeating its claims that military atrocities had been committed only in isolated incidents; that Fretilin had provoked the attacks; and that the death toll was greatly exaggerated.[23] The United States abstained from most of the U.N. resolutions censuring Indonesia and used its influence to dilute them. Australia also supported Jakarta, and in 1978 Australian Prime Minister Malcolm Fraser granted de jure recognition to Indonesia's integration of East Timor, the only Western country to do so.

Not all Americans and Australians supported their governments' policies. When it became clear that American military equipment had been used in the invasion of East Timor, in contravention of arms transfer agreements, Congress held hearings on the matter in March 1977. Human rights groups took up the issue in both the United States and Australia. Over time, however, the news blackout of information from East Timor, its relative isolation from major power centers, and Portugal's failure to take up the cause forcefully meant that Indonesia's invasion of East Timor and the plight of the Timorese people receded from the international agenda.

INDONESIAN FOREIGN POLICY IN THE 1990s: *DIPLOMASI* AND *PERJUANGAN*

In his 1990 National Day address, Suharto declared that is was time for Indonesia to once again play a more *aktif* role in international affairs.[24] Suharto's decision to extend the scope of Indonesian diplomatic activity from his earlier focus on Southeast Asia, Japan, and key Western allies demonstrated his confidence in Indonesia's domestic economic achievements, confidence in Southeast Asia's stability, and confidence in his own foreign policy skills.

Suharto's quest for global leadership coincided with the end of the Cold War and the dawn of the era of globalization. The strong congruence of interests between Indonesia and the West in matters of ideology, economy, and security that prevailed during the Cold War would not outlast it. In the United States, the Clinton administration made the promotion of the ideology of liberalization the primary framework of its foreign policy. According to what became known as the Washington consensus, economic liberalization not only promoted economic growth but also created demands for political liberalization. Inasmuch as it was commonly believed that democracies do not fight one another, the Clinton administration argued that demands for political and economic liberalization would in turn help create peace. The United States, therefore, became more willing than ever to condition economic and military assistance on the promotion of human rights and democracy. As the West increased its pressure, Indonesia increasingly adopted *perjuangan* tactics against it. At the same time, Indonesia discovered it had a growing convergence of interests with some old allies from the Sukarno era and it embarked on a strategy of *diplomasi* toward them.

Indonesia Reacts to the Washington Consensus

The emphasis that the West placed on political liberalization and human rights in the 1990s could not have been more at odds with the interests of the Suharto administration. Suharto and his allies did not agree that Western-style democracy was an ideal to which the country should aspire. Instead, they viewed it as a threat. Writing during the Suharto era, Dewi Fortuna Anwar stated:

> The Indonesian government sees a growing danger in the efforts of Western governments and international organizations to promote universal acceptance of democratic and human rights principles. Such notions are dangerously attractive to the intellectual community and nongovernmental organizations at home, and thus present a political challenge to the authoritarian political system.[25]

Indonesia reacted to pressure on political issues by joining with other Asian states to rebut the concept of universal civil and political rights by articulating a concept of Asian values. Proponents of Asian values argued that the Western emphasis on civil and political rights focused too much on the individual while ignoring community rights. In the Asian values debate, Indonesia joined forces with Singapore and Malaysia and even found common cause with China. The Asian values debate is rightly viewed as a defensive reaction or *perjuangan* tactic against Western pressure. Absent such pressure, it is highly unlikely that Indonesia would have devoted significant attention to this issue. At the same time, many Indonesian reformers welcomed such external pressure.

Indonesia occupied an unusual position during the heyday of globalization. On the one hand, it ranked among the most successful economic development stories of the preceding three decades. It was therefore held up by international economic institutions and proponents of capitalism such as the United States to rebut the criticism of antiglobalization protesters that the international system was rigged in favor of the developed countries and against developing ones.

But Indonesia rejected this view and helped create the Group of Eight major developing countries to oppose it. It also rebelled against the tendency of Western countries to condition economic assistance on issues such as labor rights and environmental protection. According to Indonesian Foreign Minister Ali Alatas, linking "extraneous issues such as environment, labor laws" in trade and economic cooperation agreements was simply "a new and insidious" way by which Western countries were undermining the economic potential of developing countries."[26]

The Dili Massacre

Indonesia's search for international recognition also coincided with the Dili massacre. In November 1991, Indonesian troops opened fire on a peaceful funeral procession in Dili, East Timor, killing 271 unarmed civilians and wounding many more. Foreign journalists witnessed the event and film footage was smuggled out of Indonesia. The foreigners bore witness to the atrocity and the film made a mockery of Indonesian claims that blame for the massacre lay with the demonstrators.[27]

The Dili massacre, and Indonesia's refusal to acknowledge it in the face of credible evidence, elevated East Timor to the agenda of the international community. The European Community condemned the event and within weeks the Dutch, Canadian, and Danish governments had suspended aid programs to Indonesia. The facilitating role that U.S. weapons played in Indonesia's actions received great publicity, and Congress responded in 1992 by severely restricting Indonesia' s access to American military education and training.

From the perspective of Jakarta, it was difficult to understand why the international community was willing to sacrifice good relations with a large, rapidly growing country for the sake of 800,000 people occupying half a remote island. Most Indonesians were flabbergasted when the Nobel Peace Prize was awarded to Bishop Carlos Belo and José Ramos Horta. They perceived the increasing tendency of Western actors to criticize Indonesia on East Timor matters, and condition aid on policy changes there, as a means of keeping Indonesia down.

Indonesia protested bitterly against the Western outcry over its actions in East Timor. In 1992, Suharto responded to the Dutch suspension of aid by borrowing a refrain from Sukarno and telling the Dutch to "go to hell with your aid." Indonesia also demanded that the Dutch withdraw from the IGGI and be replaced as chairman.[28] Indonesia responded to the American restrictions on military assistance by accusing the United States of hypocrisy, given its earlier support for Indonesian policy toward East Timor. It also began to seek new suppliers of military equipment.

A Successful Quest for International Leadership

Determined to rebut criticism that the New Order had abandoned Indonesia's traditional *bebas dan aktif* policy, Suharto set his sights on achieving a goal Sukarno would have applauded: becoming chairman of the non-aligned movement (NAM).[29] But Indonesia encountered opposition. The country's traditionally strong ties to the United States created the perception among many NAM members that Indonesia was not sufficiently non-aligned. The imperial nature of its invasion and subsequent rule of East Timor was condemned by many. Given China's status as a key third world country, Indonesia's chances of securing the NAM leadership were minuscule without the restoration of relations with China. Indonesia failed in its bid to host the 1989 NAM summit.

But Suharto persevered. Indonesia's candidacy was helped by the end of the Cold War, which Suharto argued meant that NAM must adapt or risk becoming sidetracked. He argued that the focal point for NAM in the aftermath of the Cold War should be economic development, and that Indonesia's progress in this area put it in a unique position to bridge the north–south divide.[30] Having recognized China two years earlier, Indonesia assumed the NAM chairmanship for a three-year term in 1992.

From the beginning, Suharto took his NAM leadership role seriously and used this platform to lobby the G-7 nations on economic issues important to the developing world. Sounding very much like Sukarno in an address to the U.N. General Assembly, Suharto called for the restructuring of the Security Council to include non-Western countries such as India, Indonesia, and representatives from Africa and Latin America.[31] In short, as Suharto reasserted Indonesia's international leadership role, he did so by reverting to traditional third world concerns such as economic injustice and inequality in world politics that had been prominent issues in Sukarno's foreign policy.

Indonesia's goal of bridging the differences between the countries of ASEAN and Indochina advanced significantly when ASEAN admitted Vietnam in 1995. By 1997 all ten Southeast Asian states had been brought under the ASEAN umbrella, and Indonesia was widely recognized as the organization's unofficial leader. Indonesia continued its role as a regional troubleshooter. At the request of the Philippine government, Indonesia helped broker a truce between authorities in Manila and the Moro Liberation National Front in Mindanao. When China began aggressively pressing its territorial claims in the South China Sea, Indonesia organized a series of workshops designed to keep the claimants from escalating the conflict and working toward ways to resolve it. The creation of the ASEAN Regional Forum, a multilateral institution dedicated to security issues, was also an effort to lay the foundation for regional stability in the post–Cold War era. One of Indonesia's primary motivations in helping to create the forum was to provide a venue in which China, long averse to multilateral institutions, could be socialized into becoming a responsible regional actor.

By the mid-1990s, Indonesia had adopted a bifurcated policy posture toward the international community. Despite tensions over issues of political and economic liberalization, it nevertheless maintained close working relationships with the West and key international organizations such as the World Bank and International Monetary Fund. At the same time, it had once again taken a prominent role on the global stage on behalf of postcolonial states and had reestablished relations with China. Throughout, Indonesia maintained a strong regional leadership role in ASEAN. For the first time ever, Indonesia enjoyed solid working relationships with virtually all key foreign countries and international institutions.

The End of a Regime

Economic success was the foundation of Indonesia's international leadership role. It is therefore ironic that Suharto, the father of development, was driven from office by the 1997 Asian financial crisis. When the financial crisis hit Indonesia, Suharto turned to the International Monetary Fund, just as he had in previous downturns. The Fund extended financial support but demanded a host of reforms to Indonesia's economy that, if enacted, would have brought serious economic pain to Suharto's family and cronies. Placing personal interests above those of his country, Suharto failed to meet the conditions. When Suharto announced a few days after signing a second Fund agreement that he was ready to serve a seventh five-year term as president and that his preferred vice presidential candidate was B. J. Habibie, the international reaction moved into the political realm.[32] Habibie was an aerospace engineer whose grandiose high-tech schemes had long been denounced by mainstream economists. United States Treasury officials threatened to cut off aid if Habibie was appointed, and President Clinton dispatched former Vice President Walter Mondale to Jakarta to reinforce that message. During his March 3, 1998, meeting with Mondale, Suharto complained that he was being "victimized" and that implementing the International Monetary Fund reforms would be "suicide."[33] For a time, Suharto defied this international political pressure and on March 11, 1998, Indonesian's rubber-stamp MPR (Madjelis Permusyawaratan Nasional) duly elected Suharto and Habibie.

Suharto's defiance could only last so long. Indonesian opposition leaders blamed the crisis on Suharto and used the outside pressure to bolster their demands that Suharto must go. When Suharto announced that government subsidies on gasoline would be cut immediately, resulting in a 70 percent increase in the price of gasoline, large-scale rioting and looting resulted. Over the next two days, mobs burned hundreds of homes and looted shops, targeting those owned by ethnic Chinese. As Jakarta went up in flames, even those most loyal to Suharto realized he was part of the problem, not the solution. On May 21, 1998, Suharto resigned. At the end, Suharto had adopted a policy of *perjuangan* against his traditional allies in the West but the struggle defeated him.

THE *REFORMASI* ERA

In the six years of Indonesian *reformasi*, the country's relations with the outside world have undergone dramatic shifts. Indeed, it is difficult to think of another country whose international reputation has shifted from respected international leader to international pariah and back again in such a short period of time. After Suharto's downfall, the opportunity to help Indonesia become the world's third largest democracy and restore its economy led the international community to pledge significant support to the new Habibie administration, which was warmly welcomed by Jakarta. Hopes for a new era in Indonesian relations with the outside world came crashing down following the wholesale destruction of East Timor in 1999. The international community responded by condemning Indonesia, halting economic assistance, and demanding an international peacekeeping force. When Abdurrahman Wahid replaced Habibie as president, this process was repeated. Wahid's credentials as a democratic reformer led the international community to embrace him wholeheartedly. But less than two years later, Wahid's attempts to use military support to protect him from impeachment made a mockery of these credentials, while corruption scandals led international institutions to cut aid and frayed ties with other key external actors.

In August 2001, the presidential transition from Wahid to Megawati, like all of the previous ones in Indonesia, occurred in the midst of economic and political crises, with the country's relations with key actors severely strained. During her three years in power, Megawati restored a fair degree of stability to both Indonesian domestic politics and foreign relations, but failed to significantly advance the reform agenda. When Megawati handed the reins of power to Susilo Bambang Yudhoyono (SBY) in October 2004, it was the first time an Indonesian president took office during a period of relative social, political, and economic stability, with the country's external relations on solid footing. The inauguration of a directly elected president who has pledged to tackle issues that are high on the agenda of the international community, such as corruption, legal reform, and conflict resolution in Aceh and Papua, has led it to embrace SBY, just as it did his predecessors in the *reformasi* era.

Indonesia's dramatic *reformasi* transformation was clearly reflected in Indonesian foreign relations. In part, this was due to the lack of institutionalization of Indonesia's foreign policy–making process, which allows significant scope for the president's personality and policy preferences to set the tone and content. However, the dispersion of power from the executive branch that was the hallmark of the *reformasi* era also occurred in the realm of international affairs. The DPR held up ambassadorial appointments, refused to provide funds for what it viewed as excessive and unnecessary foreign policy expenses, and demanded answers to foreign policy questions—all of which would have been unthinkable during the Suharto era. Public opinion, albeit often manipulated by political elites for their own purposes, was also a new constraint on foreign policy.

The lack of coherence in Indonesian foreign policy also reflected the dramatic shifts that had occurred in international political affairs. In contrast to the relative certainties of the Cold War environment facing both Sukarno and Suharto, subsequent Indonesian leaders were forced to grapple with significant changes in both global and regional environments. The most fundamental, of course, was the war on terrorism. It is hard to imagine a set of circumstances any Indonesian leader would wish to avoid more than having to respond to the Bush administration's doctrine of preemptive war and U.S. military action against countries with large populations of Muslims. At the regional level, the rise of China and decline of Japan posed new policy challenges for a country more comfortable with the previous status quo. The economic and political fallout of the Asian financial crisis in Southeast Asia, combined with the radically different stances countries of the region took toward the war on terrorism, complicated Indonesia's relations with its ASEAN neighbors. Most recently, international relief efforts in the wake of the December 26, 2004, tsunami created the possibility for greater cooperation with countries such as the United States and Australia, but hold the seeds of potential conflicts as well.

Habibie as President

Upon assuming the presidency, the accidental president, B. J. Habibie, adopted a policy of *reformasi* domestically and *diplomasi* internationally in an attempt to legitimate his government with the Indonesian populace and the international community. While Habibie was accepted as the constitutional successor, his status as Suharto's protégé meant he was not accepted as a legitimate President by many in the *reformasi* movement. Acutely aware of this, Habibie moved quickly to demonstrate his democratic credentials. Habibie freed the press, released political prisoners, lifted restrictions on labor organizations, and promised free and fair elections. In meetings with foreign officials, Habibie was quick to point out that his administration was implementing political reforms long advocated by Western critics and that Indonesia welcomed foreign assistance in these endeavors. Western countries eager to help promote a democratic transition in Indonesia strongly supported the Habibie government's reforms. The highlight of *diplomasi* in the political realm was the enormous international involvement in the June 1999 parliamentary elections, Indonesia's first free and fair elections since 1955.

Habibie and the International Monetary Fund

Like Suharto, Habibie took over an economy in crisis. In May 1998, inflation was rising at 80 percent per annum, output was down, the rupiah hovered at one-third its precrisis value, and the price of rice had tripled.[34] Indonesia clearly needed external assistance. Habibie quickly took steps designed to resume the flow of international aid that had been suspended when Suharto refused to take measures demanded by international donors. The International Monetary Fund and World Bank quickly resumed disbursement of the $43 billion rescue package.

Despite Habibie's swift moves to restore relations with foreign donors, some of his political appointees had long promoted an economic vision at odds with the free market ideals of the International Monetary Fund. Many Indonesians viewed the economic crisis as a historic opportunity to restructure Indonesia's economy. A key goal was to reduce the economic holdings of Sino-Indonesians. Adi Sasono, a Muslim activist appointed minister for cooperatives, called for a redistribution of wealth that would benefit the poor Muslim majority. Sasono was dubbed "the most dangerous man in Indonesia" by the *Asian Wall Street Journal*. Secular voices also supported calls for economic restructuring but advocated greater state intervention in the economy.

Ultimately, however, it was not differences of development strategy that led the Habibie government to adopt a strategy of struggle against the International Monetary Fund, but the same issues of corruption and personal economic interest that had undermined Suharto's relations with the Fund. These came to light in the Baligate scandal, which involved close Habibie associates demanding bribes in exchange for a promise of government influence.[35] When the International Monetary Fund demanded that Indonesia publish a report on Baligate written by the international accounting firm of PricewaterhouseCoopers, Habibie refused. Habibie, like Suharto before him, chose to struggle against the fund rather than pay the domestic political costs of appeasing it. The International Monetary Fund once again halted its aid program.

Habibie and Singapore

If Indonesia under Habibie moved quickly to repair ties with the West, relations with Indonesia's immediate neighbors were more problematic. In Singapore, Senior Minister Lee Kuan Yew had registered strong objection to Habibie's appointment as vice president.[36] Habibie later responded "there are 211 million people in Indonesia . . . Look at that map. All the green area is Indonesia. And that red dot is Singapore."[37]

The deterioration of relations between Indonesia and Singapore during the Habibie administration was not wholly a function of personality clashes. Indonesia's relationship with Singapore revolves around economics and ethnicity. The Asian financial crisis brought to the surface long-standing Indonesian resentment against Singapore's role as the banking and trading center of Southeast Asia.[38] This resentment is built on the belief that Singapore exerts undue influence over the Indonesian economy. Racial tensions also arose. Many believed that economic development had benefited Sino-Indonesians at the expense of the great majority of Malay Muslims. Some of this anti-Chinese attitude spilled over into Indonesia's relationship with Singapore.[39] In the wake of the May 1998 riots in which Chinese homes and shops were destroyed and Chinese women were the victims of systematic rape, many Indonesians of Chinese descent fled to Singapore. Included in this exodus were many Chinese tycoons. Some Habibie administration officials demanded that Singapore "bring back to Indonesia economic criminals seeking refuge there."[40]

Indonesians believed that Singapore was benefiting economically from Indonesia's misfortunes and expected bountiful assistance from its richer neighbor in its time of need. Singapore initially committed $5 billion in economic assistance to Indonesia. But when it became clear that Indonesia wanted the money with no strings attached, Singapore refused to disburse the funds. This led to recriminations on both sides that revealed fundamental differences regarding both countries' sense of obligation to their neighbors as well as their citizenry. The Suharto and Habibie administrations expected that Singapore would provide the money, not only as a symbol of its "good neighborliness" but also because economic troubles in Indonesia were bound to spill over into Singapore. Singaporean authorities, however, insisted that because the money promised to Indonesia was taxpayer money, they had a fiduciary responsibility to ensure that it be used solely for economic recovery and not lost to corruption. Troubles flared when Singapore refused to disburse the money.[41] As one high-ranking Singaporean minister remarked privately, "If we just give them the money, we are no better than their own cukongs (local Chinese partners)."[42]

Habibie and Malaysia

Habibie's ties to the Islamic community should have ushered in an era of close Indonesian–Malaysian ties. Habibie's high-tech programs found inspiration in Malaysia's heavy industry policy, while many of the Islamic intellectuals around Habibie admired the way Malaysia's New Economic Program (NEP) benefited the Muslim community in that country. Sporadic rifts between Indonesia and Malaysia in the 1990s had been largely a function of personal clashes between Suharto and Prime Minister Mahathir Mohammed over the mantel of regional statesman. Habibie described the closeness of Indonesia's ties with Malaysia as "one breath, one racial group . . . In times of difficulty, I know who my friends are."[43]

But Mahathir's sacking and arrest of Deputy Prime Minister Anwar Ibrahim created friction in Indonesian–Malaysian relations. Anwar had many supporters in Indonesia who viewed Anwar's *reformasi* movement as akin to their own. They condemned Mahathir's actions. Mahathir's attempt to smooth over the issue by sending Tun Ghafar Baba, a former deputy prime minister and close confidant, to "explain" the situation backfired when Ghafar lost control in front of a hostile Indonesian press corps and told them: "If you think Anwar Ibrahim is so important, you can take him and make him your leader. Maybe he is more fitting to be a leader in Indonesia because I heard that it is okay to be homosexual here, but in Malaysia, it is against the law."[44]

The Indonesian outcry over Ghafar's remarks illustrates how historical stereotypes are influencing public debate and relations in the *reformasi* era in Indonesia. Sukarno's patronizing views of Malaysia were echoed in an editorial in the *Indonesian Observer*, which stated:

> We cannot remember a time that a foreigner . . . had the temerity to say insulting things to our face. We must therefore have patience with the likes of Mr. Baba who comes from a country which, despite its modern appearance, is actually a feudal society, which received independence on a golden platter. This puts us in a different category from Malaysia because we are Revolutionaries who fought and died to achieve our independence. It is now the beginning of the end for feudalistic establishments which will be swept away by the new wave of reform initiated by Anwar Ibrahim.[45]

The tensions raised by Habibie in Indonesia's relations with its closest neighbors were limited by Ali Alatas, Indonesia's longest serving foreign minister. Alatas agreed to stay on under Habibie and provide continuity in Indonesian foreign policy. His close ties with the other ASEAN countries and his stature as one of Southeast Asia's senior statesmen kept Indonesia's foreign relations with its ASEAN neighbors on track during Habibie's tenure. Moreover, because Habibie chose not to appoint a vice president and the political situation was so fluid during his tenure, Habibie almost never traveled overseas. Alatas, therefore, continued to represent Indonesia's interests abroad.

East Timor Again

But Alatas could not prevent his voluble president from undermining years of diplomatic efforts to craft a solution to the East Timor issue that would remove it as a constraint on Indonesian foreign policy.[46] Alatas had hoped to formulate an agreement under which Indonesia would withdraw its troops, release Fretilin leader Xanana Gusmão from jail, and grant East Timor "special status" with a high degree of autonomy during a transition period after which a referendum on the territory's status would be held. Xanana Gusmao, from his cell in Cipinang prison, largely approved such a plan. With Suharto gone, negotiations were coming to fruition under U.N. auspices.[47]

In February 1999, Habibie ushered in Indonesia's most serious foreign policy crisis in decades by unilaterally announcing that Indonesia would permit a referendum on self-determination in East Timor. The leadership of the Indonesian armed forces was furious. In addition to opposing the potential loss of East Timor, it feared that the referendum would serve as a precedent for other restless provinces and ultimately threaten the territorial integrity of the Indonesian state that the military was sworn to uphold.[48]

As is well known, Habibie's attempt to remove East Timor as an obstacle to good relations with the international community went horribly awry. On August 30, 1999, the citizens of East Timor voted overwhelmingly in favor of independence from Indonesia in a referendum conducted by the United Nations. In the aftermath of the vote, pro-Indonesian militias and members of the Indonesian military unleashed a wave of terror: attacks on U.N. personnel, attacks on religious leaders and institutions, the forced movement out of East Timor of tens of thousands, and the wholesale burning and devastation of East Timor's physical infrastructure.[49]

The atrocities in East Timor were swiftly condemned by the international community. The U.S. Congress responded by adopting the Leahy Amendment, which prohibited the restoration of military ties with Indonesia until a series of conditions were met. The Leahy Amendment called on Indonesia to permit the return of East Timorese refugees who were forcibly displaced from their homeland, to assist in investigations of human rights violations by the Indonesian military and militias, and to use "effective measures to bring to justice" those members of the Indonesian military involved in aiding or abetting militia groups and those directly involved in human rights violations themselves. Under intense international pressure, including threats to cut off economic aid, Indonesia reluctantly agreed to permit a foreign peacekeeping force authorized by the United Nations into East Timor to restore order. Given Indonesian sensitivity to foreign intervention in its affairs, this decision was viewed as a national humiliation.

Many Indonesians were stunned at how quickly foreigners, particularly Westerners, were ready to treat Indonesia as a pariah state. Lacking access to independent sources of news about East Timor, most Indonesians expected the referendum would be favorable to Indonesia. International condemnation over East Timor, coming shortly after the International Monetary Fund threatened to cut off aid in response to Baligate, came as a shock and triggered a rise in nationalism and *perjuangan*.[50] Top political leaders contributed to a discourse of *perjuangan* that portrayed Indonesia as the victim of hostile external forces. Prior to his election as president, Gus Dur called for an "anti-UN Jihad."[51] Megawati, who owed much of her political support to the popularity of her father's staunch nationalism, had initially opposed the East Timor referendum. In an opinion piece in *Newsweek* at the height of the crisis in 1999, Megawati wrote that the first step in improving relations between Indonesia and the international community lay with outsiders. "First, the international community should halt the demonization of the Indonesian people. We know too well about violence and human rights, but as victims, not as perpetrators."[52]

Australia, not the United States, bore the brunt of Indonesia's nationalist backlash. Some Indonesians blamed Habibie's decision to permit the referendum on a January letter from Australian Prime Minister John Howard. More critically, Australia was the leading advocate of an early insertion of a U.N. peacekeeping mission into East Timor, which many Indonesians perceived as a threat to invade Indonesia.[53] In the nationalist backlash against Australia, Habibie abrogated the 1995 security agreement that Suharto had signed with Australia.

The East Timor crisis revealed fundamental differences among Indonesia's key international supporters regarding their priorities toward Indonesia at this time of political upheaval and economic crisis. Japan, long Indonesia's most important economic supporter, valued stability over political liberalization and feared that tying economic aid to political reform in general, and East Timor in particular, was antithetical to that goal. A Japanese spokesman stated that Japan would not suspend aid to Indonesia in protest of East Timor due to "the impact of such steps on Indonesian stability, its people and the Asian economy as a whole."[54] In contrast, the United States pressed, both publicly and privately, for a peacekeeping force and supported the decisions of the International Monetary Fund and World Bank to halt disbursements of economic aid until Indonesia allowed the peacekeeping force into East Timor.

International demands that Indonesia prosecute those responsible for the violence in East Timor continued to condition aid from many quarters. In October 1999, a month after Indonesia acquiesced to the imposition of a U.N. peacekeeping force in East Timor, the MPR rejected Habibie's accountability speech and later elected Abdurrahman Wahid and Megawati Sukarnoputri as president and vice president respectively.

Wahid as President

The unexpected election of Abdurrahman Wahid as president was greeted enthusiastically by the international community because he appeared to represent a clean break from the past. A Muslim cleric and leader of Indonesia's largest Islamic organization, the Nahdlatul Ulama (NU), Gus Dur, as he was commonly known, had long been a proponent of democratic values and religious tolerance. In the eyes of many, Gus Dur's personal history provided him with a unique legitimacy with which he could mediate social conflicts such as those in Aceh, Papua, and Maluku. It was also hoped that a partnership between Gus Dur and Megawati Sukarnoputri would give Indonesia a stable political coalition that represented the aspirations of the country's Muslim and secular constituencies. In the end, Gus Dur squandered his opportunity. His failure to tackle the country's pressing problems, his erratic behavior and willingness to sacrifice the national good for his personal interest led the MPR to remove him in July 2001.[55]

Almost immediately after ascending to the presidency in October 1999, Gus Dur embarked on a series of international trips, which he argued were necessary to repair Indonesia's international reputation after the East Timor crisis and secure the international support that had been cut off because of it. In visits to the United States and Europe, Gus Dur argued that the new government was serious about promoting Indonesia's democratic transition and economic recovery and requested international assistance for these efforts. Gus Dur's strategy of *diplomasi* was supported by a series of symbolic gestures. The appointment of Juwono Sudarsono, a well-respected civilian, as defense minister was viewed as a signal to both the military and the international community that Gus Dur was serious about reforming the institution responsible for the East Timor debacle. Gus Dur made an early visit to East Timor, where he pledged to support the territory's transition to statehood. The international community responded positively to Gus Dur's diplomatic offensive, resuming disbursements of international aid and promising support for Indonesia's territorial integrity. Only Australia among Indonesia's key Western allies was excluded from this diplomatic offensive. Wahid expressed a desire to repair relations soured by the East Timor experience, but domestic opposition prevented Wahid from visiting Australia until the waning days of his presidency.[56]

Had Wahid limited his foreign travels to his initial forays and buckled down to the tough work of addressing the country's challenges, his foreign policy—and his domestic legacy—might have been radically different. But it soon became clear that Gus Dur was an erratic leader, who preferred the prestige of foreign travel to the hard work of domestic reform. During his twenty-one months in office, Gus Dur visited more countries than Suharto did in thirty years, becoming the most traveled of all Indonesian presidents. Wahid's frequent absences from the country meant that difficult decisions were not being made at home.[57] Foreign policy can secure promises of external support, but without the political will of Indonesian officials to deal with critical problems, it can contribute little to their resolution. For example, after securing the support of the international community for the territorial integrity of Indonesia—which meant no international support for Jakarta's opponents in Aceh and Papua—Gus Dur failed to address the problems on either end of the archipelago seriously. In fact, he exacerbated matters with off-the-cuff statements. Gus Dur responded to Achnese demands for a referendum on the future of the province by stating that if a referendum was possible in East Timor, why not in Aceh? Similarly, he attempted to curry goodwill in the country's easternmost province by renaming it Papua and permitting the flying of the "Morning Star" or Papuan flag, long a symbol of resistance to Indonesian rule. Gus Dur made these comments knowing full well that they would be opposed by Indonesian nationalists of all stripes, particularly the army. More importantly, there was no substantive effort to craft political solutions in either case.

Indonesian foreign policy was also weakened by Wahid's dismissive attitude toward Indonesia's foreign policy establishment. Clearly preferring to function as foreign minister himself, Wahid appointed Alwi Shihab, a close political confident with no foreign policy experience, to the position. The lack of professional backstop to Wahid's foreign policy manifested itself in little attention to Indonesia's traditional foreign policy planks and a series of initiatives that undermined them. Wahid broke long-standing ASEAN tradition that the first foreign visits of ASEAN heads of states are to member countries. He further undermined ASEAN by proposing that East Timor and Papua New Guinea join the organization, despite well-known opposition to such proposals by other members. When this was brushed aside by Lee Kuan Yew, Wahid claimed Singapore was "greedy" and "anti-Malay."[58] Wahid also made a series of far-fetched proposals. In a throwback to the Bandung alliance of Asia's "big three," Wahid proposed an "Asian axis" among Indonesia, China, and India to counter Western domination. This proposal not only antagonized the West but also inspired resentment in Japan, Indonesia's top economic supporter.

The wide range of initiatives Gus Dur proposed created confusion and disarray in Indonesian foreign policy. Moreover, the goodwill obtained from trips to the United States, for example, was quickly offset by trips to countries such as Cuba. Domestic analysts such as Kusnanto Anggoro criticized Wahid's foreign initiatives as "a policy of no policy," while Meidyatama Suryodiningrat of the *Jakarta Post* held that "We can only hope that the consistency of the past has laid a strong enough bedrock to withstand the confusion of the present and the uncertainties of tomorrow, particularly in ASEAN."[59]

Furthermore, Gus Dur failed to live up to a number of commitments he made early in his tenure, particularly in relation to East Timor. In an attempt to give the new administration breathing space, the United Nations had agreed not to seek an international tribunal to punish those responsible for the atrocities in East Timor as long as they were brought to justice by Indonesian authorities. In cooperation with international experts, Indonesia's Human Rights Commission undertook a credible investigation of the atrocities committed in East Timor. But the government did not take steps to bring those implicated to justice. Nor did it take concrete measures to resolve things on the ground. In September 2000, a full year after the referendum, an estimated 130,000 East Timorese refugees who had been forcibly displaced remained in squalid refugee camps in West Timor. On September 6, 2000, armed militias attacked a U.N. office in the Atambua camp, killing three U.N. workers, one an American.

The killings triggered a U.N. resolution calling for the disarming of the militias, a resolution of the displaced persons problem, and steps toward accountability. The international community adopted a tougher stance toward both Wahid and Indonesia. In Jakarta shortly after the Atambua incident, William Cohen, U.S. secretary of defense, warned that Indonesia risked losing foreign economic assistance if it failed to act.[60] Cohen's message that the militias must be controlled was reinforced by James Wolfensohn, president of the World Bank, who warned that if Wahid did not take action before the CGI meeting scheduled for October 2000, "the donors are going to react."[61]

Once again, the Western decision to link economic aid to political conditions triggered an angry response from Indonesian leaders. MPR Speaker Amien Rais lashed out at Cohen, saying Indonesia "should not accept pressure from William Cohen or any other 'Cohens' because we are independent and sovereign."[62] Even Emil Salim, a respected technocrat and vice chairman of the United States–Indonesia Society, opposed such conditionality. According to Salim, "The international community should not use Indonesia's economic Achilles heel to extract political concessions. That would be interpreted as blackmail."[63]

The West largely maintained its hard-line stance. In part, this reflected Indonesia's lack of action toward rectifying the situation in East Timor. In part, it reflected the Wahid government's own mismanagement of economic affairs, exemplified by his dismissal of highly regarded economic officials such as Laksamana Sukardi and their replacement by Wahid cronies. The Bulogate and Bruneigate scandals, in which Wahid and figures close to him were accused of using state money for private purposes, tarnished Wahid's image as a moral force and served the same political function for Wahid that Baligate had for Habibie. They also led the United States to reconsider its previous support of Wahid. The United States had named Indonesia one of four key democratizing countries that it was prepared to support generously and gave Wahid breathing room to enact the reforms he claimed to favor. But as opposition to his ineffective administration led to impeachment proceedings against him, Wahid took actions demonstrating that he was more interested in safeguarding his own political position than his country's fragile democratic reforms. Appallingly, Gus Dur appointed military and police leaders he hoped would support a declaration of a state emergency, which would give him the power to dissolve the DPR and MPR, thereby preventing them from impeaching him. The logic that the West must support Wahid because he represented the best hope for democracy in Indonesia had been completely discredited.

By July 2001, Indonesian politics were at a state of brinkmanship. The MPR was determined to remove Gus Dur, who already promised not to leave the palace and was calling on NU members to physically protest his "illegal removal." Crisis was averted with a face-saving formula that had Gus Dur leave Indonesia for medical treatment in the United States.[64] Like Sukarno, Suharto, and Habibie before him, Gus Dur left office largely bereft of international allies.

Megawati as President

Megawati became Indonesia's fifth president in July 2001. Hamzah Haz, head of the Muslim United Development Party (Partai Persatuan Pembangunan) and the man who had blocked Megawati's path to the presidency in 1999 by arguing that Islamic teachings prohibit women from becoming leaders, became her vice president. Once again, many hoped that a partnership between representatives of Indonesia's centrist secular and Muslim groups would foster sufficient political legitimacy and social stability to deal effectively with the country's myriad challenges.

As in every previous presidential transition, Megawati assumed office with the task of repairing Indonesia's relations with key international actors. The International Monetary Fund had refused to release $400 million in response to the Wahid government's failure to implement its commitments. The West in particular was frustrated with Indonesia's apparent unwillingness to prosecute those responsible for atrocities in East Timor. International human rights groups were mobilizing against continued military abuses as well as social violence in places like Maluku.

In the weeks between her inauguration and the September 11, 2001, bombings of the World Trade Center and the Pentagon that would create a host of new foreign policy challenges for Indonesia, the Megawati administration moved quickly to demonstrate a new era in foreign policy. In contrast to Wahid's neglect of Southeast Asia, Megawati declared that ASEAN was the cornerstone of Indonesian foreign policy. She underscored this statement by reverting to ASEAN tradition and making her first official trip a series of whirlwind visits to all her ASEAN neighbors. Megawati announced that Jakarta's conflicts with Aceh and Papua must be resolved politically rather than militarily. She signaled a desire to repair Indonesia's frayed relations with Australia by inviting Prime Minister John Howard to visit Indonesia. Indonesian economic officials held early meetings with their international counterparts. In short, with the exception of bringing those responsible for military atrocities to justice, Indonesia made significant strides to put its relationships with key international actors back on track.

The international community responded positively. The International Monetary Fund quickly resumed lending. Australian Prime Minister John Howard traveled to Indonesia in August, becoming the first foreign head of state to call on President Megawati. The Bush administration was engaged in a strategic review of Indonesia, and key officials such as Paul Wolfowitz, deputy secretary of defense and a former ambassador to Indonesia, were arguing for the resumption of military ties.[65] The initial foreign policy moves of Sukarno's daughter were infused with Suharto's pragmatism.

The War on Terrorism

The attacks on the World Trade Center and the Pentagon thrust Indonesia high onto Washington's agenda. Once the United States had declared war on terrorism, Indonesia's status as the world's most populous Muslim country made it a critical ally. Making a previously planned September 20, 2001, visit to Washington, Megawati became only the second international leader and the first leader from a Muslim majority country to meet President Bush following the events of September 11.[66]

In Washington, Megawati condemned the "inhumane" attacks on America and vowed to cooperate with the international community in combating terrorism.[67] In return, the George W. Bush administration pledged to work with Congress to secure at least $130 million in bilateral assistance, providing $10 million for police training and additional sums for displaced people in Maluku and Aceh. The two leaders also focused on long-standing sources of tension in the bilateral relationship. Bush called for the peaceful resolution of separatist conflicts, while emphasizing that the United States "does not support secessionist aspirations anywhere in Indonesia."[68] Megawati pledged to pursue peaceful solutions to secessionist conflict but also made it clear that "the integrity of our country is of the highest importance and we will defend it at all costs."[69] In Washington, Megawati reminded her audience that Abraham Lincoln resorted to force to maintain the unity of his country and asserted that Indonesia would defend its territorial integrity "as did Lincoln."[70]

Why did Megawati support the American position on terrorism immediately after September 11? In large part because Indonesia had been a victim of terrorism itself. Since the fall of Suharto, the Jakarta Stock Exchange had been bombed, a large number of churches and mosques had been attacked, and there had been bombings of other sites.[71] Hence Megawati could portray her support for the war against terrorism as one of mutual concern rooted in domestic events.

But Megawati was walking a delicate tightrope between American pressure for wholesale support of its war against terrorism and sentiment among the Indonesian populace that the war would morph into an anti-Islamic crusade. Bush tried to allay such concerns by stating that "the war against terrorism is not a war against Muslims, nor is it a war against Arabs . . . It is a war against evil people who conduct crimes against innocent people."[72] But as *Tempo* magazine reported, Bush's "blundering talk about a 'crusade' not to mention his mobilization of the U.S. military machine against Afghanistan for an operation called 'Infinite Justice' was perceived by many as a challenge to the Islamic world as a whole."[73]

Islam in Indonesian Foreign Policy

Islamic concerns have traditionally been absent from Indonesian foreign policy. The absence reflects the historic marginalization of Islam in domestic politics under both Sukarno and Suharto. Sukarno viewed Islam as a divisive factor that had the potential to thwart national unity among Indonesia's plural society. Sukarno viewed fellow Muslim states not through the lens of religion, but according to whether they were members of the nonaligned movement.

Once Suharto's Islamic allies had helped him eradicate the PKI, he also sidelined political Islam. In 1972, Indonesia refused to sign the charter of Organization of Islamic Conference (OIC) on the grounds that it was not an Islamic state. It was not until the rise of the Organization of Petroleum Exporting Countries (OPEC) that Suharto viewed Middle Eastern countries as potential contributors to his development goals. As former Foreign Minister Adam Malik commented, "Indonesia did not regard that region as important, except for pilgrimage every year. With the exploitation of oil, we then became aware of [its] importance."[74]

Even after OPEC, the Suharto regime's fear of political Islam led it to approach international Islamic issues and the countries associated with them warily. Indonesia has always refused to recognize Israel and supported the Palestinian cause, but it justified these policies on the right of the Palestinians to self-determination, not religion. In the 1991 Gulf War, Indonesia supported the coalition to remove Iraq from Kuwait because Iraq's invasion of Kuwait violated international law. Indonesia is home to the world's largest community of Muslims, but its role in the Islamic world was traditionally a peripheral one. Amien Rais observed that rather than identify with its religious brethren in the Middle East, "the government tends to identify Indonesia as a country closer to the Far East."[75]

But the *reformasi* era provided much greater political space to Muslim voices. The confluence of a rise in Islam in Indonesian domestic politics, the war on terrorism, and the war in Iraq made it likely that Islam would play a larger role in Indonesian foreign policy in the future.[76]

Once the United States began bombing Afghanistan, Megawati found herself under intense pressure to distance Indonesia from the American action and adopt a policy of *perjuangan* against it. There were calls for Indonesia to break diplomatic ties with the United States, embargo American goods, and kick Americans out of Indonesia.[77] Echoes of Suharto's pragmatism could be heard in voices of moderate Muslim leaders condemning the bombings in Afghanistan while urging restraint among their followers.[78] The leader of Muhammadiyah, Syafi Ma'arif, argued that anti-American actions were irresponsible because "if America reacts and stops economic assistance, our country will be bankrupt."[79]

The political risks to Megawati were very real. Vice President Hamzah Haz reacted to the events of September 11 with the observation that the violence might help the United States "expiate its sins."[80] In late September 2001, the Indonesian Council of Islamic Scholars (Majelis Ulama Indonesia, or MUI) issued a declaration stating that if the United States attacked Afghanistan, all Muslims were obliged to join a jihad against America.[81] Both Hamzah Haz and the MUI were forced to distance themselves from these controversial statements. But they clearly illustrated the lengths leaders in the Islamic community—who had successfully blocked Megawati's ascension to the presidency in 1999—were willing to go to weaken her government only weeks after it had been formed.

Megawati responded to the attack on Afghanistan by stating that the Indonesian government rejected any attack launched by one country on another in the pursuit of terrorists. She stated that international regulations and conventions should be followed to ensure that the war on terrorism did not become a new form of terrorism itself. In short, Megawati was trying to distinguish the goal of eradicating terrorism from the violent strategy used in pursuit of that aim.[82] Not surprisingly, Megawati's comments were greeted warmly in Indonesia but coolly in the United States.

The American designation of Southeast Asia as the second front in the war on terror raised new sources of tension between Indonesia and the United States as well as with its closest neighbors. Surprisingly, it was in tightly controlled Singapore, not lax Indonesia, that the terrorist threat next appeared. In December 2001, Singaporean authorities learned of plans by local radicals to bomb Western government targets, including U.S. naval assets and the Australian embassy. Singaporean authorities quickly arrested a number of Muslim Singaporeans. The plan was discovered in part by evidence found in Afghanistan, leaving no doubt that those arrested in Singapore were part of a transnational terrorist network.

Intelligence findings that those arrested in Singapore were members of Jemaah Islamiyah led to demands that Indonesia take action against the group. As Robert Hefner explains in chapter 2 of this volume, Jemaah Islamiyah is a loose network of Islamic radicals throughout Southeast Asia whose spiritual leader is Abu Bakar Ba'asyir.[83] The group's stated goal is the creation of an Islamic caliphate that encompasses the states of maritime Southeast Asia.[84] It was responsible for attacks on churches in Indonesia, the home of the Philippine ambassador to Indonesia, and Christian communities in Maluku, Poso, and elsewhere.[85]

Prior to the October 2002 Bali bombings, many Indonesians dismissed the terrorist threat. Indonesia's police chief denied there were terrorists in Indonesia,[86] while Foreign Minister Wirayuda claimed Indonesia had "no hard evidence" against Ba'asyir or other radicals.[87] The international community was exasperated by the manner in which many Indonesians reacted to the terrorist threat. Attempting to make political capital out of international pressure that Indonesia clamp down on Ba'asyir and his followers, Vice President Hamzah Haz made a public visit to Ba'asyir. When Indonesian authorities finally arrested an al-Qaeda operative named al-Faruq, the fact that much of the evidence against him came from the Central Intelligence Agency (CIA) led many Indonesians to question both the validity of the evidence and the motives of the Americans.[88]

The United States deemed intelligence regarding threats of terrorist activity in Indonesia sufficiently serious to close its embassy in Jakarta for five days in September 2002, but Indonesian authorities downplayed the allegations.[89] American authorities were particularly dismayed at the official investigation into a September 23, 2002, grenade explosion outside an American embassy house in Jakarta. Western officials said the blast was a bungled attempt by Islamic militants to attack an American target, but the Indonesian police dismissed the incident as a debt collection effort gone awry.[90] Similarly, although Indonesia signed both an ASEAN declaration on counterterrorism as well as a three-way pact with Malaysia and the Philippines to pool efforts to fight militancy, many of its Southeast Asian neighbors were frustrated by Indonesia's failure to act on intelligence they provided regarding suspected terrorists in Indonesia.[91] It took the Bali bombings to convince many Indonesians of the presence of terrorists in their midst.

The Bali Bombings

On October 12, 2002, bombs destroyed two nightclubs in Kuta Beach, Bali, killing 202 people in Indonesia's largest terrorist attack ever.[92] Most of the victims were foreign tourists. Indeed, the bombers chose their target with the goal of killing as many Westerners as possible; they later stated they had hoped the majority of the victims would be Americans rather than Australians. Another bomb targeting the U.S. consulate in Bali was also set to blow up at roughly the same time as those that destroyed the nightclubs in Kuta but failed to detonate.

Indonesia and the international community condemned the Bali bombings. The carnage in Bali confirmed that Indonesia's porous borders made it ripe for terrorist infiltration.[93] But extensive debate broke out over whether the terrorists were homegrown or foreign. Ba'asyir and others argued that Indonesians couldn't possibly be behind the Bali bombings: "Indonesians don't have such powerful explosives . . . I think maybe the U.S. are behind the bombings because they always say Indonesia is part of a terrorist network."[94] Most mainstream leaders urged their followers not to make accusations until credible evidence had been found.[95] But the climate of suspicion between Indonesia and much of the outside world was not helped by the tendency of many Indonesian leaders to once again blame foreigners for problems inside Indonesia.

Fortunately, Indonesian officials placed the investigation of the Bali bombings in the hands of I Made Pastika, a native Balinese who quickly took up offers of foreign assistance.[96] Pastika's speed in compiling a credible case against the bombers—all Indonesian nationals—and arresting them was exceptional by Indonesian standards. Nevertheless, many Indonesians remained unconvinced that their fellow countrymen were sufficiently evil or skillful to carry out such an operation. In an attempt to dispel these beliefs, Indonesian police staged two bizarre news conferences in which police officials joked on camera with the confessed bombers before leading them through a discussion of how the bombings were organized and implemented.[97] The sight of the Indonesian police making small talk with those responsible for the death of so many was viewed with revulsion outside of Indonesia, particularly in Australia. But the interviews served a critical domestic purpose by convincing a skeptical public that the perpetrators of the Bali bombings were local, not imported from abroad.

In the wake of the Bali bombings, the Indonesian government took a number of steps long advocated by outsiders. On October 19, it arrested Abu Bakar Ba'asyir.[98] It enacted a new terrorism law that gave the authorities greater power to act against terrorists. And intelligence provided to Indonesia by the West and its Southeast Asian neighbors was treated seriously.

Indonesia's post-Bali willingness to respond to the terrorist threat removed a critical obstacle to good working relations with many key supporters. But measures taken by foreign governments to protect their citizens created new sources of tension. The Malaysian decision to expel illegal Indonesian workers in part due to fears of terrorist infiltration raised tensions between the two countries. The decision by many governments to issue travel advisories warning their citizens to defer travel to Indonesia was damaging to tourism and Indonesia's image to foreign investors.[99] The American decision to include Indonesia among a group of mostly Middle Eastern countries whose residents in the United States must register with the Immigration and Naturalization Service caused an outcry in Indonesia. But it was the Bush administration's war on Iraq and doctrine of preemptive war that raised new obstacles for Indonesia's relations with the United States and allies such as Britain and Australia.

IRAQ AND PREEMPTIVE WAR

It is difficult to imagine a greater foreign policy dilemma for an Indonesian leader than the Bush administration's call for a preemptive war against a Muslim country. Indonesian nationalists condemned the doctrine of preemption as a violation of international law and national sovereignty. They argued, "There is a basic question that hasn't been answered by the U.S.: who has the right to punish a nation? The United Nations or the U.S.?"[100] Moderate Muslims, who agreed that Saddam Hussein should comply with the U.N. inspections, were outraged at the idea of an attack on a Muslim country. Both secular and Muslim leaders worried that an attack on Iraq would be confused with "religion in the minds of some people."[101] They feared that an American war against Iraq would provide an opportunity for Indonesian radicals—both secular and Islamic—to hijack Indonesian politics in ways detrimental to the interests of both Indonesian moderates and the United States. Moderate Muslims launched campaigns to denounce the use of Islam for violent ends. Although protests against the Iraq war in Indonesia were smaller and better controlled than expected, according to the Pew Global Attitudes Project, 85 percent of Indonesians now held an unfavorable view of the United States, due largely to its actions in Iraq and its support for Israel.

Separatism on the Periphery

The war on terror overshadowed but did not remove other issues from Indonesia's foreign policy agenda. International actors retained an interest in how Indonesia dealt with the separatist movements in Aceh and Papua, as well as with those responsible for the postreferendum violence in East Timor and the Atambua killings. Megawati's nationalist credentials provided her with the legitimacy to take unpopular steps to resolve these issues. Unfortunately, she was not willing to do so.

On May 19, 2003, Megawati declared martial law in Aceh and the Indonesian military launched a new offensive designed to eradicate GAM once and for all. Jakarta's actions ended the fragile five-month peace that followed the December 9, 2002, cease-fire agreement between Indonesia and GAM.[102] That agreement, brokered by the Henri Dunant Center after three years of painstaking negotiations, was to have been the first step in a comprehensive plan to resolve the twenty-six-year-old conflict. Despite intensive mediation efforts by the international community, the peace process collapsed.

Both sides contributed to the breakdown of negotiations by failing to live up to previous commitments. Jakarta failed to fully implement the special autonomy status it granted to Aceh in 2001. It also refused to offer GAM the prospect of a formal political role in the province. For its part, GAM refused to put its weapons in cantonment. Most critically, despite accepting special autonomy in the December 2002 agreement, GAM leaders viewed autonomy as a stepping-stone to independence, an outcome wholly unacceptable to Jakarta.[103]

Many international actors hoped that the war would be short, successful, and conducted without major violations of human rights or disruption of economic activity. Previous conflict had led Exxon Mobil to shut down its natural gas operations, which accounted for 11 percent of Indonesia's oil and gas revenue. In the past, the international community condemned Jakarta's military approach to the conflict in Aceh and the human rights abuses that accompanied it. But well-documented atrocities committed by GAM, combined with its refusal to accept anything less than full independence, led to a decline in international support for the separatists.[104] Key states reiterated their commitment to Indonesia's territorial integrity, implying tacit support of Jakarta's strategy. According to a senior American official, "The U.S. will not lose sleep if the military's operation is successful."[105]

After a year of martial law, Indonesia downgraded the status of Aceh to civil emergency, claiming its 40,000 troops had made significant progress in its battle against GAM's estimated 5,000 fighters. According to the TNI (Tentara Nasional Indonesia), it had killed almost 2,000 GAM members, arrested another 2,100, and taken the surrender of 1,276.[106] Following the government's announcement, GAM released twenty-two hostages in a deal brokered by the International Committee of the Red Cross. These moves by both sides held open the prospect for further steps toward resolving the conflict and ending the suffering of Aceh's 4.4 million people. During the remainder of the Megawati administration, however, no further progress was made.

The Megawati administration never embarked on a serious effort to address the legitimate grievances of many native Papuans. Instead, a number of initiatives taken in Jakarta combined with actions of national authorities in Papua dealt serious blows to the prospect of a peaceful solution to the conflict in Papua.

The Organization for Free Papua (Organisasi Papua Merdeka, or OPM), the armed wing of the Papuan independence movement, has waged a long but low-level struggle against Jakarta. In 2001, the DPR passed a special autonomy law that many in Papua, Jakarta, and the international community believed provided a new foundation for Papua's relationship with Indonesia. The legislation called for Papua to receive 70 percent of its mineral wealth and for certain key governmental posts to be occupied by native Papuans. With support from the local community, key Papuan leaders formed the Papua presidium, which pledged to work with Jakarta to implement autonomy.

But hopes for peace dimmed in late 2001 when Theys Eluay, head of the Papua presidium, was murdered. Members of the military have since been convicted of his murder. After dithering in the implementation of the special autonomy law, Megawati signaled its death knell when she issued a decree dividing Papua into three separate provinces in early 2003. This decree not only served as an obstacle to Papuan collective action but also rendered implementation of the special autonomy law nearly impossible. These actions undermined the willingness of many Papuans to work with Jakarta.

Recent military abuses also led to increased international attention to Papua. In August 2002, two American employees of Freeport-McMoRan were murdered in Timika, Papua, with the military once again the lead suspect. The United States said that a credible investigation into the murders was a prerequisite to good relations with Indonesia.[107] In 2004, Indonesian authorities arrested Antonious Wamang, who confessed to the murder, and the FBI indicted him. The FBI indictment means that Indonesia has formally met the above-noted condition set by Congress for improving relations. But Wamang has not been turned over to U.S. authorities for prosecution, and many observers contend he was likely acting under the direction of the TNI, given the heavy military presence in the area where the murders took place. Human rights groups and their congressional allies view the Timika case as another example of Indonesia's unwillingness to prosecute military personnel for gross violations of human rights. In their opinion, the FBI indictment is an attempt by the Bush administration to circumvent congressional restrictions on military relations with Indonesia. From Indonesia's point of view, the unwillingness of human rights groups and Congress to treat the FBI indictment as credible is simply another example of American bad faith: every time Indonesia meets an American demand, the bar gets moved.

The East Timor Trials

In an unusual twist, Indonesia's prosecution of those accused of atrocities in East Timor will be measured against a standard set in the United States, where Indonesian General Johnny Lumintang was found guilty of crimes against humanity by a civil court.[108] The court found that Lumintang, who was vice chief of staff of the Indonesian army in 1999, "along with other high-ranking members of the Indonesian military—planned, ordered and instigated acts carried out by subordinates to terrorize and destabilize the East Timorese population and to destroy East Timor's infrastructure following the vote for independence."[109]

To date, Indonesia's prosecutions have fallen far short of the American precedent. In large part, this is due to the belief held by many Indonesian nationalists that those accused of atrocities were Indonesian patriots, not criminals. Key military figures such as former General Wiranto, who was armed forces commander in 1999 and finished third in Indonesia's July 2005 presidential election, claimed, "We did not do anything wrong." He illustrated the disconnect between Indonesians and outsiders when he stated, "We invited about 4,000 foreign observers and reporters to observe. . . . Not a single monitor died. How can we have committed human rights abuses when there were foreign observers and reporters before and after?"[110]

To ward off calls for an international tribunal, Indonesia set up an Ad Hoc Human Rights Court on East Timor in Jakarta to hear cases against those responsible for the postreferendum violence. To date, the Court has announced twelve verdicts. All of the Indonesian military and police personnel have been acquitted. Two East Timorese, including the most notorious militia leader, Eurico Guteteres, have been convicted of charges including crimes against humanity but remain free on bail.[111] Human rights organizations denounced the trials as a whitewash and called for the United Nations to set up an independent tribunal. East Timor has publicly opposed the creation of a tribunal, ostensibly in the name of reconciliation with Indonesia, but in reality because it does not want to antagonize its larger neighbor. Officials in Jakarta desperately want to avoid an international tribunal but find themselves caught between international pressure for convictions and strong domestic opposition to such a move. Arief Budiman doubted that more senior generals such as Wiranto would face trials because, he wrote, "Indonesians see these convicted individuals as sacrifices made to appease the international community. But if the government does more than that, it risks creating domestic problems for itself."[112]

Reassertion of ASEAN Leadership

The Megawati administration deserves credit for working to restore Indonesia's traditional leadership role in ASEAN. ASEAN had been rudderless since the Asian financial crisis, which forced all Southeast Asian countries to focus on domestic recovery, and deprived ASEAN of an elder statesman. Neither Habibie nor Wahid had much interest in ASEAN, but Megawati's term in office coincided with Indonesia's assumption of the ASEAN chairmanship in July 2003 and its hosting of the ASEAN Summit in October 2004. At that summit, ASEAN approved a series of Indonesian-inspired proposals, the most important being a commitment to the creation of an ASEAN Security, Economic, and Social and Cultural Community.

Reestablishing its leadership role in ASEAN did not necessarily translate into good working relationships with all of its ASEAN neighbors. Indonesia took a hard-line stand toward Myanmar, urging the ruling junta to release Aung San Suu Kyii and take steps to implement its own "road map" to democracy. Indonesia demonstrated its leadership on this issue by appointing former Foreign Minister Ali Alatas as Megawati's special envoy and sending him on several trips to Rangoon. Indonesia's quest for leadership also created some tensions with Thailand. Thailand initially opposed Indonesian plans for an ASEAN Security Community, in part because Thai Prime Minister Thaksin would like to play the role of ASEAN leader himself. But tensions between Indonesia and Thailand have also arisen due to the heavy-handed manner in which Thaksin's government has dealt with the Muslim insurgency in southern Thailand. Despite these tensions, Indonesia's relations with its Southeast Asian neighbors are much improved from the early days of the *reformasi* era, when they worried about the balkanization of Indonesia and the negative consequences that would have created for them.

The Inauguration of Susilo Bambang Yudhoyono

Having won 60 percent of the popular vote in the September presidential runoff with Megawati, SBY was sworn in on October 20, 2004, claiming a mandate for change. SBY has pledged to take steps to eradicate corruption, reform Indonesian's legal system, and promote economic growth. He has also stated that resolution of the Aceh and Papua conflicts require political, not military solutions. SBY appointed a mostly reformist cabinet and retained Foreign Minister Hassan Wirayudya, a much applauded move that signaled approval of the steps Wirayuda has taken toward restoring Indonesian prestige abroad. On key issues, the new cabinet ministers enunciated policies that were congruent with the interests of the international community. Indonesia's new justice minister, Hamid Awaluddin, promised tougher antiterror laws and zero tolerance of graft.[113] Juwono Sudarsono, the country's civilian defense minister, has outlined an ambitious plan to exert civilian control of the military by folding the TNI into the Defense department and bringing the military's economic enterprises under state control. Once again, the international community embraced an Indonesian leader for the reformist ideas he appeared to embody.

As this book goes to press in 2005, the December 26, 2004, tsunami disaster that is currently estimated to have killed over 100,000 people in Aceh and the international response to it have created opportunities to put Indonesian relations with the outside world on a new footing.[114] At the same time, the high international expectations for SBY combined with the intense international scrutiny of Indonesian behavior toward the crisis held the potential for negative fallout as well.

First, the natural disaster added impetus to moves toward a peace agreement between GAM and Jakarta. An informal cease-fire between Jakarta and GAM already existed and the government had called for talks to be held by the end of January 2005.[115] Nevertheless, both sides continued to hurl accusations at each other. The government accused GAM of attacking relief convoys, and used this as justification for continued counterinsurgency actions that it claimed had killed 120 rebels during a two-week period in January 2005.[116] GAM denied attacking aid workers, offered to cooperate in the relief effort, and claimed that 100 of the 120 killed by the TNI were unarmed civilians, not combatants.[117] While the tsunami provided a catalyst for conflict resolution, hard-liners on both sides could easily scuttle a deal. Although many civilian members of the Indonesian government may favor a negotiated solution, many military figures, who have significant economic stakes in Aceh, prefer a hard-line approach. The challenge facing the SBY administration was to craft an agreement that made sufficient concessions to the Achnese to secure a peace settlement, but not so many that the TNI would feel compelled to scuttle it on the ground, as in East Timor. A second challenge is for the government to engage Achnese civil society and convince the traumatized population that its best hope for the future lies with Indonesia.

Second, the tsunami opened the door to a new era in Indonesia's relations with the international community. The traditional Indonesian suspicion that outside powers want to weaken Indonesia was reinforced by the international reaction to the 1999 violence in East Timor. The outpouring of international support for Indonesia may help overcome such suspicions. Indonesians of all stripes were on record as welcoming the foreign assistance. Nevertheless, old attitudes also were on display in reports claiming foreign militaries were spying in Aceh or were after its oil and gas. Official sensitivity to such suspicions was behind the announcement that all foreign troops must withdraw from Aceh by March 26, 2005.

The participation of so many foreign soldiers in the relief effort, often working side by side with their Indonesian counterparts, presented an opportunity for Indonesia to meet a long-standing goal of restoring military relations with the United States and Australia. Members of the Bush administration, particularly Paul Wolfowitz, lobbied hard for years to upgrade relations with the TNI, but Congress opposed such a move because of Indonesia's lack of accountability for military abuses. While on a tour of damaged areas in Aceh, Secretary of State Colin Powell announced the U.S. decision to partially lift its arms embargo to permit the purchase of spare parts for Indonesia's Hercules C-130 transport planes so they could be used to deliver relief supplies. Powell stated, however, that he hoped this decision would not lead to renewed attacks on GAM. With Aceh open to the global media to an unprecedented degree, there existed the possibility that military abuses there, recorded by journalists, could scuttle the attempts of political leaders to upgrade relations.

PROSPECTS FOR THE FUTURE

Despite the dramatic shifts in Indonesian foreign policy since independence, a number of striking continuities, described in this chapter, are likely to influence Indonesia's stance toward the outside world well into the future, including a tight linkage between Indonesian domestic politics and foreign policy, strong opposition to conditionality, a fervent belief that Indonesia has an important role to play in international affairs, and a conviction that the world is a hostile place. Precisely because these factors have influenced Indonesian foreign policy across time, however, they cannot account for the dramatic swings between *diplomasi* and *perjuangan*. Instead, the choice between these strategies has been largely determined by the congruence of interests and attitudes between Indonesia and other key actors in the international community. Ultimately, Indonesians will chart their own foreign policy course. Because this course will be influenced by Indonesian perceptions of the attitudes and interests of key members of the international community, however, there is some scope for outside actors to influence the outcome.

Resentment against Conditionality

Indonesia's strong objection to conditionality—particularly to the practice of linking political conditions to economic aid—has led the country's leaders to sacrifice desperately needed material assistance to political ideals in every era of Indonesia's history. Those who argued that Indonesia's need for economic aid would prevent it from taking the politically popular step of terminating its relationship with the International Monetary Fund were ignoring a long history of Indonesian leaders doing precisely that. This opposition to conditionality is a manifestation of the *bebas* component of Indonesia's foreign policy doctrine and is unlikely to change in the near term.

A Hostile World

Indonesians are united in the belief that the world is a dangerous place. This perception has a number of components. First, that the rules of the international system are defined by the great powers as a way to maintain their supremacy and keep secondary states down. Second, that the ideals on which the great powers claim to base international rules are simply fig leafs for the pursuit of their own national interests. These beliefs are a product of Indonesian experience. Despite its rhetorical commitment to self-determination, the United States supported Dutch efforts to restore colonialism and retain Papua. The United States, Britain, and the Philippines intervened on the side of the rebels in the outer island rebellions. The Suharto regime viewed the Western promotion of human rights as an encroachment on Indonesian sovereignty. To the extent that support for human rights today involves calling attention to the plight of groups such as the Acehnese or Papuans, it continues to be viewed as unwarranted interference in Indonesian domestic affairs.

Entitlement to Leadership

The almost universal belief that Indonesia's size and history entitle it to an international leadership role has traditionally been a driving force behind the country's foreign policy.[118] Sukarno's leading role in the Afro-Asian movement and Suharto's dedication to ASEAN are cases of this variable leading to a productive role for Indonesia in foreign affairs. But the denial of a desired leadership role has also led Indonesia to adopt policies inimical to stability, such as Sukarno's *konfrontasi*. A sense that Indonesia should play a leading role in international affairs is a product of the *aktif* component of Indonesian foreign policy doctrine and will continue to influence that country's stance toward the outside world for many years to come.

Concerns for Social Cohesion

Indonesia's stance toward many international issues has been driven by a concern for the country's social cohesion. The *bebas dan aktif* principle and Indonesia's nonalignment were adopted in part because they would not exacerbate Indonesia's fragile social consensus. If these were defensive stances, Sukarno's *konfrontasi* is a classic case of a diversionary policy designed to overcome domestic divisions by creating an international scapegoat. Indonesia's reluctance to embrace the war on terror was driven by concerns about a domestic backlash. In short, Indonesia's social cleavages serve as both a constraint on policies that would deepen these cleavages as well as an impetus toward policies that would bridge them.

Less Coherence in Foreign Policy

Until the *reformasi* era, Indonesian presidents were largely insulated from public opinion on international issues, giving Sukarno and Suharto wide autonomy to craft Indonesian foreign policy as they desired. Such insulation no longer exists. The rise of electoral politics makes it difficult for Indonesian leaders to back policies to which voters might object. The shift in power from the executive to the legislature makes it much more difficult for Indonesian leaders to pursue policies that not long ago would have generated little opposition. The DPR responded to an American decision to resume some military aid to Indonesia by summoning Defense Minister Matori Djalil for clarification. Legislators asked, What conditions were attached to the aid? Would human rights be a consideration? Was aid given so that Indonesia would support America?[119] That moves toward a resolution of a long-standing policy goal could come under fire by the DPR indicated the degree to which Indonesia's political opening has expanded the number of players who can influence foreign policy decisions. This will make it more difficult to achieve coherence in Indonesian foreign policy in the future.

Role of Personality

Indonesian foreign policy has traditionally reflected the personality of the Indonesian president. Foreign policy under Sukarno was militant, nationalist, and romantic. Under Suharto, it was pragmatic, low key, and deliberate. Each *reformasi*-era president has also put a personal stamp on foreign policy. It is difficult to imagine any leader other than the voluble Habibie taking the decision, almost universally opposed in Indonesia, to hold a referendum in East Timor. Megawati may be Sukarno's daughter, but her low-key persona has often prevented her from building relationships with key foreign officials. Megawati's refusal to take a phone call from Colin Powell in October 2001, because she thought such a task should be delegated to Foreign Minister Wirayuda, is a case in point. SBY's supporters claim that his steadiness of character will be a positive influence on Indonesian foreign policy while his detractors claim that his indecisiveness will impact it negatively. Given Indonesia's weak institutions, the country's foreign policy will likely continue to be influenced by the personality of its president.

Personal Interests

More than their different approaches to Indonesia's broad national goals, however, it has been the particular political interests of Indonesia's leaders that have led to the breakdown of relations with key international actors. Sukarno's decision to wage *konfrontasi* against Malaysia—which ultimately led to the suspension of economic aid, tens of thousands of commonwealth troops on the border, and Indonesia's withdrawal from the United Nations— was driven partly by a desire to unite the otherwise antagonistic PKI and army behind his regime. Similarly, it was Suharto's refusal to put national interests before those of his family and cronies that led the Western powers, international economic organizations, and some ASEAN allies to withdraw support they had provided for more than thirty years. Both Habibie and Wahid ended their presidencies at odds with the international community in part due to corruption scandals such as Baligate and Bulogate. Indonesia's pervasive corruption and lack of strong institutions have provided numerous opportunities for its leaders to pursue policies that benefited the few at the expense of the many. SBY made the eradication of corruption a key plank of his policy platform, and required all of his cabinet ministers to sign a clean government pledge. Only time will tell whether the new president is capable of resisting the temptations of office and making a sharp break with the past.

Congruence of Interests and Attitudes

The key factor determining whether Indonesia's relationship with the outside world will be one of *perjuangan* or *diplomasi* will likely be the extent to which there exists a congruence of interests and attitudes between Indonesia and key international actors. For the bulk of his rule, Suharto operated in an international environment that was largely supportive of his economic, ideational, and military goals. It is hard to imagine a scenario in which Indonesian goals and the interests of outside actors could be as congruent as they were during the period from 1965 to 1990. This congruence, however, was the function of a shared negative ideology: anticommunism. There has traditionally been much less congruence between the positive interests of Indonesia and the West at other times. The two sides have never agreed on a similar domestic structure. Sukarno argued that the Western notion of democracy in which 50 percent plus one has the right to govern is inimical to Indonesia's communalism; Suharto's use of propaganda with regard to *pancasila* democracy reflected similar concerns. None of the *reformasi*-era presidents has promulgated a vision of Indonesia's political institutions and state–civil society relationship based on an Anglo-Saxon model. Similarly, despite a congruence regarding the desirability of economic development, Indonesia and the West have remarkably different visions of the ideal relationship between states and markets. Particularly in the wake of the 1997 economic crisis, there is little support for liberal economics, while the West is traditionally the world's most ardent promoter of unfettered markets.

It is important to note that national interests—or at least the strategies to pursue them—are not static but open to reinterpretation in response to changes in political leadership at home and events abroad. As the United States reinterpreted its interests in Indonesia over the past decade, it alienated many erstwhile supporters in that country. The Clinton administration's decision to limit military-to-military relations throughout the 1990s and then cut them off completely following the 1999 referendum in East Timor alienated the renamed Indonesian military (TNI) but was welcomed by *reformasi* activists. The push by the Bush administration to resume military ties with the TNI under the principle of fighting terrorism then alienated these advocates. To many Indonesian activists and their allies in human rights networks and governments in the West, the TNI is itself a source of terror. By what logic, they ask, is an institution with close relations with terrorist organizations such as Laskar Jihad going to help fight terrorism? Bush administration officials such as Colin Powell argued that support for the TNI in the war on terrorism was compatible with the protection of human rights. But to many Indonesians, Powell's attempt to square the circle simply underscored the degree of alienation that had occurred. The TNI might welcome the restoration of American military aid, but Indonesian officers will likely remain wary of their American counterparts. Similarly, *reformasi* activists will continue to seek American support, but they are unlikely to put much credence in the lofty rhetoric that often accompanies such aid.

Attitudes toward the United States

It is not only the growing divergence of interests that is likely to make Indonesia's relations with the United States prickly in the near term; there is also a growing disenchantment with each other's attitudes. As one keen observer of Asian attitudes noted, the American policy shift from deterrence to preemption did immense damage to the U.S. image. Among Muslim Asians in particular, there exists "animosity toward what they see as an overtly anti-Muslim campaign drummed up by Christian fundamentalists and other pro-Israel elements in Washington."[120] The increasing American resort to unilateralism was also viewed as a "revival of Western imperialism, with other predominately white English-speaking nations, Britain and Australia, playing supporting roles."[121]

Indonesia, like most of Southeast Asia, traditionally viewed American hegemony as benign. The U.S. strategic goal of ensuring that no other power exerted geostrategic dominance over Southeast Asia long served as a unifying force with an Indonesia that traditionally viewed China as its long-term strategic rival. But the doctrine of preemption, espoused by both the United States and Australia, was adamantly opposed by Indonesian nationalists of all stripes. The war against Iraq was a rallying point for Indonesian nationalists and Islamists, two groups that traditionally had been antagonistic toward each other. It is unlikely that opposition to American policy will serve to unify such groups. Instead, the danger is that elite politicians may use the issue to mobilize Indonesians behind their own agendas. And the agendas of some Indonesian elites are detrimental to the interests of the United States. If American policy enables corrupt, power-hungry politicians to rise to power by playing both the Islamic and nationalist cards, then it will have helped bring about the very radicalization of Indonesian politics that the United States professes to abhor.

Indonesia in Southeast Asia

Traditionally, ASEAN has been the vehicle through which Indonesia exercised its regional leadership role. During the Cold War, anticommunism, a commitment to economic development, and the fear of China were the common interests that bound ASEAN together. In the 1990s, the end of the Cold War, the Asian financial crisis, and ASEAN's expansion to include all ten members of the region have undermined the organization's cohesion. Once dominated by countries of maritime Southeast Asia, ASEAN now has half its members located in mainland Southeast Asia, where China and India are exerting growing influence. Burma and Thailand have close economic and security relations with China, and Vietnam is engaged in a rapprochement with its northern neighbor. The changing geography of ASEAN and China's growing prominence make it unlikely that Indonesia will be able to lead the organization as it has in the past. If Indonesia's desire to reassert its traditional leadership role generates increasingly strong opposition from its ASEAN partners and other regional actors, Indonesia may be tempted to adopt strategies of *perjuangan*.

Indonesia's ASEAN partners may have divergent interests regarding the role Indonesia traditionally played in fostering regional stability. What they fear is that continued domestic problems in Indonesia will spill over into the region. Indonesian economic migrants are already a hot button issue with Malaysia and Singapore. Piracy in the Strait of Malacca is already the worst in the world, with most attacks occurring in Indonesian waters. A further collapse of the country's administrative structures and economy could turn Indonesia into a force for regional instability. It would also provide fertile ground for terrorism.

Indonesia in the Asia–Pacific

Indonesia is likely to find the changing Asia–Pacific environment less hospitable in the future. Japan, for decades the dominant economic power in Asia and Indonesia's chief supplier of aid and investment, was widely expected to emerge as the key regional leader. But a decade of economic stagnation and feeble political leadership has undermined that expectation. Instead, China is emerging as the region's economic powerhouse. Given its warm relations with Japan and its historic animosity toward China, Indonesian leaders strongly prefer Japanese leadership.

Indonesia and International Donors

One of the key questions facing Indonesia and the international community is how long donors will continue to support Indonesia and at what levels. Indonesian ire at the international donor community has focused on the

International Monetary Fund. Tensions in Indonesia's relationship with the organization were rooted in the belief that fund policies helped deepen and prolong the economic crisis. Indonesians also resented the conditions the fund imposed, particularly the political ones. These frustrations manifested themselves in widespread calls for Indonesia to terminate its relationship with the International Monetary Fund when the Fund's second three-year program expired in late 2003. In the event, Indonesian and Fund officials negotiated a peaceful parting of the ways. By removing such a focal point for Indonesian anger against conditionality, the termination of Indonesia's relationship with the Fund might reduce the calls for economic *perjuangan*.

A CRITICAL JUNCTURE

As this book goes to press, Indonesia stands at what could be a critical juncture in its relationship with the international community. The tsunami disaster that struck Aceh only two months after SBY ascended to the presidency created a crisis that will test his leadership. Perceptions of how well SBY and his administration handle it may have far-reaching effects both at home and abroad. Domestically, successful handling of the crisis could generate political capital that SBY could then use to push his reform agenda. Internationally, competent administration of the relief effort, a concerted effort to ensure that money is not lost to corruption, and a good faith effort to negotiate an end to military hostilities in Aceh would go a long way toward convincing the international community that SBY indeed was the Indonesian leader who could move his country forward.

For the United States, the tsunami disaster provided an opportunity to broaden its attention to Indonesia beyond its focus since 9/11 on military responses to international terrorism. If key foreign policy goals of the Bush administration are winning the war on terror and promoting democracy, then Indonesia is a critical partner. In 2004, Indonesia consolidated its status as the world's third largest democracy with three separate elections that were free, fair, and peaceful. The war on terrorism will not take place in a vacuum. It will take place in countries with which the United States shares basic political values. The majority of Indonesians want their country to become more politically open, economically strong, and socially inclusive. The congruence of interests that has led to cooperative relations between Indonesia and the West in the past appears to exist at this time. The United States can and should respect Indonesia's efforts to pursue these shared values in its own very different domestic context. Is this too much to ask?

NOTES

1. Michael Leifer, *Indonesia's Foreign Policy* (London: Allen & Unwin, 1983), 105.

2. *Pemuda* literally means youth, but during the revolution it took on a deeper connotation of activism, militancy, and patriotism.

3. For a discussion of the views of the older nationalists and *pemuda* leaders, see J. D. Legge, *Indonesia* (Englewood Cliffs: Prentice-Hall, 1977), 141–42.

4. For views of the nationalist leaders at this time, see George Kahin, *Nationalism and Revolution in Indonesia* (Ithaca, N.Y.: Cornell University Press, 1952).

5. The suppression of a communist uprising in Madiun by Indonesian forces helped make the Indonesian nationalist movement more acceptable to the United States.

6. Leifer, *Indonesia's*, 26.

7. Rizal Sukma, *Islam and Foreign Policy in Indonesia: Internal Weaknesses and the Dilemma of Dual Identity*, Asia Foundation, Working Paper no. 11, San Francisco, September 1999, 11.

8. Herbert Feith, *The Decline of Constitutional Democracy in Indonesia* (Ithaca, N.Y.: Cornell University Press, 1962), 199.

9. The U.N. vote was forty in favor, twenty-five opposed and thirteen abstentions, including the United States.

10. The seminal work on American involvement in the outer island rebellions is Audrey R. Kahin and George McT. Kahin, *Subversion as Foreign Policy: The Secret Eisenhower and Dulles Debacle in Indonesia* (New York: New Press, 1995).

11. For the seminal work on the role that Indonesian foreign policy played in domestic politics during this period, see Franklin Weinstein, "The Uses of Foreign Policy in Indonesia" (Ph.D. diss., Cornell University, 1972). Weinstein's published works also make this argument, albeit with less detail. See *Indonesia Abandons Confrontation* (Ithaca: Modern Indonesia Project, 1969).

12. For the full text of the speech, see Herbert Feith and Lance Castle, eds., *Indonesian Political Thinking, 1945–1965* (Ithaca, N.Y.: Cornell University Press, 1970), 466–70.

13. For these figures, see Leifer, *Indonesia's*, 113; and Harold Crouch, *The Army and Politics in Indonesia* (Ithaca, N.Y.: Cornell University Press, 1988), 334. Of Indonesia's total debt of $2.3 billion at the end of 1965, $1.4 billion was owed to communist countries, including $990 million to the Soviet Union, Indonesia's largest creditor.

14. Leifer, *Indonesia's*, 115.

15. Franklin Weinstein, *Indonesia Abandons Confrontation*, 75–76.

16. Ann Marie Murphy, "From Conflict to Cooperation in Southeast Asia, 1961–1967: The Conflicts Arising Out of the Creation of Malaysia and the Establishment of ASEAN" (Ph.D. diss., Columbia University, 2002).

17. Leifer, *Indonesia's*, 115. The IGGI later became the Consultative Group on Indonesia (CGI).

18. ASEAN Document Series (Jakarta: ASEAN Secretariat, 1979). Such Indonesian sentiments reflected the country's experience during the outer island rebellions and its strong desire to prevent a reoccurrence.

19. Adam Schwarz, *A Nation in Waiting* (Boulder: Westview, 2000), 201.

20. Schwarz, *Nation*, 204.

21. See John Taylor, *Indonesia's Forgotten War* (London: Zed, 1991), 73–74, for a description of the "act of integration," which reveals the extent to which it was an Indonesian-managed affair, not one of self-determination.

22. Taylor, *Forgotten*, 203.

23. See Taylor, particularly chapter 5, for a wealth of data that rebuts the Indonesian claims.

24. Sukma, *Islam*, 36.

25. Dewi Fortuna Anwar in Muthiah Alagappa, ed., *Asian Security Practices* (Stanford, Calif.: Stanford University Press, 1998), 498–99.

26. Ali Alatas, speech to the Group of 77, January 13, 1998.

27. Schwarz, *Nation*, 213.

28. The IGGI was succeeded by the Consultative Group on Indonesia (CGI) under the leadership of the World Bank.

29. Rizal Sukma, *Indonesia and China: The Politics of a Troubled Relationship* (New York: Routledge, 1999).

30. Leo Suryadinata, *Indonesian Foreign Policy under Suharto* (Singapore: Times Academic, 1996), 175.

31. Suryadinata, *Indonesian*, 178.

32. John Bresnan, "The United States, the International Monetary Fund, and the Indonesian Financial Crisis," in Adam Schwarz, ed., *The Politics of Post-Suharto Indonesia* (New York: Council on Foreign Relations Press, 1999), 93.

33. Bresnan, *Politics*, 95.

34. Hadi Soesastro, *Globalization, Governance, and Sustainable Development* (Jakarta: CSIS, 1999), 2.

35. The bribes were collected for the purpose of buying votes for Habibie in the October 1999 MPR session responsible for electing the president.

36. Singaporean leaders had long-standing contact with Habibie and his family due to their prominent roles in Batam island. Disagreements over a number of Batam issues as well as dismay over the level of corruption there did little to endear Habibie to the Singaporeans.

37. Bilveer Singh, *Succession Politics in Indonesia* (New York: St. Martin's, 2000), 252.

38. This resentment dates back to the days when Chinese traders in Singapore essentially set the value of the Indonesian rupiah. One of the reasons that even well-trained technocrats such as Mohammed Hatta and Mohammad Sadli supported Sukarno's economic embargo of Malaysia and Singapore during *konfrontasi* was the belief that Indonesia needed to reduce its economic dependence on Singapore and the ethnic Chinese.

39. Many Sino-Indonesians maintain homes and bank accounts in Singapore and send their children to school there.

40. Singh, *Succession Politics*, 256. The statement was made by Adi Sasono.

41. Singh, *Succession Politics*, 250.

42. Confidential interview with Singapore cabinet official.

43. "We Are Like Malaysia: Habibie," *Straits Times*, July 9, 1998, quoted in Singh, *Succession Politics*, 244.

44. Singh, *Succession Politics*, 245.

45. Singh, *Succession Politics*, 246.

46. The tendency of many countries to condition their policies toward Indonesia on changes in Jakarta's relationship with East Timor had long frustrated Indonesian diplomats.

47. Singh, *Succession Politics*, 243.

48. Why Habibie made the decision on East Timor at this time is a matter of debate. Some argue that Habibie's decision was made in a fit of pique after a January 1999 letter from the Australian prime minister that urged such a course of action. Others claim the decision reflected the anti-Christian sentiments of some of Habibie's Muslim advisers, who asked why Indonesia should continue to support the ungrateful Christian province.

49. Dan Murphy and John McBeth, "East Timor Scorched Earth," *Far Eastern Economic Review*, September, 16, 1999.

50. Derwin Pereira, "Jakarta Cave-in Sparks Anger," *Straits Times*, September 14, 1999.

51. Keith Richburg, "Humiliated Indonesians Direct Anger at the West," *Washington Post*, September 19, 1999.

52. Megawati Sukarnoputri, "Blame It on Habibie and Suharto" *Newsweek International*, September 20, 1999.

53. "Many Indonesians Think Australia Is About to Invade," *Australian Financial Review*, September 11, 1999. When the United Nations and Indonesia authorized a U.N. peacekeeping mission, Australian troops were the first to arrive and an Australian officer was put in charge of the operation.

54. "Japan Not Studying Change in Aid Policy toward Indonesia," *Dow Jones Newswires*, September 12, 1999.

55. Dewi Fortuna Anwar, "The Tragic Ending of Abdurrahman Wahid's Presidency" (paper presented at the Mini Update Conference, Indonesia: Challenges of History, Jakarta, July 26, 2001).

56. Wahid visited Australia in June 2001, a month before he was removed from office. Michael Malley, "Indonesia in 2001: Restoring Stability in Jakarta," *Asian Survey*, January 2002, 130–31.

57. The costs for Wahid's traveling—typically with a large entourage—also became an issue in Indonesian domestic politics. Seemingly oblivious to domestic opinion at a time of economic crisis, Wahid exceeded the presidential travel budget early in his tenure, and not only requested an increase but also the purchase of a presidential aircraft to make his travels more comfortable. Wahid's domestic opponents used this issue against him.

58. "Foreign Policy Open to Ridicule," *South China Morning Post*, January 13, 2001.

59. "Foreign Policy Open to Ridicule," *South China Morning Post*, January 13, 2001.

60. "US Cohen, Indonesia's Wahid Discuss Attacks on UN Workers," Associated Press, September 18, 2000.

61. "World Bank Chief Backs US Warning to Indonesia to Control Militia," Agence France Presse, September 19, 2000.

62. "Indonesian Islamic Party forum Advocates Embargoing American Products," *Detikworld*, September 21, 2000.

63. "Jakarta Against the World," *Time Asia*, September 25, 2000.

64. The U.S. State Department actively assisted the creation of this face-saving formula.

65. The U.S. military began direct reengagement with the Indonesian military in May 2000, when some Indonesian officers observed U.S.-sponsored Cobra-Gold military exercises in Thailand. The following month, members of the Indonesian navy, marines, and coast guard trained with their American counterparts in a joint exercise. In late 2000, the United States lifted the ban on spare parts for light aircraft, followed by that on parts for Hercules cargo planes and commercial aircraft.

66. The two sides discussed postponing the meeting, but the United States urged Megawati to come as planned.

67. "Indonesian President Decries Attacks," Associated Press, September 19, 2001.

68. See text of joint statement: "U.S. and Indonesia Pledge Cooperation," September 19, 2001.

69. Transcript of the address by H. E. Megawati Sokarnoputri, president of the Republic of Indonesia at the USINDO gala dinner in Washington, D.C., September 19, 2001.

70. Megawati, transcript of address, September 19, 2001.

71. "Blast Rocks Jakarta's Atrium Plaza," *Jakarta Post*, September 24, 2001.

72. "US Reassures Indonesia Retaliation Will Not Be Anti-Muslim," *Australian Financial Review*, September 20, 2001.

73. "Jihad Jive," *Tempo*, October 2–8, 2001. Just as Bush's unfortunate use of the word "crusade" caused consternation in Indonesia, the call of some militant Indonesian Islamists to engage in "jihad" against the United States in the event of the attack on Muslim civilians caused consternation in the United States. Jihad means "righteous struggle" and is often used by Indonesian Islamists in much the same way that Indonesian secular nationalists use the term *perjuangan*. But many Americans confused the term with the foreign jihadis, who proved to be among the fiercest supporters of the Taliban in Afghanistan.

74. Sukma, *Islam*, 15.

75. Sukma, *Islam*, 21.

76. Rizal Sukma, *Islam in Indonesian Foreign Policy* (New York: RoutledgeCurzon, 2003).

77. "Muslim Groups Hunt for Americans," *Jakarta Post*, September 24, 2001.

78. "Muslim Groups Hunt for Americans," *Jakarta Post*, September 24, 2001.

79. "Jumping the Gun," *Tempo*, October 23–29, 2001.

80. See comments by Robert W. Hefner, testimony before the U.S. House of Representatives, Committee on Internationals, Subcommittee on East Asia and the Pacific, December 12, 2001.

81. Hefner, comments, December 12, 2001.

82. "Diplomatic Gloves Off!" *Tempo*, October 23–29, 2001.

83. Ba'asyir is an Indonesian who fled to Malaysia in the early 1990s to escape prosecution by Suharto and returned to run a *peasantran* in Central Java following Suharto's downfall.

84. See "Al-Qaeda in Southeast Asia: The Case of the Ngruki Network," International Crisis Group Indonesia briefing, August 8, 2002.

85. "How the Jemmah Islamiyah Terrorist Network Operates," *International Crisis Group Asia Report*, December 11, 2002.

86. "Confessions of an al-Qaeda Terrorist," *Time Asia*, September 15, 2002.

87. "US Wants to See Indonesia Combine Democracy and Islam: Wirayuda," Agence France Presse, August 5, 2002.

88. "Authorities to Continue Drive against Terrorists," *Jakarta Post*, September 20, 2002.

89. American ambassador Ralph Boyce held numerous briefings with Indonesian officials. In addition, Karen Brooks, an Indonesian specialist at the NSC and an old friend of Megawati, traveled to Indonesia to personally convey the distress of many Americans that Indonesia was lightly dismissing threats that the United States viewed as extremely serious.

90. "Death Toll in Bali Attack Rises to 187," *Washington Post*, October 14, 2002.

91. See, for example, "SE Asia Ministers Ready Counter-Terror Declaration," Reuters, July 29, 2002.

92. Many of the victims were young Australians, shattering the sense of security provided by Australia's geography and leading Australian Prime Minister John Howard to become one of the staunchest international supporters of the Bush administration's policies.

93. "Nation Unites in Condemning Bombing," *Jakarta Post*, October 14, 2002.

94. "Indonesia: The Enemy Within," *Asia Times*, October 15, 2002.

95. Syafii Ma'rif of Muhammadiyah, "Nation Unites in Condemning Bombing," *Jakarta Post*, October 14, 2002.

96. Pastika had undergone police training in Australia. His appreciation for the scientific tools Australian investigators could provide as well as the way in which they approached investigations has been identified as critical in the relatively smooth working relationship between the Indonesian police and their Western counterparts. The desire of the police to rebut TNI criticisms regarding their ability to handle such cases is another reason that international assistance was accepted without the usual nationalist backlash.

97. There were two separate news conferences. The first, with one of the planners, discussed the logistics of the bombing and the motives of the bombers. In the second, with a technical expert, the police even provided the bomber with a truck similar to the one that blew up in Bali to demonstrate how the bomb was constructed. In both

cases, there was a distinct sense of pride that an Indonesian possessed the wherewithal to carry out such a large-scale operation.

98. Sidney Jones, "From War on Terror to Plain War," comment to *Le Monde Diplomatique*, November, 2002, accessed at mondediplo.com/2002/11/04indonesia.

99. "Bombing in Bali Seen As Opening a New Front in Fight on Terror," *New York Times*, October 14, 2002.

100. "Voices of Moderation Lose Sympathy for Bush," *Financial Times*, March 6, 2003.

101. "Indonesia Warns U.S. Against Attack on Iraq," *Jakarta Post*, August 10, 2002.

102. "Aceh: A Fragile Peace," International Crisis Group, March 26, 2003.

103. See John McBeth, "Military Offensive in Aceh Causing Economic Disruption," *Far Eastern Economic Review*, June 5, 2003.

104. Sidney Jones, "Avoid Past Mistakes if Military Option Inevitable," *Jakarta Post*, May 5, 2003.

105. John McBeth, "Military Offensive in Aceh Causing Economic Disruption," *Far Eastern Economic Review*, June 5, 2003.

106. Saman Zia-Zarifi, "'Stop Violence' After the End of Martial Law," *Jakarta Post*, May 19, 2004.

107. In an unusual move, Indonesian authorities permitted the Federal Bureau of Investigation to travel to Papua in connection with the investigation.

108. United States legislation allows American jurisdiction over acts of torture committed outside the country if the defendant is served with legal papers while in the United States. Lumintang was served while on official business in the United States and tried in abstentia.

109. "US Judge Slaps 66 million dollars in Damages on Indonesian General," Agence France Presse, October 4, 2001.

110. "Indonesian Ex-military Chief Calls E. Timor Trials Unfair," Associated Press, January 9, 2001.

111. "Justice Denied for East Timor," Human Rights Watch, March 11, 2004.

112. "Justice," March 11, 2004.

113. Achmad Sukarsono and Dean Yates, "Indonesia Minister Backs Tougher Anti-Terror Laws," Reuters, November 1, 2004.

114. It is unclear how high the final death toll may rise. On January 24, 2005, it was reported that the confirmed number of dead in Aceh stood at 94,584, with as many as 132,000 still missing. There are, however, strong suspicions that the number of missing may be grossly overstated. See Jay Solomon and Andrew Higgins, "Indonesian Relief Faces Graft Claims, Watchdog Says Officials Inflate Numbers In Attempt to Get More Aid," *Wall Street Journal*, January 24, 2005.

115. "Indonesia Plans Talks with Aceh Rebels at End of January," Reuters, January 19, 2004.

116. Daniel Howden, "Indonesian Army Ignores Ceasefire to Attack Rebels," *Independent*, January 21, 2005.

117. Daniel Howden, "Indonesian Army Ignores Ceasefire to Attack Rebels," *Independent*, January 21, 2005.

118. Michael Leifer was the first scholar to describe Indonesia's view of its international role as one of entitlement. See Leifer, *Indonesia's*, 173.

119. "The Ups and Downs of American Military Aid," *Tempo*, October 2–8, 2001.

120. Philip Bowring, "East Asians: Reluctant Fellow Travelers," op-ed, *International Herald Tribune*, October 14, 2002.

121. Bowring, "East Asians," October 14, 2002.

Epilogue

The Indonesian crisis of the late 1990s and the transition from it spanned the better part of a decade as the chapters in this volume were completed. The timing was propitious. The Indonesian people had taken major steps toward reforming institutions that were among their most significant national legacies. Communal tensions had subsided and counterterrorist policing was seemingly effective. The electorate traversed a year of voting in 2004 that was notable for its scale, complexity, and orderliness. The gross domestic product was reaching levels the economy had enjoyed before the crisis. Leaders were beginning to consider what role they should play in the region of Southeast Asia and beyond. Only the December 2004 tsunami and the devastation it caused in Aceh contributed a major negative element to this largely positive picture.

In the near-term future, which is to say the next five years or so, much remained to be done if Indonesia was to complete the agenda its first popularly elected president set for his administration in late 2004. President Susilo Bambang Yudhyono (SBY) promised to deal with corruption by means of "shock therapy." He made it a national priority to run down known terrorists who remained at large. He vowed to raise economic growth to 6.6 percent during his five-year term. He promised to resolve differences with separatists in Aceh and Papua. He said that in time he would place the armed forces under civilian control. He and his cabinet began a new initiative to bring Indonesia back to an active role in regional affairs, and international responses to the tsunami opened a new prospect for positive movement to resolve the rebellion in Aceh. If there was any question about this agenda, it was whether popular expectations might be raised to a level that the SBY government would find impossible to reach.

Large questions remained for the longer term. What does the future hold for Indonesia's territorial integrity? Indeed, what holds Indonesia together? The contributors to this volume find multiple answers to these questions. Emmerson's exploration of Indonesia's ethnic and linguistic diversity is a reminder of how fundamental this diversity is to the study of Indonesia and how difficult it is to know what Indonesia is and is not. He finds the national language highly effective in engendering a spirit of commonality among most Indonesians, even as he notes that it can be used against that spirit too. Hefner underscores the importance of the shared history of living together in the great archipelago over thousands of years as contributing to a national sense of solidarity among most Indonesians, even as he traces out the vast array of cultures described in the anthropological literature.

Both contributors find the coming of Islam one of the great movements in Indonesian history, uniting people in an overwhelming majority of the population, reinforcing ethnic differences for many minorities, and yet open to major cultural differences among the Muslim majority as well. Hefner and Clear attest to the role of Islam in civil society, providing the leaders and organizations that created the reform movement that followed the fall of a long-serving autocrat in 1998. They also find that most Muslims are "religiously neutral nationalists" in their politics, and that even nonmilitant promoters of Islamic law are a small minority.[1] Nevertheless a struggle continues over precisely what role Islam is to have in the public sphere.

The use of armed might by the state and by private interests is a continuing concern. Emmerson credits the modern phenomenon of borders, and the ability of the state to enforce its will within them, as the principal reasons for the possibility that Indonesia might survive, more or less as we know it, for a second half century. Hefner argues that communal harmony is particularly vulnerable to leadership appeals to narrow interests, and underscores the essential need for leaders of state and society who can reach across the great division between self-consciously devout Muslims and the rest. He also calls attention to the great danger that the growing presence of paramilitaries presents to orderly society.

Several of the contributors note that the experience of East Timor demonstrated that a weak government in Jakarta, such as followed the fall of Suharto, is itself a threat to Indonesian unity. The challenge may be greater in Papua. The underdevelopment of eastern Indonesia as a whole is tellingly set forth by Emmerson, and the condition is especially evident in the case of the Indonesian half of the island of New Guinea. Physical and cultural differences also separate the indigenous people of western New Guinea from most of the rest of Indonesia. Emmerson recalls that the United States and the United Nations played roles in giving recognition to the Indonesian claim to

Papua and suggests that both may well find themselves the object of appeals to reconsider their actions. Papua represents a challenge to the leaders of Indonesia that is beyond solution in the absence of a change of heart.

In the case of Aceh, the interest of the international community in reconstruction and rehabilitation in the wake of the tsunami was a factor that favored a peaceful resolution of the rebellion. Other factors did not favor its retention as an integral part of Indonesia, however. Its embedding in the world of Muslim Malays did not distinguish it from neighboring Malaysia, where many Acehnese have found acceptance as exiles. Aceh was long designated a "special" province, but the implied benefits never materialized. Its natural resources have consistently been exploited for the benefit of others. Many of its people had already lost all hope of ever obtaining justice from Jakarta. The degree of army repression exercised against the Aceh rebellion further complicated the resolution of the problem the region poses for the national leadership. Having failed to find common ground with the rebels, some in Jakarta welcomed foreign efforts toward a resolution. But contributors to this volume observe that a major test of wills between the SBY government and the Indonesian army was in prospect. Indonesia still faces a major challenge in designing a political infrastructure that will enable all its peoples to live peaceably within its national borders.

The deep ideological divide that separates some Muslim visions of the nation's future from the visions of secular and religiously neutral nationalists is a second major challenge. As Suharto's position deteriorated in 1997 and 1998, bitter rhetorical attacks by army hard-liners and conservative Muslims on minority Christians and Chinese led to outbursts of sectarian violence of a magnitude that Hefner describes as "never before seen in modern Indonesia." He attributes these outbursts to a conjunction of factors: a diminished capacity on the part of the state to function, factionalism at the level of the elite, and "sectarian trawling by leaders of state and society." Bresnan also sees the flight of Chinese Indonesians and of capital from Indonesia as a major factor in the significant decline of productivity in the economy. It remained a test of political strength whether the SBY government, or any Indonesian government, can attract this capital back as reinvestment in Indonesia's future.

Is this what Indonesians have to look forward to? Given a leadership that has the requisite skills and resources, state capacity can be rehabilitated, but it will take years to build and rebuild the necessary institutions. Factionalism among the national elite, inasmuch as it reflects the behavior of large numbers of people, also does not seem amenable to change in the short term. If factions are the largest groups that can be mobilized at present in Indonesia, social and economic recovery may be distant. As Hefner, Clear, and Bresnan make clear, elections are only the beginning of democratic reform. Coalitions are essential to legislative majorities. Self-restraint is essential to good governance. Not only an end to ethnoreligious violence depends on leaders of state and society reaching across the state–society divide. As Hefner notes, good governance also depends on it to do so to enhance collaboration, stabilize political competition, and strengthen popular adherence to the rules of the new democratic game.

There is a need now for such reaching out to take place at local levels as well as at the level of the nation. Violence broke out in many localities with the fall of Suharto. Much of the violence reflected the upsetting of local balances of power by social change made rapid by the boom economy. But frequently there was a connection with events taking place at the national level. Most egregious was the case of Maluku, where Muslims were pitted against Christians once again. Here the level of violence was raised by the injection of a paramilitary force known as Laskar Jihad, which was trained in Java and shipped to Ambon over the objections of then-President Wahid, with support from financial and military sources bent on unseating him. Some 10,000 lives were lost in Maluku during the peak of the violence, and sporadic fighting continued to break out there and elsewhere into 2005. This case and many others smaller in scale that occurred in the late 1990s and early years of the twenty-first century suggest that paramilitaries and sectarian violence may be acquiring a vicious hold on Indonesian society. The trauma already caused may place burdens on social, political, and economic institutions in Maluku and other localities for years to come.

The Bali bomb blasts of October 12, 2002, thus occurred in an environment in which violence in the name of religion was already widespread. The combination of Wahhabi teaching from the Arabian peninsula, weapons training in Afghanistan, and the aim of creating an Islamic state in Southeast Asia, which came together in Bali, nevertheless represented a significant ratcheting up of violence in the name of Islam in Indonesia. Many Indonesians at first tended to see Bali in the context of the plethora of violent communal events that occurred around the country from the mid-1990s onward, in which Muslims were not always the instigators. The Indonesian government was slow to accept the fact that such violence was created by its own people. But it did eventually take decisive action. The potential for such violence appeared to have lessened as a result of effective police action.

The reforms of political institutions in the first years of transition are remarked on by all five contributors to this volume. Clear notes that the transformation of the framework of governance in Indonesia is not complete, and will not be complete until the chief justice begins his proposed reforms of the judiciary and the minister of defense begins his proposed reforms of the armed forces. Even then, the actual reforms will be spread out over many

years. Also, the achievements, while real, face limitations. Controls on freedom of speech and assembly were abolished, but a wealthy personality could
still take a major newspaper to court for damages over a news account. Political parties grew by the score, but all the large ones were holdovers from
the New Order. The lower house of the legislature was filled by elections
that were judged free and fair, not once but twice, in 1999 and again in 2004;
but rules governing elections had yet to give equal opportunity to new parties. A constitutional change introduced direct election to the office of president in the latter year, and Susilo Bambang Yudhoyono won a popular mandate with 61 percent of the vote, but his new party had only 10 percent of the
seats in the legislature. A second house of parliament was inaugurated to provide a forum for representatives of the provinces, but critics complained that
it lacked teeth. A massive program of decentralization transferred resources
and authority from the center to local governments, but there was widespread confusion over conflicts of interest between them. The army was
shorn of its claim to social and political responsibilities, of its reserved seats
in parliament, and of its access to civil posts in government, but resistance
was expected to the proposal by a civilian defense minister to convert the
corporations owned by units of the armed forces into state corporations with
independent auditors.

Learning how to make all the new and reformed institutions work for the
benefit of the people would, understandably, take time. The political structure
has been changed, but not the political culture. Changing habits and playing
by the rules of the new democratic game may take years, even decades. Nor
is it likely that Indonesia will move in linear fashion toward a Western style
of democracy. As Murphy notes, none of Indonesia's presidents has suggested
such a model. The nation might more likely in time settle into a mixed political system that has similarities with other nation states that share its stage of
development but is still very much its own.

Public opinion reflected in several private polls had helped the drive to
amend the constitution to make way for the president and vice president to be
elected directly by the people for the first time. The electoral rules nevertheless enabled three large parties surviving from the New Order to dominate the
parliament elected in April 2004. SBY was himself a product of the New Order. Jusuf Kalla, elected Vice President, never severed his ties with Golkar,
the governing party of Suharto, and subsequently became its chairman. Thus
continuity triumphed over change; Golkar, a product of the Suharto era, had
the largest block of seats in parliament. But the vice president, not the president, was in nominal control of Golkar. The political prospect was thus two-
fold. The president was politically experienced, had a hands-on approach to
governing, and was a good communicator. These characteristics set SBY

apart from the previous post-Suharto presidents. At the same time, he was widely seen as indecisive. The stage was set for a delicate relationship between the president and his vice president, for which there was neither constitutional provision nor historical precedent. The relationship might facilitate a politics of negotiation and compromise, but there was no assurance that this would be the case. A politics of stalemate and frustration also was possible.

The reform of political institutions was, in any case, well advanced. The new institutions were peopled by many individuals who also were new to politics. The institutions were not likely to function exactly as had been hoped by those who championed them. Indeed, the expectations of the new popular presidency and parliament probably were too high; public institutions might for some years be unable to meet popular expectations. There is no substitute for time to enable political institutions to grow strong through the repeated exercise of their functions.

Prospects for recovery of the economy were clouded by a mixed picture in regard to structural reform. Indonesia's near collapse, Bresnan finds, flowed from political uncertainty and policy mismanagement that occurred at the very time that predictability and adherence to the rule of law were most needed. Recovery was slowed by the damage done to both public and private institutions and by the size of the government's debt, domestic as well as foreign. Sales of nationalized banks proceeded more or less as planned, with foreign buyers figuring prominently among the purchasers. But sales of state-owned enterprises to strategic foreign buyers proceeded at a slow pace, inhibited by strong nationalist objections to their loss to non-Indonesian hands. Sales of formerly private corporations were accompanied by much opinion in the marketplace that many were being bought by third parties on behalf of their former owners. The government faced years of heavy payments to service the public debt stemming from the bailout of the banking system.

Meanwhile, lawbreakers among former bank owners appeared to be escaping criminal prosecution in the interest of giving them a major incentive to repatriate funds they were holding abroad. There was a clear conflict of interest here, and the challenge that faced the government was to resolve it without recreating a structure of ownership that had already been found to be socially undesirable and politically unstable. That most of the wealthy private parties involved were members of the small Chinese minority, so frequently made scapegoats for the actions of others, underscored the seriousness attaching to a resolution of this conflict that is fair and is seen to be fair.

Indonesia is a nation, Murphy finds, that has since its revolutionary period pursued strategies of diplomacy and "struggle" in its dealings abroad. The key factor in determining the balance set between them has been the extent to which there exists a congruence of interests and attitudes between Indonesia and key international actors. Murphy finds there has usually been much less congruence between the positive interests of Indonesia and the West than obtained from 1965 to 1990, when there was a shared ideology of anticommunism.

Indonesia and the West have never agreed fully on domestic political structures. The two sides have very different visions of the ideal relationship between states and markets. There was also, from 1990 onward, a growing disenchantment between Indonesia and the United States. In particular, as government in Jakarta grew more open, public opinion there began to matter more. There was growing hostility in Indonesia to American policy in the Middle East, which many Indonesians saw as overtly anti-Muslim. The increasing U.S. resort to unilateralism was viewed in Jakarta as a revival of Western imperialism.

There is a strong potential for further growth in the divergence between Indonesian interests and those of its neighbors and the United States. American policy was alienating both Muslim and nationalist constituencies in Indonesia, opening the possibility of its contributing to the very radicalization of Indonesian politics that the United States would prefer to avoid. Southeast Asian neighboring states, once led by Indonesia in the handling of regional issues, came to fear that Indonesia's internal problems, if not well managed, could spill over into their own societies.

There are thus many reasons why it is important that Indonesia continue to make a transition from a politically autocratic and financially corrupt past, which nevertheless provided widespread social and economic benefits, to a new era of electoral politics in which the people's social and economic welfare is at least minimally assured. There is much to be done in the near-term future to build upon the new political freedoms if they are to be made secure. There is a great deal to be done over the longer term if the reformist ideas unleashed by the national trauma of 1998 are to result in a government that is, to use the currently fashionable terms, transparent and accountable.

It was urgent that employment opportunities and per capita incomes be increased as well. The issue was how far the government could go in stimulating the economy by deficit spending without losing the confidence of the financial markets that had been won by years of tight fiscal policies from 1997 on. The tsunami of 2004 intruded to insert a new demand on government: that it help rebuild the physical infrastructure of Aceh with equal urgency.

With so much to be done, the Indonesian people will be heavily dependent on the quality of the individual leaders who rise to prominence in the state or civil society. Political institutions are not strong enough to function in a predictable manner in the economy of scarcity that will obtain. Savings and investment within the economy will not be sufficient to create the employment or to support the social services the population requires. Will the new generation of Indonesians rising to leadership include men and women capable of turning such challenges into opportunities to improve the working of the state and the welfare of the society? Indonesia will have to be fortunate for that to be so, and it cannot be taken for granted.

Is Indonesia fated to remain something other than a "normal" country, with much being made of its "otherness," its exceptional qualities, its differences from more familiar nation states? To think so is to see Indonesia as too static, the contributors believe, too untouched by the globalization of information and ideas. In fact Indonesia has been changing very rapidly in recent decades, economically and socially, and much of that change has been heavily influenced by contact with the rest of the world. Since 1998 that change has also been political. The "great transition" the contributors describe is creating a more accessible nation–state. If readers, as students of history and social science, begin to approach Indonesia as a "normal" country, the contributors will feel they have achieved the principal goal they had in mind when they began to write the chapters that compose this book.

John Bresnan

NOTE

1. See chapter 2, note 90.

Index

About the Contributors

John Bresnan has for many years been a senior fellow/senior research scholar of the Weatherhead East Asian Institute, Columbia University. Previously he was an executive of the Ford Foundation. He is the author of *Managing Indonesia: The Modern Political Economy* (Columbia, 1993) and most recently a series of reports on contemporary Indonesia under the title *Transition Indonesia* (Weatherhead East Asian Institute, 1999–2001).

Annette Clear is assistant professor of politics at the University of California, Santa Cruz. Her Ph.D. was awarded by Columbia University, and her B.A. in East Asian Studies by Yale. She is currently completing *Democracy and Donors in Indonesia*, analyzing the effects of donor strategies on the process of democratization in Indonesia.

Donald K. Emmerson is senior fellow, Stanford Institute for International Studies, and director, Southeast Asia Forum, Stanford University. He is most recently the editor and coauthor of *Indonesia Beyond Suharto* (M. E. Sharpe, 1999).

Robert W. Hefner is professor of anthropology and associate director of the Institute on Culture, Religion, and World Affairs at Boston University, where he directs the program on Islam and civil society. His most recent publications include *Civil Islam: Muslims and Democratization in Indonesia* (Princeton, 2000) and *Remaking Muslim Politics: Pluralism, Contestation, Democratization* (Princeton, 2005).

Ann Marie Murphy is assistant professor at the John C. Whitehead School of Diplomacy and International Relations, Seton Hall University, and adjunct research scholar at the Weatherhead East Asian Institute, Columbia University. She received her Ph.D. from Columbia University. She has been a visiting fellow at the Institute of Security and International Studies, Chulalongkorn University, Bangkok, and the Centre of Strategic and International Studies, Jakarta.

Studies of the Weatherhead East Asian Institute
Columbia University

The Weatherhead East Asian Institute is Columbia University's center for research, publication, and teaching on modern and contemporary East Asia regions. The Studies of the Weatherhead East Asian Institute were inaugurated in 1962 to bring to a wider public the results of significant new research on modern and contemporary East Asia.

Selected Titles
(Complete list at: www.columbia.edu/cu/weai/publications/html)

The Merchants of Zigong: Industrial Entrepreneurship in Early Modern China, Madeleine Zelin (Columbia University Press, 2005)

Science and the Building of a Modern Japan, Morris Low. Palgrave Macmillan, Ltd., 2005

Kinship, Contract, Community, and State: *Anthropological Perspectives on China*, Myron L. Cohen. Stanford University Press, 2005

Rearranging the Landscape of the Gods: The Politics of a Pilgrimage Site in Japan, 1573–1912, Sarah Thal. University of Chicago Press, 2005

Reluctant Pioneers: China's Expansion Northward, 1644–1937. James Reardon-Anderson. Stanford University Press, 2005

Contract and Property in Early Modern China, Madeleine Zelin, Jonathan K. Ocko, and Robert P. Gardella, eds. Stanford University Press, 2004

Gutenberg in Shanghai: Chinese Print Capitalism, 1876–1937, by Christopher A. Reed. UBC Press, 2004

Japan's Colonization of Korea: Discourse and Power, by Alexis Dudden. University of Hawai'i Press, 2004

Divorce in Japan: Family, Gender, and the State, 1600–2000, by Harald Fuess. Stanford University Press, 2004

The Communist Takeover of Hangzhou: The Transformation of City and Cadre, 1949–1954, by James Gao. University of Hawai'i Press, 2004

Taxation without Representation in Rural China, by Thomas P. Bernstein and Xiaobo Lü. Modern China Series, Cambridge University Press, 2003

The Reluctant Dragon: Crisis Cycles in Chinese Foreign Economic Policy, by Lawrence Christopher Reardon. University of Washington Press, 2002

Cadres and Corruption: The Organizational Involution of the Chinese Communist Party, by Xiaobo Lü. Stanford University Press, 2000

Japan's Imperial Diplomacy: Consuls, Treaty Ports, and War with China, 1895–1938, by Barbara Brooks. Honolulu: University of Hawai'i Press, 2000

China's Retreat from Equality: Income Distribution and Economic Transition, Carl Riskin, Zhao Renwei, Li Shi, eds. M. E. Sharpe, 2000

Nation, Governance, and Modernity: Canton, 1900–1927, by Michael T. W. Tsin. Stanford: Stanford University Press, 1999

Assembled in Japan: Electrical Goods and the Making of the Japanese Consumer, by Simon Partner, University of California Press, 1999

Civilization and Monsters: Spirits of Modernity in Meiji Japan, by Gerald Figal, Duke University Press, 1999

The Logic of Japanese Politics: Leaders, Institutions, and the Limits of Change, by Gerald L. Curtis. New York: Columbia University Press, 1999

Contesting Citizenship in Urban China: Peasant Migrants, the State and Logic of the Market, by Dorothy Solinger. Berkeley: University of California Press, 1999

Bicycle Citizens: The Political World of the Japanese Housewife, by Robin LeBlanc. Berkeley: University of California Press, 1999

Alignment despite Antagonism: The United States, Japan, and Korea, by Victor Cha. Stanford: Stanford University Press, 1999